October 31, 1943: Indoctrination at University of Arizona: "Still a wee bit afraid I wasn't cut out for the military what with mustering for this & for that; capt's inspection etc."

November 7, 1943: "We stood the last Capt's inspection this afternoon I hope—then took a short nap to make up for the time I spent in the head last night preparing for the last two examinations—one in Fundamentals and Ships & Ordinance—maybe they will spring us in the Navy next Tuesday but can never tell."

August 1944: Onboard the *Scurry* during shakedown along the California coast: "Since Herney is a junior officer aboard and with less practical experience of any aboard he takes pretty much of a razzing. Have requested permission of the skipper to send a dispatch to Bupers asking to be reassigned to the Rebel as they <u>might</u> be glad to have me. The request of course was denied.

"Am just as enthusiastic as ever about the tour of duty aboard the Skurry. Hope eventually to feel fully at home on her and not a first class tenderfoot, and that in not too distant a future."

October 13, 1944: Onboard the *Scurry* in the Asian Pacific: "Guess by the time this particular cruise is over I should be just salty as hell—if for nothing else from taking salt water showers. Really you take a shower & you're sticky—really don't which is worse feel stickey or smell yourself from around the corner. The engineer is being close with the water. Cant blame him for it would be his neck if we should run out of water for drinking & washing purposes."

October 26, 1944: "The idea of loosing a whole day in matter of a split second is a bit upsetting—especially when there are so many things that you should do & just haven't time nor the energy to do. Don't know if we will get the order of the Golden Dragon or not.

"Last Sunday we enjoyed our first rain. Everyone who wasn't on watch got out with their soap and washrags & took a fresh water shower. Since I was on watch no shower & thought a salt water shower would have to do. However later in the day about sunset we had more—nothing would do but to get out in gods clothes and enjoy the rain—did feel good to get a fresh water shower for a change—Really you try to get along without a shower until your so of-fensive to yourself & then you just give up & take the salt water shower. Was funny besides enjoying the rain everyone was catching water in all the buckets they could find for washing clothes.—caught two buckets & did my washing last Monday—really had quite a bit of laundry too though you don't put on clean linen every day. Have learned can't afford to wear a clean pair of soxs every day."

October 29, 1944: "Occasionally someone will come forth with—Do you know what I would like right now—always something in addition to be-ing home for that seems to be understood. Some would like a cubesteak sandwich—etc. a glass of beer, a coke or the like.

"Can't imagine what you aren't thinking because you haven't received any mail before this—please don't be too hard on me for it really isn't anyone's fault—just circumstances. Have thought about all of you a great deal & I guess will think more & more as time passes. Do hate to see Susie & Steve getting older without being able to see them both grow."

"The boys aboard have started a newspaper—called the 'Scurry Bugle.' This I am sending to you under separate cover 'Free' so don't be expecting it right soon. Everyone is hoping that we will be getting some mail real soon—of course that goes for me too as well as the other officers.

"Got to take another shower on deck with nothing on but Gods clothes evening before last as we had just a very short rain—felt good but before the evening was over smelt almost as bad as before I had the shower. Will I appreciate a tub bath again—will soak & soak and won't need a beer to enjoy it either."

January 4, 1945: "Haven't been doing much of anything except working hard at the job Uncle gave me—Wondering & worrying at times too if I'm doing things right. Can't say that it wouldn't be right but so damn many things to do & be responsible for.

"The new year is well on its way to a good start—didn't get to Mass but did have a little meeting with the flock.—Many of course seem interested & possibly wouldn't make the effort without a suggestion. Am so glad however that Xmas found us where we could have the privilege of attending mid-night mass."

"The Cap't elected me as mess treasurer for the coming quarter. Just a few more things to do I can assure you & very possibly hear all of the complaints about what is wrong with chow—Will be glad when the next three months are over. Have been compensated however by the fact that Ensign Bezold has assumed some of the duties I formerly had & am grateful for it—besides I readily admit I know very little about it.

"Schnabel still hasn't heard about being a new papa or what he's a papa of— well overdue too for it should have arrived about the 10th of Dec.

"Gates made an alnav the first of last month so he is J.G.—Really he is a delightful person & it is difficult to imagine what we would do without his humor. Really a godsend for when things get tense he can come thru with things that make one drop off with petty stuff.

"Capt has sort of settled down—the responsibility of it all has been a justification for much of his irritability & possibly we would be the same way or worse."

April 1, 1945: Easter Sunday, beginning of the Okinawa assault: "Easter was spent in a manner very much different than any I've spent before—of course the routine as far as service life is concerned—was so busy all day that any thought of Services were forgotten. However I'm sure that the Almighty will forgive each of us for not having spent the day in his way. If I'm wrong about that he will let us know in good time but we can only wish for the best."

June 2, 1945: "The letter this morning was interrupted by a trip so will finish here before the boat shoves off on the mail trip & me on it Damn it—

"Really I've taken so many trips in that boat that it will be one hell of a time until I'll even step in a rowboat when this is over.—Then when getting where your going there are about 16 dozen other places for the boat to be so you wait—you know how impatient I am. Left the ship this morning at 8 15 and got back for lunch at 1 00—they fortunately saved if for me tho the word was they didn't know whether I would be back—The last word I passed was that I would be back & ready to be picked up at twelve—Really hate to hit port—as does the mailman for it means so much extra work for him—me too—This is & is intended to be bitching—or did you guess?

"Your remember Mother—& her planning. All one had to do was to mention going someplace & wingo—everybodies problems were yours—that's just the way it is here—nobody seems to want to go—so Schultz who has to go generally gets stuck—naps are nice & can get one if somebody else does it for you—yep still bitching—hope you don't mind."

June 5, 1945: "If you would like to know how it feels to be more or less water bound—just ask me—haven't had foot ashore since the first part of March when at Saipan—really enuf to drive one a bit looney to say the least—at least however I've been off the ship—but as I've said before that is no pleasure either for all it means is that you go from one to the other—there is the compensation of seeing some new faces."

June 8, 1945: "Sweet feel like a meanie in not being able to comply with your suggestion of sending the Pride & Joy some gum—but since there is a regulation against doing so—foodstuffs including candy & gum shipped to the Islands and beyond are not to be remailed to the states. We don't allow the men to do it so don't feel that I am at liberty to do so either. Would very much like to however & I'm sure that Susie will forgive me for feeling this way about it. Will write Chuck R & ask him to send her some if you wish."

July 12, 1945: "What I wouldn't give for a sight of you Susan & Steve—however the next best thing is to take out the pictures I have & wish & maybe do a bit of day dreaming but then its such a shock to come back to realities. Life away from my family is hell. Should take consolation in the fact that there are many thousands like me—but that's just a bromide."

August 11, 1945: "The very good news we heard early last evening means one thing—that [the end of] my separation from you and the youngsters is in sight. Just when the dept will see fit to say 'Go home to your loved ones' can't be too soon for me that is still undetermined. There is however this hope that at least one of the factors—can be transposed from the unknown to the known columns. Don't see how the Allies can do anything but accept the Nips offer.

"The news came during the movie...No one was interested in seeing the rest of the show but took in the spectacle which was unfolding before our eyes here in the harbor, truly a beautiful sight. Searchlights, crisscrossing against the heavens, running lights, adding their bit, pyrotechnics of all descriptions and various colors parachute flares, whistles tooting sirens contributing to the din.—Gave one the impression of standing in the center of a huge gigantic carnival. Don't believe I will ever forget it but irrespective of what the sight did to the emotions there was some deeper meeting Sweet—at that of course meant—'home' with all its blessings—you Susan & Steve would again be a reality rather than just a hope—tears were close as they are now from the mere joy of the thought."

August 25, 1945: "Since the Reserves fought & won the war for the Regulars I can see no need why the Reserves should continue to be held finish up the work so they, the Regulars, can immediately take their leaves & when their ready return to the good old days of keeping the guns in good order."

September 22, 1945: "We finally got a break today for we were given the opportunity to see the effect of the atomic bomb. [truck tour of Nagasaki] Complete & utter devastation with the exception of few buildings in the area—they of course are mere shells—no windows or roofs. Steel framed buildings with no walls & the frame works twisted and bent—some still upright but askew. Frame or brick or masonry level to the ground—exposing portions of the machinery or equipment housed. Rather grotesque to see still standing granite archway among the rubble—Saw pieces of china & tile which I would have liked to recover but weren't permitted to leave the truck. No crater or excavation since the bomb was to have exploded prior to reaching the ground.

"Everyone including children seems to be busy cleaning away rubble or otherwise engaged in doing something useful. All along the road passed all types of both sexes coming and going."

September 28, 1945: "I'm glad I.J. didn't write you that I was going to be at Okinawa. It wouldn't have helped you knowing we were there. It wasn't pleasant I can assure you but that's all over now & of the past. A bit amused tho for you should have known that being in on the Iwo deal we were probably would have been in on Okinawa as we would have been in on the next one too if there had been one."

October 12, 1945: "Don't know how long or what will come after this but for sure am getting so sick of this horsing around. Symptoms of war fatigue, delayed, are becoming even more evident. Somebody is fooling themselves if they think this is being done in an expeditious manner. Maybe one can put it down to 'Service' and let it go at that—Doesn't help much however if you don't want to stay in it but have other plans for living."

November 3, 1945: "Have been out in the East China Sea. If you can spot 30 degrees north and 127 degrees East that is just about where we have been—not moving out of the immediate location."

November 9, 1945: "The status of the querrie—When are we going home has been further complicated by discovery that our Administrative/Command seems to have no conception of just what his problems are or are going to be & as a result no plan tho expressing a policy—intangible as hell—snafu is a mild term to be used & in fact used."

November 17, 1945: "Well at last the Scuttlebutt has boiled itself down & out to the simple equation of homeward bound soon. In fact sometime the first part of next month. This then is to be our last operation.

"Are now out in Tsushima Straights sweeping a few more—In about the same area we were before—west of Iki Shima Tsushima Island—made up of two islands—Kamino and Shimano Shima. Shouldn't be too difficult to locate."

December 2, 1945: "Here we are back at Toushima Straits. This time we have been working in the western part of the Straits—anchoring in Tadei Po anchorage in Koje To—Korea. Koje To for your information is a small neck of land extending out into the Straits from Korea just south of a line between Fukoka Kyushu and Fusan Korea.

"Just when we will complete this little job is still a question. Expect to be darn soon so that we can spend a few days at Sasebo & then homeward bound. Ho hum please God make it quick."

January 3, 1946: Western Union telegram to Dorothy

"LEAVING THURSDAY AND NO EAST COAST AIR THE CIVIES AND COOL THE CHAMPAGNE
    LOVE.
    ALWAYS.
    AL
                NAVCOM PEARL"

STEADFAST

stead·fast

adjective
adjective: **steadfast**

Very devoted or loyal to a person, belief, or cause: not changing.

Merriam-Webster Dictionary

STEADFAST

Compelling Firsthand Accounts of Two Parallel Journeys in World War II.

Susan A. Herney

ISBN: 1511530995
ISBN 13: 9781511530996
Library of Congress Control Number: 2015905189
CreateSpace Independent Publishing Platform
North Charleston, South Carolina

In loving memory of Dorothy and Albert Herney, with appreciation of the character and values they modeled so well; and with thanks for the support of family, friends, and community who helped sustain their commitment; and in recognition of the essential role of minesweepers and their crews.

ACKNOWLEDGMENTS

THESE MEMOIRS OF Dot and Al Herney document their wartime journeys seventy years ago and would not have come to light without such methodical retention of even the smallest memento or paper record. Their generation has been characterized as having a propensity to save and protect possessions, perhaps as a residual imprint of their coming of age during the Great Depression. I am in awe of their foresight.

Two of Dot and Al's contemporaries mentioned in the manuscript are my eldest cousin, Patricia Herney Menke, and lifetime friend, I. J. Stadler, both now in their nineties. Each of these incredible ladies received a copy of the earliest draft of the manuscript in hopes they would be reminded of the important roles they played in the lives of my parents.

I am grateful for the assistance and generosity of my brother, Stephen, and his wife, Donna, who photographed Al's military ribbons and insignia, which greatly aided my research, and for the loan of family photographs to help enrich the illustrations.

My friend and mentor, Patricia Penn, always a cheerleader, provided insightful advice and enthusiasm for the project; Marshall Kornblatt, a lifetime friend, creative collaborator, and Vietnam-era military veteran, read the entire draft manuscript and provided constructive suggestions as to how I might make the relationships in the story easier to follow; another dear friend, Ann Wonder Dempsay, researched potential publishing leads on my behalf; former colleague and author Traude Gomez Rhine generously shared the story of her own journey to publication with helpful advice; business advisor Douglas Barker, a former Navy SEAL, has been enthusiastic throughout the project, providing updates and encouraging stories of his other client-authors.

To Ross R. and Lisa Veal, my son and daughter-in-law, I express my gratitude for their help and patience tutoring me through the technical steps contemporary publishing requires. Others who provided avid support, enthusiasm, and belief in this project include generous friends Verna Wefald and Ted and Lidia Martinez, whose talents and integrity I admire tremendously. I also appreciate Gaylyn Boone and Jim Dorcy, who introduced me to the National World War II Museum and have become the dearest of friends. My thanks also to Jeffrey Sachs for his interest, advice, and enthusiasm for this work.

"Bright star, would I were steadfast as thou art."

Keats, Sonnet, *Bright Star*

CONTENTS

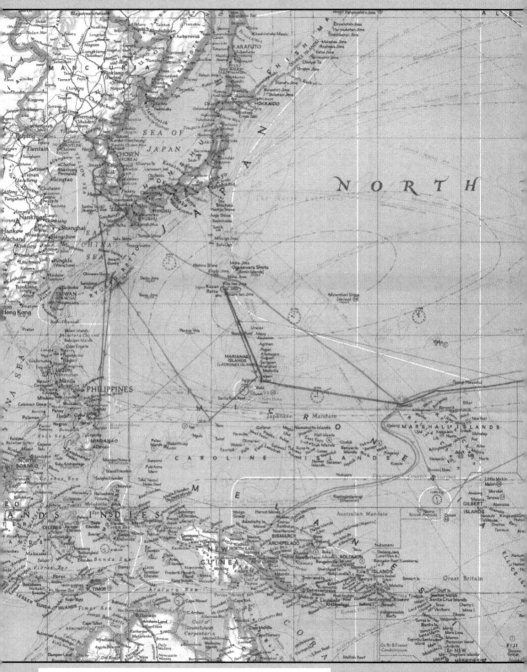

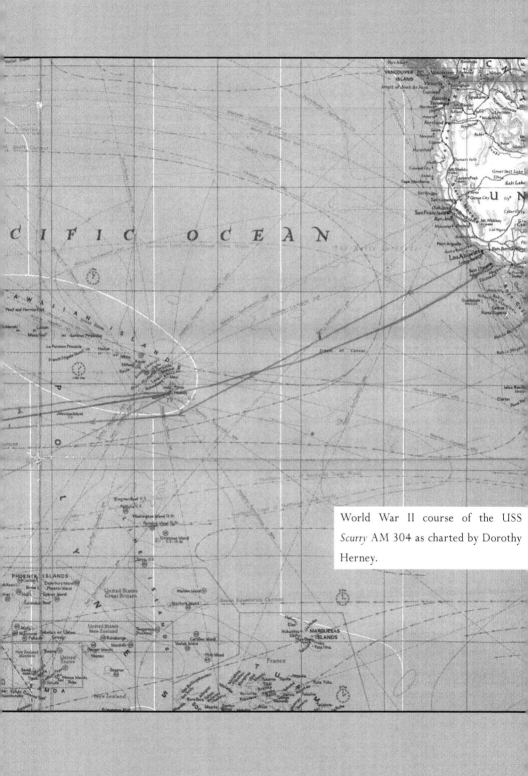

World War II course of the USS *Scurry* AM 304 as charted by Dorothy Herney.

INTRODUCTION

A CACHE OF LETTERS, photographs, magazine articles, ration stamps, books, news clippings, Al's USNR personnel jacket, and other ephemera provided the inspiration for this WWII story of Dot and Al Herney, told largely through their own words. As I sorted through the collection that had been stored for decades in the bottom drawer of an old file cabinet, I considered its potential interest for purposes of historical documentation, especially in light of the current focus on seventieth anniversary events commemorating major World War II battles in the European Theater and the approach of similar commemorations of the war in the Pacific.

It is my hope that *STEADFAST* will provide those interested in that generation with the story of the impact World War II had on the individual lives of everyday participants, their contributions to the war effort, and insights into their personalities and character. I also believe that others, including scholars researching various aspects of that amazing time in history, will find the stories, documents, and illustrations useful primary-source material. The collection has been accepted as a donation by the National World War II Museum in New Orleans where it will be available for research purposes. The critical work of minesweepers seems to be largely overlooked in military history. Perhaps this work will help elevate the reputation of their contributions, or as Al would say, of the "little fellers."

A first step was to organize the volume of paper and other items into a logical sequence. Many of the letters were dated only with the day and month. A few were attached to envelopes with postmarks. Using calendars from 1943, 1944, and 1945, I found clues using references to the days of the week to catalogue the letters into chronological order.

Next I developed three parallel timelines: one for major events in the war, one to chart Al's duty assignments and ship's locations, and another for Dot's whereabouts. Then I organized the other materials, including all photos and other items, into chronological sequence. Some assumptions were corrected and new discoveries made as the story unfolded through the transcription process.

Transcribing the letters was a laborious process due to the challenge of Al's penmanship, his made-up words, and outright misspellings. Although there should be some consideration for the rolling movement of the small ship, Al's handwriting was always nearly illegible, and there remains one word I was not able to decipher. Al's letters were subject to censorship from the time he boarded the *Scurry* in August 1944 until after Japan's surrender a year later. As a result, the text required annotation to clarify the ship's location and mission at the times some letters were written.

The ship's first-year-anniversary booklet, *The Saga of the Scurry*, a mimeo produced July 29, 1945, was especially useful. I was able to locate sufficient other information to provide additional context for the letters, including the Salazar interview, Spangler's work on Ulithi, and US Navy records regarding staffing patterns during the war in the Pacific. Other useful information was discovered upon closer inspection of the material: one example is the photo of the church in Tacloban, Philippine Islands. Because it bears the stamp of the ship's censor, and because it was referenced in one of Al's letters, it is now placed in its proper sequence.

Dot's address book yielded the easy-to-read, complete names for many of those mentioned in the correspondence. Other memorabilia, such as the items Al crafted while the ship underwent overhaul in Leyte, have been in my possession for many years. However, I did not fully understand exactly when or where they had been made, or with what provenance.

Thus, the manuscript developed into this true World War II story of commitment to duty and fidelity, as revealed through the lens of personal correspondence during Al's service as communications officer aboard the minesweeper USS *Scurry* (AM 304). The *Scurry*'s mine squadron zigzagged across the Pacific, first as a convoy escort during the late months of 1944. They next performed mine-clearance operations for invasions at Iwo Jima and Okinawa in 1945 and other mine-clearance and patrol duties throughout the Asian Pacific during end-of-war demobilization.

Prolific correspondence between Al and Dot (and others) begins with Al's commission in the US Naval Reserve as he departs for military indoctrination in October 1943 and continues through his discharge from active service in January 1946, after sixteen months at sea. His wife, Dot, is his psychological lifeline as she writes chatty and generally upbeat letters from home. As one of the 88 percent of US naval forces who were not "regular" navy serving in the Pacific, Al was a typical reservist attempting to acclimate to the navy's way, although often frustrated and impatient as he vents writing his opinions of military inefficiency and bureaucracy.

These letters reveal the parallel development of each of their accommodations to the realities of separation and war as they cope with the unknowns ahead. The letters also share family and shipboard drama, illustrate the importance of humor, and demonstrate strengths of character each writer possessed.

The USS *Scurry* was one of the decorated Minesweeper Squadron 12, which made an important difference in the war in the Pacific. The story provides a unique first-person account that chronicles daily life aboard one of the navy's smallest wartime vessels and shares humorous vignettes of shipboard incidents. It also provides an entertaining narrative of one everyday couple's relationship as it evolves through the framework of significant events.

Attributed historic reference material is incorporated to elaborate and provide context when censorship rules prevented Al (it is ironic that he was the ship's chief censor) from writing details of the *Scurry*'s specific location and mission at the time. Herman Wouk's classic work, *The Caine Mutiny*, is a well-known fictional account of a minesweeper in World War II, based upon Wouk's service aboard a destroyer-class converted minesweeper. Although life aboard the USS *Scurry* was very different from the fictional *Caine*, Al's letters provide a reality-based frame for understanding the challenges of service and command under trying and sometimes humorous circumstances.

Al's accounts of the celebratory sights and sounds in San Pedro Bay at Leyte, Philippine Islands, when news of Japan's surrender reached his ship; his observations of Nagasaki and Sasebo; his descriptions of combat invasions he witnessed; as well as details of life at sea during much of the war in the Pacific, continuing through the challenges of demobilization, provide insight into typical service aboard one of the smallest ships in the fleet.

This ordinary couple (along with legions of others) made an important difference during this challenging time in the nation's history. I hope readers who share this journey will enjoy Al's sense of humor and Dot's storytelling as the letters reveal each correspondent's personality and values. Readers will also experience Al's frustration with his unrealized determination to be released from active duty soon after V-J Day but will be cheered by his final joyful telegram home to Dot in January 1946: "Air the civvies and chill the champagne."

Author's Note: Misspellings have been reproduced as they were written. Notes in [brackets] provide clarifying information. Names in { } are pseudonyms.

Top photo: Al, Susan, and Dot Herney, October 1943. Bottom photo: Al in uniform with Susan, Dot, and family pet Nickey in front of their Chula Vista home, late 1943.

THE

PRESIDENT OF THE UNITED STATES OF AMERICA

To all who shall see these presents, greeting:

Know Ye that reposing special Trust and Confidence in the Patriotism, Valor, Fidelity and Abilities of <u>ALBERT FREDERICK HERNEY</u>

I Do Appoint him

<u>ENSIGN</u>

in the Naval Reserve of the United States Navy to rank from the <u>FOURTH</u> *day of* <u>JULY</u> <u>1943</u>. *He is therefore carefully and diligently to discharge the duties of such office by doing and performing all manner of things thereunto belonging.*

And I do strictly charge and require all Officers, Seamen and Marines under his Command to be obedient to his orders. And his is to serve and follow such orders and directions from time to time as he shall receive from me, or the future President of the United States of America or his Superior Officer set over him, according to the Rules and Discipline of the Navy.

This Commission to continue in force during the pleasure of the President of the United States for the time being.

Done at the City of Washington this <u>THIRD</u> *day of* <u>AUGUST</u> *in the year of our Lord One Thousand Nine Hundred and* <u>FORTY</u>-<u>THREE</u> *and of the Independence of the United States of America the One Hundred and* <u>SIXTY</u>-<u>EIGHTH</u>.

By the President:

FRANK KNOX

Secretary of the Navy

199719

PART ONE

TERRA FIRMA

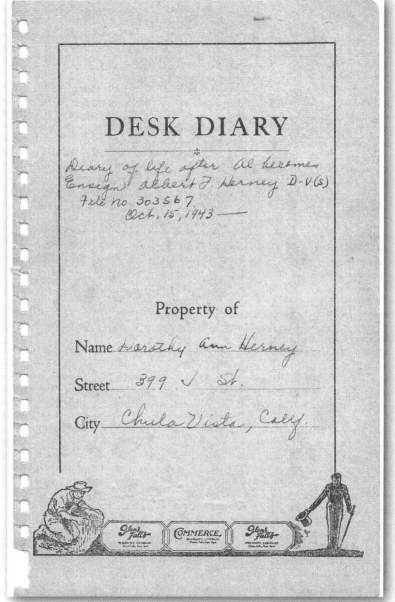

DESK DIARY

*

Diary of life after Al becomes
Ensign Albert F. Herney D-V(S)
File no. 303567,
Oct. 15, 1943 ——

Property of

Name *Dorothy Ann Herney*

Street *399 J St.*

City *Chula Vista, Calif.*

Dot began a desk diary, recording her feelings and experiences during the war.

1

AND SO IT BEGINS

1943
From the desk diary of Dorothy Ann Herney: "Diary of life after Al becomes Ensign Albert F. Herney D-V (s) File No. 303567 Oct 15, 1943—"
Al goes in the Navy—to school at Tucson

Thursday, October 14
Well, we're off. We arrived at Consolidated Plant at 9 a.m. Al was given a pass to see Captain Hunter so we went to gate 10. I couldn't go in so Susan [Dot and Al's daughter, age 14 months] and I walked up and down outside the fence. As soon as his passage was assured, he came out and stayed with us till 10 of 10. Then he bid us goodbye. Susan waved & said 'Bye Bye' and she and I went back to Western Airlines where we could see the field. There we watched planes come in & take off until 11 when 4 big bombers came up the runway and took off. We couldn't see him but I feel sure he was in the second one. So we came home and now I am fighting tears because it's such a lonesome feeling to know he won't be home. We had dinner with Ruth & Harvey [Cole, next-door neighbors]. There is a beautiful moon. Received commissary card.
Round steak - .45
Dog meat- .20

2 cans grapefruit juice - .30
1 large can peas - .18
2 cans baby food - .19
¼# butter   .15
1 avocado   .25
1 loaf bread   .10

            _____

            1.82

Friday, October 15

Well, its 10 o'clock already and I don't seem to have done much of anything today. Susan has taken a <u>lot</u> of steps today—so many more than usual that I think she won't do much more crawling. Evelyn Miller called—she got back Tues. from Carrie's. Said Bradley really has a temper.

I had French toast, peas and avocado for my supper—wonder what Al had.

Had no word from him today but will hope for some tomorrow. Walt Carrell [friend, son of CV pharmacist "Doc" Carrell and his wife, Marie] called to see if Al got off alright.

Saturday, October 16

This is <u>not</u> my idea of 'how to spend Sat nite'! Believe me if I get much lower I'll be chinning myself on my shoe tops. No letter yet. Bob Norton says all mail to Tucson goes by way of L.A. whether straight or Air Mail so he might as well be in Chicago. I stuck close to home tonite thinking he <u>might</u> call but no luck. Susan broke the back off her bathinette today and got a black and blue mark on her forehead from the fall. Also the front venetian blind is on the blink—don't know what to do about that. Talk about the calm after the storm this is it and I repeat—I don't like it.

yarn .50
oranges .25 (dz)
Dog Food .20
Dress & slip 5.10 (Mode 'o day) - Black sheer
Guilbert's Bill - 9.09

Gas Bill - 6.69

    ———————————————

    21.83

Water bill 6.12

    ———————————————

    27.95

Sunday, October 17

    I am a little more cheerful tonite. I went to S.D this afternoon after Susan's nap to Marie Hanneman's [one of Al's cousins by marriage] tea for Aunt Anne's [Al's aunt] birthday. Marie is to have a baby within 10 days—her Mother is coming from Tucson—She has a duplex in back yd.—½ of which is empty being painted & reroofed—Marie is going to write her Mother so we will see 'if' and " 'anda"—had dinner at [Al's sister] Julia's. Susan was so good. She ate what we did—mashed potatoes, roast beef, jello salad & mashed peas. Joanne & Hank have bought a sailboat $3800!!!

    If I don't get a letter tomorrow!

———

From Ensign Albert F. Herney—NTS University of Arizona—Tucson

October 17 Sunday Morning:

Dear Dot & Susie Q—Here it is Sunday and not much of anything to do except completing squaring away.

- Friday was all spent in having the papers processed—getting a billet no. having sheets blankets et al issued & bunk made up. Didn't get out till @ 10:15—waited until about 11:45—taken to <u>Old Main</u> for the above—just about in the door and & advised to come back after chow—yes—just like registration at school & with a little organization—thanks <u>god</u> had most of it taken care of by 5 P.M.

  Up at 5:20 yesterday <u>morning</u>—thanks god no callth. As its colder than hell—chow at 7:40—& then off for some drilling—Some general orientation—drilled from 10 to 12—then muster for chow & back to drilling until 3:15 & is that son hot during the later part of morning & early afternoon.

- Went into town after showering & putting on the dress blues—had dinner in town & visited a few of the bars.
- It is something new for me to be housed in the manner we're housed here & subject to all this routine—guess it must have some point to it.—
- Some 750 men are housed in this gym 500 juniors & about 250 seniors—known as 13 & 12 Battalions respectively—the boys in the 12th seem rather fed up with the place after a month of it.
- Oh—what a life—nobody seems happy about none of it.
- Guess you had better send the <u>whites, the w shoes</u> and wrist watch— would suggest also that you go to the Columbia outfitters & get a couple more shirts—size 14–32—
- Plan on doing some washing today sox & underwear & hankerchiefs as the laundry is awfully slow.
- If I should get some time later in the day will drop the family a short note—if not call the family & give them my regards—forgot to call Carl and Sal and say goodbye to them—
- Do miss not being at home and guess it will get worse & worser but then things are tough all the way around.
- The address is as follows
  Ensign Albert F. Herney USNR
  NTS—13 Battalion No 21–41
  Univ of Ariz
  Tucson Ariz
- Am fortunate in not having a bunkey so that the <u>whole </u>locker is at my disposal—
  With much love to both of you & regards to the family & all the friends—
  Al
  P.S. Classes start tomorrow & part of the shots this week—sometime—
  - Love Al.

—◆—

Monday October 18
First Rain of the Season
Meat   .68
Piggly
          Baby Food (19)
          Potatoes
          Squash
          Lima Beans
          Dog biscuit
          Butter (1/4)
                              3.18
          Soap & Bananas   .40
          Water Bill   3.12
          _____ 7.38

—◆—

October 19 (Tuesday) Postcard
Dear Dot & Susie:

Just a note to let you know I'm still on the loose & able to write.

The schedule started in full on Mon—'hit the decks at 5:20 out on the field at 5:30 for exercise—partly stiff from same but will get used to it.

Thanks so much for your letter received it <u>today</u>—walked to the post office as not brot to ship as no <u>roster</u> made up as yet—<u>will</u> write in full to you on Sunday next—

All my love to both of you,
As always, Al.

—◆—

Tuesday, October 19

Another letter today—and at <u>least</u> an address—

Ensign Albert F. Herney U.S.N.R. NTS 13th Battalion No.21-41

Univ.of Arizona, Tucson, Ariz.

I have to send him 2 more grey shirts, shoe ration book—so it begins. This was written Sunday night, so am a good deal quicker than others. Eleanor Moon came down to dinner tonight & I lent her small radio. Went to lunch at Louise's—Evelyn was there. I was so upset at Susan's lunch behavior before I left here that I was crying when I got there. From now on if she doesn't want milk I will not fight about it. Am going to bed a bit early—am so tired tonight. Y.W.C.A. membership 1.00

Wednesday, October 20

Received 3rd Letter—mailed 3rd letter, mailed suit, wrist watch & ration book.

Got new No. 4 Ration book

Postage	.68 (Packages to Al)
Piggly	.50 groceries
Cookies	.24
Magazine	.15
Baby Powder	. 15

—————————————

$1.72

Thursday, October 21

I really started clearing out today—but have a long way to go if I don't move faster than I have been. Have been trying to do a little toilet training with Susie…but think it's gonna be a long process. Susan has done so well on the milk the last two days that I don't know whether it's the psychology of my not caring or whether it's the teeth for the laterals are really coming thru. Actually had a nap today. Susan slept good—from 1:30–4:15 and I slept too from about 3 on. We go to the Dr.'s tomorrow for 2nd Dipth. Shot.

Friday, October 22

Overslept this a.m. so really had to tear to get Susan fed, washing out & on my way to Dr. by 10:30. He gave S her second shot & said she needn't drink milk if she didn't want it. Went out to Beth's [a friend]—fed S & put her down for nap which she took nicely. Sandy & Paula played so hard with her that she was worm out. After her supper & ours just put her to bed & she was glad to go. Paul went to meeting & I stayed till about 10:30. A card from Al today—said he got my first letter. Sort of stiff from the calisthenics. Haven't heard from Marie Hanniman yet.

———

Sunday morning October 24

Dear Sweet & Susie Q:

Just another note this morning before getting to studying—didn't get any done yesterday as went into town to buy the pair of shoes—didn't wait for Susie's coupon as didn't need it.

Received the 1st tetanuss (?) & typhoid inoculation & scarlet fever scratch—gave both at once in the different arms—T in the left with vaccination & typhoid in right arm—hence impossible to watch the procedure—did watch however that when processing the fellow before me that the needles were stuck in plenty deep.

Mustered for the first captains inspection yesterday at 2—didn't take too long but long enuf—had several boys fall out—yep faint—didn't feel that way at all—

The arms aren't too sore this morning nor were they yesterday—possible will later on—was conscious that the arms were touchy when rolling over in bed.

There are only about 750 fellows housed in the ship—double bunks—in tiers—the seniors being given the benefit of the upper bunk—duty of the jr. to see no such trunk Pennants—no dust etc on locker or bed—Unfortunately there are only about 250 in the Seniors battalion and I do not have a <u>bunkey,</u>

this partially compensates for by the fact that the <u>whole</u> locker is available to me—

Your letters have all reached me—notice of the receipt of the registered package arrived yesterday but too late as the post office on the base here closes at 12:30 noon.

Have not as yet looked for Blouemant or Daney; tho have a <u>Landis'</u> from east of McCook here in my platoon.

Every week the Platoons of the Battalions Senior & Junior (12th and 13th) compete among themselves—Academic & Military qualities being considered. Platoon 21 was the winner for this week which pleased us very much as most of us are good & green recruits.

Sorry to hear of Marie C's [Carrell] bad luck but guess it's something that will have to be considered. Damn shame they didn't give her more consultation when they knew her condition.

In case I didn't tell you about last Saturday—we had no caleth. But we did have drill—2 hours A.M. & 2 P.M. & oh what tired dogs—Then off to town for dinner & a few drinks—returned to ship about 10:30,

My love to both of you Al always,

Al.

———

Monday, October 25
Wrote Al—5

Worked so hard yesterday & today that I am all tired out. Also cleaned out garage a good deal but have more to do. Hope I have the energy to keep it up. Called Marie Hanniman yesterday to find out about Tucson & she is in hospital with a baby girl so I called and talked to her. Her Mother's place was rented as I suspected but maybe something else will turn up. Susan very fussy today—must be teeth again. Charles & Blythe Reed [friends] stopped by last night and stayed for dinner & the evening so my Sunday night wasn't as lonely as it might have been.

———

Sat. nite (October 31, 1943)

Dear Sweetie o':

Here it is and two weeks of the eight gone by the bridge, & had the second typhoid this morning—The arm is somewhat sore but then do guess that it will get over that before long.—Not much fever or reaction yet so guess I'm plenty lucky.

Still a wee bit afraid I wasn't cut out for the military what with mustering for this & for that; capt's inspection etc.—Oh yes, the vaccination has taken but not much scab so guess it won't be too long—

Received a nice note from Marie [another of Al's five sisters and his law partner]—do hope they can find out what the hell is wrong—also received the letter from Mother which you addressed.—Tell Marie also that Bill Mahedy & Arnold Kalus were over this week to address the Regiment—but couldn't get to see them because of the mustering—tried my damnest on Thurs. night after a very delightful 2 hours listening to Col. Carlson of the Marines (remember he organized the 2 Raider Battalion & oh what a sense of humor. First he gave us a lecture on leadership, then during the question period was asked to relate some of his experiences—(beautiful paragraphing, isn't it?)

Haven't written any checks on the account & won't do so unless I inform you—still have $50.00 $40.00 of it being in the travellers checks—Won't need to write any since I plan on paying the board & room bill out of the first pay here & send you the rest. Would like to know how the account stands.

This week started out OK—with a 4.0 in fundamentals—dropped to 3.5 in ships & ordinance to 2.7 in seamanship & 3.0 in navigation. A new week starts brand new so will try to see what the hell happens.

The schedule of 'watches' has been posted.—Have watches for Nov. 7th which is Sunday—Nov 15th & Nov 25th—the first already passed October 25th. Would of course be very pleased to have you come—will look forward to it—I understand that the Hotels will accept reservations from outsiders coming into town but not from the boys here.

Harm's wife is here this week & the hotel put the room in her name—Will have to [make] damn sure not to get on the tree that weekend for if you're on the 'tree' you are restricted till 8 o'clock. Don't plan on Nov 7th at that day must be here for muster at 1:30 p.m.

Am very pleased to think that Susie Q hasn't forgotten she has a daddy. Am sure that if she misses me as much as I miss both of you she has a great big <u>miss.</u>

Have you had the pictures developed which were taken on Wednesday before I left.——Would like to see them.

Do hope that Susie's pictures are as good as those taken on her sixth [month] birthday.

Might be a very good idea to have Harvey [Cole] clean out the furnace not less than once every 10 days & remind him to flip the valve checks several times to see that the float won't stick. Given them both my very best regards & tell them I miss running in to see them.

Don't work too much on the yard honey & don't overdo—especially with the dirt—surely the kid who is to cut the lawn can help you with it—has the reconveyance come thru as yet—

Please call all the family & give them my love. Miss you very very much and sorry I can't be home with you.

Love, Always—

Dagwood—

P.S. Enclosed find Susie's ration book as I didn't need it—

Love, Al

Wed. Nite (11/3/43)

Dearest Sweet & Susie:

Haven't heard from you for some time. Know I haven't been very diligent in even dropping you a card.

Will plan on calling you on Saturday nite from the Ship or in town will call collect which will save time & getting a mess of coin.——

Have wished many times that I were back with you both for I love you greatly yes—both of you.

Wrote this in a hurry before chow as I must <u>study</u> navigation tonight.

Received Virginia's [Capterton, secretary in the law office, also called Gee Gee and/or Sweetie Pie] letter—call & thank her.

Love Always,

Al.

Saturday Afternoon (11/6/43)

Dearest Sweet, Susie & all:

Here is another week gone—really they do pass in one hell of a hurry in one way and drag another.

Capt's Inspection is over & on the way to town for a little relaxation.—honestly one begins to wonder how in the heck you can do what they plan to have one do.

The ship has been in one big uproar due to the fact that most of the boys received their orders this afternoon.

Inclosed is a money order for $300.00. They paid today including the $120.00 allowance.—The other $100.00 is to be paid from the Bureau by check—They evidentially paid to date—the total was $335.00—Paid 29.60 on board and room (yes all they asked to date) & have kept the balance of $5.40.

Do with this as you feel you want to do—or you can put the $150.00 back in the box tho—the taxes will have to be pd. & the life insurance premium is due the 17th of this month.

Graduation is to be the 12th of December—so for as your staying a full week is entirely up to you. You know I do want you close but then the week would be bound to be plenty slow.

This next week is bound to be a heller—comprehensive—ships & ordinance—ship & plane recognition.

The <u>watch</u> is a 16hr deal.—assment of the decks—no chance to study or do anything else.—will have to do as much as I can on the morrow.

Received a nice note from Mother this morning. So sorry to hear about Bobby [Gawers, a nephew, son of Al's eldest sister, Josephine, and her husband, Hank] but think the rest and all will be best for him.

Do hope Marie is getting along & that the time at Scripps will be well spent.

Thank you for the two letters—was beginning to wonder what the hell—the shirts have not arrived as yet.

Love to all especially to you & Susie

Love

Dag.

P.S. Understand this is the last money we receive before being detached in Dec.
Love
Al

—•—

Sunday, November 7

There is a bad brush fire out Otay Lake way & so dark at 2 P.M. I must keep the lights on to see. Al called last night and we had a good talk. I have my train reservation for next Friday but no place to stay in Tucson as yet. The folks think they are coming out between Dec 1–15 so don't know if they will get to see Al or not. Jane [a family friend] is going to take care of Susan. Ben Alice is to be at Oceanside, Camp Pendleton but don't know yet when she arrives. Susan has an invitation to David's birthday party.

—•—

Saturday Afternoon (12/4/43)

Dearest Sweetie & Susie Q:

Knew you wouldn't mind my not writing before this since I have been awfully busy.—I like everyone else would wish to tell you that the 'orders' have been received & that they were just what we wanted but no such luck—very few have received their orders.

Was very much surprised to learn that you had called Lois but know that you are very anxious. Haven't had a chance to talk to her but plan on doing so tonight.

We stood the last Capt's inspection this afternoon I hope—then took a short nap to make up for the time I spent in the head last night preparing for the last two examinations—one in Fundamentals and Ships & Ordinance—maybe they will spring us in the Navy next Tuesday but can never tell.—

Ordered six pictures 8 ½" x 10" & two small full face and two profile—none of the proofs were to good—one was really the cats meow—Ed

— 14 —

suggested that I have one taken to show the <u>crew</u> in case I get armed guard.—
Won't pick them up till next Thurs. will write a check to pay for them also
will write a check to pay for my ticket since we won't get pd until graduation
day—might suggest that you get some jack from the safe deposit box if the
account is very low—before we forget it you had better deduct $10 for checks
I wrote last weekend.

Al's official photograph.

Did have a very nice week end last week—will tell you about it when I get
home—everyone was sorry you couldn't have been there.—Lois has kidded
me much about the commander.

Was sorry to learn about Fred Wallace—he has been awfully sick for
some time you know & not in the office at all—Lowell carrying the whole
load. Thanks for writing me about Jim—Dave told both Bob Burch & Alex
Cory [friends and San Diego lawyers] & both very pleased.—Guess I will get
so see Jim before he goes.

What in the world is the story about Jo going to Wash—doesn't make sense.

Meeting [Dot's] Dad & Mother in Oceanside and having lunch with Ben Alice [Day, Dot's cousin] will be nice—much relieved you aren't driving to L.A. Of course you don't plan on taking Susie Q with you.

Will check & get Warren Campbell's billet number & look him up. Thank god I'm just not starting—

Does Jerry's [Cawby, Dot's longtime friend] mother still run the apt house in L.A.? If so would like the name and address as one of the boys in 21 has thru orders to L.A. for communications & is looking for some place to live with his wife who has reservations for the 20th—would appreciate an immediate reply to this so I can pass it on to him.—

Received a bill from Nelson-Moore for the shirts today—will return it <u>to them</u> & notify them that the shirts have not arrived—

Do hope to be home a week from this time having been picked up at San Ysidro:

Miss you both greatly. Tell all the family to have the home fires burning & do have a fire in the fireplace for me if it isn't too damn warm outside—that will about top off the homecoming.

Love you both always

Al.

P.S. Will call you just as soon as I receive any word about orders. Plan on leaving here Fri nite with "Gregory" also from S.D. will get tourist as don't expect to sleep much anyway. Will plan on you meeting me at San Ysidro one week from today—a long week but will eventually pass.

Love Always

Al.

Platoon Twenty-One, Thirteenth Battalion Naval Training School, Tucson, Arizona, November 1943

Al Herney is second from left in the third row from the bottom.

Tues nite (12/7/43)

Dear Dot Susie Q, [Dot's] Mother & Dad

Just think three more days & I will be on the way home.

Haven't sent an invitation before since they were just passed out this afternoon.

Would of course be very glad to have you here but the ceremony is simple & short which is much to my liking.

Carl [Stadler, longtime friend] seems to be very happy about his assignment—of course he is disappointed like myself that it isn't Los Angeles as then we would be close to home & the climate not near as cold as the east. Will have sufficient time to discuss whether the family will be better off by your staying in Calif. [while Al goes to Boston for NTS Communications School at Harvard University]

The schedule for the train indicates it should arrive in S.D. on the 11th at 11:30 a.m.—of course it would be too much to expect it to be on time.

With love to all of you as I love you very much

Al.

P.S. The invitation can be given to Mother & Dad as I have one which I intend to keep for Susie's book.

Love always,

Al.

P.S.S. Ed has not as yet rec'd his orders—only about as many came in today as were in yesterday.

We are to get out Thursday afternoon from 2 PM to 9 PM. Ed promises that it will be necessary to pour him into the ship if he doesn't get his orders—sorry you won't be here—Love always Al.

"LET ME PREMISE HERE

that the bedrock of a naval service is organization;

its soul, honor; its necessity, subordination;

its demand, courage; its inspiration,

love of country; its crown, honor."

Admiral G. E. Balknap, US Navy

Included in the program of graduation exercises, Class 4-44, Naval Training School (Indoctrination), University of Arizona, Tucson, Arizona, December 10, 1943.

Dec 12—Al gets home from Tucson

Dec 20—we leave by car for Lincoln

Dec 23—we arrive in Lincoln

Dec 25—we leave Xmas nite on Zephyr

Dec 26—Meet [Carl and I. J.] Stadlers in Chicago—take same train for Boston

Dec 27—Arrive in Boston go to Copley Plaza Hotel

Dec 28—look for a place to live!

Dec 29—Move in at 8 Miller Ave Cambridge

Dec 30—Carl comes down with cold

January 3—The rest of us come down with colds!

HARVARD
AND THE
SERVICE SCHOOLS

Al was assigned to the navy's service school for communications officers
at Harvard University, Cambridge, Massachusetts.

2

CAMBRIDGE TO SEATTLE

January–July 1944

*Al hanging Susan's diapers in the frozen yard of the apartment the Herneys
shared with fellow officer Carl J. Stadler and his wife, I. J., at 8 Miller Avenue,
Cambridge. They rented in a sublet arrangement from a Mrs. G. Manley, who was
cantankerous and later alleged the Herneys and Stadlers damaged a sink.*

Left photo: Al Herney and Carl Stadler; right photo: I. J. Stadler and Dot Herney.

Al and Susan at Boston war memorial.

Dot's desk diary continues in Cambridge:

Jan 20—Regimental Ball
Jan 27—Drive to Plymouth Rock
Febr 14—Valentines Day—we get candy—Susan gets animal crackers from Daddy
April 28—We leave Boston <u>Hurrah</u>!
April 30—Arrive in Lincoln

Top photo: Susan and Al with Dorothy's parents in Lincoln; Bottom photo: Al and Susan, April 1944.

May 4—Al leaves in car

May 5—Mother [and Susan] and I leave Lincoln for Kansas City

May 6—Susan & I leave for San Diego from Kansas City

May 8—<u>Arrive</u> in San Diego. [Stay with Al's sister Anne Tex on Uvada Place in San Diego.]

May 16—Al leaves for Frisco & Orders

[Dot stays with Al's sister Anne in San Diego through the end of May, as their Chula Vista home had been rented during their time in Boston.]

———

Dot's letter to Al from San Diego:

Wednesday nite, May 17 (to Whitcomb Hotel, San Francisco)

Dearest,

Well, at least I can write to you someplace—when I heard Billie [next-door neighbor to Anne Tex. She had a telephone in her home.] call I knew it was you & tore over. So good to hear your voice even if you only left yesterday. I was sort of blank all the way home. We stopped and let Virginia and Marie out at the parking lot and stopped at Sears for Anne to see about her corset (they've lost it!). While parked there Janet Hopkins walked by—it is she who's getting married a week from Sat. We also stopped at [Al's sister] Jo's to 'air' Skippy—then took Grandma [Herney] home, got our car and came on home. Anne & Jo went and voted. Bev [Koening, a friend who lived with Dot during this time. Her husband, Hank, was also in the navy] & I got dinner. I was so tired I could hardly wiggle but wrote to Mother & Jerry and we were all in bed by 10. I really slept hard. Susan didn't awaken till 8:15 so I felt rested this morning. I certainly haven't done much all day—went shopping this morning and had Susan outdoors for awhile. She was in much better humor today so guess she was just tired too. I took a nap when she did and slept hard.

Anne came home & then went downtown & went to a show with a friend so she won't be home until about 10. Susan seems to have a special liking for Joe [Tex, Al's nephew, son of Anne]—after dinner we went outside & the boys were playing basketball—she wanted to be beside Joe all the time.

Billie said to tell you to all at any time and it was perfectly alrite with her so you shouldn't hesitate. I don't' plan to be gone at night at all until I know more about your plans. I finally located Mr. Horn by phone tonight after you hung up and I am going to meet him at 10 A.M. Friday at the house. He said he couldn't do it until June 1. He asked where I was going to get the lumber——I told him I thought I could get it—but would have to know <u>what</u> to get so at least I can talk to him and find out what the score is.

Bev got 2 letters from Hank yesterday and two more today—she got sort of weepy after she read one last night & I told her she's better be careful or she'd turn on my water works too. Susie kissed her Daddy's picture goodnight last night. Bev was putting her to bed when I came back tonite & was having a hilarious time on the bed.

Hope time doesn't drag too heavy on your hands—of course I won't be sorry if they keep you there for a long time but I know it's hard to wait around. I might call Jerry tomorrow night in L.A. but if not—you'll see her probably & can tell her how things are.

At any rate will get rested up if nothing else—but it sure is a let down. Will be happy over any letters, cards, phone calls etc. you see fit to make and now I don't think of much else.

All our love Sweetheart—Dottie and Susie

Meant to tell you—will you please no. your letters number after date and start new at beginning of each month—that way I can tell if there are any letters I've not gotten & you can the same. It's a good system—just don't forget what last number was. This is my <u>first.</u>

You can read in bed <u>these</u> nights can't you??

Thursday, May 18 9:20 p.m.
Dearest Sweetie-Pie: (Sent to Hotel Witcomb, Market St. S.F.)

Having put Suzie to bed for the <u>4th</u> time I'm ready to go myself. Don't know why but she kept crawling out and banging on the door. Might be the phonograph Anne picked up an electric portable for the boys & some nice records and we have been playing it so that might have disturbed her.

I seem to be tired tonight too & shouldn't be for Suzie & I slept till 9 this morning but seemed I was getting dinner from 3:30 on today—Anne was baking 2 cakes while I was getting dinner & guess that's what made it so complicated.

I mailed your blue cap cover this aft. You should have it tomorrow or Sat at the latest. Am wondering how fast you get my letters. Bev mails them when she goes in the A.M.

And they are picked up at 7:15. I think there is a plane at 9 so it's possible you could get then in the afternoon of the day they are mailed. It poured again early this morning and has been very cool all day although sun shone from noon on.

By the way tonight's paper carried death notice of Lena Merch's father so will drop them a condolence card—wondered if it was sudden as she didn't mention him being ill when we saw her last week.

Anne called your Mother tonight & said Julia had gone to Chula Vista so wondered if she & Jane had gone to see the King house. Jane was here the other night with Mrs. Campbell & Johnny. She came to bring a large jar of Betadine ointment for the family so we will divide it.

Will have to get up some earlier in the AM. if I expect to get to Chula by ten. I have something concrete to report about the fence tomorrow night.

Had such gas pains last nite—didn't get to sleep right away—felt alright at 2 A.M. when Susan cried out and I woke up and turned her over, went to the john, and went back to sleep.

Billie came over for awhile this evening—she is really a riot—we had the back door open listening for the phone, in case that you should call—really didn't expect it tonight but we listened just in case.

Well, Susan should be asleep so guess I'll go too. Bev didn't get a letter today—but is still perky.

All our love Sweetie—Suzie & her Mama

From Albert Thursday night, May 18, 1944, Whitcomb Hotel, San Francisco Dearest Sweet & Susie Q: (addressed to Dot at Anne Tex home on Uvada Pl. in San Diego.)

Must write you tonight so that you will receive it not later than Saturday. Would apologize for not writing last night but know that you will forgive me.

Since I called you, you knew that I hadn't received any orders. Still haven't today but will try to let you know as soon as the fate is known. Very few of the boys had orders when they arrived. Some were assigned to ships, in communication & some to C&IO's (two) and about four to a pool here in Frisco and three including Young to Honolulu. Carl didn't his, however.

Spent this morning in conference with Lt. Stone of the Comm. Off staff. Was told about the staff and what would be expected of us while here for or during temporary duty. Have planned a detailed program for us covering most every phase of the workings of the Comm Office. Will get toted around——i.e. transportation provided which is a help.

Since we had this afternoon off contacted Knopp—Carl I J came down to see some films but instead went down to the yard with him and saw a ship—a friend of his took us through & saw quite a bit. The chap really put himself out & it was surprising how much nomenclature one is able to absorb in such a short time. Had dinner with him and they, including I.J. are seeing <u>films</u> now. Just to be on the safe side better not to mention the latter.

Scuttlebut is that orders should be in before two weeks are up—can't quite see how one can tell when they will be received but guess that they will in good time. Would like to get off the pan however. That is one reason and the big one when I said I hoped they had a ship waiting for me.

Tried to get into the BOQ which is furnished free to married men but the Chief who checked me in said wasn't eligible since assigned to temporary duty at the Comm Office. The room is costing me $2.50 per day & sharing it with a chap Ensign Joe Lynch—just out of midshipmen school.—20 yrs old—home in Iowa and a Catholic boy—a very nice kid who volunteered for amphib & is awaiting transportation.

We are going to Mare Island tomorrow on our own—do hope to get to see Elmer [Cawby] if only for a minute. Didn't call him tonight thought possibly that I might go over Saturday nite if they would invite me & stay part of Sunday since I don't have to report on Sunday. Forgot to tell you that the senior officer of each group might call in each afternoon to check on orders.

It is needless to say Sweet how much I hated to see you & Susie and all of the family see me go by-by. Do believe however that it will all be easier this way for both of us unless of course there is a chance of a C & IO job so that you & Susie can join me unless your condition is such that it wouldn't be safe for you to risk it.

Went home right after dinner last night—took a hot bath—washed a couple pairs of sox & talked to Joe whom I met for the first time when he showed up. God would have given much to be with you too.

Don't know whether I left any papers lying around on any of the dressers. If I have & not knowing what they might be might suggest that you destroy them for me. Ann likes the fireplace used for burning trash anyway.

Being a navy wife now for 6 months or more & realizing much about what can & can't be said don't feel bad if I won't be able to advise you fully on what is what & should I call you don't ask questions but let me do the telling & only as much as possible—not that I wouldn't like to let you know the all.—

Don't know if the letter will get by on all of the price of one airmail but will give it a try.

Forget to tell or <u>ask</u> Sweet-pie to copy the attestation clause from <u>wills</u> out of the maritime 'law' digest volume for Nebr. & send to Dad & Mother. I will write them to add it to their wills & have it witnessed.

Don't forget I love you very very much sweetheart & that product of ours also.

Many kisses and much love to you both.

Thank Ann for that nice note & the donation.—

My love always

Al & Dada

———

May 21—Al arrives back in SD. with orders to report to San Pedro on May 25.
May 25—Al leaves again

———

Sunday afternoon, May 28, 1944 (from Roosevelt Base, Terminal Island SCTC San Pedro, CA)

To Dot at Anne's at Uvada Place in San Diego:

Dearest Sweet & Susie:

While the girls (?) Are getting ready to go out for dinner will drop you a note.

Arrived safely at the Island about 1:30—without any lunch. Decided I'd get checked in before worrying about dinner or lunch—Didn't get any thing to eat until about 6:30—ate at Officers Club—had steak dinner for $1.05 with trimmings including dessert.

General mess—where you have no choice provides breakfast for 20c—includes breakfast food bacon & eggs—fruit, rolls & coffee—; lunch .04—soup, meat vegetable bread & pie—supper for 20 c. Haven't tried that as yet but will let you know Plan on eating at gen. mess to see how much can be saved.

Room 104 occupied by two double bunks—only three have occupied so far as the fourth chap went to amphib at Small Creek. Don't envy him respective of what "Dutch" [Higgs, a friend and San Diego lawyer] says.

Don't as yet know what the schedule of training will be when the Commanding Officer & Exec. Check in.—Did meet two of the officers assigned—Lt. Farell and (JG) Hetzber (?). The latter expects to come to S.D. for some training.

Tomorrow start helping (JG) McCarl in the Comm. Division indoctrinate the chaps assigned to him for training in communications. Frankly advised him would do my best but never taught & might blotch it. Undoubtedly my schedule will be changed when the CO & Exec. Arrive.

Was notified by Miss Alderson of Officer Personnel that she had a modification of orders for me. Have been reassigned to another craft being constructed in Seattle so will be going there. That will mean I will be probably leaving here about the last of June.

Was a bit disappointed at first to get the news but guess that it will all work out.

Will see about getting leave.—50 mile limit next weekend. Don't plan on asking for additional time—Ask Mac [Julia's husband, McAllister] what he can do to get me on any bus I can catch out of Long beach sat night to return

Sunday nite—can imagine what it would be like to be getting out of Long Beach on the bus.

Life at the BOQ is much as Lee described it—not bad but a communal head—not at all crowded except yesterday morning when most everyone including myself were getting ready for Capt's inspection at 8:30—were there until about 9:45—can't imagine why so much time is wasted on these inspections.

Have applied for permission to vacate the base from the Capt.—Don't know if he will grant it but there are a good many men here who aren't on per diem so quarters are provided free except if unmarried. If move in with another chap—will save about 16 per week on rent and which not as convenient as living on the base can undergo some inconvenience to have some jack.

Thanks for getting off the coat & papers—meant to take both but didn't know I would need copies of the orders until the pay clerk said he needed them.

Do miss not being with my family but we ain't no longer a first class or even a private citizen.

Lovingly & lots of it to you both—

A

Western Union Telegram: June 9, Long Beach, California
WILL ARRIVE ELEVEN FIFTEEN TRAIN SATURDAY NIGHT STOP
WILL YOU MEET ME LOVE AL

———

Dot's desk diary continues from Chula Vista:
June 3—Bev, Susan & I move home to 399 J St—what a wonderful feeling. Al arrives on 11:15 train for the weekend. We unpack
June 10—Al comes home again for the weekend
June 17–18—Al home for Father's day & for the last time
June 20—Al calls from L.A. leaves tomorrow for Seattle

———

Sunday afternoon June 25, 1944

Dearest Sweet, Susie & all:

Must get note off to you before doing anything else. Meant to do so earlier than this but then always had something to do.

Left L.A. at 5:30 pm. On Wed. Found out that morning that I had been routed through Portland—didn't go to Frisco. The train I found out after getting on was pretty much like the milk train between L.A. & Frisco—stopped at every town—pulled off the tracks when any and all trains desired to pass going the same or other direction. The <u>colored</u> gentlemen (?) porters and all were snotty—indolent, and nothing like one finds on the mail trains— Would seem the problem is plenty deep.—

While waiting for the number to be called at the station (ticket office) in Long Bach early Wed. afternoon started talking to a Merchant Marine one striper—found out he was going to Seattle his home after completing a cruise. Turned out he & I were occupying the same car—I the lower & he the upper—Had lunch together & spent a good part of the time on the trip together. He told me that since things were pretty tough to find that he would like me to spend the night with them & that during the wait at Portland (3 hours) had called his wife and told her to be prepared for a guest—Both Ernest & Babs (Emel) are much fun. They invited me to spend the weekend with them so did so.

Will see this afternoon about accommodations at the College Club—605 Seneca which will be more convenient to the yard, the Emels living just outside the city limits.

Glad that you would be happy about it but greatly disappointed as that would mean sitting & not feeling that a lot was being done.

Expect to be able to send you a money order so that the insurance premium on the car will be taken care of—remember that is one of the things I mentioned the tax refund would take care of it if and when it was repaid.

When I get settled will send you a night letter as 'Arrived safely— address————etc. in that way avoid any question of a personal greeting until further notice send gen'l delivery but for heaven sake make no mention of <u>craft</u> but merely as Ens. AFH USNR Gen'l delivery or College Club—Seattle Wash.

Do hope you are feeling OK and ready for the big push. I'm sorry I won't be very close when the time arrives but can't & know that you will be brave about it & incidently if it is a boy any combination of <u>Edwin William</u> will be ok with me or anything else you wish. You did a damn good job naming the first one.

With all my love to you & Susie—P.S. I miss you much.

Al—

Thursday morning June 29 Special Delivery

Dearest Sweet & Susie:

Must get this written and in the mail or it won't be there for the Big Day of July 3rd" [their wedding anniversary].

Thought of moving into town "College Club." Moved in on Tuesday and moved out on Wednesday since they had gotten things all messed up and ended up by having two of us for the same bed.—since he was a <u>him</u> decided no place for me Ernie and Babs wondered why I should move in the first place and when I had dinner with them again extended the invitation to live with them the rest of the time so accepted—they helped move me so will be there from now on.

Really in the thick of things.—The next few weeks will be busy ones—but am beginning to be a bit more optimistic about things rounding out.

The more I see of the skipper and the rest of the complement the happier I am that the assignment was changed.—Of course don't know any reason that the first assignment wouldn't be just as pleasant.

While down at Per #91 yesterday laying some groundwork saw a gal who had been out at [San Diego] State when I was there—Shot the breeze with her for awhile but still don't know her name—you know me and names <u>but</u>.

Possibilities are that we won't be where we expected to be when we expected to be there—schedules sometimes can't be met but guess it is all for the best.

Haven't had time to look for an Ann. Present Sweet—enclosed is a $50 money order made payable to me but endorsed to you. Take $25.00 of this if you which & expend it for something for the occasion. Wouldn't do for me to buy anything requiring much time & effort in packing. Last year you were away on the 3rd—remember—guess this is my turn and don't like it one bit.

Will be drawing some more per diem (the $50 was pay for the 1st to the 15th) and sending you some more. Prospects are that no pay will be received until after commission date but can get along on per diem.

Will plan on calling you Sunday nite.—

Do miss both of you very much Sweet and wish this thing were soon over so we could take up a normal life again. Love always to both of you & the moistest of anniversary greetings.

As Always,

Al & DaDa

P.S. Endorse money order where marked x on face only as Dorothy Ann Herney.

P.S.S. Promise to write more regular from now on

Love, Al

P.S.S. Stay with Mr. & Mrs. Ernest Emel Tele. (Scheridn) SH 7231

Office address

Ensn A.F. Herney U.S. N.R.

% Associated Shipbuilders

Harbor Island Plant Seattle (4) Washington

Telephone (Eliot) El 2072

Western Union Telegram June 29—Seattle Washington

STAYING WITH ERNIE ADDRESS ON LETTER WILL CALL SUNDAY NIGHT MISS YOU AND SUSY LOVE AL

Friday nite July 1, 2014

Dearest Sweet & Susie:

While waiting for the water to get hot—coal furnace will drop you a note.

Was much surprised when calling at the P.O. to find three letters—a jack pot if you want to know. Do appreciate it much, tho haven't written that many—This of course will be #3.

Have been working for the last two days at the Comm Office at the Dist Hdqts. The work has been for myself & will be a big relief when it is done. However quite tedious but must be done.

Ernie and Babs took off for Hoods Canal yesterday—Don't know when they will be back—maybe one or two weeks. It isn't as convenient because of transportation but I enjoy being here.

Went out to dinner Wednesday nite—unique—ate outside in booths. The carrying of the food is up to you. The order is put in—they give you a number & wait it to come up. Then drove around the north end of the lake— Lake Washington—You remember the body of water to the left of highway 99 on which we came into Seattle.

The weather here has been much the same as that in Calif. Not much of a summer overcast much of the time but never yet have wanted to wear the top coat.

Ernie and Babs are outside the city limits. Just a block from here a creek runs its course. Heavily wooded along its banks. Took a walk Monday nite— then out to a tavern for a beer. Applied for a license today—said to come in Monday and pick it up. Can't get too drunk on one qt of whiskey every two weeks.

Hope Dr. Myers [the family doctor and Dot's obstetrician] is going to be gone the first part of July—Would be a swell note to have you producing while he was gone. It was good to hear that you were in good shape tho don't know why you shouldn't be as you were OK when examined after Susie was born.

Susie must be getting into that possessive stage. She hadn't better forget her daddy—Would make me feel bad about it all—Both of you didn't miss me more than I miss being there.

Sorry you won't be going to the Mts [Palomar Mountain cabins] as I know that you & Susie would have enjoyed it. Much of the country here is like it— Still give me S.D. for the year round climate.

Nice for Carl to be in the Islands for awhile. Give him a chance to get oriented to Comm. Know I would prefer to have such a chance before assuming the responsibilities. Will drop him & Hank a note real soon.

Off to take a bath. Do hope I could be home for a shower & be able to sleep in my own bed.

Again, a happy anniversary sweet—do miss not being there. Regards to all & love to you & Susie.

Al

P.S. <u>Sat Morning</u>—It rained last night & is raining now—don't like it so well. Love Al

Tuesday nite—July 5 1944

Dear Sweet & Susie:

After the shower and before hitting the sack will drop you a note.

Worked yesterday—yes all day and today too—started about 8 A.M and worked till 5 pm—all paper work and the eyes do get a bit tired.

Last week while waiting for the bus was picked up by a chap who was going to the pier at which I am working this week. Told him I expected to be there this week—he said he would be keep his eye open for me & he has—get a ride down and back—quite a break as I would have to transfer down town if I didn't get the ride.

Sorry to hear that Mrs. Cole's mother hasn't been feeling too well and that Harvey had his accident—glad that there was some bourbon to give him the shot. Do hope he hasn't suffered an injury other than a temporary strain or sprain.

Today was a very pleasant day—with the sun shining all day.—just now getting dark.—really is pleasing to have such a long evening tho don't do much but sit.

Cut the lawn last Sunday for a bit of exercise. Watered the garden tonight while doing some washing—can't leave too many socks build up.

Can't quite understand Carl being transfered to amphib. Tho on the other hand all of us will be in it in one phase or another. Don't believe that Dad & Mother [Stadler] would be too upset as Carl Hasn't been assigned to landing craft or shore party has he?

Forgot to tell you that when I arrived there was a letter from Madam Manley [landlady in Boston] addressed to the Commandant of the 12th Naval District. Have partly drafted the answer which I am to send her direct. The interesting part reads as follows "While here they chipped the porcelain from a whole sink which had been given to them in good condition." The Stinker—not a word more about the facts—this undoubtedly to leave the impression that we took hammer & chisel & set to work on it. Don't worry am being moderate in my answer.

It was so good to be able to talk to you Sunday nite Sweet and to hear the offspring say "Hi"—would have liked to have spent the day with you at the beach but I just was too damn far away.

If anything, plans will be delayed later than expected. Just when or how much later they will be can't guess nor would I not knowing nothing about nothing.

Will drop in to the post office tomorrow while down town to see if there is any mail. Haven't expected to hear from anyone but you up to now so if there is some mail will be surprised.

Since 6 AM comes awfully soon will say good night and that I love you both very much.

Love Always

Al & DaDa—7/5/44

Sweet—Here is another money order for $50.00. Drew some per diem and don't need all they paid me—Know you can use it—sort of equalize the insurance deluge.

Love Always

Al

Friday night July 7

Dearest & Susie:

Already 9:30 and still very light out—so light that I would object going to bed if I were a youngster, but since I no longer am will hit the sack as I am quite tired tho haven't done any physical labor.

Your letter was a big surprise. Don't see how you could have been pregnant before Tucson—that is you couldn't have been pregnant before Rancho unless I've turned out to be a Christian Scientist—Will wait for a telegram but don't expect one real soon, that is within the next two weeks.

Received a letter from Mother today—must have been written before the Caugheys [Al's aunt Julia and her husband, Albert] arrived as they were on their way. Hoped you gave Aunt Julia the bag which I had purchased for her to give away. Are they going back to Atwood [Texas]—nobody said nothing about nothing except that they had arrived and were to—

A carnival set up in business just a block away. Must go up to see what they've got to take the suckers money—Oh Yeh!—

You didn't say what you had decided on for if it's a boy—though you know I wont object. The prospects (financial) looks pretty good for a contribution if it's a Mary Martha [after his sister Marie]. Can't say that I go for Penelope—besides it ain't rymthic with Herney & who would want to bless a child with that—Don't get the impression that I'm mercenary.

Would like to be there for the party tomorrow night for the Phi Mu [Dot's sorority alumnae club in San Diego] Party—Sounds like the dinner is the usual that Ed [Mueller, Marie's husband] puts out. Know that you will say hello to all of them for me.

Worked from 8 a.m to 6 PM yesterday. Had chow on board one of the crafts here—a calls made of "Cuba" to the chap who took the pictures for the class book is the Comm Officer aboard. Don't get home until after 11 and by the time I got to bed it was after 12.—

Spent the morning at the office and this afternoon at the Issuing Office again—am beginning to see day light & if possible will go down on Sunday and get the job over as soon as possible so that some of the incidentals and the fun stage (when what) will be reached—they say things gradually get to be more difficult. What the heck did they send me to Harvard for anyway—Do think the Skipper is satisfied with my work however & the more I see of him the more I like him.

Whether Dr. Myers is right or wrong know that you will be OK and realize that I would like to be with you—as much as you would like to have me.

Regards to all of the family and all my love to you & Susie—Hope she knows that it was her daddy talking to her last Sunday—

Love always
Al & Daddy
P.S. Let me know if you got my letter enclosing the $50.00 money order.

———

Sunday nite July 9, 1944
Dearest—

Well, young fry is in bed and asleep I hope. She has had a sniffle again the last two days which may be a cold and may not—has been sneezing but hope it will disappear like the last time.

Well, last night was the Phi Mu party at Marie's [and Ed's] and a good time was had by all. There were 24, there I believe.

Shaws, Gillettes, Morrisons, Foss's, Dramis', Belchers, Reeds, Sue Beagler (Navy Dr.s wife), Margaret Campbell, Nolans (Ruth Ware & husband), Vivian, Jo Work, myself, Helen H [another of Al's sisters]. Marie, Ed. Of course it was a beautiful dinner, the roast beef was delicious and they served wine with the dinner. Besides Rose, Martha came to help but as Helen said, the two of them weren't used to big crowds as the Herney are—and Helen & Anne had to rush to the rescue t the last moment as they had enough gravy for about 8 people. Rose left early as her husband's liberty was up at 2 A.M. this morning and she thinks he's going out so I helped Martha finish up the dishes as I figured I could miss the meeting as I probably wouldn't be at the next party anyway. Ed had the men downstairs playing poker. Several left early but there were 3 tables of bridge. Marie & Cal [a friend's husband] got into argument over a bridge point, I'm curious as to who is right—I'll put my money on Marie! The moon on the bay out the window was beautiful and everyone saw Eddie's beautiful garden & Marie's too.

I came in yesterday aft. & left Susan at Janie's for the weekend as she has been after me so constantly so I went to the party with Anne & Helen came home with us. Was glad I could sleep till 11 this A.M. Got Susan after dinner tonight. The dogs sort of bother Susan but couldn't say I blame her—they bark so incessantly.

I asked Dr. Myers about Jane being with me—he said it was alrite but he didn't want to see anymore of her than possible so I'd just as soon this business came in the daytime so she wouldn't be there. I hate to do anything that might annoy him and I must say Jane gets on my nerves more every time I see her.

Ruth's [Cole, next-door neighbor] Mother & sister are leaving tomorrow—today is Ruth's birthday so everyone is gathered over there tonight. Harvey still home from work—goes to the Dr. again tomorrow. He's lost so much weight he looks ten years older since this happened. Jack Tex [Anne's other son, Al's nephew] has new glasses—just got them yesterday. They look very good on him. Honestly I would kick those kids the way they spend their Mother's money and do nothing around the house. Otherwise they are such nice kids. Thanks so much for the second money order—do hope you have plenty. Have paid the $106. To Mercy [hospital] so that's off my chest and will pay the insurance all up tomorrow—the car insurance isn't due till this month anyway.

Had a letter from I.J.—said Carl didn't seem to be getting her letters & he was worried about her. He, Carl, has been working with Buck Lyman and I.J. had a letter from her & she hadn't had her baby yet—can't figure that out as she was supposedly 3 months along when they left Tucson.

Sounds like you've gone domestic what with the yard cutting and garden watering! Dr. Myers goes on his vacation next Sat. July 15—to be gone a week. Will be glad when he's back—just on general principles. Was certainly surprised at the memo from Mrs. M. [Manley, the landlady]—guess she's gonna die a hard death! Don't worry—it isn't gonna worry me. She can chase you all over the Pacific if she wants to but she'll never get an answer out of me!

I don't seem to know much news around Chula. Carrie & a girl friend are coming down to San Diego for a week—supposed to come Wed. Evelyn M called today and said she wanted Louise & me out to lunch while they were here if we could manage so will see. They will probably come to Chula sometime this week. Am going to have Shirley [a local girl Dot hired as a helper] start cleaning Susan's room real good this week and am going to send the dining room rug to the cleaners as the spots are really bad on it.

Charles Reed said that he could have gotten transportation for you back & forth from San Pedro if we had just called him—that guy has a finger in everything—next time no matter what I want, I will call him and ask anyway! Well, think I'll go to bed—want to wash tomorrow.

Today was a beautiful day—really the best summer day we've had so far. Am enclosing the condensed version of the Tribune in case there is anything you might be interested in. We love you darling—and Seattle seems a long way aways—but as long as it's U.S.A. I'm not complaining and neither is Susie tho she misses her Daddy so much.

All our love—

Dottie and Susan

———

Monday nite July 10

Dearest Sweet & Susie:

Must drop you a note tonight as I had failed to write yesterday. This was due to the fact that I had a rather full day as I washed and cleaned the house—then ironed 3 grey shirts and a white one later in the evening. Babs & Ernie are coming in tonight or tomorrow.

Received a nice note from Virginia on Saturday—was late in getting here—evidently the postman—rural delivery was in too much of a hurry.

Didn't receive a note for you today but will overlook it as I know how busy you are with the expectation of an early birth—guess its best to be prepared than have nothing ready.

Received word today that the big day as to be the 28th of July so will be here for at least a few days after the first of Aug—which all in all should give me a chance to at least see Junior or <u>ese</u> which ever it may be.

Still down at Pier 91 at the Issuing Office. Wanted to do some work yesterday but the chap in charge—Commndr (?) suggested I put myself out & stay some evening—did it burn me as I've done that for the past week doing work which they should do—kept my mouth shut but had a hard time doing that—Won't spend much more time down here & that's a cinch—they can take a flying leap off the moon—could have very profitably spent this past week on my administrative job.

Understand that one of the other officers is in the same boat as myself i.e. an expectant father and about the same time—believe he is an ensign also he is my senior—am stressing the fact that I'm a <u>Dept Head</u> to get the lower bunk—looks more comfortable and not near to far to fall if it gets rough.

Got a liquor license last week—went to the <u>dispensary</u> to get my quota— bought a bottle of scotch, rum and gin. Scotch was the cheaper of the three— spent almost $15.00. Had a couple of "Tom Collins" Saturday night—so tired didn't eat dinner but hit the sack & awakened about 2AM—had cig and back to sleep.

The damned carnival is making one awful racket—wish that they would fold up and go to some other location quite a way away.

Jim—Ernie's youngster arrived home Friday nite—just completed a cruise (merchant marine) to the islands. Couldn't awaken me to get in so crawled in thru the basement window. My what a break as was I sound asleep tho I didn't hit the sack till 11 P.M.

Want to drop Mother a note so will say goodnight to my <u>two</u> sweet hearts.
Love Always
Al & DaDa

Tuesday morning, July 11
Dearest Sweet:

Marie finally got in touch me by phone about 10 A.M. to give me the good news that <u>it</u> was all over and that both you and him were doing well— That of course was the best news of all.

It was difficult at times to hear her but understand that you presented me with a <u>boy</u> weighing 55 & tho premature would not need to be placed in an incubator (?). Not much in size but do bet that he is all there including the tassel. Don't know why you didn't tell me that Dr. Myers didn't want you to go to Chula because of the prospective date as it really wouldn't have been such a shock to get the call this morning.

When Marie called was at the Issuing Office—So happy to hear the news that closed the books put on the hat & coat called the Skipper for permission to secure, which was granted, and went out the door heading for home and a couple of drinks of rum and soda which I am now enjoying.

Forgot to tell Marie to send you some flowers for me (guess how excited I was) so will have to make some other arrangements about that matter.

Do hope you are in a room with telephone as plan on calling you tonight—giving you time to regain a bit of normalcy after the big ordeal.

Marie also said that the matter was of a short duration—went to the hospital at 3 A.M and that the youngster was born about 8—maybe the fact that he weighed only 55 had something to do about it.—Awfully glad you didn't have as long a time in the hospital as you did with Susie.

Wonder if Mother [Charleson, Dot's mother] will have a chance of making the train for Calif on such short notice—Guess she was caught as unaware as I was about the matter—Will drop Dad a note very soon and maybe this afternoon.

You know how sorry I am that I couldn't have been with you during the event but here I am way up in Seattle—so damned far away from home and not liking it one bit.

In order that the rural delivery man will pick this up will quit—

With all my love and knowing that both you and Stephen William will be tops will say by-by—

With all my love

Your husband Al—

P.S. Forgot to mention that Stephen William is mighty fine as far as names go and will be satisfied if you tack that on to Jr...

Lovingly, Al

———

Mercy Hospital Room 614 Bed 2

Wednesday July 12 11:20 A.M.

I hope the name suits you.

My dearest—

Methinks I hear them coming with the lunch trays already so I may have to postpone this till after that. I guess I sort of pulled a fast one on you didn't I. Guess Marie told you most the facts altho I haven't seen her—just seen Anne who didn't know exactly what Marie told you. Hope it wasn't too much of a shock. I am so relieve that the baby is ok—that nothing else matters. Since last Tuesday I have been so worried about it coming ahead of time that I felt I was walking around with a crate of eggs inside of me. I was so disgusted last Tuesday when Dr. Meyers had me come in for a check & then sent me up here to the hospital and so relieved when I was able to leave Wed. but he told me to say in town [San Diego] and not go back to Chula.

Then too he leaves on his vacation this next Sat. & he seemed concerned the baby would be here before Aug. & I was scared to death it would happen while he was gone. He promised to have Dr. Black on hand from the beginning. I was so afraid of its being so premature (5 weeks) so often they don't survive. However, the <u>baby</u> or should I say Stephen William, our son, is doing fine. Dr. Black skipped town on <u>his</u> vacation & his brother-in-law from someplace North—also a pediatrician, is taking over. He came in this morning and said the baby was fine. He is just above the premature line, 5# 1 ½ ounce so is not in an incubator but is in the premature room and believe it or not, I haven't even had a good look at him. They showed him to me before I left the delivery room but I couldn't focus my eyes enuf to see anything but a blur. Julia says he looks like you and Carl [Herney, one of Al's three brothers]. I am to start nursing him tomorrow so can tell you more about him then.

It really was short & snappy. I got to the hospital at 4 A.M. and it was all over at 8—born at 7:50 but those 4 hrs weren't any tea party. Jane wasn't there. She came last week with me but the tension was just too unpleasant when Dr. Myers was in the room so I told Anne when we left for the hospital we'd just tell her there wasn't time. Julia was with me and such a comfort. Dr. Myers came about 6:30 and got a little disgusted I think—said I wasn't working hard enuf—so he left to go down stairs to get a cup of coffee and on the next pain Julia & I really pulled and grunted and things popped & they took me right to the delivery room. They were a little worried he wouldn't get there I think for I heard one nurse say, "<u>Where</u> is he, I wish he'd hurry." I don't think they gave me much ether for I came to & heard Dr. Myers say "Once more Dorothy" then they gave me some more but I could hear voices, heard the baby cry and heard him say "It's a boy Dorothy, isn't that swell?"

I have felt fine—yesterday had quite a few after pains which is normal with short labor. Dr. Myers came in the A.M. and said everything was ok.

Later

It is so much nicer up here on 6 very quiet, more service I believe and not so strict. Aunt Julia & Julia sneaked in with some pansies just as I was finishing my lunch and stayed about 15 minutes. Anne came to see me last night. I wish you could have heard her description of Joe Tex getting Susan up. Anne told him to dress her—laid out her clothes for him & pack her things & give her her breakfast & then call Mac to come & get her. She said Joe said she woke up & said 'Go Go' so he put her on the toilet. She cried for "Mama" so he told her, her mama had gone 'bye bye' to get her a baby and she stopped crying. He fed her and then called W4455 and the sum total of the conversation was "she's fed and dressed, come and get her" whereupon he hung up. Can't you just <u>hear</u> him? Susan adores him anyhow. Anyway she's back at Julia's. She was there all last week until Sat & had the time of her life. She's very fond of Uncle Albert [Caughey] and follows him constantly.

Marie called Mother and I guess she was so surprised she didn't say much so hope she wasn't too upset. Did say she would try and come out as soon as she could.

I received your telegram yesterday aft. & as soon as a nurse came in asked her about the possibility of a telephone call & she said there was no way I could talk to you so hope you weren't too disappointed.

This room is on the back side of the hospital toward the south end—so have a nice view of east San Diego—can practically see Julia's—<u>can</u> see Aunt Anne's.

The girl in the room here is very nice—her baby died—breach birth— her husband is a Marine—has been overseas & now stationed at Marine Base. My eyes are sort of tired so think I'll rest a little as it will be visitors hour before long & I <u>might</u> have company.

I'm really glad its all over—just so by the time you see him he should be getting filled out. Miss you so sweetie—and now you have 3 of us. Your Dottie

Both money orders received & deposited.

———

Wedn Morning July 12
Sent to Mercy Hospital
Dearest Sweet:

Will try to get off this note this morning before really getting to work so that you will receive it not later than Saturday.

Was very disappointed last evening to find that you had no phone in the room. Got in on quite a bit of the conversation at the hospital as to whether or not you could receive the call.

Called Marie last evening to find about you & the offspring. Relieved to find out that both of you were still both fine and nothing to worry about. Said Anne had been to the hospital and had seen you & the <u>junior</u> and again said no incubator was necessary.

Spent the afternoon just relaxing—of course had a few rums between the horizontal exercise—took a drive with the neighbor.

Ernie & Babs returned hoped last evening—very much thrilled about their vacation & did nothing but sit.—Have purchased a 10 acre tract for $300 has an outhouse on it but no house. Plan on building log cabin and selling the house here in town and moving out there next spring.

Aunt Julia & Uncle Albert are to say until the end of the month. Nice that they are going to be able to have that much time. Do hope that mother [Herney] doesn't try to go to Frisco as that would be like setting a babe down in the woods & very probably crushed to death by the herds rushing by.

Understand that Susie was disappointed when you didn't produce last week on the false alarm. She should be happy now with "Baby" but hope she is isn't too spoiled to really be a problem about it all. Guess however that now is the time to get the young lady <u>learn't</u> that she isn't the only one.

Don't worry about my financial condition for I wouldn't have sent the last money order if I hadn't had sufficient to get me by—Will be able to turn over the majority of the pay which has been accumulating since the 15th of June—However it does cost to live doesn't it.

Wish that I could drop in to see you during each visiting period.—Do think about you (<u>all three now</u>) very much.

With All My love
Your's always
Al & Da Da & goo

Thursday morning July 13—Sent Special Delivery to Mercy Hospital
Dearest Sweet:

The best time to drop you these notes seems to be bright & early & before the days endeavors really begin.

Spent quite a hectic day yesterday. Didn't seem to get much accomplished but tried hard. Did however dispose of one matter that had been bothering the skipper. Do guess it is better to follow up & complete one thing when it its <u>tail.</u>

Received your note written Sunday & mailed on the 10th—arrived on the 11th—quite good time.

Know that you are feeling in the pink by this time (and of course that <u>he</u> is still red as I haven't learned any thing to the contrary.) Didn't call last night to find out that nothing had changed.

Went to see "A Guy Called Joe" with Babs & Ernie—He is much like George F—takes a year & a day to get him started. Insisted on taking a shower and as a result we were late to the show—no matter for we didn't miss much.

They are going back up the canal for a couple of days with a friend of theirs who is going to do some clearing (timber) for him. Wanted me to go along but since I haven't time to take off in the middle of the week have to pass it up.

Must get to work or we might be sunk later on—
With all my Love
Yours Always
Al

Friday morning July 14—Special Delivery to Mercy Hospital
Dearest Sweet:

Since I <u>did</u> get up before the alarm (set for six) went off while have time to drop you this note before my driver comes along.

Yesterday was another of those days when most of it was spent accomplishing little or nothing. The morning was a total waste of time. The more one deals with most of the boys doing shore jobs the more one appreciates they don't care for same including me. Had a conference yesterday morning with several of the men regarding a training program for part of the crew while here—didn't know nothing & evidently did nothing & find out—sat on their fat ———: Disgusting. Of course it is always the outsider who could make some changes and suggestions.

Thought maybe I would have a letter yesterday & was a bit disappointed to get home & find there was none but guess that if you were up to it you would have written. Since I have had no word to the contrary assume that everything is all right.

Get home every night tired as the devil—can't say that a CIO job is at all easy. From all I gather from the boys immediately before me they are still walking around land after commissioning—expect to work but plan on having things pretty well in shape before getting to that stage.

Expect to go to school next week which of course will mean little other will get done as the other offices will be closed by the time classes are over.

Had a conference with Cotepac's communication—a red-haired Lt. by name of Clark. Strictly on the ball & very helpful—just mentioned the training program, he was on the ball right off—some satisfaction at last.

Will try to call again tonight to see if <u>they</u> put you in a room with a telephone—would like to talk to you but it they can't arrange it will just scream a little bit.

Am to be the sole occupant again for the next two days as Ernie & Jim went to the Canal & Babs is taking her mother down to see her uncle—Nice and quiet & very conducive to Doc's <u>horizontal.</u>

Do miss you so much honey & would very much like to see what the new addition looks like—not a squirrel (?)—all red & stuff.

When does Mother [C] expect to arrive & can she arrange transportation. Still haven't written dad but will do that not later than this weekend—

With all my love to all three of you—

Always your husband

Lovingly

Al

Saturday Morning—July 15

Dearest Sweet—

Received your note yesterday. Looked in the mailbox and found nothing. Was disappointed but later found that the neighbor had taken in the mail so everything is "jako".

What a big bruiser S.W. must be at 5—one would get awfully tired carrying such a load around.

Can't understand anyone being able to see any resemblance to anyone at all at the ripe age of two days. You can tell both Julia & Anne they are slightly nuts. Do hope he doesn't have my big ears and long nose. Well only time will tell whether he will be competing with Susie Q as to looks.

Can just seek Joe—shy as the dickens taking care of Susie—including the go-go—Must give him credit for trying hard. Just like him to have carried on that lengthy conversation.

Don't know what to suggest about the youngster being baptized.—In any event doubtful if I would be here and we won't want to hurt [your] mother again by suggesting that she be in on that.

Might suggest that Uncle Mac & Aunt Marie stand—no one except Mother would know of the eligibility of both. By doing this will split up the spoils & possibly make everyone happy. Maybe it could be arranged before [your] Mother gets here.

Spent all day yesterday at the office—expect to do the same today, getting all of the paperwork done there so can go to school next week without feeling some of the administrative work is gone by the board slighter.

Must complete the final touches as the driver will be along any minute now.

With all my love to the three of you. Again sorry you dot have a phone as would like to call you.

As ever your husband Al

Sorry that your roommate was so fortunate as to lose her youngster, extend my sympathies to her. I guess our luck is pretty good huh!

Lovingly,

Al

Sunday Nite July 16

Dear Sweet:

Will drop you a note before hitting the sack.

Much of the day was spent in writing the letters, or part of them, that I've been intending to write for some time. Got one off to Dad, Carl I.J. and all. Will write Hank sometime this week. Besides doing that washed a couple of shirts linen & hankerchiefs.

Ernie and Babs got back this afternoon. Ernie bought some oysters which I helped him open and Babs bought strawberries, black berries and ? berries. She is going to be one busy gal tomorrow.

The neighborhood reminds me a good bit of the old gang on J St. For anyone who doesn't know would suspect that someone was nuts & plenty so. Having been part of "J" Street can appreciate the spontaneity of it all and pass it off. While writing "Lee" the neighbor came in with Ernie & of course wanted to contribute. Was going to call W4455 this evening to see if everything was alright but went out to dinner rather late and didn't get back until late. May call tomorrow nite.

Received a nice letter from [my] Mother yesterday. Evidently all of the uncles and Aunts want to have a young visitor by the name of Susan. Very glad she is as <u>she</u> is and love her so much—Of course, no thoughts of her mom or Steve (is that going to be permitted?)

Sorry to hear that the pains have but you& hope that they won't last too long. Isn't quite fair to have them before and after both is it?

Will close with all my love to the three of you.

Still think that both Mac & Julia are nuts to think that they can see a resemblance—

Lovingly,

Al

Monday nite July 17

Dearest:

Another note before hitting the sack.

Received your nice letter today—only the second I have received from you while in the hospital—dated July 15—are there any stray ones—not complaining but wanted to know.

Since you were planning on going home on Friday decided I would wait until then to drop the nickel in the box and ask for long distance.

Do hope that [your] Mother can get something else beside a chair car for she will be a plenty tired gal when she arrives if she does have to sit up.

It is good news to hear that Steve is gaining some weight—bet he is still plenty red and oh so small. Guess you did have some supply if he isn't taking much of his formula.

Saw a gal today who evidently would be able to take care of a few—my what a dairy—wondered why she wasn't hunch backed carrying such a load.

The nurses must be keeping an eagle eye on the visitors—must have relaxed the regulations somewhat however to have allowed people to wander in when and if they please.

Can just see the dear sister coming in to ask if you would like to go to mass. Quite a job at that to get you in position so you could go.

The specials must have made good time. Thought I would see that you got a letter on Saturday & Sunday but guess I sort of missed the boat—certainly did not want them (pen is dry) to awaken you from your nap, if any.

Won't address any more letters to you at the hospital if you are going home on Friday but will send them home.

Nice of Etta [Myers] to pay you a visit and rather mean that she didn't get to come up. Mother wrote that Steve was to get a bond from Mother Styer and that Susie was to get one also.

Must close Honey to get some of that shut eye so I won't be yawning during Convoy and Routing School tomorrow.

All my love to the three of you

As Always Your

Al & Da Da

———————

From Dorothy's Mother, Jessie C.

Lincoln, July 18, '44

Dearest Dorothy—Got your letter today and so glad you seem to be getting along so fine. I am about ready to leave. Is about 10: P.M. I have a berth for tonight but nothing more. They have been trying to get me one from K.C. but so far haven't succeeded, so don't know how I will fare. I probably won't be on that first section if not on a Pullman so likely won't connect with that first train so maybe Anne had better wait until I call her so she won't have to make an extra trip.

We went to Mr. Hamilton's funeral this afternoon. Daddy was one of the pall-bearers. Her two boys looked so nice. Franklin in his white Navy (Leut.J.G.) uniform and Clark Lt in Army. Clyde [her sister and Dot's aunt] came over a little while this morning and I took her down town.

Have to call Mrs. Q [Quiggle, friends in Lincoln] yet. They came out late yesterday afternoon but we had gone to take my baggage to check and then went to see "Show Business."

Guess this is all and will be seeing you soon. Love, Mother

Note from Dorothy's father at bottom of the letter:

Am a little late in acknowledging father's day gift which was very nice. Also to put in a nice word for Stephen William. Will be very anxious to see him when I get a chance. Glad to hear you are getting along so well.

Daddy

Didn't mean to overlook Susan but you know Stephen has to have the spotlight for a little while.

———

Wednesday Morning July 19

Dearest Sweet:

Was too tired last night to write the note so will do so now before heading for town.

Hit the jack-pot yesterday on letters, received yours—one from Marie with note on outside from Virginia & a cute card from Harvey & Ruth. Will keep it & send it to you.

Dr. Black it would seem to make up his mind and steer his course without much hesitation. Sorry that you can't continue to nurse the youngster but you remember how sore you <u>used</u> to get when nursing Susie. Hope Mother won't take it too hard.

Forgot to say that I hope Steve is a blond and very tickled that he has some hair. Would be awful to start out bald and be like his dad at such a very early stage.

Didn't know that the offering from a Mary Martha was a $500 bond. That would have been quite an inducement. Marie said she was to have Susie over the weekend (last) and she wasn't sure whether Susie or they would have the best time.

Uncle Albert must have something to be able to walk in and take over like he has. Can see Susie following him around—tho it is understandable as he does have an abundance of patience—always has had.

Nice that Marie & Helen are going to give a tea for Tanta [Aunt Julia Caughey]. She is certainly one sweet person. Know that mother is very happy that they are able to spend so much time in S.D.

Won't be too long now that quarters will be on board. Really looking forward to it since I cant be at home as the Sanfu is really always present.

Are going to have a pre-commissioning party the 25th. Will send a program for Susie & Steve—Don't know how many invitations (commissioning) I will get but will get as many as possible to send. The sponsor is to be some gal from the yard—not bad from the picture in the yard magazine.

Must close Sweet as the driver will be along (he did) so will finish while waiting for the bus to take me to town to the Exchange Bldg.

Nice for you to be going home. Assume it is OK for you to go & take Steve with you. Don't do too much. Shirley is still with us, isn't she?

Love always,

Al

P.S. Give my love to Mother. Looks like <u>Summer</u> is here. Third day that sun was out at <u>six.</u> Yesterday was warm 96o. Won't complain as I like it that way—

Wednesday nite July 20
Dear Sweet:

Didn't receive a letter today so guess you had found something to keep you busy or that you had started your drying up process & didn't feel like writing.

Went to personnel office today and made out beneficiary slip to show "Steve" in the relationship of child so that he & you will be protected if something should happen to me. Here is a copy of the slip submitted so just put it with your papers.

You should be home by the time this reaches you and all settled in 399 J St—will be good to get home won't it even tho the life in the hospital <u>often</u> isn't too hard to take with not much to do but relax—tho one does get tired relaxing too much.

Will go to bed early tonight as it was a bit late in hitting the sack last night. Hope the light isn't still too bright so as to prevent the slumbers. Was so warm when I went to bed last night threw back the covers & found on awakening that I was covered. Don't remember ever coming too & pulling the covers over me.

Really have surprised myself in writing you every day but guess that is just because I love you so much—Can't help it I guess but that is what woman does to man.

Babs & Ernie are going to take a walk. Since I'm going to bed won't join them this time.

The weather cooled off today—a bit of rain this morning with protective clouds this afternoon. Rather pleasant tho to have seen the sun two days in a row. Will be pleasant sleeping tonight as cool as it is.

Wonder how Susan is going to be at <u>home</u> after all the excitement she has had and the <u>attention</u> from her uncles, aunts, grandma & cousins. Maybe the fact that "Baby" is going to be there will help some to keep her attention. Hope she isn't too upset about another interest.

God night Sweet—My love to all three of you. If you can spare some give some to Mother.

Love Always

Al & Da Da & goo

Friday morning July 21

Dear Sweet:

Will start the letter but don't know how much of it will get write before Mr. Winchester comes up over the hill.

From the schedule Dr. Black has set up for you it would seem that you should be triplets & that a four bedroom house wouldn't be too large. Am just wondering how in the heck Steve is going to be kept isolated. Surely Susie cannot be put out of the room & can imagine her not being able to see the youngster 'baby'.

Think leaving her in town until Sunday very good one. Do wish so much that I could be there and take care of some of the feedings but then it doesn't do too much good to wish.

Thought I told you I would be going to Convoy comun. School this week. Has been rather an easy week as we are secured about 3:30 and it wouldn't do any good to go to the office at that late hour. Have taken care of some business in town and gotten home early for a change.

Today is the big day for you to be released from the (office) hospital & on your way home. Do hope that Mother has arrived and in not too tired. She didn't know what she was getting into did she?

Have been conscious recently of a new type of headgear—in all shades. They look very much like "Bra's" being worn topside on the noggin. Wonder what the designer had in mind.

Just another week of living ashore & then will get begin getting "salty". Starting with the letters written after the 28th you had better address them to me—U.S.S. Skurry AM 304 % Fleet Post Office San Francisco CA. Should reach me just as soon as before. However if you need to get in touch with me in a hurry am sure can work out some deal with Babs.

Since I am completing this in the Post Office and must have breakfast before school take up must get on my horse.

Will call tonight & see how you are with love to all think of you I am

Your Husband & Da Da

Am mailing this off % Coles in hopes you will get it by Sunday.

Saturday morning July 22, 1944

Dearest Sweet:

Possibly have time to start & complete this before the driver shows up— will try anyway.

Was awfully good to hear your voice and that of [Dot's] Mother & [cousin] Ben [Alice Day] too. At first didn't figure that Mother had gotten in & so you had not asked to be released from the hospital yesterday. If I hadn't gotten you the second time would have called the family.

Had wondered why Dr. Black hadn't suggested keeping Steve in the hosp. until he had gained some more weight but since he feels that ain't the place for him that is good enough for my money.

Speaking of money do you need some more? If so will see if I can't draw the money for salary which has been accumulating since the 15th of June. If not will wait until the middle of Aug & then see you get most of it—can be in a lump sum then.

Wonder where Susie could have picked up what she may have. Not worried about it but certainly complicates things a bit. Know that she was very glad to see you yesterday. Did she ask about "Baby" or had she forgotten about it.

Have shown her pictures around plenty—of course without the <u>aire (?)</u> of a proud papa—all seem to be very much impressed & after looking at me wonder—but then I add the maternal side has contributed much.

Would like to be informed at all times good or bad how my family is feeling which includes much. Don't appreciate the fact that you don't want to worry me as one <u>more</u> worry won't break the <u>old man's</u> back. Do mean it Sweet for I would much rather have it that way & I know that you are not an alarmist. Don't expect anything to happen I can assure you for really we have been very fortunate in our venture of living and anticipate that good fortune will continue.

Am awfully sorry that [your] Mother had such a tough trip. Was [illegible word] of her to make the trip especially on such short notice (aren't you ashamed of yourself for being in such a hurry) without having been able to get accommodations. She must care for you a lot to have stood <u>too.</u>

Don't know what I will do about the ships pre commissioning party on Tuesday nite—expect I will stag it if possible tho I suppose the entertainment committee (District Office Wel. & Rec.) will have some she male guests. Will send some invitations home.

Am very anxious for this theory to end and practice to end—Maybe I'm foolish about it but do prefer a definite routine.

With all my love to the <u>three of you.</u> Pass on what you don't need to Mother & the family.

Love Always Al

(Completing this on the bus hence the scrawl.)

———

From Ensign Carl H. Stadler:

22 July 44

Dear Al,

Was so very glad to get your very newsy letter. I have been trying to get your address ever since I left but it seems to be of no avail.

From what I gather from your letter you have a very excellent deal and don't realize just how nice it is. I can imagine just how thankful you were to see the radio technician come aboard.

So the "Madam" [landlady Manley] tracked you to the 12th N.D. If I told you here what I thought of her and that whole deal I'm certain the censor would have quite a time cutting obscene and descriptive language out of this letter. I hope you tell her to fly a kite in no uncertain terms.

I got the news of your latest arrival a couple of days ago from I.J. Dot didn't let you down this time and not have a boy. Our 'poncho' hasn't shown yet but any day now they keep telling me.

Saw Buck Lyman not long ago. He is a new poppa of another girl.

Hank [Koening] & I have been seeing quite a bit of each other lately. It is nice to have someone like him out here. I'm still bunked with Sansom & Sparks which also makes it nice.

Have a pretty nice job now and like it better as long as I learn more about it.

[Name removed by censor's scissors—likely I. J., Carl's wife]_____ sent me 2 pictures of Miss Suzan that we had in our camera from last Easter. They are certainly cute and occupy a very prominent spot on my desk. [Name removed by censor's scissors—likely I. J., Carl's wife] is going to send Dot copies so she can see them.

Well Al I hope you are getting settled in your new job and will be able to start taking it easy before too long.

I'll take that bet although I think you drive a very hard bargain on the odds. Good luck to you Al & write again.

Carl

Ens. C.H. Stadler

Sunday nite July 24

Dearest Sweet;

Writing this tonight as I'm pretty sure I won't be dropping you a note tomorrow morning as we are going to see the Miracle of Morgans Creek—which I understand is very much of a scream. Company kept us from going to an early show so will have to go to the last one at 9:55.

Didn't get up till noon today—really very lazy. Babs sister Billie spent last evening and night here—played cribbage until late and didn't get to bed until 2:30. Spent this afternoon working in the yard with Ernie and sense it was warm decided to go to the lake, within a few miles for a swim. Was very much surprised to find the lake [Washington] very pleasantly warm. Didn't stay in too long as the wind was short and dinner was waiting for us.

Have really felt good since leaving SCTC—guess it all was nervous indigestion & have used very few of the Amphojels which I bought on Marie's suggestion. Have been gaining back some of the weight I let slip by.

The pants since the adjustment seem to be a bit large in the waist. The blouses however seem to be a bit snug still.

Spoke to the Skipper the other day about wearing apparel. He said he had made a mistake and would not take any blues or whites with him this time so don't be surprised if you will have to find storage for them at some spot there at 399J. Plan on buying another blouse and 2 prs pants (work) as that is what I will probably be wearing a lot. Think it best to get another cap as the "Go to Hell" one far from practical for sea duty. Will have sufficient to take care of these expenditures.

Won't be able to advise you when we are leaving here but know for certain that we will be south before going wherever we will be going. Very possibly I will have an opportunity to see Carl sometime in the future, not to near. Don't believe that his assignment will be any worse for him—many of the boys intended for "hauling Panties" get special training & doubt if Carl as or will get it as they don't generally waste Harvard men that way.

Have been wondering if Susie has or has not. Guess she might as well start getting those child diseases if she is to get them so as to have the bother with them in the past—Will be interested to find out.

Would very <u>much much</u> liked to have spent the weekend with my family.

Love to all <u>three</u> of you.

As Always,

Al & Da Da

Tuesday nite July 26

Dear Sweet:

Just a few more days remaining till I will no longer be a dry land sailor. Things have been fairly well whipped into shape. The Skipper and Exec. Seem to be fairly well satisfied so that is a big relief.

The Schnabels couldn't find anyone to stay with their youngster. Decided that since I didn't have a partner & really wasn't interested in having one decided it would be just as well if only one didn't go to the party rather than two. Mr. S wasn't very receptive because he felt I wanted to go but Mrs. said she would like to see what it was all about. Hence I'm spending the night as nursemaid. Will spend the nite with them.

Called Babs to inform them that I wouldn't be home and asked if there was any mail. A bit disappointed to find there wasn't some. Do hope the mail man will be good to me tomorrow for I am anxious to hear about the progress of S and that of my Susie Q.

The Exec. Advised me tonight that I had drawn the first watch from 11 A.M. Sat to 8 A.M. Sunday. Will have to be on board but of course will be permitted a bit of sleep & relaxation. The selection boiled down as between myself and the other ensign & he thought I was more capable of handling. Don't believe it was soft soap so feel it somewhat of a compliment. The J.G's weren't figured in the elimination as they both have their wife here. Expect to be given the breaks if and when the Skurry is in at S.D.

Sometimes one is ready to say the H with it from the much buck passing which one sees. Tried to get some special flags & pennants which one requires—understand they had been ordered—only to find out they hadn't been made & couldn't get them for two weeks—expect to be here long enough to get them but it does get under the skin. It's no wonder a thinking person doesn't want a shore job & the more I see of it the less I would be happy with one—(Maybe I'm a moron but can't see it any other way.)

Am sending two copies of the programs to the party tonight & invitations under separate cover—which I thought you might want to put in Susie's & S books (when you have time). The gal on the program is sweeping a mine in case you can't make it out.

If I don't hear from you tomorrow will call. Know that you are awfully busy and will write when you can but would like to hear.

Love to all three of you

Al & Da Da

P.S. Just received your letter of last Wed. last evening. The addressed the same as the others evidently had been delivered elsewhere—Can't understand why but one other letter was made to suffer in the same way.

Lovingly

Al

P.S.S.

Do wish that you could be here for the big event & come aboard for the refreshments.

Love Al

The ship's precommissioning party program.

Thursday nite July 28

Dearest Sweet:

Must get a note off to you before going to bed. Ashamed I neglected to write you yesterday but know that you will overlook the neglect.

Was much relieved to learn that everything and everybody was alright. Was a bit worried since I hadn't heard since last Saturday except forgetting that late letter of Wed. a week ago.

The weather has been quite warm the last few days & in fact gets hot. We have gone swimming.

Will mail the invitation to the Commissioning under separate cover. Have sent only one of the cards required for admission as the other I gave to Ernie & Babs. Have sent one to the Herneys & mailed one to Dad for Dad & Mother. Someone made a mistake and ordered too few.

Received a nice letter from Carl S today together with your letter written on Sunday—can't understand why it took so long to arrive. Carl's letter has date of July 22nd which isn't bad time at all. Had two deletes as you will note & fitting in the pieces both were references to I.J. which appeared earlier in the letter but was not deleted.

Time that your husband is going to be a land lubber is really running short. Am really anxious to get on board for the work. Has been hard work and will be hard work for the next few weeks before things will really be whipped into shape.

The party must have been a huge success as all of the officers except the Schnabels stayed to the last. The Schnabels took a walk out on the party but waited for the Hetzlers (Exec. Off) since Mrs. S expects an addition on about Dec. 12. Their little youngster awakened about 11:45 and cried until 12:30 when Mother & Dad got home. Suppose you can't blame the youngster being upset seeing a strange man trying to quiet him at that hour. Even my singing didn't help. Can't say that I didn't think Susie wouldn't do that.

Ironed three greys and one white shirt pls some hankerchiefs which Mrs. Emel was kind enuf to wash for me—took me about an hour & a half. Guess I'm not quite what I used to be on the ironing. Do want to move aboard with as little dirty linen as possible.

Don't think I couldn't do for a sight of you Susie & Steve. The letter seems to have hit the jack pot on gifts. Sweet of Dad & Mother Stadler to have remembered Susie as well as Steve, and of course the beginning of the nest egg from Dad & Mother was a big help—Did Steve thank his Grandmother.

Will send this care of Coles in hope you will get it by Sunday.

Love you three Always

Al.

P.S. Can't understand why most of the letters get delivered & others are delayed or returned.

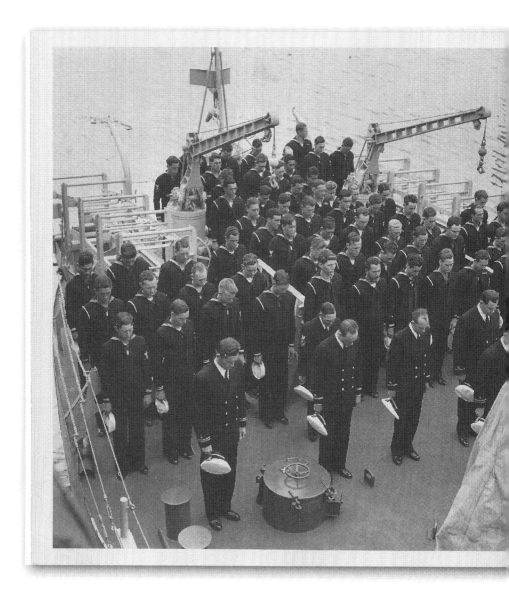

The invocation during the commissioning ceremony of the USS Skurry,
*July 29, 1944. Ensign Albert Herney is third from the left in the row of
officers. The ship's name was later changed to the USS* Scurry.

SHIP'S OFFICERS:

        Lieut. C.E. DUNSTON, Commanding

        Lieut. W.F. HETZLER, Executive Officer

        Lieut. F.K. SCHNABEL, Sonar Officer

        Lieut. (jg) D.F. GOSCH, Gunnery & Minesweeping

        Ensign A.F. HERNEY, Communications Officer

        Ensign F.L. BEZOLD, Radio-Radar Officer

        Chief Bos'n C.D. KRAUSE, Damage Control Officer

        Machinist L.C. HANNA, Engineering Officer

The USS Scurry AM-304.

From Dictionary of American Naval Fighting Ships*:*

Scurry (AM-304) was a steel-hulled Admirable class Minesweeper constructed for the U.S. Navy during World War II. She was crewed by sailors who were trained in mine-sweeping, and quickly sent to the Pacific Ocean to clear minefields so that Allied Forces could invade Japanese-held beaches. For this dangerous work, often under enemy fire, she was awarded four battle stars.

She was laid down on 24 May by Associated Shipbuilders, Seattle, Washington, launched on 1 October 1943; sponsored by Miss Winette DeLaye; and commissioned on 29 July 29 1944, Lt. Charles E Dunson in command. The spelling of her name was changed from Skurry to Scurry on 3 August 1944.

General characteristics

Class & type:	*Admirable-class minesweeper*
Displacement:	*650 tons; 945 tons (full load)*
Length:	*184 ft 6 in*
Beam:	*33 ft*
Draft:	*9 ft 9 in*
Propulsion:	*2 x Cooper Bessemer GSB -8 diesel engines, 1,710 shp*
	National Supply Co. single reduction gear 2 shafts
Speed:	*14.8 knots*
Complement:	*104*
Armament:	*1 x 3"/50 calibre gun*
	1 x twin Bofors 40 mm guns
	6 x Oerlikon 20 mm cannons
	1 x Hedgehog anti-submarine mortar
	4 Depth charge projectors (K guns)
	2 x Depth charge tracks[i]

Friday nite July 29, 1944

Dear Sweet:

The last note that I will write you before all the correspondence will be censored. Not that I object to that phase of the matter as have tried to censor my own mail. Tough at times however.

Have packed earlier this evening, then a shower. Must get to bed soon as I have been up late for the last few evenings.

Won't be leaving here yet for awhile so don't think I'll be going right out. If Steve keeps picking up he will have filled out somewhat before I get to see him.

Received your letter written on Tuesday. Seems to have arrived in good time.

Susan must have been quite a problem—with her interest in "baby" and wanting to touch. Hope that she will continue being so interested and helpful. Suppose that Mother can't help spoiling her as we seemed to do a good job of it ourselves and then life is always so touch or a youngster not old enough to understand.

Both Susan and Steve seem to have found a Godmother in Mother Styer. Will drop her a note thanking her for the gifts. Marie wrote that she (Mother S) planned in getting a bond for each of them since the drive in Coronado had been lagging.

Will advise you of the procedure to be followed if you must get in touch with me in a hurry. Generally you will contact the Commandant of the 11th N.D. advise him (or one of his assistants) of name rank & activity to which attached (never however advising him as to where the skurry is even if you know) & if within the Continental limits will pass the information and message. Give you specific details later.

Would have liked very much to have been home with you, Susie & Steve Sweet but that will all will have to come later.

Was wondering how Nickey [Al and Dot's dog, a German shepherd] took to the new addition. Appreciate the fact that he as yet hasn't been allowed to wash Steve's face but has he had the opportunity to know that someone new is in the house. Will have two to guard now instead of just one. Does he like the retainer (fence) or isn't he content to remain within.

Worry to hear that Harvey hasn't been feeling too well. Will be nice for them as well as for Lee & Virginia to have them so close.

Do hope that Miss Turner [Shirley, the helper] won't get too independent. Ask her to say hello to all of her family.

Will hit the sack so as to be fresh for the big day tomorrow.

With all my love to the three of you—Tell Mother I won't mind if she spoils Susie just a little.

Your Salty Sailor Husband

Al

P.S. It is my understanding that as soon as one as a F.P. address that 6c airmail for half ounce is permitted.

P.S.S. What is Mrs Styer's first name?

Saturday nite July 30 1944 (a typewritten letter)

Dearest Sweet, Susie and Steve:

Now that pre-and commissioning is all over the residence has been taken up aboard the part of Uncle's Navy to which he assigned me. From all that had been experienced by the men who have preceded us here it would appear that the work is only now really beginning. No object is make to work if you can see that there is being accomplished and wont mind it a bit.

The ceremony yesterday was short, sweet, and to the point, even to the Chaplin. While simple it was much as expected and can't say that I was at all unhappy or disappointed to be a part of it even if it was such a small part. Enclosed is a copy of the ceremony program.

All of the festivities were over by two, including the luncheon to which the guests were invited. Didn't get to eat till late as there were several Navy inspectors who decided that it might be a good time to come aboard about that time to check on the equipment; since it was in the Comm. dept. wanted to see what it was all about.

After all of the guests had departed the fun began trying to start a bit of organization out of the chaos which is bound to be inherent, something like moving into a new house. Nobody knew about nothing, where it was or how it got there. All you had to do was sit down and start to do some thing and then someone was looking for you to straighten out a problem that was bothering them or one of the yard crew had a matter to be straightened out. Really more fun and a quick ticket to the bubby hatch.

In order to get a bit more familiar with this new home, new in many ways, stayed aboard last evening as I did most of the day except for a trip into town to get the mail. Found your letter of July 27 which helped take away a great deal of the feeling experienced when you move into strange country. Not bad on the delivery considering that it was sent to the skurry % F.P.O.

Don't let the difference of opinion respecting Susie's bed problem upset you too much. Allow Mother to try her way first and see what she can do. Since she is there and wants to try her sure fire way give it your best. Sounds like Susie is too, with the competition she is running with Steve on the diapers. If it isn't successful then fall back on what you thought would work.

Sorry the adjustment seems to be so hard for her but then the addition is so new to her and will be for some time as yet and we can't expect too much for a very small youngster. Then also you hadn't better be too tough on my pride and joy and if you are plan on being treated awful when I get back to being a first or any class civilian just so it is of a civilian nature.

Plan that you will make provision for [my] Mothers birthday which will be within the week. Will drop her a birthday note but will leave the gift up to you. Something else I have missed and will in the future too, is the many clan gatherings for the many and numerous birthdays and events.

Do wish you could have been here to have witnessed the Commissioning Sweet, but 1700 miles is a long way off isn't and such a problem with a family. Invited Ernie and Babs but since his sister had a program at the same time didn't get to come.

Must get to bed so that some co (n) structive work can be accomplished in the next few days.

With all my love to the three of you.

Al

Albert F. Herney

Ens. U.S.N.R

PART TWO

AT SEA IN THE PACIFIC
ON USS *SCURRY*

3

ADJUSTMENT TO SHIPBOARD LIFE:
SHAKEDOWN AND CONVOY MISSIONS

August 1, 1944—December 31, 1944

From "Saga of the Scurry: The First Year," the ship's first-anniversary program:
Commissioning—

Wartime earnestness marked the colorful military ceremony staged on board fleet
minesweeper SCURRY moored in a Puget Sound shipyard one year ago today. Assembled
at division quarters topside, the ship's one hundred officers and men stood at attention
to orders; a band sounded off with the National Anthem as colors were hoisted to the fore
commission pennant to the maintruck—The SCURRY was ranked "UNITED STATES
SHIP"...and pledged to the work of war.

First cruise—

Fitting out and trials were completed with alacrity in the home waters of of shake-
down the SCURRY sailed south to fleet operating waters off Southern California. Drill
discipline and training interspersed with succulent liberties in Los Angeles, Hollywood,
San Diego...such was the magnificent strain of shakedown. The conditioning of men
and machinery for overseas duty was accomplished during these six weeks. A first cruise
establishes alliance of ship and men and therein is wrought the "character" of the ship,
foreverlasting. The Captain reported his ship ready to join the fleet.[ii]

From Dictionary of American Naval Fighting Ships*:*
Following shakedown between 15 August and 19 September 1944, Scurry departed
the west coast on 1 October escorting a convoy to Eniwetok. After arriving there on 3
November, Scurry escorted convoys in the vicinity of Eniwetok and Manus until return-
ing to Pearl Harbor on 13 December.[iii]

According to NavSource Online: Mine Warfare*, Scurry's signal code name*
was "November Quebec Sierra Foxtrot."[iv]

— ◆ —

August 18, 1944 to Dorothy from George Herney [Albert's brother] from Ft.
Worth Texas.
Our Dear Dorothy

Of course you know that we always include Susan Ann, Stephen W.
and Al. Dorothy we Herneys' are more than proud of you and your two fine
Children. As for me no one can take the place of that sweet angel child you
yours. Then again you gave us a fine Boy. He will have lots to do along with
Gregory [Herney, Francis's son] to carry on for our departed Father. I don't
know whether you ever met our Dad or not, but take it from me, he was a
kindly, fair, home loving and brilliant man. How proud he would be of all of
his in-laws and the grand children.

He too would be proud of Al and his many successes. Its tough I know
your present separation, but God Grant that it not be for long. I had a long
letter from Uncle Albert reporting on the health and doings of the Herney
Clan. He tells me that Mother is not at all well, Please dear give me a detailed
report as I am worried.

I am enclosing a pocked Medal for Al. Have it blessed if possible by his
Parish Priest and get it to Our Dear Brother. My sunken chest extends with
pride whenever I think of him and his fine family.

Well Dear, Mike [Leonore, George's wife] joins me in wishing for you
and yours everything Good Always. And our prayers for Al's speedy and safe
return to you.
With Love

Geo
1200 West Rosedale St.
Fort Worth (4) Texas

Thursday night [August 1944, undated]
Dearest Sweet, Susie, Steve & Mother:

Haven't been at all diligent about writing but know that you will forgive me. By way of explanation, not excuse will say that there really hasn't been much time left for correspondence, since horizontal exercise isn't enjoyed until the late hours. It is now after midnight.

Received only one letter from you since commissioning. Realize that you have been very busy with your added family duties and you not yet entirely recovered from the effects of presenting me with a son. Will be content with what correspondence you can find time to write.

Mother wrote giving me the news on <u>him</u> saying that he was progressing satisfactorily—sleeping well and gaining his weight. Hope he keeps it up so that if he even wants to get in the navy he will be free from the worry of putting on weight stuffing himself with an excess of oatmeal, nice, bananas and drinking half & half.

The meals we have been getting are first rate—the first class cook assigned is first class. The food always seems to be prepared rather than cooked which goes a long way to keep a man partially happy. We are eating general mess so eat the same as the crew. They all seem to be very contented with the food as much as we have been.

Since Herney is a junior officer aboard and with less practical experience of any aboard he takes pretty much of a razzing. Have requested permission of the skipper to send a dispatch to Bupers asking to be reassigned to the Rebel as they <u>might</u> be glad to have me. The request of course was denied.

Am just as enthusiastic as ever about the tour of duty aboard the Skurry. Hope eventually to feel fully at home on her and not a first class tenderfoot, and that in not too distant a future.

Was wondering how soon it would be before it would be possible to have a family group picture taken. Don't believe you had had one since your announcement picture. Of course Steve would be just a bundle and would rightly refuse to smile when the photographer said look at the birdie—but then Susie's 2nd birthday will be along soon too.

Has Dad had any luck at all in getting some vacation time arranged? Mother had said that he had hoped to sometime soon. Would be nice if he had a chance to get out so he could see his new grand child.

Have written Mother a letter tonight too but haven't written Mother Styer as don't know her first name.

Will close so that I can have a shower and get a bit of shut eye before 6:15 rolls around.

Miss the three of you so much—with all my love to you three & Mother. Give my regards to Bev & the neighbors.

Al & DaDa

P.S. Understand we are to get some pictures of the commissioning which I hope to be able to pass on to you.

Thursday nite August 15

Dearest Dot Susie & Steve:

Feel like a heel for not having written you more recently but the work still is pressing and into the wee hours—seems like there is more to do more than ever. Do hope the pressure will let up soon so a balanced routine can be followed. Hate to think that this could go on forever.

Have made only 6 liberties since moving aboard—Once a week ago Sat nite and then last Thurs. when attended the Burlesque with Mr. Kinnickle, his wife & Mr. Hetzler. The Burl. wasn't any worse than the Vaudeville which we saw the Sat. nite before with the exception of a few jokes.

Your letters are all coming through in good order. Thanks Sweet for taking time out to write. Wrote Ann a birthday note the other nite but couldn't drive myself to do more writing.

The check for travel was $246.00. Can't imagine you not being able to keep track of all the things especially with the problem on your hands. Keep the check for the Tax Refund and will endorse it later as there is no big rush about it.

Made out a new allotment to you the other day. After figuring everything up—the allotment for bonds & insurance figured you could have $175.00. Knowing you realize you won't be extravagant & there is no sense in me drawing too much for more than will be left me.

Sorry to hear that you have another problem on your hands—can't quite understand Fern and in fact it has always been hard for me understand any of the {Thompsons}.

It is too bad that the Pages are leaving as they were nice people. Wonder if there just aren't going to be any more concrete barges. Give them my best and tell them I will be sorry not to have them in should the occasion arise.

Glad to hear that Nicky is much better. Feel that losing him would be a blow but Sweet never hesitate to get rid of him if he is in any way a danger to our offspring.

What a disappointment that Dad isn't going to get to come west. Don't blame Mother for wanting to go home under the circumstances and she has been with you for quite a spell. Do hope that you won't be squeezed for hands & that you might find some help.

The information about the OPA is a scream—Can't imagine why they waited this long. Believe that they intend to reduce the rent & are notifying you to that effect or does the statement say that the rent is $60 as of 1 Aug.

Would appreciate it if you would call Mannie and ask him to procure a stock—3 qts of Scotch and 3 of Bourbon—Don't know but what it might come in handy sometime and its my recollection that our supply is low.

With love always to the <u>three</u> of you.

Al and DaDa

P.S. The news on Steve's weight is powerful good news—Al

Sunday Nite August 20, 1944

Dearest Sweet, Susie, Steve & Mother:

Wouldn't be able to go for sack drill tonight without first writing you a note. The mail man was a bit slow on most of your letters for I received five of them today. Since I hadn't received any for a week was beginning to get a bit worried—now am relieved to know that you all are well.

You haven't marked the five letters received today so assume that you have written six addressed c/o Fleet Post Office, is that right. The last postmark is Aug 4 written Thurs nite (not bad time on that letter.)

Didn't mean to give the impression that the watch for the day meant on the feet for the full time for not at present anyway we get to secure—of course available to be called at any time the presents itself.

Wrote Mother a letter not sure she got it in time for the days did slip by in such a hurry—they always do especially when you have so much to do with so little time to do them in.

Glad to know that Susie is growing quite fond of her grandmother tho don't see how she could do otherwise. Didn't expect her to spoiling Susie just a little. Do hope that Susie is orienting herself to the fact that Steve being so little requires so much of her mother's time.

So Steve is slowly but surely growing up and no longer looking like a little bare squirrel. Thought he had a good bit of hair and awfully sorry he has my hairline—please expose it (his head to the sun) so as to active the hair for I could stand it for him to have as little as his Dad. You should see the picture of the Prayer [at the commissioning ceremony.] The photographer took it from above and oh how bald your husband appears.

Was wondering if you have figured in the travel money I received from Cambridge to San Francisco—Can't imagine that you would make such a mistake of some $200. If there is that much am very pleased. Can you cash the checks for the insurance refund, the $156 portion is a nice amount. Cash it if you can and buy Susie a $37.50 bond for her birthday. Think you should save the rest for the personal & real property taxes coming up this fall & would like the exterior of the house painted.

Would like very much to have been home for the party for Uncle Albert & Aunt Julia & Mother's birthday. Mother wrote that there is a possibility that they would come to Calif. to live. Think that fine for them and very nice for Uncle Albert, Tanta & Mother was well as Unke & Aunt Ann.

Your suggestions for mother's birthday are excellent ones and practical. Have wondered if you did get to Ann's for if you didn't go I'm sure they would have been disappointed.

Am not at all surprised that Ed likes Susie for he is fond both of you and myself. Has she warmed up to him any more—if she hasn't her Daddy will feel badly about it.

Wonder if Dad doesn't get a chance to have his vacation this summer. Sent him an invitation for he and Mother. Suppose he is awfully busy as usual. So can't wonder that they might not give him time off.

Your news about the examination is rather pleasant and hope that there will be no need for a touching up. It would appear that the schedule both for Mother and yourself is a full one. Please don't forget to give Steve a feeding as we do want him to get fat on him. The gain seems to be constant & good to hear.

So sorry to hear about Dad Hutton. Both are such nice people and so very very pleasant. With Mother's handicap it isn't hard to appreciate the hardships of such an affliction. Will drop them a note.

Have discovered that there were some invitations left over—didn't know until several days ago. Will send them to the family with a short note. Maybe some of them will be glad to receive them as a souvenir (?)

Life onboard has just about reached the stage where there is no longer that feeling of complete chaos but some semblance of order and routine tho there yet remains much to be done. Most of the men in my division and under my supervision are cooperative, interested & pleasant to work with which helps a whole lot.

Have arranged to have the laundry done on board. Wash day is scheduled for us—one of the crew washes (yes we have a washing machine) and one of the mess attendants does the ironing. Am now reduced to having my work greys washed. Do hope they don't shrink—especially the work greys (must be getting awfully tired for my spelling is generally bad but not this bad.)

The quality of food is the same as the first several days so plan on putting on some weight if the amount of food consumed is an indication. However there is always the possibility that the pressure might be burning it up. (Letter is much longer than I thought it would be—surprises me too and its now 11:45 PM.)

Haven't really had a chance to do any reading especially Time which I haven't seen for weeks. Maybe I'll get out of the habit but will have to take it up again to get in on the news as haven't read a newspaper for some time either.

Your thank you notes which you must write reminds me of the letters I should write—Nice of Mrs. Brown & Mrs. Leman to remember Steve. Of course Sweet pie would come thru. Should drop her a note. Steve seems to be on the receiving end and oh too small to be appreciative of that fact.

Thanks for enclosing the note from the Huttons & Bernice. Would appear that George has finally settled down to something. Can't understand him being at one thing for such a long time—good news of course to hear that he is sticking with it.

You should stop by the Brown's sometime when out that way—show off the new addition, the Pride and Joy and the bananas when ripe. That's where we got the slip, wasn't it.

It is sort of an uncomfortable feeling to know that the happy "J" street gang is again going to be broken up. Tell each & all of them hello for me.

Must wind this up Sweetheart for some of that horizontal experience.

Love always to the three of you, Mothers (both) & the family—

Your husband and dada—

Friday nite: (August 25, 1944)

Dearest Dot Susie & Steve,

The possibilities of getting home for Sunday is & are small. However it may all be for the best and very good possibilities for a longer stay and more actual time at home in the future.

Tried to call early tonight only to find a two hour delay. Since there was work to do came back to the ship to do some work. Just finished for the night & did get something accomplished. Will try to call Sunday afternoon when all of the family is at Julia's & will get an opportunity to say hello to all of them there.

Didn't get a present for any of the birthdayites including my one & only. That as usual is falling into your department—including all the other burdens on your shoulders.

Was very happy to (see) learn that Steve is getting on the plump side. Enjoyed your description of the operation and the results of same. It is good that it has been taken care of at this early date.

Possibly the christening can be delay until I can be home if you wish but if you want to have it taken care of sooner feel free to do so. What is to be done about <u>Spouses</u> is something?

Received the letter & medal you received from George. Must drop him a note that I can assure you the only letters written since I came aboard have been to you & the ones to Mother & Ann. Possibly will get some written soon.

It is surprising just how little one can accomplish in a day. Things do move fast especially when there is so much to do—seems like everything except time to work on the Pubs and becoming entirely familiar with them. Haven't as yet acquired the name so richly deserved while at Harvard but Snafu is slowly driving it to me.

Guess Carl must have tied on when he heard about the offspring. Can't blame him but think he is missing something by not having the first one a girl. Well maybe we all good.

Do hope the loss of Shirley or what she was doing irrespective of how little isn't putting too much on your shoulders and trying to too much. Do try & get some help for it will do somewhat (???) taking some of the hardship out of such a large family. Enjoyed your comment about Sundays.

Will send this to Julia's so you might probably get this Sunday.

Wish all the celebrants a happy birthday for me—a big hug and kiss to Susie and much love to all of the family & especially to <u>my family</u>.

Lovingly Always Al & DaDa

Ens.A.F. Herney

Inclosed is a birthday note to Susie.

Al

P.S. Note the spelling of the <u>Scurry</u> changed from <u>k</u> to <u>c.</u> —Why—I don't know.

Al

Friday nite:

Dearest Susan Ann:

Just two more days and you will be all of <u>two</u> years old. It has been fun to grow up and very much of a pleasure to see you develop. You know your Daddy hasn't liked being away from you, Mother and Steve yet there isn't much that can be done about. I was hoping that I could be there for the Big Day but that won't be possible. Will have to postpone the pleasure of being home on your Birthday till next year.

Was a bit disappointed the other night to find that the Sandman had already claimed you for the night. We must do something about these busy circuits to San Diego for I tried to call again tonight only to find a two hour delay.

Everyone tells me what a good youngster you are. Do hope that you will continue to be a good girl in the future and a help to Stephen in that way.

Must drop a note to Mother and its now 11:30 so must close.

With lots of love and a very happy birthday to you

As always your loving father

DaDa

Ens. A.F. Herney

———

Continuation of notations in Dorothy's desk diary:

Sept 12—Al arrives in San Diego on his ship and comes home to see us! Is home till Sat A.M. I take him in and ship goes out for a day—he is home again that nite and take him in Sunday—ship out—home again Monday nite and leaves Tues. 19th.

Sept 21—I go to Long Beach leaving Susan & Steve at Julia's. Have room at Calif. Hotel. Al comes every nite. We see show "Janie" on Thurs. nite—Friday nite Band Concert—Sat nite have dinner with Helen in L.A. and go to Turnabout theatre Sunday nite take a walk. Monday nite eat late—go back to Hotel. Tues I go to L.A. & spend a day with I.J. That night we see "Going my Way" with Bing Crosby.

Wed. I sweat blood as Al not sure he'll be back, also I catch cold. He comes finally and that is his last night with me. I leave Thurs A.M. and spend that nite with Helen Rice and home Friday to my children.

Sept 30.—Al calls much to my surprise—he is still in San Pedro.

Oct. 1—Al calls for last time—almost a yr. since he left for Tucson.

Continuation of text from "Saga of the Scurry: The First Year," the ship's first-anniversary program:

Aloha—

Final departure from the continental United States came as a routine sailing in a military sense; in the hearts of the men it found a twinge of undefined significance... inevitable avulsion. The last liberty had expired at midnight, the preparations made for getting underway. Silently the SCURRY slipped through misty harbor and out to sea toward the descending sun...a long voyage had begun.

Convoy—

Thirty-two days after the coastline of the U.S. faded from sight astern of the ship, we made our first landfall—Eniwetok Atoll in the Marshall Islands. Put on convoy duty, the ship was now assigned several long trips in rapid succession. After all, the SCURRY is a versatile ship; classed fleet minesweeper she is built to also combat enemy submarines, aircraft, and surface craft (up to her size; anything else she can bully). As an escort of convoys she covered many thousands of ocean miles the first several months overseas, and visited islands and ports widely scattered over the Pacific. In the course of travels, young sailors on board were inducted into the "Ancient Order of the Deep" as Shellbacks by Neptunus Rex, and into the "Imperial Domain of the Golden Dragon" by the phenomenon of time and distance.[v]

Thursday nite Oct 5, 1944

Dearest Sweet—Susie & Steve:

Must get off a note to you through I don't know how soon it can be mailed.

The weather is rather pleasant but a bit different that we would be enjoying at home this time of year. It is rather difficult to explain the many shades of blue one can observe and feel at the same time.

Your box from Bullocks was received on board last mailday. As I promised I haven't opened it nor will I until such time as Dec 25 rolls around, which shouldn't be too far away the way the days are rolling by.

My hopes of seeing Hank real soon won't materialize—got fooled this time but then there is always the future to look forward to.

It is surprising how much ones comfort can influence a man and effect his proportion of fairness and not assuming an equal share of the less desirable phases of a career. Guess it would be advisable to organize a club, other than a "Bitch" club and call it something like everyone needs, intends, well, endeavor to observe kindness—Oh hell who's nuts—I guess its me.

Don't guess that any of the family have missed my being one as much as I miss being gone—you at least have each other while _me_—what have I got but the Scurry and the shipmates. Still believe this is better than a shore job.

What with the watches rotating the sleep has been anything but regular. Do guess the time would come when even the two oclock feeding wouldn't be too much of a strain. Definite routine would be preferable but then guess you can't have everything.

Have wondered what has been done about the roof and the paint job. Sorry that I had to leave that for your shoulders too honey. Guess you have been having Harvey take care of the furnace so that it won't go out on you.— Will come in handy this winter with both Steve & Susie.

It has been surprising the amount of mail the crew writes every day— don't wait & no writing till the last nite before hitting port. Getting it written regular like—Two big questions are when will get to mail our letters & will all be waiting for us when we get to our Destination—The answer to both questions is something none of us know. Do hope mail will be waiting for us.

Will add a note later in this same envelope tho it may be same few days later.

My love allways to the Three of You

Al & Dada

AF Herney, Ens. USNR.

Typewritten letter from Al's mother, Helen "Nellie" Herney. Note: She was nearly sightless at this time.

Oct.12/44

Dear Al

Believe it or not we have had 2 letters from Julia; we told her cards would satisfy but along come 2 long letters; she is having a grand time and the Styers in Washington are as human as mother Styer is The Gen and wife meet them at the station and after the second glance at Julia he realized it was not Marie asked if all the Herney girls are cut out after the same pattern; so glad they like her but how could it be otherwise with the clothes she bought and what Marie had to offer she feels well dress for and at every occasion.

Sad she called for Elenor but as usual she was out; Got Julius Kellers address from Dot; so glad to hear he is married attain; he loves and home and deserves one too.

Think we will have the pleasure of having your tots over the weekend and Ed goes to the mtns do not know if Mac is going along or not.

Talk about company; tonight we have Susan tomorrow Dora she is to help Sheilah [Al's niece, daughter of Julia and Mac] do some sewing what it is I did not ask or have I been told.

Last night as I came out of church a lady asked where is your little grand daughter; she isn't sick is she; No, she is home in Chula with her mother at the time she was with us her daddy was up at San Pedro and her mother went to spend a few days with him; she was so good in church and such a friendly child; she may be with me Sat night.

Mrs. Heard was in the other day and said she would be willing to give all long beach back to the Indians; wants Frank to be surveided out so they can go back to S.D. He does have a lot of trouble with his legs; guess at that he is better off than many other fellows;

Bob [Gawers—a young nephew] is back in bed has been out of school all week; he will not mind that; the school nurse was over and said she could not allow him in school as long as he carried that much tempeture; suggested having a teacher come to the house and teach him so that he does not get to far back poor kind I do feels so sorry for him will have to go to [army] Camp

Callen and have more tests made; Dr. ?ose said he had some obstruction in the form come from that; Funny I come to the end of the line and paper before I realize it;

Had a letter from Geo wants to know what we are doing about the election the negro questions is glooming mighty black for them so he seems to think. We knew it was coming and I cannot help but think it will adjust itself.

So glad of one thing; found out it is F.D. fault that Guam was not fortified; such talk gives me the backake if nothing worse;

You know I never did know anything about it yet but I do like to have the truth told once in awhile;

You know your old mother don't you, wish I was good for something instead of just talk; you have heard of the story of Jo Herney getting her dress dirty and all she did was just talk; unnoticed herself as she leaned up against the fence and every board was marked across the front of her dress so she told Aunt Emma I never knew before that just talking makes a dress dirty.

Mac is taking Jo and Bobby out to Camp Callen tomorrow hope it will be the last time they will have to go;

God Bless you will write the results of the card game tonight
Love from all mother.

———

Sunday October 15th
Dearest Sweet, Susie & Steve:

Will make double use of the time, what little there is to take in a bit of the cool & shady portion of the boat deck and write you a short note.

Really when you come right down to it isn't one hell of a lot to write about when for days all you have seen is endless expanses of water—daily routine much the same, tempers short at times, & same faces in & out.—the routine wouldn't be too bad if the watches didn't change & there was regularity about them but that can't be because of one chaps selfishness—God Bless the little man (?)—

Since there are several Catholic boys aboard most of us gathered last Sunday nite and followed the mass—rather odd time to do it but then it was better than nothing. Plan on doing it again this afternoon. Tried to squeeze in Rosary sometime during the week—Odd isn't it & me of all people.

Sweet from all appearances I doubt if I will have the opportunity to do any Xmas shopping at all. Being fooled wasn't such a pleasant surprise but guess we will have to grin about it. Wish that you would purchase something nice for yourself. Know that as usual you will do the honors for the rest of the family.

Rather good news about the attacks on Formosa. Do hope that our losses haven't been any greater than they want us to believe. Looks possibly like there might be steps to bypass the Phillippines or that the invasion of them is to begin. Big things should begin to happen anyway. God only knows it should if we are going to do China any good & ourselves too for if landline is established control of the sea lanes won't be worth a damn.

Guess by the time this particular cruise is over I should be just salty as hell—if for nothing else from taking salt water showers. Really you take a shower & you're sticky—really don't which is worse feel stickey or smell yourself from around the corner. The engineer is being close with the water. Cant blame him for it would be his neck if we should run out of water for drinking & washing purposes.

Gave my shin—right leg a good scraping going up the ladder this last week. Can get around but my is the thing just sore as hell. Will have to learn to be a bit more careful.

The sea this morning is relatively calm—yesterday had quite a bit of swell to contend with—damned odd this sea. Don't really feel that I'd care to continue to be a seafaring man after this is all over—it is good to think of home & the pleasant time enjoyed especially that horizontal exercise.

Yesterday would have given a lot for a good hot tub bath—a good back massage & neck pull & then a cold bottle of beer—Pleasant to think about anyway.

Might suggest that the Navy supply some deck chairs for the comfort of its officers & men. After a short while it gets rather uncomfortable sitting on the deck Even when you have a little padding as I have.

Should write a lot of letters but really haven't the urge drive or will power—hope the rest who should receive but don't get won't feel too badly about it.

Sweet you know how much I miss you & Susie & Steve—This thing can't be over too soon for me so as to get back to leading a normal decent life & so you can tell a man to go to if you don't like him or his lip.

Lovingly Always

Al & Dada

Ens. A.F. Herney USNR

Oct 24

Dearest Sweet, Susie & Steve:

Have neglected to write you more often than I should Honey but hope you won't mind too much.

October 26

Started this letter last evening before chow—then hit the sack since I had the 2000 to 2400 watch and was a bit tired. Still haven't been able to get used to such a change of hours and definitely have very little ambition to do any thing but sit.

The news we have received has been very spotty—this evening however we did get the news that the Jap fleet was found & was pretty well pulverized we loosing one first line carrier with damage to some battleships & support units. Not a bad price to pay if the Japs have in fact received the damaging blow. Do hope so however that that will mean that much less for all of us to worry about.

Have the church festivities organized into a regular program. Follow the ritual of the mass at 10:30 Sunday morning and the Rosary at 18:30 on Wednesday evening. Have made use of the Rosary and Prayer Book Mother produced for me. Surprised at the fact that so many of the fellows fell in with the idea of the Rosary services on Wednesday evenings.

The idea of loosing a whole day in matter of a split second is a bit upsetting—especially when there are so many things that you should do & just haven't time nor the energy to do. Don't know if we will get the order of the Golden Dragon or not.

Last Sunday we enjoyed our first rain. Everyone who wasn't on watch got out with their soap and washrags & took a fresh water shower. Since I was on watch no shower & thought a salt water shower would have to do. However later in the day about sunset we had more—nothing would do but to get out in gods clothes and enjoy the rain—did feel good to get a fresh water shower for a change—Really you try to get along without a shower until your so of-fensive to yourself & then you just give up & take the salt water shower. Was funny besides enjoying the rain everyone was catching water in all buckets they could find for washing clothes.—caught two buckets & did my washing last Monday—really had quite a bit of laundry too though you don't put on clean linen every day. Have learned can't afford to wear a clean pair of soxs every day.

Occasionally someone will come forth with—Do you know what I would like right now—always something in addition to being home for that seems to be understood. Some would like a cubesteak sandwich—etc. a glass of beer, a coke or the like.

Can't imagine what you aren't thinking because you haven't received any mail before this—please don't be too hard on me for it really isn't anyone's fault—just circumstances. Have thought about all of you a great deal & I guess will think more & more as time passes. Do hate to see Susie & Steve getting older without being able to see them both grow.

Will close for this time and will write again in the next day or so—yes that is a promise Sweet for I know you do want to hear from me even if it is just a short note.

With love to the three of you

As Always

Al & DaDA

AF Herney

Sunday afternoon Oct. 29

Dearest Sweet Susie & Steve:

Since this is to be a day of rest or is it (?) will take time out to drop you that additional note I promised you.

Still isn't very much to report. The life is as usual the same—which you can get tired of most of the time. Hope that it will be a bit different in the very near future—change of scenery would be appreciated.

The boys aboard have started a newspaper—called the "Scurry Bugle." This I am sending to you under separate cover "Free" so don't be expecting it right soon. Everyone is hoping that we will be getting some mail real soon—of course that goes for me too as well as the other officers.

The SCURRY BUGLE

VOL. 1, No. 2   U. S. S. SCURRY (AM 304)   Sunday, 5 November 1944

NIPS STILL ON RUN

During the night of 1 - 2 November, two enemy twin-engined bombers, presumably from bases in the Bonins, bombed and strafed Isely Airfield on Saipan and the northern airfield on Tinian. Three of the enemy raiders were shot down, one by night fighter aircraft and two by anti-aircraft guns. Our personnel casualties were four killed and one seriously injured when one of the enemy planes was shot down and crashed on the field. Minor damage was suffered at both airfields.

An enemy reconnaissance sea plane attacked Peleliu Island on 31 October, but was shot down by one of our Hellcat night fighters.

One of the Third Fleet Carrier Groups was attacked by enemy fighters (turn to page 7)

SHIP NEWS: The staff of the "Bugle" wishes to take this opportunity to thank those who gave us such encouragement and praise on our first edition. At the time, we were not quite sure just how well our efforts would be received by the officers and members of the crew, but now we are assured that you liked the paper, and will contribute materially towards its success in the future.

— —

Details concerning the forthcoming boxing exhibition to be sponsored by this paper appear on the sports page of this edition. We are glad to note that the event is being planned as a direct result of our suggestion in last week's paper. Such an event is just what is needed to fill the recreation needs of the ship.

— —

The turn-out at last week's Divine Services was indeed disappointing. These services provide the only means for Sunday worship available and those of the various religious faiths should take advantage of the opportunity. The Divine Services to be held on (censored) Sunday, November 5 are as follows: Catholic Services 0700 Casu Chapel; 0900 Headquarters Chapel; 1030 Acorn Chapel; 1630 Headquarters Chapel. Protestant Services: 0800 Acorn Chapel; 0900 Casu Chapel; 1000 Headquarters Chapel; 1900 Headquarters Chapel.

This is an opportunity not to be passed by. The boat departures will be announced throughout the day.

"The Scurrier" was one of two newsletters produced onboard the USS Scurry and was likely printed on a spirit duplicator "ditto" machine.

Got to take another shower on deck with nothing on but Gods clothes evening before last as we had just a very short rain—felt good but before the evening was over smelt almost as bad as before I had the shower. Will I appreciate a tub bath again—will soak & soak and won't need a beer to enjoy it either.

Forgot to mention in any of the earlier letters (three that you will have to take care of the information he needs—You can tell him that I received per diem in the amount of $372.00. I doubt very much if this has to be included but you can never tell. Also you should ask him about the income (?) from "Bere"—You have a copy of my basic orders calling for per diem in case they need to know more, Doubt if there will be any tax due this year but would prefer to start early.

Believe now that I would have been very smart to have left all of my Blues—white shirts, whites including shoes at home for don't see how or when I would even put them on. Run around most of the time without a shirt, tho have it with me—haven't worn a tie since I left and don't expect to for some time. Would appreciate having a sun helmet but guess I can pick up one in the near future.

Had thought of mailing more than one letter in an envelope—did the first two letters but guess it isn't such a good idea of one of the envelopes wouldn't reach you.

For dinner today we had soup, turkey—peas and dehydrated potatoes. Since we no longer have crackers had bits of bread slightly toasted and thought of my "Pride & Joy" calling for "toas". Damn how I do miss the three of you—sometimes so much that it hurts. You know I was pretty much of a house boy—when I do get home you're going to have to pry a whole lot to get me out Sweet—we'll be a complete picture of a man with immavitis or sititis whichever you prefer. Won't run a chance on getting away from home and not getting back.

Should it ever be necessary to contact me in a hurry I might suggest that you get in touch with Chuck for he might be of some help to you in that regard to he won't be able to advise you of where he will know how through the proper channels of course.

Have been wondering if you have heard anything more of Carl—wouldn't doubt a bit but he was in on the Phillippine deal—if so sort of envy him seeing that much action tho his little chickadee I know would be far from happy about it.

Has Julia & Mother Styer [of the Coronado and military Styer family, no relatives but good friends of the Herney family] returned from the East as yet. Do bet they had a good one having a good time even though the purpose of their journey was not the pleasantest! Was nice for Julia to be able to make that trip for it really has been a long time since she has had any kind of a vacation. Can guess how much fun the rest of the family is having with the boss away—do hope Sheliah doesn't get out of hand.

Have written a lot more than I thought was possible & haven't said as yet that I love the three of you very much—

With all my love

Al & Dada

A.F. Herney

November 2, 1944—No 5

Dearest Sweet, Susie & Steve:

Haven't written in the last few days so will see what can be done to drum up something to put down on paper other than that which you already know "That I do love the three of you very much."

Have had some rain for the last few days each day—has tended to make things a bit more pleasant. Took another one of those showers ala nude on the deck yesterday evening—does help the moral somewhat to get the stench off you. Wasn't fortunate enuf however to catch some of the rain to do some washing.

Was wondering if I have left one of my pipes at home?—Can't find the damn thing anyplace so assume I did. Don't send it even if I have for it possibly never would get here.

Thought you might call Bob Saunders to find out if my insurance allotments are coming through. Don't think they aren't but you can verify it anyway. Might also suggest that all notices respecting the insurance be sent to

399 instead of to 1240. Also ask what I must do to change the beneficiaries on my insurance to include Steve. This has not been done on either of the policies I have with Business Mens Ass. Co.

Should you happen to have any extra shoe ration stamps I would like a pair of "Romeo's" or...Size 8 ½ would do—in black of course. Have suddenly remembered how comfortable they are especially when the dogs get tired.

We have had no word recently about what who is doing what to who in this battle of survival. With the start made do guess that things are picking up and carrying right along. Would like to know the dope however.

Unless you have been experiencing a heat wave remember that a fire in the fire place is quite satisfying about now. Would give a whole lot to be there enjoying it with you. Of course that would mean you might be a bit irked by my jumping up & down a lot but I know that you would overlook that.

The other night while on watch was impressed by the extreme calmness of part of this great big Pacific Ocean. Really was so calm that you could see the reflection of the stars on its surface. Of course there was the moon too which might have aided in some romance, almost forgot I'm practically devoid of that any more. Oh well?

In addition to missing many of the comforts of home have a yen for a good massage & back rub. Would like to have that that vibrator along to give the neck somewhat of a massage. Don't mean for you to send it—just a wish, could be something more to cart around.

Do hope that you will get the letters before too long. Know you have been waiting for Bob to deliver something & no letters.

Chow is almost done and I do need to wash my face before gracing the table.

With all my love to the three of you—wishing I could at least drop in on you for a short time if not longer.

Lovingly,

Al & Dada

AF Herney Ens. USNR

The Scurry *arrived in port in Eniwetok on November 3, 1944.*

Saturday Nite Nov 4—No. 6

Dearest Sweet Susie & Steve:

Today was a big day for I received letters 1 thru 11—two from Mother & one from Virginia. Do wish you could have gotten the letters I have written you, not however as many as I received from you. Can assure you I was plenty long in reading all of the mail—just digging out the last morsel of news.

Haven't received any of the packages mentioned—but do hope that they will catch up with us for they do sound interesting. Will let you know if & when I get same and the dates of mailing. Don't expect any real soon as all of the mail we have received so far is airmail. Your last letter was postmarked Oct 24—which is plenty good.

Was ashore today for the first time in many a day. Felt rather odd to be terra firma or something. The water close in to be beach is almost the color of the stones in the bracelet I gave you for our anniversary a year ago. In the deeper part of the bay the blue Pacific has in itself nothing to compare, really Susie's eyes are a good comparison. Too bad I can't give you a complete picture.

At the communications office ran into a class mate from Harvard. He has been here about a month. Said Lee had been here sometime back and had mentioned that he had gotten to see us. For the life of me I can't remember his name & too damned ashamed to ask him. Will go over the alphabet several times & will get it—odd name too.

Sorry to hear about Anne. Until I read letter #11 wasn't sure what the whole story was. Little Annie would love to have that added to her other problems. Will try to find some time to drop her a note in the next several days. Agree with you about the boys—should have taken it on myself to have had a talk with them. They have improved a lot as far as public relations are concerned.

Really ashamed that I haven't written Mothers—ie Herney & Charleson. Will promise to do so before we get underway again.

Was much amused at your description of your visit with Helen Rice. Can't say that you chose the best companionship for being in a blue mood. Didn't say anything about it at the time but then it was your problem.

Do hope you don't think I was bulling when I wrote that last letter from L.B. [Long Beach]. Meant it all honey & again will so state.

Glad to hear that you have arranged for the policies for the youngsters. It is more than agreeable that you are named on the policies—will let it stand. Wrote in my last letter that you should see about taking care of change of beneficiary on my insurance. Assume that the $50 covers both policies.

Don't know how I can describe the operation of the furnace from this distance. You will find all of the directions to the damn thing tucked behind the wires inboard of the studding just to the left of the pit. The directions aren't too complete I know but then I learnt by doing. Do hope you don't have too much trouble with it. It is amazing that the pilot would use up 50 gals in a month's time. Possible the control for the flow is too high—then too the float should be cleaned every time you clean the furnace. This is accomplished by releasing the little lever on the control receptical—see how damn difficult it is?—Reading the directions might help clean up this confusion. Don't see how drawing pictures will help.

All of your letters are so darn newsy plan on reading them again tomorrow to get all out of them. Do guess that little Pride & Joy is going to be alright after all. It is so difficult to realize that Steve is an integral part of the family. That of course is the fault of not being home to assist in the tougher part of the rearing so you really get to appreciate them.

Odd that you should mention enjoying the fireplace. Have often thought about the possibilities of you doing so and so damn sorry I could not be there to help you do it.

Where did Julia get the idea I'd be home by Xmas. From here it looks like many a moon just to get there—much & many more than this Xmas. Pipe dreams are sure nice to have but what a let down if they don't materialize.

From Hanks letter do guess that he is about due for some sea duty. Haven't quite been able to see how it has been as long without it. Can't say I would relish duty below as well as above the surface.

Wonder if Mama {Butler} was glad to see Howard—would be like her to be complaining that he had spent most of their money to come home to see his family. Doubt a whole lot if he will be in the Caribbean much longer tho it is nice duty. Hetzler had duty there before being assigned to the 304.

Must close Sweet for this time—will try to write again tomorrow— With all my love to the three of you.

As Always

Al & Da da

A.F Herney, Ens.

Sunday nite Nov. 5–No. 7

Dearest Sweet Susie & Steve:

Will drop you only a short note before hitting the sack.

Today was a day mostly at rest. Took 11 of my folks into mass at the base. The chapel was packed by the time mass started. The schedule on Sunday is as follows. 9:00 oclock 10:30 and 4:30 P.M. Daily mass is at 4:30 quite a schedule what?

Part of the crew went ashore for the recreation this afternoon, brother Gates took them. I take a group tomorrow. The base allows each man about three cans of beer each. While they have some recreational facilities they are limited to baseball & volleyball. However the beer seems to be the most attractive especially since it is so warm.

Enjoyed the cartoons so much Sweet especially the one about Sad Sack. Put it up on the Board in the ward room. Possibly it is not such a bad idea but is carrying things a bit far.

The ship we have been tied up alongside has a projector & a movie every nite—last nite Quiet Please, Murder & tonight "The Hard Way" with Ida Lupino. Both were stinkers but something to do. Ho Hum. There is always plenty of work to be done but God who wants to do that.

The mailman brought no mail today—a bit disappointing to all but then were not stateside so can't expect too much—maybe he'll be good tomorrow.

Thinking much of all of you & wishing I could be with you always.

Lovingly as Always

Al & Dada

A.F Herney Ens.

P.S. Forgot to say that it was a nice week-end with Beth & Paul [friends, the Shaws]—Don't blame you for wanting to do it again.
Love
Al

Tuesday Nov 7–No. 8
Dearest Sweet, Susie & Steve:

The mailman was again very good to me today for he brought me a letter from my radio technician's father and three 12–13 & 14 from you. My what nice long & newsy letters & one hell of a big surprise—yet you guessed it "concrete".

The letter from Warrens father was very nice—thanked me for showing him the ship one day when he called to take Warren home with him but Warren had already left & secondly for sending Warren home for the night before we shoved off. Will keep it & show it to you some day!

Your letter "12" was very much a surprise—not because it was "12" but because of the contents, (the boys are playing "I'm getting Sentimental Over You" on the phono—<u>mistake</u> I'm crying over you so I might be a bit jumbled up.) especially to think of concrete 50 by 30. Boy that is one hell of a lot of concrete. Think only a part of it would do but then I'm not there to do the 'saying' so guess I better be happy about it. Thank <u>God</u> Sweet you didn't do the heavy work or that you aren't going to lay the cement. There would not be much of you if you did. Know you wouldn't do it if we couldn't afford it.

You didn't mention the amount of the county taxes. Since they weren't as much as last year with $1300 in the savings box. Ho hum. Don't forget to pay them for heavens sake.

From you report the Pride & Joy is really loosing up both with her tongue and initiative. How I had looked forward to seeing her grow—there will be time for that however I hope. Too bad her reaction to Nickey needing a bath isn't so—how I would love it. Would love to see her in the outfit Grandma made for her—no doubt but that she looks <u>sweet</u> as hell in it.

What are you doing to Steve to make him grow so fast. If he keeps on doing what he is doing he is going to be one awful big clunk when I get home & too damn big to tote around. So now he is finally going to get fed on milk, even tho canned. Wonder how he will take <u>to it?</u>

Glad to hear that Ann is doing better & that Mother is over her cold. It was <u>Xmas</u> last year when she had the flu—remember. Wrote both of them a note today & will try to drop Mother C a note tomorrow.

Do hope the <u>flyer</u> on the pictures taken in National City won't be a disappointment for I do want one or more of <u>you, all, or any</u> of you. Take those I have out often & look at them tho I know that both of the youngsters are constantly changing. Incidentally don't see any harm in Rockababying Susie if she likes it—that is after the attention is paid to "Him". Can just see her acting up the other evening—she will soon have to learn that she isn't the only one in the <u>family</u> or her little nose will be bumped and bumped hard.

Your mention of Mrs.{Dirks} sounds like her & further she is just the kind of person who generally gets others into trouble by her blabbing. Don't wish the youngsters any bad luck but there is always the good chance.

Why worry too much about the {Coopers} Sweet—if you haven't time so what. Of course it's always nice to have them down (personally they drive me nuts) but you have two youngsters—no old man & that is something. Do wish you could get another youngster to help you even if it is just the cleaning.

Your evening with Peggy sounded as if you had enjoyed it a good bit. As for doc you can tell him for me he doesn't have to wait for Steve to make a face before he looks like me.

You can tell Hank for me that should I get anywhere close to where he is located I would be sure to get in touch with him.

Honey as for keeping a memo of your questions as I read your letters I'm so hungry for them the questions just go by—You have been awfully good about writing & have enjoyed them all—the last three have been especially good & long too huh? Write only when you have time for I appreciate that you have quite a job.

I do love you <u>all three</u> very much especially you Sweet even tho you plan & possibly have cemented <u>all</u> of the back yard.

Love you Always

Al

A.F. Herney, Ens.

Tuesday Nov 7, 44 [written to his mother and family]

Dearest Mother & Family:

Being lazy it is always a chance to write—but since I like to receive a note now & then must decide not to be too lazy.

Received your two letters dated Oct 2 & 13. Just when they arrived I don't know but assume they beat me here. You can use 6 cent airmails incidently——a saving of two cents.—Did enjoy them so much & know that there will be more. Thanks much Mother Dear for taking the time.

Life aboard and underway has been a bit strenuous at times.—in fact damn tiring but guess that isn't too bad in comparison. The rotation of the watches were such that the schedule was such that the schedule was always different—routine is a good bit of habit but a habit to my liking.

Have seen a good bit of the Pacific so far. The sunrises and sunsets we, as landlubbers have enjoyed can't begin to compare to those seen at sea—nothing but water 360 degrees of the horizon—various shades of blue of the sea and sky—The other morning the suns rays on the clouds to the west was such that you expected the "Christ Child" momentarily to appear & use the formation for a halo—

The water where we are at the present is of a very light blue—much like the color of Susie Q's eyes, in the deep portion of the bay and an exquisite blue green close to the shore much the color of the stones in the bracelet I gave Dot for our anniversary a year ago.

Have made several trips ashore strictly for business. The plans for tomorrow however include an indoor game against the officers of another vessel here. Will go to the Officers Club afterwards for a beer or two—not more than that for its too hot to take on a load.

The rosary and prayer book you gave me have had some use. The crew has a few Catholics among its number, about 16. We meet on Sunday morning to following the Mass and on Wednesday nite for RosaryDidn't ever think I could be a guiding light to get the thing organized but that seems to be it. Took 10 of the flock to Mass on the Island Sunday Morning. The place really was packed too which was a big surprise to me. Didn't get to meet the Padre as the transportation was due right after services.

Just a short interlude—mail call—three letters from my Sweetie—wish she had received some of mine but that is out of the question. Soon though I hope. My what a surprise to find that we are going to have a cemented back yard—hope she isn't going to cement all of it as that would be a bit disconcerting—no place for garden?

Word also is that Julia has returned home—awfully nice that she should get the opportunity to take the trip & nice for Mother Styer to have been along. Know they both had a very grand time & saw everything there was to see.

Was very much upset to hear that both you & Ann were not feeling well—you with a cold that kept you confined for a week & Ann in hospital with gen stomach—both of you had better take better care of yourself.

Am awfully appreciative of your taking care of Susie & Steve so Dot could be with me in Long Beach. It has helped a whole lot out on the briney deep to know that the family is there to give Dot a hand if needed.

Chow is about down and want to drop Ann a short note.

With much love to you Mother & all of the family.

Lovingly as Always

Al

A.F. Herney Ens.

———

Final entry in Dorothy Herney's desk diary:
November 8—First Letters Arrive.

———

Wed. Nov 8 (No 9?)

Dearest sweet, Susie & Steve:

Will get off another note to you this evening. Will write you before giving Mother & Dad a break so that if the urge gives out you at least can get one.

Am enclosing two $100.00 money orders. The sums made up as follows $140.00 from brother Gates & $60.00 from my own funds. We were paid today but someone was awfully screwed up as to amounts drawn or paid whichever you will. Hetzler & myself underpaid $40 each & Gates over $100.00. Which is the reason he has not reimbursed me for all—plan on sending you the balance of the $229. + the first of next month.

Some of the fellows were lucky & received mail today and a few packages—me—none but didn't feel too badly about it since the mailman was good to me yesterday.

Went swimming today in the lagoon. The water is unpleasantly warm & while it is good exercise is not near as refreshing as if the water had a bit of a nip to it—also the water seems to be a bit more salty with the temperature as high as it is—but then it still is part of the Pacific.

Think you should check each month to see that the allotments are coming thru for my insurance with Saunders as you might advise him to report to you if the payments do not come thru for I had like the devil to think that that insurance would lapse—be sure also to keep my health insurance in force.— Hell of a thing to be thinking about isn't it?

Plan on buying some dungarees & blue shirts to use when underway—they can be washed but do not need ironed—can save greys for whenever in port—which won't be too much I know but then there is always hope.

The more I think of the concrete the more I'm sure your going to have a lot of concrete in that back yard. Do hope that the next owner will appreciate it.

Will close so I can get a note off to Mother & Da—

With all my love to the three of you.—

As always

Al & Dada

AF Herney, Ens

P.S. The returns from the election out to be coming in soon—no doubt as to who will be president.

P.S.S. Really not much of a letter I know so please forgive me—also have lost track of no. on have I ? Still think the club I organized is a good one but guess I'll have to form another as the <u>boy</u> doesn't seem to appreciate this one.

Al always—Al

Thursday Afternoon Nov. 15, 1944 No. 10

Dearest sweet, Susie & Steve:

Won't offer any excuses for not having written soon Sweet but just didn't feel like it at all. Don't know if it were the heat or what.

Received three packages just a week ago—one of the little round ones from the Pride & Joy—one from Mother H. and one from the E.A's [Muellers, his sister Marie and brother-in-law Edwin]. Of course only opened the one from Susie—the can had been partially bashed and the sealing chipped off but on the whole in pretty good condition. The cookies were still fresh—the hard candies stickey (?)—the fudge very soft some of it & other dried out. Not complaining for you did ask for a report. Enjoyed it much just the same.—Thought of you to take time out to make & pack the goodies.

Haven't had a chance to drop in to see about mail since last Thursday. Know there was some mail for us but then one can't worry too much about mail when there are things to be done. Will be able to tell you all about it some day.

Wonder if Hank is on his way as yet or whether he is bidding his time. Maybe if he should be given a change of duty I might stand a greater chance of seeing him to I don't wish him any bad luck—his duty hasn't been too bad even tho he can't have his family with him. Remembered the name of the chap I was telling you about Klaman & yes I didn't have to ask him. His original duty was on the east coast—looks like the Theatre has shifted huh.

From all reports the boys are giving Jap. convoys hell.—The elimination of more & more of them is hope for as that will mean everything is closer to being over & oh what a joyous day that will be.

Enclosed are the two receipts for money orders mailed in my last letter— in case the two money orders don't come thru you can check on the stubs— of course they were purchased thru Fleet Post Office—Don't see why you shouldn't get the orders but just in case.

You really don't know what I would give for a quiet few days at home— with all the hot water baths, massages and (do)—be required to do nothing— my my but a wonderful pipe dream.

Will you please tell Mother & Ed their packages arrived—will try to get off a note to them but won't promise to do so today.

Don't think you would love your old man very much in his present condition—Ive had little enuf hair & to make it worse had a compulsory haircut.—My what a sight—Don't think a photo would be at all flattering.

With all my love to the three of you.—As always Al & Dada
AF Herney Ens.

16 November No 11 (?) (Thursday)
Dearest Sweet:

Have forgotten whether this is No 11 or 12 so will take a chance on the lesser as I have been lax in my notes to you.

Tried to get something today for you and our two off springs as a small Xmas offering but no such luck. Thought possibly there might be at least a small gift but no such luck. Since that is the case want you to take some of the money I sent you via money order and get yourself something nice—While you are at it if there is something you would like the youngsters to have feel free to buy it for them.

Has been rather an unusual day today—overcast most of the days and a bit of rain. Went ashore for publications, supplies and to look for something for you. Was raining at the time & since there is no pavement waded thru a bit of mud—wouldn't have dared enter 399 J Street with the shoes I can assure it. With the heat which is not unusual you felt stickey all over—ho hum guess that will be an old story soon but know you won't mind.

Thought we might have some mail today but no such luck—but then it is possible that we might have some again soon.

Wondered if you would be kind enuf to call Chuck R. [Reed] and ask him for the name of the officer in charge of R.P.I.O. (Registered Publication Issuing Office) there in San Diego. A chap here would like to know & I told him I would try to find out for him. Of course you will remember to give him & his chickadee my regards. Do hope they are still as happy as ever about their expected.

It was just bout this time last year wasn't it Sweet that you visited me in Tucson and him "Steve". My my what a time that was/ especially Rancho

Grande Rancho—Old sure shot doesn't miss but then then you haven't done too badly yourself.

Have been keeping my eyes open for some more of the class mates from Harvard but haven't seen them as yet—they or some of them must be out in the Pacific area.

After taking care of the business ashore today stayed to patronize the ice cream parlor, where beer is also dispensed to the enlisted men. Two lines formed one for beer & the other ice cream. Really both the lines were about of equal length. Understand that they use powdered milk in the ice cream—not at all bad. With the verdant green of the foliage & the amount of I do think they would bring in a herd of cattle—maybe however there really isn't anyone here who is a farmer at heart & wouldn't care to bother. It was surprising to see so many young fellows in line for beer—some I know that couldn't get any in the States but then there here doing there part too so who am I do say they shouldn't have it.

It is getting late my love so I will close with the usual and meaning every bit of it. Not much of a letter I know but you have said even a card would do.

With all my love to you three—

As always

Al & Dada

AF Herney. Ens. USNR.

———

Nov. 18 '44 Saturday 12:30 noon Letter 10

My dearest,

This will be the hardest letter I've ever had to write to you. Because I have to tell you now that Grandma died this morning in her sleep about 7 A.M. I called Charles Reed at 8:15 and he said he'd see that you got a message as soon as possible and that an airmail would reach you within a very few days so I hope you won't have to wait too long for this because I know the grief you will be bearing and not knowing or being able to find out will make it harder for you. My only hope is that you won't be angry with me for not warning you ahead of time. It has been a burden on my mind for the last month for everyone said I shouldn't tell you how ill she's been—even Charles said that—and I finally decided it was best—since the Dr. said she might last quite awhile and I knew what a worry it would be you out there so far away— not hearing for maybe weeks—and at the time she was so bad—I hadn't even heard from you yet and didn't know when you'd get my mail.

Grandma had really gotten over her cold but about 2 or 3 days before Julia got home from the East she got worse and when Dr. Myers came he said it is an Edema in both lungs caused by a badly enlarged heart—they took X-rays to find that out. And at that time (about Nov. 4) Dr. Myers warned us that she might go. An edema means that the heart does not carry of the waste fluids in the body and they collect in the lungs—leaving only a small space to breathe—and she gasped for air all that first week. They had a night nurse and a hospital bed and she had digitalis shots every day. Then Dr. Myers gave her something to dehydrate her which meant the bed pan every 5 minutes to drain the liquids from her. She improved so much that she was able to sit up a bit each day—and had had a bell by her bed which she could ring for someone—we (Anne & I) went to see her everyday—but only for a few minutes—as she was supposed to save her strength—and then when she got a little better—we would read to her. I read one afternoon to her while she was being dehydrated—from "My Family Right or Wrong" and Anne read to her from "Low Man on a Totem Pole" and she did enjoy listening so much and you know how Grandma always wanted someone around. I would take Susan in for only a minute or two—and she would say "Grama sick abed—too bad— get well quick Gramma." That was the reason really I stayed in at Anne's last week—but since she was so much better I came home last Sunday. I was in yesterday and took her the pictures of Susan, Stephen an me and she was so pleased—and said she was glad to have one of me alone and when I left she held my hand and said "God Bless you Dottie."

She didn't suffer Sweetheart—of that you can rest assured.—Julia said she had been in with her at 6:30 a.m. and she was alrite and then at 7 they went in (she was in Sheila's room)—and she was on her side with her hands tucked under her face and holding her Rosary and peacefully asleep. Dr. Myers said we must remember she was 72—and had had 9 children and not a quiet life but a very full life and that you must remember too my dearest—for I know of noone

one who has enjoyed life more or made fuller use of it for herself and for others so we must be comforted by that and I know your Dad has been waiting along time for her and how she must have missed him all these years. I am so very glad she had the chance to have Susan & Stephen near that week I was with you—she did enjoy them so—and tho' they won't remember her in years to come—they did their part in giving her happiness. I am so glad too that she received your letter this last week—for she talked every day about her son Albert and you know she was always thinking of you as of all her family.

They had not been able to get hold of George yet this morning—but they had called him before when she was so bad and I don't believe he is coming tho' I don't know. —I just called and talked to Marie—and she says George is not coming—and that the Rosary will be Monday night and the Mass Tuesday morning at 9. Eddie has Susan at the moment but I'm taking her out to Beth Shaw's tomorrow so I won't have both of them—have Steve here—and am getting ready to go into Anne's now and will stay thee till Wed. afternoon before coming home.

I wish I could be with you when you receive the news because I know how hard it will be for you alone out there but please know I've thought of on one else these last few weeks and did what I thought best in telling you. She didn't know how sick she was and was planning on Thanksgiving Day at Marie's as Dr. Myers thot she could go she was so much better so up to the last my dear she was looking forward to a family gathering.

I'll try and write again tomorrow and know you will take this as you have your other trials and stand up under it.

All our love Sweetheart,
Dottie

Wednesday. Nov 22 '44 Letter 11
My dearest—

I have missed a letter to you, but hope that you will understand that only because of what has been happening I lost out—there was just too much confusion and all of us much too tired to think of putting anything down on paper I do so hope you will be reaching port soon to receive my mail so that you won't be sitting out there without a word.

The Rosary was held Monday evening at Good body's Ivy Chapel as every-one said, Grandma looked like a Queen surrounded by the bower of flowers and the flowers were all so beautiful. Grandma wore the lovely rose dress she looked so nice in. There was a nice group of people here and I shan't list them here—you can read the list when you come home. It would, of course, as you know, hit Marie and Julia and Jo the hardest—I stayed with Jo most of the time. Grandma would have smiled to know that <u>all</u> of her flock—strayed or not—recited <u>all</u> the prayers and never missed. Our Susie and Steve had an old fashioned bouquet of asters and Sweet Peas for their grandma which was very sweet and looked like it came from children.

It was a <u>glorious</u> sunshiny day Tuesday Morning, clear and quiet and beau-tiful. Billie Eichenlaub kept Bobbie [Gawers,] and Stephen. Father Cotter conducted the services himself and he said a very brief but sweet service and commented on the fact that your Mother need have no worry—she had led a good Christian life and had had the last sacraments two weeks ago even tho' she had no idea how ill she was, which was true. Father Cotter went to see her and she was so pleased because she hadn't been able to go to Communion in so long and he told her he would give her the Last Sacraments—to make her get better. The pall bearers were Clifford Jackson, John Hanley, Chas Tex, Bill Lingelbach, Ace Snyder and Doc Carrell. Father Cotter also went on to say that we here living should prepare for the next world and that we 'couldn't take it with us"—Eddie told Helen he guessed the talk was directed at him. I saw Mrs. Olivier at the funeral but no chance to speak with her. Mrs. Myers was there, Jo Work and many people I didn't know. Mrs. Frazier (club woman) and so many, many flowers—from our friends as well as your Mothers—Parvins for one. I think dear Pat Herney made the most apt com-ment when she said, "Well, we know someone is up there now to say payers for all the rest of us" and isn't that true? There isn't much more I can tell you dear, it was a lovely as you could have wished and all of your family are bear-ing up splendidly because they can live with the beautiful memories herself of how much she enjoyed everything. Julia was so sick all day yesterday because she was suffering from two bad teeth which she had to have extracted yester-day at 4—her jaw was swollen so terribly she had to hold her coat over her face—it is still swollen some but not as badly.

I took Anne to the Dr's this morning.—I've been taking iron shots too to get a little more pep and it leaves us with the nastiest taste in our mouth. I've got a little neuralgia in one hip too—so Anne and I sort of lean on one another and say we think they ought to take us out and shoot us!

I'm going out to Beth's tomorrow to get Susan and then going on home. There will be no family Thanksgiving—and Harvey invited Bev & us for dinner so think I'll go home. I was nearly frantic on Saturday trying to get here—had everything in the car and the car wouldn't start—Harvey happened to be home so he pushed me to Ralph Paxton—the distributor points were so dirty it wouldn't make contact—& Harvey says the spark plugs need cleaning and says he will do it on his next day off. So I hope the old Studebaker holds together! Anyway I got here alrite and she seems to be perking alrite so will keep my fingers crossed. I talked to Bev on the phone and she said Hank wrote that maybe the first place you stopped was Saipan. Well, maybe so and maybe not—anyway you must be enroute someplace else and I just hope it isn't 38 days till the next letter.

I helped list the flowers today and the cards. The picture of the monk is yours, you know.

There doesn't seem to be much else to write you Sweetie. I'll be glad to be home again tomorrow—located a colored gal to come and help me clean next week and I've bought Louise Morehouse's baby crib for Stevie so will be rearranging again! Well—as always I can still keep saying, if you were only home—but we know its harder on you than on us here at home so will sit tight and try and be patient.

Goodnite Sweetie and I hope I've answered all the questions from your side—but if there are others just ask and I'll try and answer. I have your letter you wrote her—she had kept it because she wanted a copy for Susie & Stevie because she thought you had written such a beautiful description of the "Christ Child" in the clouds—she had asked many time to have the letter read and reread to her so she got a great deal of pleasure out of it and you can be so thankful tomorrow for that and so I wish you as Happy a Thanksgiving as possible dearest.

All our love,
Your Dottie,
Susie,
Stevie

———

Wed. Nov 22 No. 12

My Dearest Sweet, Susie & Steve:

Must get you off a note—haven't written for nearly a week—why—just haven't felt up to it physically.

Received only one letter from you today—that one the 1st for Nov. Understand the airmail has been delayed. Did however receive your Xmas package and one from Sweetie Pie—[nickname for Virginia Caperton] her's it seems has had a bit of rough handling but still didn't investigate it.

This morning stopped in to see Klaman. Said I had missed Lee Jordan by just two days—that is Lee showed up while out on a cruise. Word is that <u>he</u> Lee had seen Hank & they were both waiting for me to show but no such luck. Would very much have liked to gotten together with them but then it seems someone had other plans.

Don't know what will be in store for us in the near future but guess it will all be for the best. Can't imagine Xmas being so close and I so far from all of you—doesn't seem normal.

Can imagine you with all of your small problems on the "Home Front". Wouldn't do any good to worry about them—do hope however that they won't get to be too many or too much for you. Would like to be there to help you with some of them.

This Pacific is certainly unpredictable. The sea at times is so calm that the reflection of clouds is very apparent on the surface and then also the stars glistening on the sea's really something to see.

Since I want this to get off with the mail man will cut it short promising to write you again today or tomorrow.

With all my love to the three of you.

As Always

Al & Dada

AF Herney Ens USNR.

Sunday Nite November 26 '44 No.13

My Dearest Sweet, Susie & Steve:

Your husband like this Navy is rather unpredictable. Promised to write you last Thursday or Friday but as you see—no such thing occurred. Could have written but you would not have received it any sooner than you are to receive this.

Have been quite a busy boy even when in port—Yes the life of a communicator is a hellish one but may soon have it compensations if the proposed plan works out. Will keep my fingers crossed—not to dissolution you however—it wouldn't mean being able to be any closer to you physically however but a bit more desirable as far as routine is concerned.

Was so busy last week when I wrote you that I didn't get ashore except for business—yep and there were some women to take a look at too—ho hum… from all reports however they were practically all of the less attractive type so guess I didn't miss much.

Will send you letters under separate cover—one for & to the family & one to the Phi Mu's. The one to the family is not to be opened till Xmas Eve & you must promise before opening it that you will not give it to anyone them for they might hold it against me & <u>read</u> it to me at some future date. You however may keep or destroy it afterwards as you see fit. The letter to the Phi Mu's you of course will take to the Phi Mu Xmas Party.—The letter for the family will be addressed to Mrs. <u>Albert Fred</u> Herney & the letter to the Phi Mu's will be addressed Mrs. A.F. Herney—everything clear?

Must drop sweet Pie a Xmas letter—also Mother & Dad—Ernie & Babs & oh how many more. You really don't know what a chore it all seems but guess I can get myself up to the chore.

Have the mid watch tonight so must be hitting the sack very soon—did have a nap this afternoon which of course will stave off shut eye for a bit but will try to relax a bit anyway or don't you think that is possible.

Do hope that the mailman will be very good to us soon and bring us all lots of letters for he has rather forgotten us of late.

Do wish you would send the pictures taken at National city as soon as you receive for I do want to see what all of my family looks like. After about two months absence not that I can't & often do picture all of you when remembering what pleasant times I have had with you.

My love to the three of you

As Always

Al & Dada

AF Herney, Ens USNR.

P.S. You need not tell the Family that they are getting a family letter.

Love,

Al.

Tuesday Nite (no date)

My Dearest Sweet Susie & Steve:

It hasn't been a month Sweet since I heard from but it has almost been a month since the date of your last letter. Was very much disappointed today as was all the rest of the crew that there were no letters for us. Why no one seems to know—Did look forward to having some. Guess you have gotten some of the few I have written you by this time.

Was invited aboard another ship here this evening to see their movie —"The song of Bernadette"—quite old but since not having seen it before enjoyed it, especially helps to keep one's mind off things that you miss & aids one in not getting too blue.

Spent most of the day in doing what I was trained to do—can't say I enjoy doing paper work anymore now than I ever did but must do it since there is no one else that says "let me do it for you." Have wondered how it would feel to have that happen.

The chaps had had several visits to the officers club. I however have not as yet done—if I do go I plan on staying with the soft drinks—sounds funny doesn't it—but haven't had a drink since that last beer with Schnabel in Long Beach—do guess I won't get to be a drunkard after all.

Started today in taking some exercises—commenced easy like but will be doing or planning on doing plenty of Hello darlings within the week.—The lack of exercise just seems to tie one up like all hades—yep could stand a neck massage & neck crack tonight. Do you feel up to it?

How I've rattled on without saying much Sweet—but you know I miss all of you much & would give much to be with you—Wonder what I could do about it?

Must hit the sack as tomorrow always seems to come so damn soon.

With all my love to the three of you and love to all the family.

As Always

Al

AF Herney ENS USNR

P.S.—Will just add a good morning Honey before turning this over to the mail man.

Love Al.

Wendesday Nite (the day before Thanksgiving—Nov 22)

My Dearest Sweet, Susie & Steve:

Must drop you a note before getting some sack drill for in that way can make myself believe that I'm spending a least a few minutes with you. Yep it would be swell to drop in on you three.

Spent most of the day trying to get a few supplies to do a slight alteration respecting gear under my cognizance. As usual you meet up with Navy Red Tape—first one question then another until finally you feel like jumping up & down—of course you don't because you are supposed to be a gentleman. Ho hum—finally made out with some success. Time alone with tell.

Was again invited over to another ship this evening and say "The Butler's Sister" with Deanna [Durbin]—The chaps have been lucky to have gotten two decent pictures in a row. Do hope our projector finally catches up with us for it would be rather pleasant to sit on your own forecastle & see a picture. Not complaining too much if the invitations continue. Guess we should be thankful for something. Won't get to see what's showing tomorrow for I have the duty & it being Thanksgiving.

Speaking of Thanksgiving that seems to mean one thing to me—another family gathering of the Herney clan at someones domicile & hell I have to miss it. Shucks—and some more. The heavens were good & we have some turkey left so will be having the festive bird at least. Should help the bluish feeling of all of us.

Still no mail—prospects are for tomorrow—for some to arrive but not be distributed—wonder what the hell has been holding it up—maybe we'll never know, and care less when we do get same. You know what a help it is to get a note or so once in a while I'm sure. You however have our two offspring to help keep your time very busy—however I now it gets tiresome at times too Honey.

Must get a few more notes off so will close for this time. Goodnite Sweet to the three of you—With all my love

Al Always

AF Herney Ens. USNR.

P.S. Just an added not this morning to wish you each—all the family & friends a very happy Thanksgiving.

Love Always

Al.

Saturday Morning December 1, 1944

My Dearest Sweet, Susie, Steve & Family:

The mailman was good this morning in bringing several letters together with a dispatch that contained anything but pleasant news. Of course you know how it hit me for the first inkling (envelope addressed to Communication Officer AM 304) were "Ensign Albert Fred Herney from Dorothy Herney via San Diego X Mother Died Morning November 18." But your letters no's 8-9-10 & 11 were also received giving more of the details which have helped somehow.

From one of your earlier letters had sort of an inkling that all was not too well with Mother & should have been all set for a bit of news that I have received. Do you remember a promise you made to me Sweet that I wished to know even the bad news. I will forgive you this time but please, please never do it again. Can't blame your forgetting in view of all the worry you all had yourself & the advice you were given but again my Sweet Please don't do it again.

Can't understand why it took so long for that dispatch to be delivered—will do some checking on it from this end. Really don't know what I would have done if I had received it without also receiving your <u>Sweet letters</u> at the same time.

Am very pleased that Mother got some enjoyment out of the letter that I so condescendingly took time to write tho I am sure she didn't expect any—really she expected so little & got so very much out of so little, tho at times we thought she was asking a lot. Sweet—thanks for being so very good & considerate to her. Thanks for enclosing the newspaper clipping.

Received a nice card Xmas from the Quiggles [friends of Dot's family in Lincoln, Nebraska] with this morning mail as a letter from Marie dated Nov. 16. Also without a word as to what to expect. Thank her for taking time out from her busy days to drop me a note—did and do appreciate it very much.

Can readily understand why there wasn't any Thanksgiving festivities this year. Do feel however that there would be the Xmas Eve party for I'm sure that Mother would have wanted it & as a Xmas present to me from all the family ask that it be held.

Am enclosing in this letter the first part of the Xmas letter I was in the process of writing. Will of course revise it. As to the original letter enclosed here you may keep or destroy as you see fit.

My Sweet you don't know how much I would have liked to have been with you both during Mother's illness, after her death & now also my love. We will all have to bear up under our loss which I am sure will be much to all of us.

I do wish that you would thank all of the Pall Bearers for rendering Mother their last respects & all that assisted at the family's time—especially Paul & Beth for taking Susie. As you say I do hope Susie can remember a bit of her grandmother for she as the rest of the family could take much from her in the way of learning how to live.

Can't understand George [his brother] not coming for the <u>services.</u> He possibly feels that he now is much more of an outsider that before which of course is as much my fault as anyones—we could have at least been a bit more generous in our attitude toward him.

Am very glad that Mac has been out to do those little things for you that I would be doing if I were home—is nice of him & do appreciate it. Thank him for me for taking his time. Have you gotten in the concrete as yet—Doubt it with all of the added burden everybody had.

Must close this my Sweet for I must get busy and do some more of the things expected of a communicator.

With all of my love to the three of you & much love to all of the <u>Family</u>

Lovingly as Always

Al & Dada

A.F. Herney Ens.

P.S. Thanks for enclosing the pictures will look at them again this afternoon when I haven't so many blurry spots before me. The Stadlers youngster looks like Carl doesn't he?

Love

Al

P.S.S. Sweet, do you remember what I told you when we were deciding about spending Xmas in Lincoln last year? No request Sweetheart but possible a premonition.

*Photographs of Al's family, taken November 1944, which he kept in
a folding leather frame while onboard the USS Scurry.*

Dec. 2, Saturday No. 2

My dearest Sweet Susie & Steve:

Received your missing letters No 2 thru 7 together with No's 12 & 13 also the pictures of yourself, Susie & the three of you all of which I may say were very nice and did appreciate them together with the other snaps enclosed with some of the letters.

Sweet you really don't know how much of a thrill the letters have been to me and really nearly like everything all of which I want to know about especially all of my family. Did enjoy the drawing about the <u>concrete</u>. Do guess there will be room for some gardening in the back yard.

Do guess that our Pride & Joy is really growing up and comprehending a lot of things we didn't think would be a problem to her parents quite as early as this. Do think it rather smart of her & very sweet also to connect the stars and ships where her grandmother is now staying—think your explanation about Grandma an intelligent one and very satisfactory. Do guess she is pretty much of an angel to be so loved by all of the family.

As to your trip to Nebraska the problem is one for you yourself to decide. Can't say sweet that the prospects for getting back to the States very soon are at all bright so don't let that deter you tho it would be irony to get to the coast to have you halfway to delightful Boston. Can't blame Mother & Dad for wanting you and their grandchildren so if you don't feel that the trip would be too much for you plan on the trip. However don't think you should plan on being gone for too long a time and under no circumstances to rent the house. Check with Ted Stark about the insurance however as that is an important thing—have a house vacant for any length of time.

Can't say your decision about the change has my disapproval in the least. Believe it to be a smart thing for you to do now more than ever. Guess it wasn't such a smart thing to start with but then you never can tell about these things.

Very glad you haven't broken down to play for Xmas services. Possibly Father Brown [former pastor at Saint Rose of Lima in Chula Vista] could have invited you to do so but doubt if the present Padre has it in him. I'll bet he wonders what kind of parishioners we have been in the past. Have the masses been as well attended since he took over? Do think that we should lend some financial support & would also like several masses said for Mother. Would you take care of this for me or rather for us. As you say you really have become it & will promise to take much of it off your hands when I get back.

Think your plans or wishes for a gift from me to you satisfactory. Do know that you aren't extravagant & if you want the outfit feel free to buy it.

The bank balance is pleasant news. Does that include the $200.00 I sent you. Had hoped you would put that in the savings account for a rainy day for we still haven't returned that amount to Marie & as you remember she said to keep it for an emergency. Hope I don't have to write a check tho I may be somewhere I can cash a check & I am getting a bit low. If I do write one it will not be in excess of $25.00.

May give <u>myself the pleasure</u> of calling you (and Xmas present) just when I can't say nor from where but should the opportunity present itself will do so as there is so much I would like to say but please don't be disappointed if my hopes don't materialize, of course will make it collect or do you mind?

Received the long interesting box from Susie today—though haven't received but a total of four from you including the one from L.A. only one of which I have opened & that was the one round can mentioned in an earlier letter. Haven't received the one from Mother C as yet though have received the one from 4140 Park Blvd. & one from Ed & Marie & one from Virginia.

Thanks for getting the information from Chuck for me—will pass it on. Know you will tell him also I appreciate his efforts to get the word to me—something went wrong somewhere & its doubtful whether we will ever find out what.

Thanks for your many sweet letters My Sweet—know writing is quite a chore for you. I should be ashamed for not writing you more—do believe you have gotten all or most of my letters—don't think I wrote for that 8 day period in Nov. while at sea.

With all my love to the three of you & much love to all of the family.

Lovingly

Al & Da

A.F Herney Ens. U.S.N.R.

Sunday Nite Dec 3 No. 3 Dec.

My Dearest Sweet Susie & Steve:

How nice it would have been to be with you today to spend a relatively quiet Sunday enjoying a bit of your work and then a fire in the grate. Know you wouldn't mind my getting up occasionally to replenish the wood that had grown into embers. However instead the Deck was mine which meant taking care of many things and really getting very little accomplished.

Forgot to mention that the trip to Whittier sounds exciting though I hope not to much for you especially since you now have two instead of one to worry about. One of you of course will insist on crawling all over you & the other as you say has his pants problem. Know you will have a good time.

Forgot to mention also that Virginias (Sweetpie) does have a bit of trouble & know that you will extend to her my most and deepest sympathy. Tell her also have started a Xmas letter to her.

Marie wrote that Rose [Marie and Ed's housekeeper] is to bless the world with an offspring. Know they are very happy about it (Rose & her husband) tho it is tough on Marie & Ed. If it isn't war work, impossibilities it's a prospective family so what the hell—you just can't win.

Don't like the way you said that the School bond had carried. Remember my love if you're a taxpayer you catch it in the neck & oh how it can hurt. Wait for the tax bill next year.

Can quite understand why Bob {Davis} was defeated—he does try to be a good egg but you just can't carry high pressure business methods over into everyday life and expect to get by with it.

Was wondering the other day what had become of Dutch [Dewitt Higgs]? Is he still at Camp Pendleton for it he is I know he is damn unhappy about the whole thing.

Many of the boys have purchased bracelets of sea shells from the boys on the beach. Haven't considered one for you as they may be a novelty & you would say see what Al sent me from somewhere but don't think that is anywhere worth what they are charging for the things—then too doubt if their wives have an aqua marine or whatever it is.

No mail today but you can't expect some every day especially when your last letter was dated & postmarked Nov 27 which I received yesterday. Damn good time isn't it (redundancy).

You sort of confuse me when you mentioned in one of the letters that the "Monk" is mine. If you mean that the picture of the Monk is or was given to me by Mother do think that Ed should have it if he wishes for the picture originally came from him. He too was fond of Mother and very good to her and she fond of him so if you don't mind you may pass on the thought. Don't misunderstand that I wouldn't very much like having it & it pleased me much to think that Mother wanted me to have it. Will not in any way feel that Ed is unjust should he indicate that he would like it.

Have not mentioned before that if there are expenses it is only fair that we share them with the others. What with your good management, fell that it will be ok & you and our offspring won't starve. Pease ask the family about the finances and take care of our share.

Must close my sweet as I am to be called even before the crew in the morning. Yes its my pleasant to duty to see that they hit the deck.

With all my love to the three of you and much love to all of the family.

Lovingly

Al & Dada

A.F Herney Ens USNR.

12/4/44/P.S. Mothers package arrived yesterday still I pretty good shape. Good morning my love & little Sweets.

Love Al

Scurry *arrived in Pearl Harbor December 13, 1944*

Wednesday Dec. 13 '44 Dec. No 4.

My dearest Sweet Susie & Steve:

Received Dec No 3 today only—what has happened to 1 & 2 and any after No 13 for Nov is beyond me. Must get used to having the letters packages & what have you chase you around.

I guess I was pretty much of a sailor until this trip. Was really sick for the first few days had what I thought as seasickness but oh after things started settling down decided that it was something else. Expect to have an examination to determine whether or not I've got what I hope I ain't—yep ulcers—Will do this without fail before pulling out of here.

Your letter of Dec 7 raises several nice points my Sweet—first you talk about Dr. Myers saying you were OK <u>now</u> & that you told him he didn't bargain for bring six into the world & that he ought to be glad you weren't having another—together with the fact that you have been in at Julia's & Macs—Sure what gives—don't tell me the 'Sure Shots' came thru again & in view of all the excitement you had to lose it. If so my Sweet I am sorry to hear that you have had that also to add to your many burdens. Have been thinking a whole lot about you Susie & Steve recently & would give much if I could be with you and This damn thing all over.

Have dug out Joe's address & also Kay Gates "Willie"—don't know when I can get in touch with them but will try to do so soon. You gave me Joe's address & telephone no—thanks for remembering to do so.

Sweet I haven't written to you since the <u>3rd</u> of Dec—Twelve days is a lot but frankly I wasn't much caring what happened & whether the world kept on or not. Still feel like I could raise a lot of hell over a very little bit to upset me.

Haven't received any letters from anyone of the family. Do agree with you that Mother would be happier out where God's Sunlight on occasion can & does give one so much moral as well as physical warmth.

So the little Pride & Joy has really gotten to the point of knowing the meaning of candie—How did the whole thing start after our good intentions. Must watch the candie dish for sure for it really wouldn't do for her to get sick on it.

Steve must be a powerful big boy by this time. Wonder if he will remember me—oh nuts guess what? Would very much like to be there Honey to see him smile but will just have to imagine it.

Forgot to mention in my last letter that the insurance allotment was to commence on Aug 1.—Wonder what has happened to the allotments for Aug Sept & Oct. Check with Bob about this at your first opportunity—I'm sure that I haven't been paid those sums each month as it is drawn as a deduction on allotment.

Here I've covered four pages & haven't said much—It's times like these Sweet that your love & my happy recollections help pull me along.

Lovingly as always

Al & Dada

A.F Herney Ens USNR

V-MAIL message to Al's son, Stephen, conveyed a patriotic message.

Thursday Dec. 14 No 5

My Dearest Sweet, Susie & Steve:

The mailman was good today for he brought no's 14 & 15 for November and No's 1,2 & 4 for December plus a nice note from Mother & Dad, a card from aunt Heral [Dot's aunt, sister to Mother C.] a sweet note from Marie &

Helen & Virginia—which all adds up I know to say that you all do love me— which I will assure helps a great deal.

Your letter of Nov. 30th Sweet was very enlightening and clears the air a whole lot. Honey here I am with just a few worries to bother me and you having everything on your shoulders. Can quite understand just how you felt about it all and can't say that I blame you one bit. How I would have loved to have been there to help take some of the problems off your shoulders, and wouldn't for the world have wanted to have been the cause of all the trouble—but then I always have been pretty much of a demanding person when that urge hit me & oh how often. I too my dear say thank goodness we aren't having another just now. Can well imagine your relief.

Your arrangements regarding & about the young couple are satisfactory with me and do hope that it will be of some help to you. The young fellow does seem to be quite a sensible chap when you come right down to observations. Would suggest you call Mannie to see if O.P.A. would be interested in the deal. Don't feel so but then you should make sure. Do remember them both for me.

The purchases for the Meyers are more than agreeable with me & Sweet I didn't whistle. Think you'd better take both the offspring with you when you deliver the presents & be sure to extend to both of them my sincere wishes for the nicest holiday season to them. They're nice people & Lloyd has done much for us. I haven't written any checks as yet and don't think I'll do so & don't give a damn about the checking account.

Marie didn't say anything about the expenses for Mother's last rites. No need to mention it again but didn't know what the story was about Mother's affairs but did feel we should do our part if there were any expenses.

The phone call is out of the question Honey so it was, it seems a pipe dream but I did have much fun in hoping it were possible. Tried also to send you an E.F.M. (Expeditionary Force Message) but no sope on that either right now except in case of death, illness, marriage & the like.

Word has it that we were sunk with only 7 survivors. Don't believe it Honey for we were all having a grand life on the Scurry as part of the fleet—well anyway we were on the Scurry—all wishing it were possible to be home with our loved ones.

Did so enjoy the letter relating about Carl S.—received a Xmas card from IJ. With a picture of their Steve—looks to be quite a young man too doesn't he? Must drop Carl a note. It's too bad Hank had to leave for I might have saved myself that letter I must write him.

Poor Virginia is having one hell of a time poor dear—finished a Xmas letter to her last evening only to find from your letters today she must have more. Will write her again. Her letter about Mother was dear—as you might well know.

My letter of last night Sweet was a very poor excuse—but will try to do better in the future & not bother you with my problems. You can see since I didn't have the missing letters I didn't' see what you were doing in town so much—not that I minded a bit.

With love to the three of you forever

Al always

Al & Dada

A.F Herney, Ens USNR.

P.S. Have mailed you the letter <u>Xmas</u> to the family with a special note to you—same directions not till Xmas eve—won't write P.M.'s as Xmas party is over. Your last letter mailed Dec. 11 received today—good time huh?

P.S.S. Do sympathize with both the Carrels especially Marie—give them my love with you

Al

Friday 15 Dec Dec#6

Dearest Sweet Susie & Steve:

Have just written Mother & Dad, George and Ernie & Babs—Can't of course neglect the three of you but won't promise much of a letter.

I am quoting part of my letter to Dad & Mother so you will be fully advised —"Dot has written me about your wishes that she bring your grandchildren to Lincoln for a few months stay this Spring. She has my approval for I think it only fair that you too have the pleasure of enjoying them tho I'm sure the "Pride & Joy is getting to be somewhat of a problem. No doubt being spoiled by all of the extra attention being shown her by her uncles & aunts. Please appreciate however that Dot's decision is rather a difficult one for you never can tell about the "Navy".

This of course leaves the decision up to you but a way out too if you don't feel you wish to take the chance. I will say that the last sentence of the quote is no intimation nor is it intended to be of what I or anyone else can expect, tho I would very much love to hope there was that chance.

Sweet I'm afraid you would blush with pride and feel warm all over if you knew what else I wrote your Mother & dad about you but simply it boils down to the simple basic fact that I love you so damn much I hurt all over and I'm not meaning in a base way either. The way you've taken it all has given me more an urge & the drive to come <u>home </u>hell, high water or anything else the Japs have to offer.—and Sweet I think that is about the highest compliment that can be paid to Mrs. Herney or any woman.

I have gotten so much pleasure my Sweet out of the abundance of pleasure I've had in the years you've been mine—not so much from the possessive sense but the companionship you've offered—the willingness to add to posterity and the two darling youngsters you have presented to me. Know always Dottie that I do love you.

Am much relieved for (I) got to see the Med today & was assured that from the symptoms all I had was a bit of bowel irritation & could not in any way be ulcers. The Med really got sore at me for my insistence & do believe he thought I was looking for a shore job or survey—was tempted to tell him to go to hell but then he was only a Lt. Commander & I've been told you don't say that to Lt (JGs) if you're an Ensign much less to a commander. Wonder if he was such a meanie when in private practice for if he was doubt he was liked even tho he might have been good.

Your analysis about the possibility of change of duty was way off. Was informed this morning that my deck duty while at sea as such was over & could concentrate on communications which will be one big break—definite routine most of the time and something I am looking forward too to say the least. This is of course the result of the new officer who has reported aboard & has a good general background

Did I tell you in my letter of last night that I had enclosed a short special Xmas message in the letter for the family. I'm pretty sure that I'll be very close to you in thought on Xmas my love so please make believe that I'm there.

Felt right proud that I've taken care of so much correspondence last nite 7 tonight—sent the kids military Xmas cards V mail—last night—will sent to Pat Monica Catherine & Sheilah [Al's nieces] tonight.

With all my love to the three of you—

Al & Dada

Ens. A.F Herney USNR.

———

Dec. 16—'44 Sat. nite Letter 7

Merry Christmas my Dearest and Merry Christmas Daddy

While Susie and Stevie are tucked snug in their beds, Mama will endeavor to write a Christmas letter—hoping it will reach Daddy about Christmas time if the planes and the Navy and God is willing.

We know that all the things we say so often can't be wished any harder than we're wishing them everyday but we do hope our letters, our boxes and our thoughts will be with you on Christmas Eve and Christmas Day in particular and if you have a tree, know that your daughter is looking at one too with shining eyes and with the eagerness that only a two year old can have—while Stevie will be blissfully snoozing and unaware of anything unusual except that there will be lots of doting uncles and aunties to hold him and talk to him.

Mama is thinking of all of the 7 Christmas's that have been or I guess its 6 before this one and I'm going to try and remember them.

The first one was Christmas 1935 and was spent at 3317 Orange Ave with Dot & Al making the cranberry frappe and snatching a few kisses when no one was looking, or were they? I gave you a ring—and we wanted to be engaged but we were in thought if nothing else.

1936 is sort of vague but I know Mom and Dad didn't come out that year. Casey and I were living in Arvilla Courts and I was at Annes' and

Tex but where the party was I don't remember. Anyway Christmas night Casey and I threw a party in the match box court and what a party! It rained buckets, Doc was tight & got out in the court and yelled "Oh Mr. McKendry" and you and Dot Cook put our guest towels in the bathtub and Dot ruined her stockings and you took up a collection to buy her a new pair, and Lloydines' boy friend was a bell hop from some hotel and a wonderful drink mixer and we had the electric malt machine from Doc's drug store & he made wonderful gin flips of some kind—there was an all red Christmas tree and we were in love!

1937 we went to Lincoln—that was a special year because we were now Mr. & Mrs. Phiss [a school chum of Dot's] joined us in L.A. and we had a rollicking good time on the Challenger chair car. We got to Denver and Anne Powell who had been on a Pullman (Plutocrat!) took us out to her cousin's & we ate breakfast and all lay down on our stomachs to rest our fannies! We caught the Zephyr at 4 P.M. on Christmas Eve to Lincoln and met a former school mate of mine and his new wife at the bar. Albert had one too many on an empty & tired stomach and got violently ill but got a whiff of zero temperature between cars and came to quickly. I was very proud of my new husband and wanted him to know all of my relatives and friends.

1938 is vague—but we were living at 288 Del Mar and Mom & Dad came out. Can you remember where the festivities were. It was your first Xmas out of law school and you hadn't really started in yet in your own office.

1939—I'm a complete blank there???

1940—Our first Christmas in our own home, and we had the Christmas Eve party and it was a big success and everyone enjoyed it and thot our home was lovely.

1941—Things were beginning to happen. We'd had Pearl Harbor and the Draft was beginning to look menacing and there was a future Herney on the way tho no one knew it at the time—not even us for sure, except Al was very confident there was no question! The festivities were at Julia's.

1942—Dot and Al and Susan spent Christmas Eve at Eddie & Marie's where the party was held. We stayed all nite and Susan behaved like a little angel—and even her aunt Marie thought she was pretty good even tho Edie put her in bed with them at 6 A.M. It rained buckets alnight the Christmas day dinner was at Julia and Anne's again and there were so many people I never did find out who they all were.

1943 found us in Lincoln again on our way to Boston—and it didn't seem much like Christmas—we'd had a very grueling 4 days of driving from San Diego and Mama wasn't in her best spirits for Mama knew that there was a junior on the way and she was a bit upset, physically and mentally, but Daddy was a good sport an didn't mind too much—he has that faculty of not getting upset at Mama's moods that Mama hasn't appreciated as much as she should till lately when she has no one to explode on.

And so we come to 1944—and our first Christmas apart. I pray it is our last apart. Because of the children the Christmas gayiety will prevail even to our hearts may be heavy and our eyes a bit misty, for we've lost one of us and another is far away and wanting to be with us but were trying to make the best of it and "carry on" as usual ad Susan and Stevie will know on some future date that in 1944 their Daddy spent Christmas in the blue Pacific, in strange places but was thinking of them as much as their Mama was thinking of him.

Again Merry Christmas my dearest—and may the New Year bring us together again.

Your loving wife,

Dottie

———

Saturday 16 Dec. 1944 No. 7

My Dearest Sweet, Susie & Steve:

Received your Dec No 5 mailed Dec 11, a nice letter from Ann—Xmas card & note from the Shaws and the information from Bob re insurance. The mailman does of course continue to be very good.

Forgot to mention in my last letter that I didn't say anything to Mother & Dad about your extreme worry—which right now is a matter of the past nor will I do so in the future. Will keep your secret.

Did so enjoy the information about going to see "Santa". Can just hear Uncle Eddie bragging & then remembering that possibly you did contribute (not also this is the first time you related it to me so no rehashing & forget it if you do.). God bless the "Pride & Joy" for saying first Bring Daddy Home & then her set of dishes.

Can't quite get over the young lady acquiring such a big vocabulary in such a short time. Do realize that I'm missing a while lot in not being there but then she will still be a little girl when I do get home, but then I will have missed much too.

Can imagine what a time she is going to have being pretty much the center of attention this year. Wonder why such a little girl should be so fortunate to have so many nice Uncles, Aunts & such nice grandparents—to say nothing of parents—but then on second thought she is an angel. It is so darling of her to say goodnight to her paternal grandfather & such a very very pleasant it is too!

Didn't mention how pleased I am that Steve has gotten to be such a big boy—must be getting to be wide away and so interested in whats about him. Don't think Sweet in no mentioning him that I don't consider him one of us but these days acquaintance isn't a whole lot. Growing up with Susie spoiled me and much of my recollection is of her of course. Susie didn't like her pablum at first either did she.

Would have loved to nestle in with you & Susie the other morning. A pleasant thought to say the least and reminds me of the three days I had at home.

Wrote some more military Xmas cards last night to get the correspondence out of the way. Solmans, Stark's the two Higg's—the "Herneys" Pat etc & Sheilah and the Paxtons for their nice attention & generosity to help make my three days at home more pleasant.

Received word today that Marie & Ed have sent me a subscription to the "Readers Digest". It was nice of them to do so though a bit sorry as we are getting sufficient copies aboard already—others have sent subscriptions in but will be nice to have my own copy. Thank them for me. Forgot to say that I received a package from "Herney" Ed of course & dying to open it for I know it is an interesting book with cartoons but haven't broken down as yet, & then Xmas isn't too far away.

Pay day today. Since we haven't been docked for two months chow already eaten didn't draw any as only $50.00 on the books—will get about $10.00 next payday. Gates however gave me $50.00 more so will keep that as I am in need of some funds $20 of which I've already kicked into the kitty for the purchase of little extras for the mess. Still have the $20 travelers check which I'm included to endorse over to you for deposit. Will see how it works out. Will have sufficient as soon as we get caught up on the back mess—one of the reasons I drew the $80.00 60 of which I sent to you.

Very glad you stopped to see the Padre & make the donation & take care of the masses. Sweet of you to do these nice little things that I would like to do buy can't. Do hope you enjoyed the card party & saw many people that you have missed in the last months.

Sorry to hear about Mary & Durban tho as you say you really can't blame her much for her decision.

Remember Sweet the only time we really had any possibly chance of a wing dinger enroute from L.A.—have often thought of how much we each would have missed had we done so. Thanks Sweet for not having decided you wanted to go your separate way.

Glad you could get the bed for Steve for he surely will be needing soon if he doesn't stop growing. Just wonder how your going to arrange all of the furniture for it however especially now that you have the young couple.

Sweet if you can possibly find time do hope you keep up with your piano—possibly our little girl will somehow grow to like it & eventually really want to learn. Maybe with the helper there now you'll have a bit more time to spend enjoying yourself.

It was thoughtful of you to offer the use of the cradle for Blythe's & Chucks expected and I'm happy they accepted. As you say it will soon have a history for this will be number 5 won't it? Will fix up the crib when I get home with the record of all of them—names & dates & do the crib over with a real finish if you want call yourself a sandpaper widow.

Would have enjoyed to be at the last Phi Mu party when Blythe & Chuck were the recipients of all those nice little things for the new one. Do guess they enjoyed it too.

Ann wrote Susie is now the proud owner of silk pants & insisted on seeing if Ann had silk ones on. My what is she getting to be a doubting Thomas?

Must drop Paul & Beth a short note before calling it quits.

With much love to the three of you always

Al & Dada

Hope this hasn't been too much of a rambling letter—

Al

A.F Herney USNR.

P.S. Will return the application for commissary card soon as received.
Al.

Monday Nite Dec 18 Dec #8
My Dearest Sweet, Susie & Steve:

Did miss writing to you yesterday but know that you will forgive me again for not taking the time. Failed to write as I really didn't have anything to say.

Received a nice letter yesterday from Marie C.—mailed Dec 5 regular so you see air mail does make so much difference in time tho 12 days regular mail isn't so bad at that.

Today the application for Commissary card renewal arrived—have filled it out & will see that it gets in the mail tomorrow direct to O-in-O US Navy Commissary Store S.D. Calif. Don't know if it will be processed & received by him by the 1st but do hope so.

While in town yesterday looked around for something for you & the youngsters. Quite a bit of junk—yes—and the clothes all seem to be made in the States so ended up by buying nothing. Have made arrangements for something for you—something I've never purchased for you since we've been married. Know they can't get there for Xmas nor no sure when but they are meant for your birthday—not much but something I do hope you'll enjoy.

Incidently ran into Dagwood & he gave me a bit of information about Joe & his new wife. Joe it seems is now doing legal work on one of the Islands and has been doing so even since he arrived. The wife while at present is in the hospital from a serious operation is recuperating and will be going home within the next few days. They are running a day nursery and doing quite well at it—from a financial standpoint & does enjoy it much. Dagwood spent the nite and next day with Joe—going to the hospital to meet the wife, younger than he expected when he had seen the stepson who was sixteen. He said she was a very pleasant person & more than Joe's first wife could have been. After getting back from the hospital Joe & Dag talked till after midnite about old times & trials. Joe invited Dag to the base for Xmas day—which he said he was going to try to arrange if possible. Gosh what a lucky egg.

Wrote Beth & Paul, Blythe & Chuck a short note nite before last when in some more of my writing mood—have really done a whole lot better than I expected but guess the pressure gets just too heavy & you can't do anything except get it off your chest.

Did I thank you for getting the information about Dutch. Am glad to know all about him for I will keep my eyes open for him & expect to run into hi somewhere out in his big broad Pacific.

Have been feeling somewhat better—have broken the diet just once——a beer in celebration when I got to see Dag- & then couldn't resist that little variance. The medicine prescribed is anything but pleasant tasting but then haven't overlooked taking it for its more comfortable without that pain.

Tell Ann I haven't received her nuts as yet but then they will be good to look forward to at some future date.

With all my love to the three of you always

Al & DaDa

As Always

A.F Herney Ens, USNR.

Tuesday nite Dec 19 No. 9

My Dearest Sweet, Susie & Steve:

Another day gone I haven't accomplished a thing. Will have to get off the dime as now is the time for some of the heavy work to be done & I've really gotten so awfully lazy its funny.

Received your #6 today—mailed Dec 15—not bad service at all. Wonder if you have gotten any of mine as yet or whether you are wondering why I haven't written within the last few weeks. Too I may have forgotten my numbers again so don't get confused if you receive two with the same number.

Forgot to tell you that Bob Saunders has been sent the insurance papers & will return them with in the next few days so that matter can be straightened out—he of course will need the policies to send in to have the endorsements entered thereon. Have wondered if Virginia has had her operation as yet? Poor dear she has had her troubles too—hasn't she? Sent her a Xmas card & will try to drop her another note.

Wrote Marie & Doc & Walt last night—really this correspondence takes one hell of a lot of time & when you can't get started until late the wee hours show up on the clock—here it is nearly 11:30 now.

Tho I don' know the {Norths} very well I'm sorry that they had had their difficulties. Sweet—people must be either awfully short sighted or very self centered and selfish when the first thinking they think of is separation. Life always has been & will be some sort of compromise—& its peculiar they often overlook small things in others than those with whom they've cast their lot entered into the best venture of living. Ho hum here I am lecturing again.

The party did seem to be a bit of fun but much of a hen party—my all the gossip that didn't pass—almost as much of it as the conversation about children.

Sorry to hear that Steve still has his cold—& with Zeta [and her husband lived with Dot during this time to help Dot with the house and children] having a touch of the flu hasn't helped either. She must be pretty much on the ball not to want to go to bed tho that is the best place for her. As for Julia spoiling Steve just give any of the Aunts a chance & the answer will be the same.

So Susie Q was a naughty girl—she does have a good bit of the old neck in her at that—that's after me of course. Of course if Dad was there he possibly would have done the spanking. God bless her for not wanting to neglect the night prayer for I'm sure it will be one big help when the time comes for that type of help.

Shore based I'm sure is Hanks idea of the duty—still can see it for I'm sure that I would get sititis & that ain't what I'm looking for.

Will forget about the Income Tax since you have had the info from Durbin—Suggest you keep all of the records so when necessary that they will be available.

With all my love to the three of you.

Al always

Al & Dada.

A.F Herney, Ens USNR.

Wednesday Nite Dec.20

My Dearest Sweet, Susie & Steve

Had the deck today so didn't get much accomplished—however worked after chow for a few hours & did get some things accomplished—very little however.

Received a very nice letter from Jack [his nephew] today—will enclose it in a later letter but want you to keep it—will answer it tell him soon after Xmas.

The mess attendants take care of the cleaning of our head. The other day after they had done some painting, shower & urinal Petteway chap you would think knew better prepared & stuck the following sign on the door—"Notice fresh paint in the shower & ernold." Thought you might enjoy it as I certainly did when I saw it.

Julia & Mac's package arrived yesterday. How I'm going to love to get into them for I know that I'm going to be just as blue as hell—your right about the time your having Xmas Eve it will still be early afternoon out here in the Pacific.

Helen mentioned in her letter to me that she is getting the Romeo's for me. Will be very welcome to have too I can assure you & easy to put on just in case its ever necessary to get the hell off of her in a hurry tho I don't anticipate that in the least.

Can't quite get over how the two youngsters are developing in such a short time.

Saw Dag again today and he said that he was hopeful of yesterday Xmas afternoon with Joe & his wife Xmas afternoon—however he is going to have to do a heck of a lot of work between now & then. Its lucky for him that the doesn't have the duty either on Xmas Eve or on Xmas day.——It seems that the breaks are with him.

Thurs Morn:

As I want to get this off it will be necessary that I just add a few more words and close as the mailman is about on his way. Am looking forward to him bringing me a letter from you.

Hope Steve is over his cold & that Zeta is back on her feet so that you will have a bit more time for yourself.

With all my love to the three of you always. Much Christmas love & oh how I wish I could be with you.

Al & Dada

AF Herney Ens USNR.

Thursday Dec 21 Dec # 9

My Dearest Sweet, Susie & Steve:

Received your very very sweet letter Xmas special today. Mailed on the 17th which isn't at all bad—don't know if mine to you is delayed a whole lot but do hope not tho I understand the mail going out of here is awfully heavy.

Your recollection of the many Xmas we've had together is tops Sweet—but then if you will count 1935 thru 1943 there are nine Xmas's. 1936 Xmas I believe was with Ann & Tex was it not for Tex was still living and we did have a Xmas at 4910. Another of the missing dates was with Julia & Mac at Collier remember? Just which one I'm not sure & my recollection goes back to the many pleasant times were had together. That party at Arvella Courts was a humdinger wasn't it.

Did I forget to tell you that Helen [his sister] wrote she was to get the Romeo's—think I did but will mention it again so don't worry about it for if she can't get them I can get along very easily.

Honey I really don't know how Mother knew how boys away from home do enjoy being invited out. I did so enjoy just doing everyday civilian things—shopping for groceries—sleeping in late. Very possibly the answer lies in her deep love for all of her family & for humanity in general. Can now readily see why she so generously always asked someone out—for dinner—the day yes and even the nite.

Did accomplish a little today—not as much however as I would like to have done but there is always someone else's problems but your own too. Well guess it will always be that way.

I'm afraid my numbers on the letters have again hit on the rough side for don't remember numbering the one written last night but mailed today. Have written however every day since the 13th with the exception of one.

Honey I don't seem to have a whole lot to say so know you will overlook the fact that this is anything but a newsy letter.

As far as the chaps aboard they are all fine—Both Mr. Johnson & Gates have hit an alnav—Bots is now a chief warrant & brother Gates a J.G.— would gladly give up a raise in rank if this damn war would be over before I expect and which won't be before Febr. 1.

Schnaebels baby is due now but he hasn't as yet had any word about it & doesn't seem too concerned. The Capt is fine & has leveled off a bit—Hetzler [executive officer] is of course still much the same—honest he does so damn little except pass on all the responsibilities its funny. Gosch of course wants to go home like all of us but can't.

Honey thanks for the nice Xmas letter—truly is one & wish I could do as well—Will be thinking hard about you all especially my own little branch— missing you oh so much—

A very big hug & kiss to the three of you & my love always

Al & Dada

A.F Herney, En.

P.S. Have you received any of my letters?

Saturday Nite Dec 23 Dec #10

My Dearest Sweet, Susie & Big Boy Steve:

Received your letter of the 19th today Sweet. Not bad time either & by this time you should have all of them or all but the last two letters written. It is good to get them—isn't it.

Was very happy to get the picture of Steve. My how he has grown a lot since the middle of Sept.—but then that was about 1 ½ months before the picture was taken. Will be very glad to see that he keeps growing to be a mighty big boy. Is that the picture they blotted you out of the picture? If so they did a nice job. However all the pictures taken would seem to be good.

Sweet—about the house—Aren't you a bit optimistic about us taking on such a load at this time with everything so uncertain and the market high-—I'm pessimistic about the price & doubting if Bob would consider any thing close to $5000.00 for ours. If you were asking my opinion—would much prefer that nothing be done by way of change of domicile until I get home.

Tickled about you suggestion to get a good dose of ulcers if I were getting some—Do believe that ulcers would be the way for a survey but <u>ain't</u> looking for a survey now when the fun is about to start nor would I have made any attempt to get out via that method—first because there is still a big job to do & further ulcers ain't pleasant.

Picked up a birthday present for you but as yet unmailed. This is of course in addition to the other thing I mentioned in an earlier letter.

The mails are rather slow especially packages—& straight mail. Airmail gets in right regular so if that continues and I get the nice letters from you Honey I won't care.

Will try to get out to see Joe on Xmas afternoon. Of course will try to get to communion on Xmas—two special reasons in addition to it being Xmas. Can you imagine what they could be?

Bev wrote me a nice note on the back of their Xmas card. She is quite a gal all in all—Didn't seem to mind your manner & said she was glad you have found someone to be of help to you. Maybe I will get to see Hank sometime soon at one of these Pacific Islands—God how many there are.

You didn't mention before just what was wrong with the Zeta & am glad she is coming along OK.

Just one night away from Xmas Eve—Merry Xmas to the three of you & do hope your eyes won't be too misty & hearts too heavy when it is time to join in "Holy night, Silent nite" But I can' honestly say mine won't—in fact they are right now.

May God continue to be good to us and bring us all home this coming year—

With all my love to the three of you always

Al & Dada

P.S. Didn't write you last night for I was correcting Pubs until the late hours.—

Al

A.F Herney, Ens USNR

Xmas Eve 1944

My Dearest Family:

Merry Xmas to each and every one of you. You all realize of course how much I would love to be with you tonight even tho our own sweet Mother is absent. How she did enjoy to have her family gathered round—creating bedlam generally but then it wouldn't be a gathering of the <u>clan</u> if that wasn't the usual.

Would or I should say I should write each of you a personal note but I don't have it in me & know that you will forgive me for not doing so—possibly sometime in the very near future.

To Julia & Mac of course special greetings this being an anniversary for them—just how many does this count up to at this time?

As for certain Santa is being good to all of the nieces and nephews. Uncle Al of course would enjoy much being with you to entertain with all the new things you received from Santa—& then it was almost my turn to be Santa this Xmas.

I've always known I had a nice family—and have grown to appreciate it more & more—your kind attentions and loving kindness to Mother and your great deal of love & protection you have shown my own little branch of the clan, off of which has helped to ease my mind about having felt it necessary to leave them for a military life which I sincerely hope is of short duration. Can't understand how Mother felt I was a poet for I'm sure I don't feel like one I the least.

With sincere wishes for as happy a holiday season as possible—much love to each of you—and much much love to my own Dottie, Susie & Steve—

As Always

Al.

Ens. A. F Herney, USNR

Xmas Eve 1944 [An uncompleted letter written before hearing of the death of his mother in November]

My Dearest Family:

Twas the Night before Xmas and all thru the house there was plenty stirring for it was Xmas Eve at a Herney's House.

The letter is dated Xmas Eve for it will be my way of being with you even for a very short time & Oh how pleasant it would be to be there. Each of you please know that I am envious of you.

I am sure that when unwrapping the many Xmas presents & packages sentimental Herney will have the kerchief handy to wipe away the ready tears.

Now for the special Christmas and New Year thoughts:

To Mother—who always has enjoyed the Xmas Season to her very heart—has taught us to appreciate them and has shown us all much about living. The merriest of Xmas's many more of them and the best of everything for the coming year.

Xmas Eve 1944

Dearest Sweet, Susie & Steve:

A special note to my one & only, my Pride & Joy, and to Steve the newest addition to our family circle. Merry Merry Xmas to each one of you.

It is rather hard to believe that this will be the first Xmas out of <u>seven</u> Sweet that we won't be together, the third with Susan and the first with Steve. While Steve can't quite as yet grasp the significance of the season it won't be long. Susan however will be there with her blue eyes big as everything—how I would love to be there if just for a short while. I've promised my self not later than '45—maybe make a date now for Xmas of 45? Maybe Santa will in fact have something under the tree for my own—will try hard to see if it can be arranged. If not I hope you won't be disappointed.

With all my love to the three of you—please miss me but don't be too disappointed that I can't be with you.

As Always,

Al & Dada

Ens AF Herney USNR

Monday Morning Dec 25 '44 Dec. #11
My Dearest Sweet, Susie & Steve:

Just back from mid-night Mass & must write you before hitting the sack. Being able to go to mid-night Mass and communion. Got there soon after eleven to go to confession—but there was so many ahead—waited until the last minute & still didn't get in so had to take advantage of the "General Absolution". It was an elevating sight to see so many men attending & going to communion. Then also there were some women with servicemen & civilians. Of course some of the women were wifes & of course I like many others were a bit jealous that they, the men, had their loved ones with them.

Sweet I've never prayed so hard in all my life. Wouldn't be for anything other than for Mother & the end of this thing that is keeping us apart. Don't why the Almighty should hear my petitions but did give it a good try. Will try again soon too.

Honey I've seen women—all kinds of—various shades of & hues but there isn't one that can compare with my "one & only." I've known that—I've loved you my Sweet but when being away from the opposite sex for a spell & then being able to come into contact with then & wanting none of them Honey you well know that there is <u>only one</u> for you.

Followed the traditional Herney Xmas Eve by opening my packages. Did so in the stateroom while the Bunkey was attending the movie—for I was sure that the memories of our pleasant Xmas's might be a bit more than I could stand without the ruse of the kerchief. Did enjoy unwrapping the parcels—all of which were in line and more than happy to receive. It was not so much what there was but the thought behind them & there was the knowledge that I was, or would be missed around the old stomping grounds. Thank you Sweet for your gifts—did so enjoy the little notes on the parcels. Thank all of the family for me. Found out that Mother & Dad had sent a subscription to Time—wondered who had done—read the thing from cover to cover in short order. Card from Esquire advises that Ed & Marie have sent in a subscription for that too as well as the readers digest.

About dinner time was a bit blue for I knew that you all would be gathering at Ed & Maries & did so wish to be there—did you get some of my mental telepathy. Hope so for I was thinking hard.

Called Joe & he is to pick me up tomorrow for a party in the afternoon so must get some sleep.

Merry Xmas & Happy New Year again to the three "Ss" of my family—(see heading) with my love always

Al & Dada

A.F Herney, Ens USNR.

P.S. Do hope you received my Xmas letter to the family & to you three—.

Al

———

Dec. 26 2 P.M. Letter 11

Dearest—

Well, here we are home again—but you sort of have to shovel yourself thru the debris—toys strung all over the front room—doll dishes, table, rocking horse—the top of the piano is covered with gifts—the dining room buffet & table covered with wrappings & string. Stevie getting a sun bath—Susan down for a nap and Zeta and I trying to get our letters written and off in the afternoon mail. I feel like I'd been on a 3 day ride on the Merry-go-round and still dizzy. Will try and go back and recount as much as I can remember.

I got off from here at 4 Saturday afternoon with the car so loaded I wondered if I could make it. Had supper at Anne's and got the kids to bed and we worked getting Anne's gifts wrapped but went to bed rather early. It started raining in the night and was pouring own by morning and kept it up. As per schedule I had the children dressed and ready to go to Dr. Myers by 10:30 and went in the pouring rain. Dr. Myers was not home yet from his hunting trip but Etta, her Mother and father-in-law were there and properly exclaimed over our children. Mrs. Myers served some cookies and Susan was so taken by her little footstool she wanted to take it home. We stayed till almost 12 but the Dr. hadn't come yet so we left as I had to get home to feed Steve. Marie had planned on taking Susan with her to make calls in the afternoon but she didn't know when she was coming so I put her down for her nap and she was asleep when Marie got there and I felt the nap was more important than the calls since Susie would be up late. Ben Alice arrived about 4:30 and such a rush as we had, getting dinner done, dishes done, children dressed & fed & off. Ben Alice and Susie, Steve & myself went in my car and I stopped at the hospital to leave our gift for Virginia—a lapel pin with earrings to match. She was feeling lousy—had had a siege of gas pains and was really all dragged out-—I felt so sorry for her. I took Susan in with me and she said "Gee-Gee sick abed—too bad Gee-Gee." We only stayed a minute.

The Mueller's front room looked like a department store gift shop as per usual. By 7:30 all of us were there and one of the two sailors (one was Eddie's 3rd cousin) dressed up in Santa Claus suit—(which they Styer's got from the fire hall in Coronado for Marie) and arrived. All eyes were on Susie—and she performed beautifully. Santa Claus asked if here was a little girl named Susan—and she said "Hello Santa Claus" tho' she wouldn't get too near him. He gave her the rocking horse and did her eyes shine! She got right on it and went to town! From there on there was such a madhouse I didn't know what was happening. Gifts kept piling up for Susan and Steve and me—Ben Alice kept them in tow—while I helped Susan with hers. Of course she wanted to take all the doll dishes out and put them on her table at once—so I had some time getting them put away and think we're missing a couple now—but they are probably at Marie's. Steve of course was upstairs asleep in Eddie's room thru all this! Ben Alice was quite overcome with all the people, presents, etc. Ice cream & cake were served and Susan had her share of Aunt Marie's, mine, Pat's Ben Alice's. I can't begin to tell you of all we received—but plan to make a list of everything to send you when I can get around to it. There was a beautiful purse from you, Susie & Steve which Marie got knowing I wanted one and that I was supposed to get it but she won't let me pay for it. She & Ed gave me a beautiful rose slack suit too—so I am really decked out—not to mention the adorable red pants & "T" shirt for Steve and red corduroy overalls for Susan from Aunt Marie & Uncle Ed—plus an elephant for Steve but I can't start telling you about gifts here or I'll never get thru. After the cake and ice cream I read your Christmas letter—which I glanced over before they all gathered as I wanted to be sure I could read it and keep my voice under control—and I assure you there was more than one pair of damp eyes in the room—and they all thought your letter beautifully written—and please know we all missed you—these 3 most of all. I got two letters from you when I got home last night—and so thrilled to know you were with Joe and hope you were able to spend Xmas with him—it should have helped somewhat. Marie called me from the office this A.M. to say there was a letter there too—so I had her open it and read it as I thought it might be something special—but know now, you were just trying to get it to me by Xmas. Your letters have been coming thru so swell—4 and 5 days is all for most of them an I haven't had time to check but believe I must have them all—the two I received yesterday were No. 6 and 7—dated 18th & 19th plus the one in at the office.

We left Marie's about 10 Christmas Eve—got to Anne's and put the kiddies to bed and as soon as Anne got there we (Ben Alice & I) went to Lucille's and Cal's for a Tom & Jerry. Their home is certainly a honey—like something out of Better Homes & Gardens Magazine. They had Judy's toys and set out under the tree for Xmas morning and that little lady was going to have plenty too—perhaps on a more expensive side but certainly not with more love—and little Susan is very happy. Judy has been quite sick with a strep throat but now alrite. Got home to bed about 12:30 and up at 7:30 Christmas morning with my angels who don't quite know the meaning of 'sleeping in". We had left all the rest of our presents at Anne's, hers to Jack & Joe &theirs to her to open that morning so we were again in a sea of paper, gifts—and Susie got her blackboard and sand bucket—so now we have chalk dust and sand to combat all over everyplace! Jo and Bobby came for dinner and also Met, Chas & Charles Allen at the last moment so Anne was really doing a lot more than she should and I'm so afraid it will hurt her recovery. She wants to go back to work on the 1st and don't think she can make it. I'm utterly no good anymore at helping out for it seems always one or the other of our two need tending so I feel I'm not doing my bit at all. About 4 P.M. Chas Tex happened to pick up the paper and discovered (None of us had had time to listen to the radio or read) that the points were going back on most of the canned stuff and all the back red points & blue were cancelled after Christmas Day and all the sugar stamps except 1 so we tore madly up to el Cajon but about a 1000 others read it before we did and what an ungodly mess. You and the crew of the Scurry can be <u>very</u> thankful you are where you are—if you had to go thru what we did trying to get a few cans you would have torn out what little hair you had left. The dirty s—of—b—in the O.P.A. that pulled that trick ought to be made to go to the front lines. Here we <u>save</u> up our stamps and go without good beef so we can have a roast or some steak & then they cancel them and the <u>sugar</u>—they even cancelled stamp <u>40</u> which was supposedly good until Febr. 28—we were all so mad and everyone in the stores were too. Butter up to 24 points a pound—it isn't that we mind going without stuff if you guys can have it but there's dirty work afoot someplace and it burns me up.

Fortunately I was about out of sugar last week and I bought 25#s with some of Zeta's stamps and mine so we will be alright but all those blue stamps I could have gotten fruit with!

We were all utterly exhausted after that trek—imagine on Xmas day! And then Susan proceeded to drop a comb down Anne's floor furnace and Joe and I practically broke our necks getting it out but finally managed. I finally got us packed up and on our way home but about 7 and was I glad someone was here to help me unpack—but you can imagine the mess this house is in—for I had to wash this morning and the icebox had to be defrosted as it was beginning to smell from stuff left in too long so we took everything out and washed it with soda—. I have two New Year's resolutions—one, to stop smoking either till you get home or I gain 10#s (whichever comes first.) and second, to get this house organized and myself so I know what I'm doing and where stuff is. That ought to keep me busy until you get home—don't you think?

Well, I'd better stop here and start the organizing business for it won't be long till Susie wakes up.

Oh—paintman came today & said we would be wasting money to paint the house outside—it didn't need it—just the windows and wood trim & that can't be done till I see if I can get new screens made for these are beyond repair—so there's another job.

It was a wonderful Christmas Sweetie—for our two babies and as nice a one as I could hope for without you. Wish you could have shared it but will hope for 1945. Mail just came and didn't have this finished. Check came from Harvard Coop Store for $10.83—not bad?

In order to support the war effort and to equalize access to almost every commodity, ration stamps were issued periodically for canned and fresh foods, gasoline, and tires. Sugar and coffee required special stamps; those who drove automobiles were encouraged to go no faster than thirty-five miles per hour to conserve the rubber tires.

Hope to hear more news of you and Joe soon. Am dying of curiosity as to what you've sent. I can't imagine. What do you think of Honolulu—did you see any hula girls?

All our love Sweetie,

Dottie

———————

Tuesday nite Dec 26 Dec #12

My Dearest Sweet, Susie & Steve:

The mailman was good to me for today he brought me a letter from you & one from Marie. If I hadn't gotten one today would have been disappointed ? (Two days without one). Was very glad to get your note even tho a short one & I know how busy one can be at this time of year.

Marie wrote she was wanting to borrow Susie the wonder girl for display & that Susie & Ed were getting along OK for which she is thankful—and so am I for you know how fond we are of Ed. So glad you were taking the children to see Lloyd & Etta on Sunday for I do know they appreciate it.

Joe came aboard with me last nite—I having spent the afternoon & early evening with them had a few drinks at the Officers Club—missed supper as none of us were hungry & just relaxed. Tried to find your letter with the picture & news of Jerry Williams but had misplaced them (now have it). Will have to call him—he too received a call from her notifying him of the fact of maybe being a mama.

During our chats when I saw him the first time he told me that they had tried to have a youngster—Jerry included & when she thought that she was pregnant she had all the symptoms of a wild woman—especially the fear of having a half Jew & Gentile—Of course she couldn't have thought of that before she showed Joe the way to matrimony. I really felt sorry for him but think he is well rid of a problem, for the future would have meant the same as for her mother. Really Joe's present wife is a honey—good for & to Joe for which Joe reciprocates. Odd too, her first husbands name (now deceased, not the name of course) was Keller.

Susie by this time should have pretty well gotten over all the excitement of Xmas. Can imagine her with a rocking horse—kindly inform me where do you put all the things.

Also today received Ann's Xmas box—haven't as yet tried the nuts but they do look good & will enjoy them later. Incidently Joe didn't get any cookies from mother so gave him half of those I received—so I know how he enjoys New Years & have an invite to Joes' if—of course no one can tell I wouldn't if they knew.

My, how these days have passed—plenty to do & haven't gotten to hit the sack till the wee hours of the morning anytime—will have to get up at 06:15.

Want to say again how pleasant it was to open all of the interesting packages Xmas eve & about all I needed to have me there would have been the many pleasant Xmas' Greetings & a bit of noise. Yes Sweet I was dreaming & hated like the devil not to have been there with you & the family.

When writing to Earl & Phys say hello for me please—

With all my love to the three of you & to the family

Al & Dada

A.F. Herney Ens. USNR.

P.S. Received Xmas card & note from Aunt Clyde & the Carrels. Did so enjoy Steve's contribution—none of which has been opened as yet, nor has a good bit of the other eatables.

Thurs. Dec 28 Dec #13

My Dearest Sweet Susie & Steve,

Received your letter dated the 23rd today. Not quite as good service as I have had but can't complain for this is only five days. Undoubtedly the heavy Xmas mails slowed things up a bit.

The Romeo's arrived yesterday—mailed Dec 5 & why Helen chose size 9 ½ I'll never know—the fit is perfect & know that I will enjoy them emensly (?) in the near future.

Since the deck & walls of the wardroom are receiving a coat of paint the letters are being written in the sack so you will understand why.—

Plan on shipping home my whites, blues & some miscellaneous junk real soon so don't be surprised if the Navy delivers a box sometime after the three months. The toys Joe insisted I take & will give Steve some pleasure.

Sweet don't want you to think that your not doing OK by the youngsters but don't like Susie running over to the neighbors by herself—she might be diverted to something of interest on J or 4th Streets & you know how careful the automaniacs are on both streets. Don't want to deprive her of the little friend north of us but I get the chills thinking about it.

There is no doubt that Xmas continues around Susie Q—Marie wrote that "Butch" pride that he is, is being shoved to the background & that Steve will likewise do the same to Susie. Can imagine just who was the most important young lady at the party. Glad you received my letter in time for tho it may have seemed a bit on the downbeat it was just about all I could say & just how I felt about the whole thing.

Not much doing except the general duties—can't get any paperwork done when you have the deck—which I have again tomorrow—really seems very foolish at times but then someone has to be boss.—yes & even bossy.

Glad to hear that the Shaws & Carrells received the letters before Xmas. Wrote also to Blythe & Chuck plus the Xmas cards—wonder how many received them.

How I could go for several weeks of the quiet & solitude of Palomar Mts—with nothing to do but just sit—you can't believe how much sitting I could do—but then there is the problem of wood so maybe I had better change it to 399 J where we have gas & the oil furnace. Incidently have you been using as much oil as before?

Forgot to send Ruth & Harvey a Xmas card or letter but will write soon— Know however that you wished them a Merry Xmas for me.

Don't blame you for shoving off to town on Dec 23rd for you had all of <u>it</u> to attend to which is no small item—what with two small ones & no husband to help & get exasperated at for not being ready etc.

Must close my love for it is getting late & there is a big day ahead of me. Plan on having Joe aboard for dinner tomorrow nite.—

With all my love to the three of you always—

Al & Dada

A F Herney Ens. USNR

Thursday nite Dec 28, 1944

My Dear Sis: (Helen Herney)

Since you are not in SD. very often & don't therefore often get to hear of me thru "My One & Only" will drop you a short note. By way of warning however, don't expect a finished letter which you and Marie are capable of writing.

Did so enjoy your letter about "Mother". The blow as a tough one I can assure you, even tho I realized that we couldn't keep her forever, much as we wanted to have her. Can fully appreciate the fact that families who have lost due to this "kill em" are hard hit when the appropriate dept. notifies them of their loss—them words Sis are cold, yes cold as steel.

The cartoon about the "California" was posted on the bulletin board for the edification of the Officers who are not from California—six of them. The Skipper being from Calif did enjoy it & made sure that all had seen it. Ed your joke about the Rabbi to brother Gates who has a delightful sense of humor. Incidently has bobby been sent home from school?

The Romeo's arrived yesterday & yes have been worn already. Expect to get a good bit of enjoyment out of them & besides in case of abandon ship they will be easy to put on for that last mad rush for the rail. So glad you got size 9 ½—good guess Sis.

When looking at some of the cloud formations, the coloring of the sky & sea, have tried to compare them to some of the lovely shots you have. However do believe that some I've seen had something that no movie has yet quite been able to record or possibly try to give you a picture of them—would really like to gather some of them to forward on to you but the "Almighty" hasn't as yet made that possible.

Missed not being home for Xmas much, for several good reasons— Did however get to go to midnight Mass and communion. Yes, I did pray like all ———, however since I haven't been too good even don't see why the King of Kings should see that the request should be granted. However tried hard.

The mess attendants recently painted our "bathroom" & the following sign l was posted on the door: "Notice fresh Paint in Shower and Eronold." Thought you might enjoy it.

Dot & the family have been awfully good about writing. Really it is difficult to understand how eagerly we wait for the distribution of mail & how disappointed one can be when there isn't even a card. I guess the same goes for those at home & something to think about.

Was invited to Joe's home a week ago—spent a nite & day with him. It was very much a pleasure & had a grand time doing the things one would do at home—sit around at your leisure, go shopping, and take care of all those little duties as the head of a family. Mother must have been humanly deep to have appreciated the fact when she had so many service men invited to the house.

Santa was very good to me—nicely wrapped parcels with interesting notes on them—but the <u>bestest</u> of all was to realize that you were being remembered.—We Herney's are darn nice people Sis & don't let anyone ever kid you.

Thanks again Helen for your nice note & the Romeo's—

Al

A.F Herney, Ens. USNR

P.S. Give my regards to all of your friends in L.A. Stilly enjoy the recollection of the "Turn About"

Friday Nite Dec 29 Dec #14

My Dearest Sweet Susie & Steve:

Must get a note off to you even tho there are so many things to be done—however can't & won't neglect my family.

Sweet got a little remembrance for your birthday—wrapped it tonight & I'll readily admit that it is anything but pretty by way of packages I have received. Thought you might enjoy it with spring coming on.

The other which I mentioned in an earlier letter (something I had never sent you before) should reach you before this package. Neither will have a note in them but I offer them hoping in these little ways to express my deep love for you.

Had Joe aboard for chow tonight. He said he intended writing you for you are due one—of course he didn't say he owned me one & no damned wonder.

No mail from you today—had hoped I would get one about the Xmas parry for I am really interested in <u>all</u>. Hope the family didn't say a second George when my letter was read—or did they?

Ran into Florian Carey who I should say looked me up.—Was glad to see him but presented a problem would have liked to invite him to lunch but couldn't & had so much work couldn't leave. He evidently understood for he soon left after a nice chat & seeing the ship. He of course was sorry to hear of Mother's death.

While they have a nice officers club here & being very close would be a temptation to get sort of blotto except Doc's orders prohibit me—did have several drinks with Joe on Xmas Day—but that & the beer were they only two times I've broken the diet.—Really Honey unless something turns up in the future your old man isn't going to be a sot.

Joe returned all of the pictures I have of the family & <u>The Family.</u> Gave them to him to show his wife & she seems quite impressed—yes even included the one taken at Shaws for it pays to show yourself at the worst—can't or haven't you ever seen [Al's brother and cousin] Fran, Hugh Caughey & myself in the yard at Deshler when we were quite young. Doubt if you would have married me if you had.

Wrote Helen a note last night after writing you—you of course are always first on my list & then if I have time to write the others.

Do hope that Virginia is feeling better & well on her way to recovery. Please give her part of my love for I'm sure you will share a part of it. She is a good egg & so glad the Dr. found no traces of cancer.

Well my love—it really is time to hit the sack but since I have some work to do will have to knock off the chatter—

With all my love to the three of you always

Al & Dada

A.F. Herney, Ens. USNR

4

PERFECTING MINESWEEPING
TECHNIQUES IN HAWAII

January 1945

From "Saga of the Scurry: The First Year," the ship's first-anniversary program:
Track lines—

In an over-all perspective of the first year, our activity can be divided into two general phases: Convoy Missions and Invasion Missions.

Tens of thousands of miles were navigated. Convoy missions have taken us below the Equator, to the South Seas, the Admiralty Islands and waters off New Guinea, to ports throughout the Hawaiian, Marshall, Caroline and Mariana Islands, and to the Philippine Islands. Invasion missions routed us to IWO JIMA and OKINAWA and into the East China Sea.[vi]

From Dictionary of American Naval Fighting Ships:
Between 31 December 1944 and 18 January 1945, the ship underwent two six-day periods of minesweeping training off Maui.[vii]

4 Jan 1945 Jan #1 (Thursday)
My Dearest Sweet, Susie & Steve:

Has been some time since I wrote I know but then time does pass & there are always so many things to be done. Know you appreciate that & will forgive me.

Only three days my love until you will be having another of those birthdays that seem to as one grows older to roll around so fast Many happy returns to my sweet. Do hope that the first remembrance reaches you on time—doubt if the other will but did let you know that it was on its way—however do appreciate that you won't be using it before spring anyway.

Haven't been doing much of anything except working hard at the job Uncle gave me—Wondering & worrying at times too if I'm doing things right. Can't say that it wouldn't be right but so damn many things to do & be responsible for.

The new year is well on its way to a good start—didn't get to Mass but did have a little meeting with the flock.—Many of course seem interested & possibly wouldn't make the effort without a suggestion. Am so glad however that Xmas found us where we could have the privilege of attending mid-night mass.

Haven't received any mail from you since the 23rd—do hope to get some soon—all in a bunch for I do want to know how Xmas came off with the "Pride & Joy" as it.

Occasionally take time out to daydream—find the many miles separating us meaningless—yes plunk right down in the old easy chair at 399 & visit with my family—Susie blue eyed & blond—Steve not quite happy because its real time and so he thinks of my One & only taking care of three charges—preparing chow or massaging the dishes—Yes Sweet it is pleasant to daydream.

The Cap't elected me as mess treasurer for the coming quarter. Just a few more things to do I can assure you & very possibly hear all of the complaints about what is wrong with chow—Will be glad when the next three months are over. Have been compensated however by the fact that Ensign Bezold has assumed some of the duties I formerly had & am grateful for it—besides I readily admit I know very little about it.

Schnabel still hasn't heard about being a new papa or what he's a papa of—well overdue too for it should have arrived about the 10th of Dec.

Gates made an alnav the first of last month so he is J.G.—Really he is a delightful person & it is difficult to imagine what we would do without his humor. Really a godsend for when things get tense he can come thru with things that make one drop off with petty stuff.

Capt has sort of settled down—the responsibility of it all has been a justification for much of his irritability & possibly we would be the same way or worse.

Hetzler is the same—hesitant to take a definite step—Executive Officers are between hell & high water anyway & hope I'm never in that position.

Gosch still carries on with his usual quiet manner—letting go occasionally to break the monotony. Johnson & Hanna still tusseling with their decks & engineering problems.

Will try to write again real soon my Sweet—

Again a very Happy Birthday to you—hoping of course that I will be with you on your next one & long before that of course—

With all my love to the three of you

As Always

Al

A.F Herney, Ens.

4 Jan Thurs. Jan #2

My Dearest Sweet, Susie & Steve:

It is nice to get two letters dated the same day—however must admit I was off the beam & was just a day early—Possibly I would like to have it that way for there is so much to do.

Wrote Sweetie Pie [secretary at the law offices] a note last night after writing you Meant to do it before but then for I do think she would enjoy a note. Knew that if I didn't write then it might be some time till she got one from me.

Had quite a busy day—All morning—afternoon & part of the night—Everything is as I wanted to find it so that helps somewhat—Can't say I don't hope I will sleep tonight for my eyes are a bit tired from so much paper work.

Have really been feeling better—however it is hard to have fresh fruit—fresh salads on the table & not enjoying them—however do feel that feeling half fit is much better than suffering with a stomach that is off beat.

Forgot to tell you that NewYears Eve was spent in a quiet sane manner without even a beer. Didn't mind for it doesn't mean much being away from your dear ones—Maybe if home we would have been stay at homes even tho I would have been able to be there—however maybe it would have been very pleasant to be just that.

Haven't as yet gotten to see Dutch [Dewitt Higgs]. Have kept my eyes open—hoping of course to see the big slug.

Have wondered if any of the folks have received the Xmas cards? Sent one to most of the people in Chula including the Paxtons for being so nice when I was home in Sept.

It is quite hard to concentrate as Gates & Hanna have been in the ward room passing the bull—am writing here as Gosch has hit the sack for a short nap.

Don't know if I'll need reading to put me to sleep tonight but can't read Time as that has already been read cover to cover—was particularly interested in the article on Lupe—much my opinion of a god many of our so "greats" from sunny Calif—incidently I'd like to see some of that country.

The table looks like the devil—glasses—cups empty of course.—had coca & not coffee believe it or not—and then some pubs of course.

Didn't sit in on the movies tonight—Life begins at 8:30—Tho Walley is a delightful character couldn't see using the eyes a lot more after a hard day.

Sweet am sorry that this isn't much of a letter but did my best.

With all of my love to the three of you—my three S's.

As always

Al & Dada

A.F Herney, Ens.

5 Jan 1945 Jan No. 3.

My Dearest Sweet, Susie & Steve:

As so glad to get your Dec 27, 29 & 31st letters. My what news one's too & just what I want to know about. The list seemed to be quite large for everyone except "Mommie" but then she of course enjoyed what the children received. Can quite imagine what 399 J Street looked like when you arrived home.

Dot you surprised me in using the language about the OPA chap. Undoubtidly he had burning ears more than once & possibly deserves it— However you must appreciate that withholding the information did what it was intended to do—prevent burning up the market. However can't see any justification for cancelling the value of any of the stamps.

Received a nice letter from George [a brother] today—However I don't believe that it was written by him but for him. He said however that he had received a nice note from you before Xmas.

Tried to call Joe [a friend stationed in Honolulu] today but he was out to lunch but will try again tomorrow. Don't know if I will get to spend any more time with him but do hope so as it is great to get off the ship for a spell. Helps to give you a new grip on life.

The mail today also brought word—Xmas card & note from Benny & George. Will try to find time to drop them a note—my this mail problem really takes a good bit of time.

Your "Tea" sounds like a good bit of goo. It was nice however that you did get to go. I have a recollection that Mr. {Carter} & Mrs. Mc had been very friendly at one time just before I pulled out a year ago. Think it was a bit hush-hush & known by just a few so keep it under your hat—evidently everything has worked out all right.

Did receive Dad & Mothers box & did write you to that effect—is unnecessary that you go back over the letters to dig it out.

It is consoling to know my love that you appreciate there are going to be times when you won't be hearing for spells. Evidently you didn't get all of my letters for Dec. for I had written you 14.—have them ticked off on the stationary folder & will continue to do so will keep the calendar however—thanks for remembering it.

It isn't going to do much good for you to worry about Susie & her wet pants. If you do get the time to rush her every few minutes so good—maybe she takes after me in that regards—gets too interested in whatever she is doing & just forgets nature.

So glad that you took time out to stop & see Virginia & taking Susie with you. Know she enjoyed it much & very thoughtful of you to do it. The description of the visit at the Myers was something especially Susie deciding she liked the footstool. Too bad youngsters have to take naps for I'm sure that she would have had a grand time with her aunt Marie.

Your faith in my faithfulness astounds me Honey—that I know that I haven't as yet even given you any reason to doubt that you are the only one & my one & only. Bet Lloyd would appreciate your opinion of his integrity.— No haven't seen any Hula's as yet & not particular to see any so that is pretty much the answer.

Don't worry about the Phi Mu party Sweet for it will be done up as nicely as every except your old man won't be there to add to your troubles & maybe having one drink too many. Don't believe however that any of the group minded my coming to the parties with a drink under the belt. Give each & every one of them my regards & tell them I'm really sorry that I can't be with them.

Glad the house doesn't need painting & the chap was honest enuf to tell you Hope you can get the screens so the framework at last can be done.

Received a movie projector today—16 mm—so now we very likely will be able to have movie's aboard & some diversion. Tho I would very much like to see the films about my family don't want you to send them to me for I wouldn't want anything to happen to them—too much of value to Susie & Steve.—

Must close & hit the sack for tomorrow is another busy day.—

Thanks my love for all the nice long letters & al my love to the three of you.

As always

Al & Dada

AF Herney—

P.S Tell Susie I hope she's right, too that Daddie's coming home on his big boat soon.

Always,

Al

P.S.S. Once again Happy Birthday my Sweet

Al

8 Jan 1945 Jan. #4

My Dearest Sweet, Susie & Steve:

Just a short note for the mailman will be on his way very shortly. Received your No. 1 yesterday together with a darn sweet letter from Fran [his brother Francis].

Thanks much for including the list of Xmas cards received—interesting to know so many of the people do remember us.

The New Years Eve party sounded like it might have been very nice & know I would have enjoyed being there—Uncle Paul [Shaw, not a relative] would think about the "Kissin" especially if he had several drinks under his belt.

Think the information about Katie's "Bill" just happened to be inserted <u>&</u> am glad to know it for I've tried the old address Katie gave me when I last saw her.

Chow is down so must wind this up—they don't like to eat without the mess Treasurer being around so all the growls can be duly noted & of course something done about it.

Do hope you can get the radio phono fixed for Susie is getting to the age when she will begin to appreciate it.

With all my love to the three of you.

As always

Al & Dada.

P.S. Yes we do get bacon—

AF Herney Ens. USNR

Early Jan 7—

My Dearest Sweet, Susie & Steve:

Tho it is early Sunday morning must drop you a birthday letter. Surely you won't receive it in time but you will know that I am thinking about you & wishing much to be with you.

Everybody except Gates has hit the Sack & he is doing just what I'm at—letters—He has a good bit too & is more than conscientious (?) about it. Of course he has dividends to show for it too.

Schnabel finally received word yesterday via airmail letter thru the Red Cross that he is the proud papa of a baby girl, born on Dec 26. Almost a Xmas bundle under the tree for him. Of course the next of the message was mother & child doing fine etc. Decided maybe he could quit now too.

While I have been busy the last few days realize & appreciate that I am going to be a lot busier within the next few weeks—How in the hell I every chose communications is beyond me—never did like paper work that well but ho hum here I am. Do hope it will pay dividends sometime in the future.

Don't know why your folks would have changed the contents of the boxes—Xmas. Were really swell & enjoyed them all a good bet. Incidentlly <u>do not</u> want you to do better for my birthday & in fact would care for nothing except letters—you all have been more than kind & faithful in writing & tho you may not get many from me understand that I love you much & think much about you. Sometimes it is easier to receive mail than to send it.

Haven't as yet shipped home the clothes but expect to get them off within the next few days. Am sorry now that I brought anything except a few essentials & my grays—Don't laugh but intend to keep my rubbers. Have worm them & have been comfortable (dry feet) while others looked with envy & asked me where I got them—yes & they weren't poking fun, either.

Don't know when I'll get to see Joe but do hope that it will be soon—Staying close & grinding puts one on edge & short temper, which I am & very likely always will be.

Haven't as yet received the letter Ed was supposed to have written to me before Xmas. Maybe it will eventually get to me tho there is always the chance that it won't—The mailman didn't bring me nary a thing today.

Have had to use scraps of stationary as I seem to have run out all of a sudden know that you don't mind.

Off to get a shower & hit the sack.—

With all my love to the three of you & hoping that you will have a pleasant birthday even tho I can't be there with you.

As Always,

Al & Dada

A.F Herney Ens.

P.S. Had intentions of trying to send you a birthday message today but didn't get away to do it. Sorry Sweet but mental telepathy will have to be the answer. Al

Jan 9, 1944 Jan#5

My Dearest Sweet Susie & Steve:

Will promise to take a little bit more time on this note than I did on the one written yesterday. Your report about Susie & Steve interfering with the music maker (piano tuner) is quite amusing. From your report Susie is to take after her dad musically of course & Steve after his mom. Wish it were the other way around for her sake however so she could & would get much interest out of it later on—why am I worrying—you may be wrong.

Talked to Joe on the phone today though haven't seen him nor do I expect to within the next few days, possibly later however.

You make me envious of Ed's trip to palomar. What do you think I would be doing except sitting when Susie & Steve took their naps—Could at least get that in so do guess that would be something at least.

If Mac turned the flow of oil on the furnace that is the answer to not getting the heat out of the thing that you expect. Can't quite understand however just why it was using so much oil when on pilot however. Read the instructions about cleaning what sediment may collect in the valve control by lifting the little jigger (?) on the front of it—(since directions east, west etc. don't mean much) on the side facing the Cole's. Not very large but should be done every time you clean the furnace. The proper position for manual operation is up.—Clean as hell I know but I can do it myself. Thank him (Harvey) for being the man around the house with you.

If you think I'm going to mortgage my soul etc for a great big whopper duper of a house Sweet it may be I can't come home—Yeh?—At least I know what to expect when I do get there what will it be—househunting right off?

Have been hoping I would get some more pictures soon. Take what I have & look at them very often—just to keep in touch with my little family.

Don't know who this Sprague is mentioned by bill. Have wondered if I would run into him. On second thought guess not. Did see Art Johnson but didn't get to talk to him—just getting (me) on a bus to attend a lecture.

Glad to hear that Mrs. Rhodes is going to assist with the dinner as surely they will all eat well as they always have & enjoyed it too. Her being there will take a whole lot off of your hands & help you enjoy the party.

Since both Carl & Hank were enlisted prior to receiving a commission they rate an advancement from the date of the issuance of their commission. Both as I remember it would be J. G's from the 1st of December. Doubt if I will make it until Febr 1 at the earliest & frankly except for the money don't care frankly.

As far as packages will be delighted to get some more cookies from you thought don't want you to take any time from your family. Did mean what I wrote in an earlier letter that mail will suffice for birthday etc. If you have time to make some cookies—don't send candy as we have bars onboard & I eat little of it you had better mail them as early as possible.

Am very much thrilled to think that Susie hasn't forgotten her daddy & do hope she continues to have that elephant of a memory. Would be very thrilling to think that she will—but won't be too upset if she doesn't. Steve I know will have to be taught that he has a daddy & very likely won't have anything to do with me at all—at least will show some passive resistance. It's my loss I know that I haven't had the privilege of knowing him like I have Susie & participating in his trials & tribulations as a wee baby.

As soon as you can divulge the information about Uncle Jim's [Farnham, Dot's aunt Heral's husband] will be very pleased to have it. Can understand the situation & while it is important it can be passed on in due time.

Have you made any plans about going home [to Nebraska where Dot's parents live]? Not that it has to be decided now but was wondering if you had given it any more thought. Can imagine that both Dad & Mother have been wondering about it tho you haven't mentioned that they have referred to it in any of their letters recently.

Glad that you could go to Marie's on your birthday & take the youngsters with you. It is a nice feeling to know that you are wanted <u>with</u> the children isn't it?

However in this case as I remember it's you bring the children and we will let you stay too. Do hope you had a nice birthday & the first of my remembrances reached you by then.

With all my love to the three of you always—
Al & Dada

10 Jan 1945 Jan No 6
My Dearest Sweet, Susie & Steve:
Received your No 3 of Jan. today—yet and on some brand new kind of stationary. As you see I have also run out—don't know which of us has run out the oftener but won't quibble about it.

Sorry to hear that Mrs.{Porter} ain't doing so good. Doubt if the Cap't would put her away Sweet as that is worse than having the Almighty take her. Possibly that would be kinder—Your info about her is vague as this is the first mention about it. Has she been molesting the neighbors more than she did last fall. Have been keeping the eyes open but haven't seen Dutch at all tho would sure well like that as you know. Would go off the diet for a night at least & the hell with work.

Your not really surprised about the {Butlers} are you? My <u>God</u> she's built for it—looks like a factory & very probably feels like one too. Don't believe that Howard will jump overboard but you can't blame him if he decided not to return to such a home. Maybe however he likes it that way. The mention also of the operation is vague as Vis's first mention of it. Haven't seen Lloyd—don't particularily care if I do—however if I run into him will see him of course but won't go out of my way any to find out where what or why.—

Am ashamed that I hadn't written Carl—have his address too I believe—Should do so soon or he will never forgive me.—Was nice of him to write you & you know darn well he won't forget his one & only.

Susie must have the maternal instinct regarding her little brother. Thoughtful of her to try to quiet him & then taking the bottle away from him.

As is usual our own affairs come last—finally sent the Application back to Bob Saunders tonight with a short note. Should have done something about it before this.

Am awfully glad that Susie wants to see "Uncle Eddie too" for I was still a bit dubious about her making up to him. She always has liked to help with the phoning—at least indicated that but possibly was a bit hesitant to talk. Do guess our little girl is growing up & fast too. Damn it that I can't be here to help.

Your letters Sweet are newsy (pen dry so will have to finish this in pencil, mind?) even tho you don't think so. Everyday things—all about <u>family</u> trials & tribulations are things we all like to hear about. Don't believe you want anything else except I haven't got the family to write about so have to be pretty well self centered in these letters. By your letters you help in giving us what we don't have.

Must do some reading—In the line of duty, Sweet before hitting the road to dreamland & thought of the three of you.

With love as always

Your Al & Dada

A.F Herney, Ens.

P.S. Found Lloyd & Etta's Xmas' [Dr. and Mrs. Myers] thank you note—evidently they not only liked your selection but our family too—they are both nice people aren't they—

Love

Al.

12 Jan 1945 Jan No 6 [This is the third No. 6 for January.]

My Dearest Sweet, Susie & Steve:

Fudging a little on the time for it is just a little after mid night. Must take a shower before hitting the sack & since I must get up bright & early in the morning will have to make this a short one.

No mail from you today—really didn't expect any since I had the letter yesterday & your letters seem to run about every other day. They are newsy ones so won't complain too much.

May start dropping you notes on V mail soon Sweet as it may be easier that way. —on my part of course & can & will be limited on writing area of course. Haven't used much of them at all as yet, tho it has been suggested.

As is usual with me have been disgruntled about delays in being served—transportation on the busses & waiting for the whale boat. Was hurrying today—one of the other Comm officers was with me—He said he didn't like to hurry—almost blew my top but didn't so guess every thing will be in its normal again by tomorrow. Really so much of a person's time is wasted in just waiting.

Gates is still up wandering around—has been writing a few letters too—can't see why he should do it but then he probably has more fortitude than I.

With all my love to the three of you as always—

Al & Dada

A.F Herney, Ens.

P.S. <u>Earlier</u> or should say later in the day "Good morning" & feel like I would have enjoyed <u>stooding</u> in bed.

    Love Al.

18 Jan Jan. No 6 [yet another January No. 6]
My Dearest Sweet, Susie & Steve:

    Had promised to write you before this but the sea makes me lazy or then too it might be that I'm not as good a sailor as I might want to be. Ho hum do hope that time will come soon. Tried to cat nap as I may have the twelve to four watch (called the mid watch) which doesn't half express how everybody enjoys it but felt restless so thought I would do my duty to you.

    Am quite anxious to now if you had received either of the two remembrances I sent. However sine I've had no mail since the letter I received on the eleventh don't know nothin about the happenings of 399 J or San Diego since then—Written I believe on the 5th.

    Know that you had a pleasant day at the Muellers [sister Marie and husband Ed]—it is rather nice to look at the bay & think that the bay is there but you are on terra firma & that is the end to it. Will have a great deal of pleasure when this is all over to look & say "Thank God"—I don't have to get in even a row boat unless I feel like it.

    Haven't written either Fran or Julia [brother and sister] a birthday note & feel ashamed of myself—however tell them I will write soon but in the meantime wish each of them a very happy birthday for me. Another family gathering which will be held & me not there. Of course it will go on but I have missed them a whole lot & will always I know.

    Virginia should by this time be well on her way to being a new woman—what with all she has had to give up—physically and mentally too. Do hope she is back on her two firm feet & feeling her own self.

    My neck for the past few days has been giving me hell again & miss those good old massages & neck adjustments—would you feel enclined to give me one via telepathy? Maybe I could be a Christian Scientist to that extent. Nobody on board ship will attempt the adjustment & really can't blame them for it.

There are times honey when your old man about blows his top & comes close to telling a shipmate to go plum to hell—of course this is the service & you don't do that—the blood pressure does go up however & doesn't aid digestion. Must consider however that there are the ups & downs & always will be. Experience is a painful teacher at times and at times would give much just to be a seaman—little responsibility and all that goes with it.

19 Jan [same letter]

Didn't get this completed last night as my energy gave out—instead took out some of your letters & reread them & renewed my acquaintance with you & the family by looking at the pictures I love—then dropped off to sleep.—

If I want to get this in the mail will have to close—. With all my love to the three of you.

Al & Dada

Albert F Herney, Ens.

18 Jan Jan No 7

My Dearest Sweet, Susie & Steve:

Was just about ready to disown you today when the first sack of 1st class mail didn't have any letters for me in it but later found four for me so feel better now. Really began to worry & think that all was not well.

Glad you received the purse—had hoped you would get it by your birthday at least—but then not too late to let you know I had remembered.

It is just as well that you have planned on going home now—however do think it might have been better for the youngsters if you could go later in the spring—must think of the acclimation—Febr does seem a bit tough for them. However if you think the situation now is best for you to go now it is satisfactory with me. What you do about the house is a problem I will have to leave with you—other than renting it—if you wish to have Clarence and his little chickadee be there while your gone I will have no objection & in fact I would prefer that someone be there to take care of the place (seem about as jumbled up as you on the whole subject.)

Don't like to think that we may loose the Cole's as neighbors. They have been nice ones and you can never tell what we would get it they do move. However do wish Harvey the best of luck & hope that he gets his transfer.

Know that my family will miss you & the youngsters while you are gone. No doubt all of them will hate to see you take them away—but not near as much as I hated to leave & be gone for such a long time with prospects of some time in the future.

Would like to know the real dope on the {Fisks}. Can't imagine a mother booting any one out but maybe Mary's mother doesn't realize what the family situation may be. Can say Mary has some gumption to take over in the house in the rear.

Sorry to hear that Mr.{Porter} is in the hospital. If you find time drop him a card for us for I do like him a great deal & he has a burden with Mrs— Little things do count with him I know & is very appreciative of them.

The group planning the Phi Mu party sounds interesting & would like to be there but as usual the old alibi—"Sorry".

I'm glad to hear that you had a pleasant time on your birthday—Your visits to the Muellers sound like you are Mrs. "Aster" plus. Someone to entertain the youngsters while Mama sleeps doesn't sound bad at all & is good for you. Susie behaving in bed is good news & do hope that she will improve. Bless her from remembering that there is where she waved bye bye to Daddy—she does have a memory doesn't she & with you think it would be swell to have you there when Daddy comes rolling in—When God alone knows but Daddy hopes it won't be too damn long.

The mystery gift could or would not have arrived by now. Will check on it with Joe for I made the arrangements thru him—don't think it's a gype game at all—however do hope I gets to you before you leave for Nebr. [Al had ordered orchids through his friend Joe to be delivered to Dot for her birthday. However, the military censors determined that was inappropriate as that would give Al's Honolulu location away. The orchids were never delivered to Dot.]

Thanks for passing on the information about Carl. Don't believe that the transfer has any significance at all—possible just routine stuff which often happens. Must drop him a note real soon but that is what I've said before isn't it.

Your suggestion about birthdays is being taken under advisement & due consideration will be given to it.

Schnabel has applied for pretty much the same thing that Walt A. is now being trained for. Thought I might apply but the after this is all over would hate to think of being in some country other than the good old U.S & specifically at 399 J Street or anywhere else in the locality that <u>my</u> family happened to be.

Received a nice note from Walt C today nicely written & pretty much the same Walt—a hell of a lot more mature than I think Marie & Doc picture Walt. Also received a nice letter from Ernest Emel in Seattle, must keep him on my list of correspondents.

Schnabels last youngster was a little "Girl"—their first was a boy so now they can quit too. Hetzler has a little girl and asked to be remembered to you.

Glad to hear that Virginia is feeling better & will be home for a time, for it is much more pleasant any where than that at the hospital.

To go back to the matter of your trip home feel as you do that dad & Mother are entitled to part of the time with their grandchildren & they have had such little time with them. Wonder if they will be glad to see you with <u>both</u> of them for it is quite a handful. Your trip on the train shouldn't be too hard since its only going to be of such a short time.

With all my love to the three of you—As ever yours

Al & Dada

AF Herney, Ens.

19 Jan (No. 8)

My Dearest Sweet, Susie & Steve:

Was very much pleased to get your No. 7 written Sunday nite & an unnumbered one written Monday today mailed on the 15th & 16th respectively not bad at all.

The report on the Phi Mu party was as I expected it for they always do seem to enjoy themselves at any of the Herneys and are always well fed. Nice of Mac to see that you had the ham. Zeta should have been surprised. Nice for you too to have had so much help & what a surprise to find the house all cleaned when you got home on Friday. Can't imagine you going to two shows in three days. Doing almost as well as myself—however have the duty tonight so will be aboard & writing you.

Sweet you & plans for going home now are working out well for you. Doubt if there should be any great worry about going and glad to hear that Clarence & Zeta will be there at 399 to take care of the place.

Your reports about the new clothes contribution for Susie sounds interesting. What is it a Mother & Daughter outfit? And what about poor Steve—you surely can't put him in the same color.

Glad to hear that Jerry & Elmer [Cawby] hit the jackpot & do hope that they do get to have it materialize. Will drop them a note but not mention it of course.

Haven't received the subscription to Omnibus but have received Marie & Eds subs. for Esquire & Readers digest. Haven't had much time for them as there is so much to read along professional lines. Hope that soon however I will have a bit more time for the skipper today said that from now on no deck watches in port or at sea unless I wanted to keep my hand in it. Really a surprise—however haven't had the time to spend on my end that I should have & think he now appreciates it.

Evidently you've forgotten the proportions of our "Pride & Joy" when she was six months old. It is good however to hear that Steve is doing as well as he is & undoubtedly will be just as fit even tho he was a bit premature & did give Dad quite a worry for being so damn small. Hope he isn't too uncomfortable because of the shots.

Expect to spend the nite with Joe tomorrow nite—Had hoped for all day with him but no sale as I've too much to do in such a little time to do it all in. Time does fly and flit when one is busy & not much of that time is your own especially when you've got the deck.

Had hoped to buy Susie a couple of dolls for her collection for the twin beds but will have to postpone that. She must have a big memory to remember so much. However the first surely is kept alive by Marie's references—her aunts & uncles too help a lot & bless them all for it & her too.

Susie must be getting to be quite a doubting Thomas tho it is quite confusing for one so young to appreciate the appearance of a dressed & undressed chicken.

Am waiting anxiously for the photos for as I've said before & will say often again it is so nice to take out the pictures & reassure myself that I do have one hell of a fine family.

Received a nice note from Helen today added to a Birthday card. She is going to be plenty early isn't she? Surprised to find that they must have saved my Xmas letter from last Xmas too. That family evidently feel that it is something to get a letter from their kid brother. Don't know who has it but you might ask. She suggested saving both of them for Steve.

Was paid today—didn't draw all of it. Gates paid me $20.00 one half of the balance due. I will keep it but am enclosing the $20 travelers check I have which I haven't had cashed. Possibly by the middle of next month I will find that I'm a J.G. & the $30 more per month of course will be sent to you for I won't need it God only knows tho I was a bit short this last month—Left enuf on the books for Dec food bill so guess that things will be OK & the financial worrys for the moment are all over. Hope you had enuf for the purchase of the ticket home & won't be too pinched for funds because we haven't a larger bank balance. Suggest that you have your allotment checks sent home for there won't be anyone there who can cash them or deposit them for you.

Also received a V letter from Aunt Clyde [Mother C.'s sister]—She really isn't anything but an old dear is she?

With all my love to the three of you as Always

Al & Dada

A.F Herney, Ens.

P.S. Haven't written Dad & Mother a thank you note—Will do so tonight.

20 January Letter No 9 [Letter #12]

Dearest Sweet, Susie & Steve:

Hope I'm not lying by thinking this is No 9 for January. Not near as well an average as in December I know but guess it will be sufficient anyway.

Received a letter today from Mother with the pictures enclosed. All of them good pictures except the one of Susie on the rocking horse in front of the blackboard which was blurred. Yes even the one of the Xmas tree with the array of presents in front of it is very good. Must add them to my collection for an occasional review.

Mother H had included some popcorn in her package (Xmas). Haven't tried to pop any as yet but will. Tried to buy some today but couldn't. Maybe if you could buy some without ration points & had the time & not to difficult would be interested for a shot of it now & then might taste good. Odd things are craved once in a while isn't it? Of course I'm taking it for granted that a lot of things could be dispensed with if I could be at home with you three.

No letter today but really don't feel too badly about it for the two I received yesterday makes up for the lack of one today.

Walked so much today & in such a hurry that I feel like somebody has rubbed my bottom with sand paper. Not sightseeing for there hasn't been time for that. Have a lot to do but suppose that will always be the story.

Didn't get to see Joe today or tonight as there was some unfinished business to take care of & no one seemed to be willing to do it. Of course it hadn't been done it would have been me who would have caught it & how.

Did some purchasing for the wardroom mess. Didn't get a whole lot for they didn't seem to have too much of what we wanted. Guess every thing is much the same everywhere so won't complain too much.

Mother didn't mention in her letter written on the 15th any thing about your going home. Maybe she thinks you hadn't as yet told me about it. Did write them last night after writing you & its odd I should have gotten her letter today. When you write, tell her that I received her letter & pictures.

Haven't as yet sent the box with my clothes. Had hoped to be able to do it within the last few days but I've had so little time for myself. Will see what I can do about it tomorrow for I don't want them, haven't used them & doubtless that I will want them in the near future.

Still no sign of Dutch but will keep looking. Also for Carl tho doubt if he would be here. Would enjoy seeing them both again & might break off the diet. Still on it & with celery on the table you know how much I don't want to have a reoccurance. The Dr. told me I wouldn't get over it in a day & know it for I've had another touch of it last week after being seasick. Have missed stepping into the club & ordering a double white rum or scotch just to help drive the blues away.

　　With all my love to the three of you as always.

　　Al & Dada

A.F Herney,

P.S. Tell Susie Daddy enjoyed her Xmas greeting.

Love Al.

From Dictionary of American Naval Fighting Ships*:*

She [the Scurry*] sailed on 22 January to support the Landing at Iwo Jima.*[viii]

From Experiencing War: Stories from the Veterans History Project, American Folklife Center, Library of Congress—Transcript of interview with Fernando Salazar, May 16, 2008. Salazar was an enlisted crew member aboard the USS Scurry*:*

…in Hawaii until early or mid January. Then we were assigned to a convoy, which was a humongous convoy made up of hundreds and hundreds of ships of all kind—mostly destroyers. We did not know where we here headed but when we got there, they told us we were in Saipan. We were there three or four days, no liberties, just assigned to our ship. Then we left from there. After we were underway they told us we were on our way to the invasion of Iwo Jima. We were to be there three or four days ahead of the invasion in order to sweep the shores of the enemy mines…[ix]

22 January 45

My Dearest Sweet, Susie & Steve;

　　Just a very short note to you before hitting the sack. Now almost one and will be getting up about four so that won't leave me much time for sleeping but will have to do.

　　No mail from you today but guess there was good reason. Did get a V mail from Aunt Heral today & mentioned Uncle Jim—the ship to which he is attached so will put that down on the list of look me outs for.

Don't know why the days have been so busy but they just seem to be here now & gone—really regret so much that you aren't near always & living apart so very much has been lost but will try hard to make up for it once this mess is all over.

Hasn't seemed like Sunday at all—everyday of course seems to be much the same—everybody in a great big rush. Can't seem to control myself either when it comes right down to it.

Missing the three of you so very much. My love Always to the Three of You

Al Always

Al & Dada

A.F Herney.

Saturday 27 Jan Jan Letter No 10 [Actual No. 14]

My Dearest Sweet, Susie & Steve:

I am ashamed that I haven't written you before such a lapse of time but since last writing have been busy from early to late & I mean that. Having all of the time without watches has given me time to apply to the job & I have been busy. Being a housewife & Mother takes time.

Have been feeling pretty good lately though still on the diet & had a refill on the prescription just in case. Have stayed on the diet which has been darn hard as it includes no raw vegetables—which included celery—ho hum but its better that way I guess.

Tonight the old moon was out early in all its splendor, big, round and yellow—just a real night for a bit of romance. If this were times for pleasure cruises there would be women & if I would be cruising during peaceful times you would be with me of course—Which reminds me of the story about the young couple on the honey moon & the husband meeting Paul Whitman—remember?

I suppose that soon I will have to be writing to Lincoln for the 11th of Febr. Will soon be here. How I envy Dad & Mother having you come visit them but then my time will come & soon I hope too. So glad you were able to get the bedroom as you really need one with that young Indian of ours—<u>My</u> "Pride & Joy" & the wee one "Steve".

It will be nice if you can find two nice gentlemen aboard this trip to help entertain Susie as you did on one trip back from Nebr when I met you in San Bernardino, for I know people enroute will take to her as most people do.—Not quite an angel but darn close to it—Yep bet you her Aunts & Uncles will say so.

Had planned on starting to use "V" mail but some how just can't appreciate that means of writing. To receive one (that is "V" letter) leaves me practically cold & I assume others have the same feeling.

Joe said he had written you a letter recently. Forgot to check with him regarding the mystery package and to tell him you hadn't as yet received it. Possibly I had better drop him a note. When last talking to him they were in the midst of more alterations—laying Masonite flooring in the nursery & had I been able to get out to see them would possibly have given them a hand— nice for a change at last.

Since I've a few other notes to write, Carl, I.J. George & Benny—Beverly (she sent me a card & note) & Hank will say as always.

With all my love to the three of you as always

Al & Dada

A.F Herney Ens.

Monday 29 Jan Jan letter No 11 [Actual January letter 15]

Even tho I wrote you last night will drop you a wee note tonight. Didn't get any more letters written except to Carl as I just gave out after the second one.

The moon isn't quite as large tonight as it was last but that probably is because it was so much higher in the heavens when I saw it tonight—but it is just as brings. Another night for romance shot to hell.

Held services on the forecastle this morning—didn't have too many attend but the regular few—Of course I had to officiate—didn't mind as it seems someone has to do it.

Am wondering if Clarence & Zeta have finally decided on what they are going to do & if he has gotten his leave. He had better take it while he can for one never knows when he will get another chance at one. Do hope they decided to come back & care for the house for it will be a big relief to me.

Haven't as yet written either Julia or Fran their birthday letter & will soon be time for Marie's to be here too—know I want to get a letter of to any of them in time but they will eventually get one.

Took it rather easy today tho should have accomplished a lot more. Did however read some official matter so didn't exactly waste the time at that. God, there is so much to do & always will be so guess there is nothing to get steamed up about.

Tho it hasn't been too hot did more than my share of perspiring today. It isn't hard to just sit & sweat—maybe one should be thankful to be able to sit for a change

This evening attended the movie—in the crew's mess hall—"Flying Fortress" an old picture but you know there are many, many old ones I haven't seen & now go to them for lack of better entertainment. It was hot so did a bit more sweating. Didn't really know that I had so much water in the old body.

Thought there would [be] some energy left to work late into the night but no such luck but then tomorrow is another day. <u>Will</u> try to write again tomorrow night—three days in a row again shouldn't be too bad a record.

Think much about the three of you & hoping that you & Susie still mention me in your prayer. With love always to the three of you Always

Lovingly—

Al & Dada

A.F Herney, Ens.

Tuesday 30 Jan. Jan Letter No 12 [Actual January letter 16]
My Dearest Sweet, Susie & Steve:

Will keep my promise by writing you the third day in a row even tho the note may be short & very unnewsy.

Took a few minutes off this evening right after chow to go topside to see the sunset. Really a beautiful night—low over-hanging clouds but with just enough heighth to reflect the sun slowly descending below the horizon. The shade was one which I don't even before sense viewing—a pink & yet not a pink—one of those now you do—now you don't affairs. The moon is out again tonight too but partially hidden by the clouds—yet sufficiently bright to break thru the clouds occasionally.

Have a book of Popular Quotations on the desk—several of which you might enjoy.

"A good husband is never the first to go to sleep at night or the last to awake in the morning." Balzac—The Physiology of Marriage—(Hm!)

"Wifes are young men's mistresses, companions for middle age; & old men's nurses" Bacon "Of Marriage & Single Life.—(He's got something)

"A husband should always know what is the matter with his wife, so she always knows what is not." Balzac. (He must have been a cynic huh)

—Started straightening out my drawers yesterday for a bit of relaxation which meant of course that the letters had to be reread before shredding & putting them in the wastebasket. Got a good bit of pleasure rereading them— makes up in part not receiving any for over a week now but then the time will always come.

Haven't as yet had the energy to box my clothes & send them. Since it takes so long will mail them in care of Julia & Mac since I'm sure you won't be home when it arrives—this is of course if I mail the damn things.

The boys have gotten quite a kick about the food. Just let them rave on. We are still on general mess & have supplementary food which was purchased at a commissary at our last port of call.—Little things added does help a good deal in keeping one's happy disposition—you well know how your old man is generally.—

Hate to think of you making the trip to Nebr with the two youngsters all by yourself but am sure you will enjoy your visit & that Dad & Mother will enjoy having the three of you with them.

With all my love to the three of you always

Al & Dada

A. F Herney, Ens USNR.

5

At Sea Headed for Combat

February 1945

Thursday Febr 1 Febr Letter #1

My Dearest Sweet, Susie & Steve:

Since I neglected you three last night will drop you a short note before hitting the sack. Didn't write last night because I read official material until 11:30 & was so tired couldn't concentrate on anything.

Just came down from the bridge as I needed a bit of fresh air before the sand man is to come. The moon is out again in all its golden splendor—hidden occasionally by a few low overhanging clouds. The sunset was beautiful again tonight—with some more of the weird shades it causes the sky to assume— However irrespective of all the beautiful scenes—cloud formations that are ever present would gladly forgo them to be with my Three S's.

Started taking some exercises today. Were announced for 1600—voluntary of course so if the crew wishes to participate they could. Only Hetzler & myself appeared. Went thru the old routine of jumping jacks & yes even some "Hello Darling." Had quite an audience to cheer us on. It seems however that some of the crew intended to participate but were a bit backward about announcing their intentions till it was all thru.—Took a shower afterwards and perspired till about an hour later. Possibly will be same tomorrow but some more of the same should help that.

Haven't written any letters to those on the list—will try to take care of it soon but really have so much that must be done that I don't feel free to take too much time for correspondence & it does take time.

Wonder if I had mentioned in any of my letters that "Katie" be thanked for her remembrance which she included in Marie & Ed's box—viz a washrag & bar of soap. Her Bill [Frazier] like all of the rest of us husbands is sorry to be away from his loved one. Do wish I might get to see him if the opportunity even presented itself—for I might even break down on the diet & have a rum with him.

Have missed you a great deal Sweet—even tho my last letters haven't mentioned it—maybe that's because I didn't want to make myself think about it too much and accentuate those blue moods.

Must be off for some sack drill as it is well after 11 o'clock—With all my love to the Three of you as always.

Al & Dada

A.F Herney, Ens. U. S N R.

P.S. Hope there is lots of mail as I am always ready to stop what ever I'm doing to find out about my nice <u>Family.</u>

Al.

Friday Febr 2—Febr Letter No 2

My Dearest Sweet, Susie & Steve:

Since I'm not sure of being able to get a note to you for Valentines Day will make this your Valentine's Greeting.

Febr 14th always means sending or delivering in person something to remind our Sweethearts that we do remember them, even tho the token be small & of very little monetary value. However the expression of love is there & that is really what counts—Unfortunately I neglected to get something for you so this note will have to be the "Thing" this year. I do love you so much my Sweet & know that it is not all one sided. The more holidays we men are away from home the more we feel that its sure hell to be deprived of our firesides and families because of fact that those that don't have want something allegedly claimed by those that have.

Was a bit stiff to day from the exercised yesterday—think I surprised some of the men as did Hetzler by arriving on the boat deck in sufficient time for another bit of the same thing. Hetzler & myself took turns in calling the count. Really is tough to call the count & do the exercise at the same time.

Today of course is Marie's birthday—known she as well as Fran & Julia will overlook my not writing to them but as I've said before & will say again have been darn busy.

Rained liked the devil this morning but since we've been a bit more conserving as far as the water is concerned have been allowed fresh water showers so didn't run out on the boat deck with soap & washrag. The sunset tonight was a complete washout & no moon but quite a number of stars are out. Hence didn't stay up on the bridge very long tonight—the air of course is always fresh & is a bit of a pick me up.

As yet I've been quite fortunate in not having caught cold—really remarkable for me. Gates has had one for the past few days.

Since I didn't get you a token of my love am enclosing three one dollar bills—Hawaii series—one for each of my Sweethearts. You can spend them or keep them as you wish. Will make up for all of my shortcomings when I get home.

Have the Coles had any further word respecting the possibility of change of duty for Harvey [a member of the US Border Patrol] and how is Mr. {Porter} progressing?

My love to all of the family, to Dad & Mother when you see them but all of my love to the three of you as always.

Al & Dada

A.F Herney, Ens.

Saturday Febr. 3 Febr letter No 3

My Dearest Sweet, Susie & Steve:

Was happy to have received your 9, 10, 11, 12 & 13 Jan letters today plus a nice letter from Marie & a note from Bob Saunders respecting the insurance. Your letters of course were newsy like all get out and carried quite a jolt for several reasons—none of which I need mention.

Regarding the matter of going home with the folks for the length of time you plan as regarding what is to be done with the house, the car and yes even with Nick are problems with you are going to have to decide. Can't say I disagree with the advice given by my family but am sure of this one thing my Sweet & that is I want you well & happy & content. I've fully realized how difficult it has been for you to have had to assume all the burdens of mother and head of the family since I've been gone. Have worried a good bit about it & should you care to sell 399 J Street & return to live with Mother & Dad for the duration you may feel free to do so & should the occasion arise that I'll get back to the West Coast before this thing is over & you aren't there waiting it will just have to be put down to the cost of this conflict. Please believe me when I say what ever you choose to do is a matter which will meet with my approval.

Marie in her letter after rereading it indicates that she feels it advisable for you to have a long stay with Mother & Dad tho I'm sure she and all of the rest of the Uncles & Aunts will miss you & our <u>Two</u> contributions to the family tree.

It was nice of Chuck to give you the reassurance about visiting Mother & Dad & take care of the package. Wondering if they did get my letter mailed the same time Paul & Beth's was given over to Uncle Sam.

The word about the two youngsters having colds & Susie's fever was a bit on the harsh side of the news respecting the family. It is good however to know that Susie is fond of her little brother & and in his entertainment tho her assistance may be at a very poor time—Don't tell me your trying to housebreak him already for that's pretty rugged for a guy his age.

Inquired of Klaman today if he had seen any of the gang including Lee— no luck & no word but do have for I would greatly enjoy seeing that swell guy & know damn good well that I'd get off this no-liquor diet and one on one hell of a good toot like I haven't been on for a long long time.

Don't get too upset Sweet about Mama & Daughter carrying on because Clarence is leaving. As you say you did damn sweet & I've been mighty proud of it, for your grit & fortitude did a lot to make it easier for me. Such pleasant memories of that last week still do much to shake away them blues.

Believe it or not it is already 0105 & quite a long day. Possibly shouldn't get so upset over some things but was mad enuf tonight to chew nails. Some chaps give up so damn easy & assume the attitude of leave George do it. When there is something to be done can't see leaving it go till tomorrow. Think I'll have to reorganize the club which I had organized before writing my first underway letter to you, or may be it would be more profitable to just sit & do as damn little as possible.

Sundays may be an awful day for you Sweet & can appreciate why. As far as we're concerned its pretty much the same as any other day as the work must go on.

Nick [the family dog] should have a good home with the Paxtons & please don't feel too bad about him—surely we all would miss not having him around. We'll see about getting him back when we all come marching home.

With love to the three of you as always and being content with whatever you decide to do—

Yours

Al & Dada

A.F Herney, Ens

P.S. Off to sack drill & dreams of my three.

Al

Febr 9., Friday Febr Letter No 4

My Dearest Sweet, Susie & Steve:

Again it is almost a week since I last wrote you & again the only excuse I have is the old one that I've been awfully, awfully busy. Was equal as busy when I wrote the last one's & where I got the energy to do so I don't know except that my love for you must have been the driving influence.

Do hope that you will get letters No 10 & 11 for Jan, & No's 1 2 &3 for Febr. Before you leave for Lincoln or they will be extra late by the time they are forwarded. In case you should receive this one first please know that the last letter written by me will free you mind about the house & your plans for a long stay with Mother & Dad.

It won't be long now till you will be on your way—in fact just another day & then for two very nice extra special days enroute with the kiddies. However

I know that our Young Lady will be a big help to Mommie & won't cause her any trouble since Steve will take a good bit of her time.

Have been awfully blue for the last couple of days & remember those days at home when I could get home & be lifted out of the dumps by my family. Would give much if just to get home for a few hours when I feel that way.

Haven't had much chance to view the sunsets & moon for the last few days as most every moment is a busy one. Do guess however that I should take time out for the bit of uplift I'd be bound to find in some of God's colors & shades.

While we haven't had too much news or taken time out to listen have heard some good news.—The Germans appear to be in the well known squeeze play & if the Russians keep on we won't have to worry too much about the west wall & what taking it would mean to our men. Doubt also that the crime Commission would have much to worry about the "Leaders" as the Russians do seem to have a quick ready answer. Of course they have much to be paid for by the Germans & the old law of an eye for an eye. Still seems to be pretty basic even tho organized modern civilizations says it ain't so.

Have been pretty regular at the physical exercise at 1600 & have gotten so tough again that the hello darlings don't keep me in pained stomach muscles (?) the morning after. However, the neck & shoulders have been tied up & got the Dr. (Ph mate) to give me a neck rub tonight so feel a bit more relaxed.

Woke up the other morning with a cold & ear ache (0200)—got the hot water bottle which seemed to relieve the ear. Still have a bit of tender nasal passages but not a runny cold thank gosh for hate like the devil to have a sore nose from the required wiping.

Haven't as et receive the cookies which you & my Pride & Joy packed for me & will let you in on a secret—have not as yet deleted your Xmas boxes for I've been hoarding them for a rainy day which may never come but nibble on them occasionally—in fact just had one.

Its been so awfully warm and I've been sweating so much I've had heat rash on my forehead. Thankful if I'm going to get it that it will be there & not anyplace else where it could be so uncomfortable.

Forgot to mention in my last letter that I am looking forward to the popcorn & even tho all it may bring even old maids to crunch on—as many things as bring home closer are really the things that can't since home itself is out of the question.

Surely you have received the orchids which are the things to be sent you. Do hope you received them before you left for home as it would be too bad if they haven't arrived as I don't know if they would last till you received them in Nebr.

Know you will be having a good time at home with all your old friends. Would bet that the conversation of all of you young mothers would be some to be listening in on when you get together. Mother of course won't enjoy taking care of her grand children while Mommie goes out for the evening for a hen party. And to think of the late sleeping hours she will enjoy is something to really look forward to.

Here I've written four pages Sweet without mentioning that I do love you a great deal & miss you immensely. As you already know I don't know what I'd do without you and thank you many times for being mine and giving me or rather us and our two fine youngsters. With all my love to the three of you & regards to Dad & Mother.

Always yours

Al & Dada

A.F Herney

P.S. It is strange to be addressing a letter to 2315 Ryons again—but suppose I will get used to it—

Al

Saturday 10 Febr Letter #5

My Dearest Sweet, Susie & Steve:

Won't promise more than a short note for its very close to 0200 military time & sack drill must go on even tho we would a times wish we could do without sleep.

Was a bit disappointed today to find no mail from you—Sugar Reports they are rightly called but guess I shouldn't complain for I received your letters written the last week in Jan about a week ago—Maybe the mailman should have held out & dished them out one at a time. However did reread them last night before retiring & after I'd written you.

After reading last weeks Time in short order picked up Lady of the Lake—took a snatch of it now & then—very much surprised how much I enjoyed rereading it & finding some awfully good passages. May reread it again real soon too.

Here it is the day that Mommie & the two youngsters start their trip to Grandma's & Grandpa's. Surely you'll get your rest when & after you arrive at Lincoln—& certainly not before for its not otherwise in the cards with a 6 months old young man and a young lady 2 & ½ years old. Do wish I were making the trip with you & you know how well I like to travel.

Tried to make provisions for a Valentine gift for you, Sweet but doubt if it will arrive anywhere near time for that day—as usual wasn't forsighted enuf to prepare for it well in advance. Hope you won't feel too badly for you know I do think about you & miss you much more.

From what you've said in your last letters about the stay in Lincoln it will be August before you plan on being at 399J Street again. Not much more of an absence than last winter when we were in good old Boston. Incidently I guess the "Old Gal" [Boston landlady Manley] has finally decided to give up following me to the end of the earth—ho hum she must be a happy individual.

Saw Coleman in the Prisoner of Zenda (?) again tonight—an old film but a good picture—he always does an excellent job & do so enjoy seeing him— Some we have had are real stinkers & very likely always will be but then one must have some diversion.

Again reassuring you that whatever arrangements you have made regarding the house & your stay in Lincoln is agreeable with me—

With love to the three you always & my kindest to Mother, Dad, the family & others in Lincoln—

Your loving hubby

Al & Dada

A.F Herney.

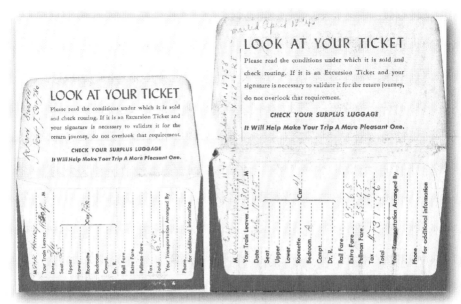

Dot's train ticket from San Diego to Lincoln was purchased as a round trip, departing San Diego
Sunday, February 11, at 6:30 p.m. Car 41. Bedroom A. Total fare of $131.56 included Pullman
Fare $35.25, extra fare $95.68, and tax $0.63. The return segment was not scheduled.

The round-trip-ticket receipt for Marie Herney from San Diego to Los Angeles indicates that Marie
accompanied Dot and the children as far as Los Angeles, perhaps to assist with changing trains there.

Sunday Nite (February 11) Febr Letter No. 6

My three Dearest S's:

Since the hour was so late early this morning before getting to hit the sack
would promise to do more than drop you a very short note—take a shower &
be off for some of that horizontal exercise.

No mail again today but can only be hopeful for the morrow. Haven't
really expected much for I know how busy you must have been—all of those
little bothersome details that one wishes someone could do for you but which
ain't at all possible. When doing them you do know that they have been done.

Can't say I don't need a shower for I'm beginning to get offensive to my
self. However don't know which is worse being offensive or being sticky after a salt water shower. However if one is good—wets down lathers & rinses
off we can have fresh water showers. The crew has been pretty good about it

too for they've begun to learn just that water ain't like it was at home—minimum per month.

Have been busy all day again & since I didn't want to bother or deprive any of the flock of the little pleasure overlooked services today. Shouldn't have done it either for they are good for all of us. Am getting to the point where I don't stumble over some of the terminology. Some however still stumps me. Forgot to mention that I was pleased that Father Brown called on you for it does show he has a warm spot in his heart for you. Think he realizes that I'm pretty much of a lost soul & that's why he smiled when you told him about my flock. Have meant to drop him a short note. Don't remember getting a card or note from him.

In Marie's last letter she said that she was to have you & the youngsters out for a weekend before you left & that she was going to send her picture home with you so Susie wouldn't forget her while she went avisiting. Do hope the young lady won't forget her Dad & know that she remembers to include him in her nightly offering to the Almighty.

Haven't heard a bit of news from the past few days so don't know what has been accomplished against the enemies that are ours. While it may be unchristian I hope it has been plenty devastating. The heavier the shorter duration & I do want to get home to my family as soon as possible—quicker too.

With all my love to my One & Only Sweetheart My Pride & Joy & to the young man. Always

Yours forever

Al & Dada

A.F. Herney

Monday 12 Febr Letter No 7 February

My Dearest Sweet, Susie & Steve:

Decided to drop you another note & after just getting started had the pen run dry—did that that stop me, it did not—& that's really perseverance—

Received your Jan 14 written on January 29 and a V mail from the Padre—who said he was remembering us in his prayers. He said he had so enjoyed his visit with you.

The word about having taken the Pride & Joy to Dr. Black for an examination is very satisfying for I was worried about it especially the possibilities that might follow a long cold—sinus for we certainly don't want her to be suffering with it. Knew she would be a good girl. Really the last time she went when I was along was such a hard time for her & she hadn't had those regular hours because Daddy was home.

Glad you got to see IJ—her [infant son] Steve & Mother & Dad Stadler. It is nice to know that he has the relief. No doubt your deal on the house will work out satisfactorily with the nephew—as well as with any other include the Litchfields. They are however nice people & do believe they <u>would</u> have been good tenants. Am very surprised that Susie remembered Carl, maybe we got something & don't know it. Have you given Susie an IQ as yet? I didn't expect that their youngster would be as nice looking as our Steve—but they think the same so what—otherwise it won't be natural.

If Clarence didn't leave before you left on the train what were the complications with his little chickadee—did they move to a hotel for they surely didn't plan on staying there.

Sorry to hear that your getting hit so hard again. Possibly its been the strain you have been under & with more rest, mental and physical you will be feeling much better soon.

As for missing me Sweetie always remember that that works both ways. There have been times when I would have given all of our worldly possessions few as they may be to have this damnable war over and be back with you three.—Your having Susie snuggling up sounds inviting & darn pleasant—About the only one who is close enuf to snuggle up with is Brother Gosch in the lower bunk & I'm sure he wouldn't be any happier about it than I would.

Once more My Sweet I'll say that I do love you with all my heart for being my wife and the mother of our two fine youngsters. Love always to my three extra special Three S's.

Al & Dada

A.F Herney

P.S. Still signing as Ens as haven't seen an Alnav which will carry me thru as JG. & don't want to be disappointed so am waiting for the dope.

Al

Febr 15, 45 Febr Letter No 8

My Dearest Sweet, Susie & Steve:

Not on the high side of life tonight so don't be surprised if I'm short & slightly on the wacky side. Have been working darn hard & many many things are on my mind so excuse please.

The more one sees of natures ways the more grows to appreciate the powerful working of the almight—Maybe also a good bit of it is due to the fact that we don't have our family to come home to at the end of a busy day and get the consolation that we want so much, & decide that since we can't have that we must look for some beauty.

No more cold but the ear still bothers me a bit. No ache but bothersome as it feels clogged up & you know how annoying that can be. Guess I'll have to see Doc about it.

Found out on the 13th that I made the Alnav but haven't had the opportunity to get a physical. Will do so however as soon as the present little Joy ride is over which I hope is over soon.

Haven't received any more mail from you since your Jan 29th letter which I'm sure I mentioned in my last letter to you. Again will say that I missed much getting some more but do guess I'll have to be patient as I know you have been and are now. We can't always regulate the deliveries of either incoming or outgoing mail.

To go back to the "J.G." business wasn't too excited about any of it except the finances which accompany it. Also at the first opportunity plan on increasing the allowance to $200.00 which will leave me with $5 per month more than I had before & believe that I can get along with that.

As usual have been getting not enuf sleep—hitting the sack after 2300 & arising about 0515 which aint enough for a little boy like I'm. Do believe I have been getting a lot less sleep than when I took watches—as I don't feel I'm entitled to horizontal exercises during the afternoon & hence haven't been taking them.

It is now after 2000 and must take a shower & off to sack drill.

Before leaving you this time my Sweet I wish again to say I love you with all my heart, am very grateful for all of the very nice things you have done for

me as my wife especially our two youngsters, for being so understandable &
for your love.

Give each of the youngsters a tremendous hug & kiss for me—With all
my love to the three of you always

Yours—

Al & Dada

A.F Herney.

P.S. Am looking forward to a very pleasant birthday—as pleasant as can be
away from you three—

Al.

From US Navy History and Heritage Command Online Library of Selected
Images:

*Battle of Iwo Jima (February-March 1945) The Iwo Jima invasion began on 16 February
1945, when a formidable U.S. Navy armada started three days of pre-landing preparations. As minesweepers and underwater demolition teams cleared the nearby waters,
warships and aircraft methodically tried to destroy the island's defenses.*[x]

*According to the Navy Department Library, WWII Command File of the Operational
Amphibious Operations Capture of Iwo Jima:*

*... [performing mine clearance prior to the invastion of Iwo Jima] were members of Mine
Group, Taskgroup 52.3, consisting of 7 Sweep Units comprising 43 minecraft under the
command of Rear Admiral A Sharp, USN Commander, Minecraft, U.S. Pacific Fleet.*[xi]

From Dictionary of American Naval Fighting Ships:

Arriving there [Iwo Jima] three day before the assault she [the Scurry*] swept the assault
and transport areas in preparation for the larger ships.*[xii]

Continuation of interview with Fernando Salazar, Scurry *crewmember, May 16, 2008:
We swept the coast of that island and we went right by Mount Suri Bachi. There were
some fireworks aimed at us, and fortunately none of our ships got hit or suffered much
damage. The sweeping was done in the daytime and the night we would head east toward
the coast, and go for three or four hours, then go back to the island again to sweep the*

next day. This went on for three or four days. We would remain in the area with the armed forces after the Marines and the others invaded the island and on occasion we would see a lot of fireworks, crashing of a plane or so.[xiii]

From "Saga of the Scurry: The First Year," the ship's first-anniversary program:
Invasion—
The highlight of the year, for us, and our real test, came in the two major invasions of 1945. In the light of the tremendous forces involved, we of course played but a small role in those battles—small but important. The SCURRY was assigned assault minesweeper with the amphibious force and operated in close proximity to enemy shore defenses. At IWO JIMA we arrived three days before D-Day and swept in ahead of the invasion...[xiv]

Sunday, Febr 18 Febr Letter No 9 [Al's thirty-third birthday]
My Dearest Sweet, Susie & Steve:

Have neglected you for several days & besides since I didn't get a birthday letter which I'm sure is not your fault will write you instead.

It (today) has been far from the Happy One's I have enjoyed in the past I can assure you. However I might say I have been doing something constructive or rather assisting in doing something constructive to end this thing a bit sooner. Have been lucky so far and expect with the Almightys help to continue to be. If I can't be home am glad I have been able to do a little toward that end.

Everyone including your hubby is has been awfully busy & a bit cross— Was up a few days ago from 0530 to 2300, not horizontal exercise & doing something every minute it seemed like. The rest of the men officers & crew had it about as tough. About the only relaxation that was mine those hours was when eating & taking care of nature. Can say I enjoyed the sack when I hit it but didn't realize enuf of it at that time. Do really believe I get less sleep since I've been on this deal than when I was standing deck watches.

The ears are still bothering me. Have had Doc washing them out twice a day & putting some drops in them. Believe I'll take a hot water bottle to bed with me to see if that will help. Gets damn annoying to have some one shouting at you, yep even the Capt.

Word has been passed that our men have landed at Bataan. Mac [Arthur] certainly couldn't miss the chance could he for it must mean a lot to take up where he left off. Really you'd think the Japs would give up & just forget that they ain't big enuf for lots of things—including being a world power.

Mother & Dad must have the situation concerning their two grandchildren well in hand by this time. Of course their mother is there to assist in their care & general custodian.

Suppose Susie was very happy about her ride on the cho-cho as much as ever & much of a Belle enroute. Am of course anxious to get one of your newsy letters concerning the trip—Just when I don't know but will have to be patient.

The weather has been exceptionally delightful not too cold or hot—after sunset however it is pleasant to be wearing a jacket. Don't think however I'll be having the boys put a blanket on the sack.

With all my love to the three of you always & regards to Dad & Mother
Lovingly
Al & Dada
A.F Herney
P.S.—Still haven't had my physical so don't know if I'll get to be a JG.—
Al

Continuation of interview with Fernando Salazar, Scurry crewmember, May 16, 2008: *...The point of Iwo Jima was to obtain air space, and give us a closer distance to Japan particularly for the airplanes, the B-29's that were bombing at the time...Iwo Jima seemed to be a very easy target, but it proved to be otherwise. It was a tiny island, something like eight miles long and five miles wide at the widest portion of that. It was full of caves, so that the forces were in the caves and it appeared that Iwo Jima was not going to be a big battle, but it proved otherwise. Of course we were all joyous when we saw the picture of the raising of the flag on Mount Suri Bachi. That's the first place on my ship [the Scurry] with the experience of seeing the Japanese suicide planes that would come down and try to hit our battleships, our destroyers.*

[One Japanese suicide plane targeted the Scurry.]We were too small of a target. The one that came to us was already on fire, and so whatever he could hit was pay dirt. Fortunately, our skipper was quite able to get us out of the way in time. It did shake the pier quite a bit. As men would say it, 'We have lost our virginity.' But that was the only time. Other times we were among the ships that surrounded the island and one of the times that I remember is that there were some missiles that were aimed at some of our larger ships. Our captain got so angry, he decided he wanted to run as close as possible and try to hit them with our biggest battery, which was a three inch battery. Pretty small compared to what they were using. Fortunately, the Commandant of the whole navy ships that were there saw that our little ship was going towards the coast and he quickly radioed and said, 'Get back to where you belong.' It was dangerous to be out there so close. ᵛ

24 February 45 Febr. 10 Letter
My Dearest Sweet, Susie & Steve:

Almost a week since I last dropped you a note doesn't really seem that long for everyone has been quite busy—of course it goes without saying that some of us at times have gotten short tempered and very unpleasant to live with or around but on a vessel this large there really isn't much you can do about it.

Have been waiting patiently for some letters from you regarding your & my family—the trip and a million other things—but guess they will be so much dearer (?) sp when they do arrive.

The dreams of late have been pleasant ones all about you and our two youngster. They do seem to help & bring me so close to all of you tho miles separate us.

For the last few days the good old rubbers have come in handy and to date the Capt & Exec are both wearing them so laugh now if you wish about my taking my old reliables with me.

While working hard have enjoyed the uninterrupted night's sleep irrespective of the length of it, sometimes short and sometimes a little longer. However it still can be anything like sleeping in the sack at home and expecting anytime to hear go-go or a lusty cry from the little feller—Ho hum here I'm day dreaming.

Have wondered what arrangements you have made about the house—don't under any circumstances wish you to have told the OPA to go to _____ for they might get a bit upset & it ain't any fun I can assure you.

Haven't written any letters to any of the family in SD so do hope you will keep them posted all the time.—Hope I can get the ambition to write a few more letters than I have written—was different of course when you were at home & could call them.

Jo's [Al's eldest sister] birthday is sometime the first of March—just when is beyond me.—Helen's [another sister] is in June also the date is blank.

Haven't received your package or anyones as far as that is concerned yet but hope it won't be too far in the future.

Do know that you & the youngsters are having a good time, resting up & getting good & fat.—That of course will be good for all three of you but a bit tougher on Dad & Mother.

With all my love always to the three of you & regards to Dad & Mother—
Love Always
Al & Dada
A.F Herney

6

IWO JIMA TO ULITHI TO OKINAWA

March 1945

From "Saga of the Scurry: The First Year," the ship's first-anniversary program:
Invasion—At OKINAWA we arrived seven days before the initial landing, for a long
period of combat minesweeping and patrol operations. It was at OKINAWA that the
SCURRY's guns, by their own accuracy and intensity of fire, splashed an enemy bomber
close aboard, and later assisted materially in the destruction of two other enemy aircraft.
Painted in red on the side of the bridge is displayed her score of enemy mines swept and
planes destroyed. We gained something else at first hand as we witnessed, from a dis-
tance, the beach head action—a sincere respect and admiration for the gallant Marine
at IWO JIMA and the fighting G. I. at OKINAWA, who were put ashore to slug it out
in close quarters with the enemy.[xvi]

From Dictionary of American Naval Fighting Ships*:*
Departing Iwo Jima on 3 March, the ship arrived off Okinawa on 25 March and carried
out a week of preparatory sweeps before the landings there. She remained off Okinawa until
8 July, sweeping mines and maintaining antisubmarine patrols around the transports.[xvii]

Continuation of interview with Fernando Salazar, Scurry *crewmember, May 16, 2008:*
We were there [Iwo Jima] until the end of February going into March. Then we went
down to some of the islands close to Guam that were not won, the Caroline Islands. There

[Ulithi] we just recuperated for a few weeks and did any repairs that needed to be done to the ship. Then we were on another convoy headed north again. This time it was the convoy headed for Okinawa. Again, our goal was to sweep the shores where the invasion was to take place. We discovered that the number of mines that were there was tremendous. I'd never seen that many mines.[xviii]

From "Ulithi" by George Spangler (reprinted with permission from the USS Laffey webmaster, A.J. Tarquino. www.laffey.org):
Its existence kept secret throughout the war, the US naval base at Ulithi was for a time the world's largest naval facility. In March 1945, 15 battleships, 29 carriers, 23 cruisers, 106 destroyers, and a train of oilers and supply ships sailed from a 'Pacific base.' What was this base? The mightiest force of naval Power ever assembled must have required a tremendous supporting establishment. Ulithi, the biggest and most active naval base in the world was indeed tremendous but it was unknown. Few civilians had heard of it at all. By the time security released the name, the remarkable base of Ulithi was a ghost...
Ulithi is 360 miles southwest of Guam...a typical volcanic atoll with coal, white sand and palm trees...enclosing a vast anchorage with an average depth of 8- to 100 feet—the only suitable anchorage within 800 miles...
The U.S. navy arrived in September 1944...every inch of the four larger islands was quickly put to use...the big island, Falalop, was just wide enough for a 3500-foot air-strip ...fly in from Guam 1269 passengers, 4565 sacks of mail and 262,251 pounds of air freight a week...Within a month of the occupation of Ulithi, a whole floating base was in operation. Six thousand ship fitters...arrived aboard repair ships, destroyer tenders, floating dry docks...Over half the ships were...towed in. They then served as warehouses for a whole system of transports which unloaded stores on them for distribution. This kind of chain went all the way back to the United States...the smaller ships needed a multitude of services, the ice cream barge made 500 gallons a shift, and the USS ABATAN...distilled fresh water and baked bread and pies. Fleet oilers sortied from Ulithi to refuel the combat ships a short distance from the strike areas. They added men, mail and medical supplies, and began to take orders for spare parts. [xix]

March 4 March Letter No 1

My Dearest Sweetheart, Susie & Steve:

Can't neglect you any longer and really let down on last month I know but just won't apologize any more.

Still no mail from you or anyone else since the last of Jan—quite a long time to wait for word from your dear one's but guess that is just part of being a sailor, even if only of sorts. Have expectations of receiving some soon however which should make up for having to wait so long.

Have wondered how much mail you have received from me. Wrote you eleven letters in Jan and ten in Febr. Maybe you will eventually get all of them.

If days like this one are many I should soon acquire & hold my title assumed at Maner B 21.—When things are rugged you expect tempers to be short & everybody wrong but Johnnie. Will have to do much to control my temper which possibly will be good for me!—Tends to make one blue as hell & [wish to be] back home as a civilian.

You three have been constantly on my mind recently wondering how much the youngsters are changing, what you have been doing,—how Grandmother & Dad have been faring with their problems <u>minor</u> ones I know but still problems. Have not as yet had the opportunity to get that physical. However since pay dates back to the time of the Alnav won't loose any pay so am not worrying one bit. Expect however to take care of it as soon as possible & the added allotment—hm with that and the next you should be Mrs. R.B. for sure.

March 5—

Dearest Sweet:

The letter was interrupted by some business & didn't get back to the letter until tonight so will try to take up where I left off. Didn't get much accomplished today—just sort of let down—guess relaxed for a bit and hate to begin doing all of the many things necessary to be done—as usual so many things I haven't done.

It is hard to realize that it has already been 5 months since we last saw each other—possibly it is good that time has gone by in such a hurry for it isn't easy to be away from you three who are the important thing—it is a happy prospect however to think that you will be there for me when this thing is over & Uncle says to all of us who wish—get going your many ways—the job is done & completely his time.

Haven't written any of the family—must drop them a note to let them know at least that I think of them or at least realize there is the Herney clan. The letters won't be long I assure you.

The news from all fronts appears to be good thought at times a bit costly—but who even heard of a war that wasn't. Wonder how the residents of Tojo's stomping grounds feel about winning the war when the Task Forces are hitting her with carrier based planes. Surely they must begin to realize that somebody bit off a good hunk then they decided we were a bit on the too soft side.

Not much of a letter my Sweet but then by <u>writtening</u> to you, you know that I do love you—as I always have and always will.

Give both of the youngsters a great big hug & kiss for me—With all my love always to the Three of you & regards to Dad & Mother.

Always yours

Al & Dada

A.F Herney—

March 5

Dearest Sis: [Helen Herney]

Your nice birthday note received well in advance of the big day which I can assure you was routine (the birthday) as all hell. It was fortunate however that it was sent when it was for I have received no mail since Jan 22—Your edibles however did not arrive with the card so should be enjoyed in the future.

The reason for the above is quite understandable for doing our small part in helping chase Tojo & his pals around (commonly called stinkers) even the best mailman would find it a bit difficult to locate us or anybody else. Am happy that Dot had the opportunity to get to go home to see Dad & Mother & now how much they wanted to see their grandchildren. They do deserve the privilege (using the term adviseably) for feel that the three might be a bit tough on them.—Can't blame Dot for planning on such a long stay either as it was a bit difficult for her in Chula all by herself.

News from all the fronts would lead one to believe that this thing will be over some day—can only hope that it will be over, giving <u>over</u> the fullest connotation possible, for it isn't a pleasant thought to think that Steve might some day be a part of a war machine even tho it is the one and only fighting for the one and only.

Doubt if Dot, the only one I've written since Xmas has fared much better on the mail than I have for being here & there might well have tended to delay her receiving it. Do hope she wasn't unduly alarmed for wouldn't want her to worry.

The months have passed since leaving the States. Really time has gone by rather rapidly. Possibly it is good that we have been busy for I'm sure that if I had much time to really sit & think things would be awfully black. What little time is available is spent in recollect—all of the pleasantries of <u>my</u> family and how nice it has been to have been of a large family and had two nice people for a Mother & Dad.—It also helps when the going gets tough.

Since I won't promise to write again before your birthday will now wish you a most pleasant one. Come to think of it I haven't written you many birthday letters have I?

With much love to you Sis & again a Happy Birthday.

From your <u>Civilian Sailor</u> brother.

Al.

A.F. Herney

March 6 March Letter No. 2

My Dearest Sweet, Susie & Steve:

Will write you another short note tonight thought don't know quite what I will say other than some ramblings.

Wrote Helen and Marie last nite—really surprised myself to have that much energy left. Can't say that the letters were much but ramblings either as it is hard to write anything like a coherent letter when one is on the dissatisfied side.

About this time last year Carl & I were beginning to enjoy our three months at dear old Harvard. However tough the "Moe" made it for us we had our families with us to enjoy the few hours we had each day to call our own. How Susie ever took the attention that was given her is beyond me. Hope she hasn't had the amount of colds she had—of course she has to have some as does Steve or things just wouldn't be right.

Every time I think of the Sunday we went sight seeing—my arms ache— and how cold we all got even poor Susie—Remember changing the disposables in Old North Church—the big questions was where to dispose of them. She really was a good youngster & much better tempered than her Daddy.

It is odd about the nature of the sea—at times pleasant as all—smooth as glass & at other times disagreeable at the very devil. Then especially do I feel that I would like to be a landlubber tho haven't been sick at all—maybe that's because I have been feeling better physically at least. However still on the diet including the alcoholic part & portion for I don't want to experience the unpleasantness of the seafaring life I did the first two weeks in December.

Must drop Joe a note to let him know that everything is on the beam & faring as well as can be expected. If it ever possible to have you & the youngsters with me feel I could bear a shore job wherever it might be. Can't blame him for being contended & happy having much of the home life to which he is accustomed.

Must be off to some sack drill for tomorrow is another day and a very busy one I'm afraid—maybe the mailman will be good to us & deliver what he has held out from us for so long a time. Do hope we won't be disappointed.

With all my love to the three of you always

Yours

Al & Dada

A.F. Herney

P.S. Forgot to say I love you very much.

Al.

March 7, 1945 March No 3

My Dearest Sweet, Susie & Steve:

Won't promise to write much of a letter nor to try to say I make heads of tales of all the news the mailman brought today—but did want to get another letter off to you.

The reaction to the Valentine's present was something like this—rambling through the pile of correspondence came upon the large envelope—open at one end & why there was any contents only God knows—pull out the card took a look—passed it around saying very proudly—take a look at this "These are my two children"—damn proudly too I will add. Don't know what you could have sent that would have pleased me more my Sweet. Can only say the "Pride & Joy" is still the same Susie Q to me, & Steve really a boy. Am so glad also that you had Cooper take them. Also received the pictures of Susie & Nick—the back yard incidently looks better than any time I can remember,—feel proud about it too—

Received either cards or letters from most of the Phi Mu's—letters and or cards & notes from Shaws, Belchers Gillette's—the letter from Paul & Beth a lengthy & enjoyable one. Mothers letter about the Valentine gift for which I was especially grateful for I understand that possibly might not arrive in time, a round robin Birthday letter from the family, a nice note from Helen (as usual & she did not mention Susie's "Sanks You Hahn" a letter from Uncle A & Aunt Julia [Caughey] with note from Uncle Geo [Burri, Al's mother's brother]—a letter from Virginia or I should say Sweetie Pie & nice letter from Ann. Cards & notes from Aunt Clyde & Aunt Heral—All & all of which goes to making life a lot more enjoyable outlooks a bit more rosey. Yes also a letter from Carl—evidently he has been looking for me as Ive been looking for him.

Sweet you don't know how happy I was that Mother was able to take care of the errand for me—tho I didn't expect you to get the least bit upset over of by it—however I did want you to know my endearing love for you always.

I am much relieved to know that you are back in Lincoln, arrived safely with no mishap other than a misplaced parcel—can't say that I blame Dad for being a bit disgruntled to find that it was a Kotex box—I do recollect however that it is the right size for packing a whole of a lot of junk. Since it contained so many necessaries very fortunate it was located.

The letter from Aunt Julia said Uncle A was to have an operation & that after he got well they would be moving on to S.D.—which I'm sure is good news & I'm further convinced that both Uncle A & Aunt J. would be much happier with the Herney's then they would elsewhere—it is odd but I can't be of any other conclusion—Do hope he is well & that the operation was a success.

Don't feel upset about your sporadic letter writing last month Sweet for I full realize that you having to do everything to do were in one turmoil. Can't realize honestly how you did it. Will remember if I see Carl about the three months deal.

Was much amused about your deduction about the locations though can't quite see why you added the second choices. However you might be right there to so what the Hell.

Do envy Dad being able to play with the two youngsters but know that he is giving them the love & attention that their Daddy would give them had he the chance & with that in mind will thank him & Mother for they're having my family with them for such an extended stay.

The weather reports about dear old Boston don't sound like its at all pleasant there but agree with you that even <u>that</u> could be stood if it would mean <u>My Family.</u>

Will write again real soon my Sweet & I'm sure a much more newsy letter.

My love to you always as ever

Yours

Al & Dada

A.F Herney

P.S. Please thank Mother for taking care of the Valentine present for me.

March 8 March No 4

My Dearest Sweet Susie & Steve, Mother & Dad:

Haven't had time to reread your letters & get myself straightened out on the sequence of events so will again write a rambler. Did however take time out to look at the two pictures of my or should I say our youngsters—Don't know about there being a sparkle in Steve's eye—but there sure is that familiar one in Susie's.

No mail today but won't complain as the mailman was so good to me before on yesterday. Haven't even had time to read Time—did however glance at Ed's contribution "Dear Sir" just like him to want to add to one's pleasure by a bit of humor. Wonder if we will be or remain two of his favorites only because we're Susie's Pa & Ma? He is one grand person and always will be.

Mother wrote that Dad Q [Quiggle, a family friend] was not doing so well. Sorry to hear this for he seemed to have a long session of it before. Even tho Johnnie may be advanced over Steve give the youngster a break—he can or should be going only one thing at a time—a cut tooth so lets give him a bit more time. Bet Steve is as good looking as Johnnie any day.

Can't quite understand why you wifes want to celebrate being widows on a one year anniversary—you should at least wait for two.

Your news about Dad is a bit upsetting. Do hope that it is not serious but just what everyone is upset about & that is so little with which to do your work—Can't you convince him to take it a bit easy if necessary—possibly having you & the youngsters there will help give him an added lift. So glad Susie likes him but hate to think she might annoy him by her tagging.

Susie might be another Pat as far as helpfulness is concerned and really mean to be a big help—later of course the piano practice will have to be at the desk time but that only follows.

Plan soon on writing you a nice long letter—all about where your "Pop" has been—losing up of censorship—where I saw the "Blue" of Susie's eyes and answer a few other questions that I know have been bothering you but couldn't answer before.—Will expect you to pass it on to the family for you know what a letter <u>writer</u> I am.—

Want to drop George H a note & also Carl S. for I do feel I might have the pleasure of seeing him soon.

With all my love to my Three & Dad & Mother

Always

Al & Dada

A.F Herney—

March 10 Letter No 5

My Dearest Sweet, Susie & Stevie:

Haven't intended to miss a day in writing for do want the letters to keep on their way to you. Wonder how you have fared on the mail so far since the letters written in early part of Febr.

Have forgotten to tell you to thank Mother for her note—It was the first letter the mailman gave me and was very much pleased to think that she received the letter in time to be able to take care of the little mission for me.

The maiden voyage of the Scurry took us to Eniwetok—just a mere thirty two days underway & explains why there was such a lapse of time before you received any mail. The atoll of which Eniwetok is as any geographical description will state—damn barren & don't know why anyone would want the thing except maybe for strategical reasons. The shades of blue inside of the atoll are many & close inshore is aqua marine if anything ever was. Then off for a short trip to Manus & what a godsend for it unlike Eni. has green cocanut groves & natives who are odd looking creatures—some came or wished to come alongside to do so bartering in their outrigger canoes but we wouldn't play ball. A November issue of Time has an article on Manus & quite interesting.

[According to the November 6, 1944, issue of *TIME*, the base at Manus, in the Admiralty Islands, was a marvel of logistics and construction, transformed from desolate island beach into a well-oiled supply station to service and repair ships as well as house and otherwise support thousands of military personnel. It was an essential part of the military supply pipeline that enabled the advance on and eventual capture of the Philippine Islands.]

Back from Manus to Eniwetok for a very short stay—then for a nice short cruise south of Eniwetok. Then finally and at last we did get to go to Pearl. You don't know how interested I was to get there having been deprived of that privilege earlier & even tho the rest of the gang had probably left Joe would still be there.

The alleged city of Honolulu is a disappointment no end. The war while it has crowded the city like all others near any war activity couldn't have caused the place to deteriorate—what a city. Practically all dumps & plenty of places to buy worthless junk much of which must have purchased in the states but people do want things to remember it by. Really Sweet, don't think we missed a thing by not going there on our honeymoon.

What has transpired since Pearl is as yet something that will have to wait but not too much longer so just be patient. Did get in on an engagement & will tell you what we are permitted to tell.—

The trip from Eni. to Pearl above mentioned that one was the damnest thing I ever hope to experience. Meeting a head on sea & sick every day tho now I'm convinced that it wasn't all seasickness. Came close at time to willingly be "man overboard" but then any such thoughts were driven for I remembered there were my Three S's waiting for me. Hope any more trips like that one won't be on the Scurry's schedule.

Here I've already written two pages without saying that I do love you and our two jumbled letters is an expression of a part of it.

Wrote Carl S & George H the eighth so only now must write to 16 dozen others. Did receive the notes from Aunt Clyde & Heral so tell them will try hard to write. Must write the family a note for the combined efforts when they were celebrating Marie's Birthday at Ann's so will give them what information I've given you here so you need not pass this letter on.

Tell Dad to get out the Atlas & trace the wake of your seagoing husband for you. Would like very much to help him do it. Incidiently I was enroute to Manus that I became a Shellback. Will send on the large certificate when I get the opportunity.

Must be off to some sack drill so I can be fresh for a big day tomorrow which will be a full one—Maybe my exam too.

With my love to the three of you as always—

Your loving H & Dada.

P.S. Give Susie and Steve an extra big hug & kiss for me with plenty of umph—

Lovingly

Al

A.F Herney.

March 11, Letter No 6

My Dearest Sweet, Susie Steve & Mother & Dad:

All of us were again disappointed today for we haven't had any mail since the 7th—really bad isn't it but there should be some for us someplace & then there are a few packages that I would like to see.

Have to go back tomorrow morning for the physical as the Dr. wanted to take part of the afternoon out & really can't blame him too much as he like everyone else was bound to have been busy recently.

Reread your letters & find that I'm missing 6 & & for Febr—have received No 8 mailed Febr 23rd. Maybe they will show up with the next batch of mail, at least I hope so.

Had hoped to run into Carl but haven't had the good fortune as yet—however won't give up hope for he may be here yet. Sometimes these things are as difficult as finding the needle but then we sometimes are optimistic.

Have so much to do don't really know where to start & haven't a hell of a lot of ambition. However will have to get down to some serious work for it must be done & not many to do it except myself. Often wonder why there is always so much paper work for everyone.

Think I about wrote myself out last night—so will relax for a spell now & finish this later on today.

Sounds like you will be well on your way not only to begin a fatty but also a well rested person—what with naps & knowing the meals that Mother puts out—all of which of course will be good for you & nice to take.

Lapses in between mail Sweet maybe long at stretches and may be for various reasons. However under no circumstances should you worry & know that you will be as brave as you were when we said goodby at Long Beach. I know that you will remember that since I have my 3 S's to come home to.— I'll get there for I'm sure that the Almighty didn't see fit to get me you three without wanting me to enjoy you. What with both Dad & Mother helping it's sure thing. Whatever is done has to be done & all one can do is say a fervent prayer that it will soon be all over.

Have wondered what kind of financial deal you made regarding the house for you didn't mention it in any of the letters I've received. Think you did a smart thing in leaving the key with Ed so he could get things out of the box if you needed anything.

Haven't added much to the letter by this second page but hated to send you a one pager—With all my love always to the three of you as always.

Al & Dada

AF Herney

March 12 '45 Letter No 7

My Dearest Sweet, Susie & Steve:

Well at least got that "Physical" & the Dr. seemed to think that I was OK—everything except the teeth. I'm ordered to get things squared away & at ease will see that the new allotment is registered tomorrow—making it as I've said before $200.00 (bucks)—Do hope you won't spend it all at one place. What I'm going to get to do about the teeth God only knows but will see what can be done.

Still no more mail & can't quite understand for others have received theirs. Maybe that mailman thinks we are still the same place we were when we left that last place—Well do hope he will come thru again real soon.—

Has been quite warm but since everyone is pretty much in the same fix can't say that it is unbearable. Really a lot more desireable that not being able to be warm—meaning of course freezing as some of the boys are doing.

Wrote the Clan a letter last night after finishing yours—sent it to Ann & the boys & asked them to spread it around. Do hope they do—It is awfully difficult to not be able to write to each of them individually but I just don't have time.

Since I haven't listened to the news for the last couple of days don't know what the latest news is either with regard to the boys over the Rhine, the Marines on Iwo Jima or the joint efforts in Indo China & then the Philippines. So easy to loose track of things.

It always seems to be so late when I get to writing my letters may be doing too much else before but then there is one's labor to be done & because of that cut you short. However know that you will forgive me for supposedly put you last but remember I don't want to end the day without dropping you a note.

This weather is awfully funny—sun bright as all for a spell—then a squall & sweetheart does it get wet—over in a short time & the sequence seems to start all over again.

Will have to make some plans for my Son's & Daughters Birthdays which tho not too soon will be here before we know I & I wouldn't want that to slip by especially since I hope this will be the last one away from them. Just an optimist I know but one can't be blamed for hoping.

Must close to go to that horizontal exercise class we all enjoy so much—please forgive this note my Sweet—With love to the three of you as always,

Al & Dada

March 13, Letter No 8

My Dearest Sweet, Susie & Steve:

Another day almost at an end & very close to the start of a brand new day & quite a long one it has been too. However was very joyfully surprised this morning to be told at 0745 that I was to have the deck for the day.—

One way to do lots of things get notting constructively accomplished is to have the deck. Really doesn't help one's disposition at all for you soon start pulling out the hair & there really is [not] much left—Can't say Sweet that we're not both ageing so don't be surprised when you do see your old man.

Am very much relieved that the allotment has been taken care of today. Made it as I told you for $200.00. The first deduction to commence as of April so you should receive the check for that sum in May. My but were going up in the world but please don't think about buying any palaces or such.—

Still no mail today & can't understand it for surely there has been some mal since that which we received at our last stop. Please Mr. Mailman be good tomorrow.

This weather is rather peculiar. Squalls come suddenly & leave as fast—odd to have a show interrupted for a few minutes because of Mother Nature only to be allowed to see the next portion after a short interlude. Almost like a serial affair—the only difference being that you don't have to wait a week.

Will be very pleased when this month is over for my turn at being mess Treasurer & having charge of the Pantry and the mess Boys will be over. Can see why some people have no patience at all with some of our Brothers. Apparently like to make big out of small which does not work at all & never will.

Hope to have some dentistry tomorrow—several fillings which I should have evidently taken care of before this but you know how I love dentists—tho didn't mind Doc Casey taking care of me & gave it to me all at once.

By this time you "Three" should be well acclimated to the Midwest climate—Susie over her cold, Steve had his "shot" and by this time cut all of his teeth—walking, & asking when Daddy is coming home. The latter question of course is one which can't be answered in any other way than He would very much like to think now but can't since the job is [not] done as yet.

Thinking about you "Three" being so far away hurts terrifically Sweet—but knowing that I have you "my One & Only" and two sweet youngsters, which you have given me waiting for me helps much & is a great consolation. I love you very deeply & always have and always will—tho at times have had odd ways of showing it.

With all my love

Always

Al & Dada

A.F Herney.

March 14 March Letter No 8 [9]

My Dearest Sweet, Susie & Steve:

Received Febr No 7 & 9 plus a short note enclosing some pictures of "Our" two (is this No 6?) youngsters plus Mar No 1 today and was it nice to receive them tho part of the news wasn't at all pleasant which I'll mention later.

Have wondered why you hadn't mentioned more about Jerry & Elmer in your last letters but guess that it is understandable since you yourself were in such a dither. It will be nice if they do have one. Will drop them a shot note soon & wish them a lot of luck.

The news about Fran [Ayres] is a bit disheartening & as far as Alice [Quiggle-Ayres] will be hard to take, the news coming the way it did however is, if true, much easier than having the news handed you from or by the dept. I do believe that it is very possible that the report might be true but that someone slipped in not getting the news to the family before the letter from the friend arrived. It is my understanding that personal letters regarding the death may be written by commanding officer or friend but only after it is reasonably certain that the Dept has done its duty. Will write them a letter soon—however can't be certain that she is a widow & Johnie a youngster without a dad—but will have to take that chance.

As far as your taking on the "Nurses Aid"—mm—no objection Sweet except that for your own sake you might have waited for a bit to see how you were going to recuperate from the problems you've had to face in the last six months & recovered from it all. However I'm sure as in all things you will do a good job of it and make every minute count. You have my consent & blessing "Sweet" & want you to know that I'm quite proud of you to think that every minute is not spent in doing or thinking of your own enjoyment. More power to you.—

Most of the pictures are very excellent for indoor pictures—time exposures—to be correct. Very glad there was one of "Mommy" included in this group. Is Steve interested or disgusted in the picture in which Susie is holding his hand? Of course he doesn't seem to be at all taken by Susie reading to him does he?

From the picture of "Steve" alone I don't see how anyone gets the idea that I passed on any of my features. Sure as all he is another Charleson ——— Ho hum—still I'll claim him. Fortunate I'm so far away what?—Only kidding as you well know.

Herney accomplished something more for himself today—viz—two teeth filled—one was a toughey & very likely if I hadn't had the work done now, would have lost it & meant another bridge which I want no part of it I can help it.

Getting back to the pictures just who is that lovely little lady sitting on the table near her Daddy's picture & some flowers? Quite a nice little Girl & her Dad's "Pride & Joy." However she is going [to] be a very good little girl for her Daddy & help her "Mommie" with "Baby Steve" because Daddy isn't there to do it.—

Very happy to think that its you describing the snow for while its warm here & you perspire no end. I've had all the snow for a steady diet that I want for some time to come.

Sweet the rest of the letter respecting Fran, is heartening and just in-dicates further what a grand gal you are & I'm sure that should something happened to me you'd go on being the same person—a big person capable & willing to meet all of the problems that "The Final Determiner of all the Facts" decreed should present themselves. So far he has been good, especially to me, & I'm sure that he would not have made me so happy and content with you & the youngsters only to cut short that enjoyment & responsibility of aiding in their education. However should he decide to do so I too "my Sweet" am very grateful for what he have had. Am sure that both Dad & Mother are on our side & will be a big help to see that "Their" youngsters will return to his family & fireside for they can't be any place but with him.

Since this has been a long day must be on my way to sack drill—Pleasant dreams Sweetheart—with all my love always to the three of you—

Al & Dada

A.F Herney

March 15 Letter No 9 [10] March

My Dearest Sweet, Susie, Steve & Folks:

Received your No 2 for March—odd that it was dated the 4th & postmarked the 6th—just who was carrying it around? Also received some more birthday cards—one from Marie & Doc Aunt Emm & Marie Burri & a nice letter from Mr Davis a client.

You didn't mention in your letter whether or not Alice [Quiggle Ayers] had received any word of confirmation from the Dept. but assume that she had. It is hard for her I know & very difficult for anyone to either console or take the sting out of news such as she has received. War & life itself is like that and something we always must remember.

Would have enjoyed seeing Dad taking care of the one and only Susie—don't loose patience with him for both Dad & Mother have been sometime without the problem of children in the house. Don't think it quite fair to have been so bold as to tell him that he was spoiled. We all enjoy being spoiled & it isn't nice to be told about it & know that you could very easily spoil me as you would have a willing subject.

Had forgotten all about the income tax—don't believe that we owe Uncle anything for this past year—should you find out that a return has to be made let W. C & R take care of it—write details to Marie & I'm sure she will try to find time to get the matter to them.—

Can't understand why you should have had any trouble buying white shoes at this time of year—except that everybody might be optimistic that that summer will eventually get here or there.

The practice baths sound interesting. The gal that quit must have been a lulu. What did she expect the prospective patients to do—walk in & take a shower. Speaking of back rubs would willingly be a subject anytime anyone wanted to practice.

Can't quite understand why you haven't received any mail since that one dated Febr 12—had hoped the mail was come thru right regular but believe that you have received the mail by this time. Post offices at times are few and far between but don't worry if they are for there isn't much to do about it but remember that I love you much & am thinking of you always.

The stories about the prisoners of the Phil's are depressing aren't they— We would have to degenerate to a great extent to knowingly allow humans to be gradually broken down by dietiary, unhealthful conditions when they are to be given certain rights under the "Articles". However we must remember that we too have conditions comparable in our own land with respect to some of our own, maybe not as pronounced but still a disregard of their basic needs—some of the cause however being their own indolence.

Sorry that Dad hasn't been getting his Time as he should—maybe it will help if he knows mine is very sporadic too—but when I do get an issue I enjoy it.

Wrote the Reeds a Xmas note. Haven't received any word from them as to whether they had received it. Do guess the "It" will be along soon & then will Pa & Ma be busy huh?

With all my love Always to you "My Sweet" & to our "Two" & yep will include Dad & Mother this time too.

Easter is close.so am enclosing $10.00 five for a gift for you from S & S & five for a gift for M & D—You of course will have to do the buying.
Love Al
A.F Herney

P.S. Don't know whether I'll get to services on Easter but I can assure you I'll be praying mighty hard for this thing to end. Happy Easer Sweetheart.
Love Al

16 March Letter No 10 [11] March
My Dearest Sweet Susie & Steve:

Either <u>If</u> I've fooled myself—or I've written a few letters to you myself already this month. However when you do get a chance for a note & possibly of getting I mailed you just hate to miss the chance for there always are dry spells.

The mailman brought me nothing at all today and as yet have not seen a package. Incidently Gosch received a Xmas package this week, a book, & you should have seen it. Looked like it had been in the drink. Really don't know if he plans on reading it.

Wonder, tho didn't mention it before just how Steve took his second shot he was to get? If he didn't like it guess Mother, his, didn't get a whole lot of sleep. As for more teeth he has to eventually have them so why not now. Put it down to experience in Nurses Aid.

Seems like Mommie will use a bit of that fat or that weight that Susie is putting on. However do guess that she can use a little too since she is growing into a young lady & must store up a bit for when she starts shooting up.

Did I mention in any of my last few letters that I received a nice birthday letter from Aunt Clyde? If not tell her I did receive it & thank her for it—interesting too for she mentioned my family. Would write now but so much to do.

The movies for the last few evenings, held on the forecastle, have been interrupted by short rain squalls. Interludes of a few minutes—dog gone interesting to say the least. Those not from Calif claim that the rainy part of the climate is just like Calif.—Ho hum. However it is, the show, about the only diversion one has except & when there is an officers club available. Did get to one last week and your old man had straight Coke's Sweet nothing more or less, tho a bottle of beer would have tasted plenty of good.

We officers as well as the enlisted men would love to tell you all about what we were doing or plan on doing but since these "Censors" say no- no

& will cut it doesn't make sense to write it only to have it deleted. However could we do so know that our letters might be very interesting to all of you. Tried as hard as we can sometimes incapable of writing a newsy letter without passing on what you've done or are to do. Of course, we can write "I love you" for several pages & its nice to hear but you would soon get tired of that very soon.

Word has it that we might get paid tomorrow—do hope so I'm getting a bit low but can get by it necessary. Have [not] had any pay since the middle of Jan but there really hasn't been anything to spend it on.

Since it is already the start of a new day must leave Sweetheart—
With all my love to the Three of you Always
Al & Dada
A.F Herney

March 17 Letter No 11 [12] March
My Dearest Sweet Susie & Steve:

Received your no ten for Febr—odd but somehow letters do just get mixed up—delays somewhere or may [be] the mailman didn't know where it send it—mm but somehow they eventually get to us.

Had hoped that the mailman would soon bring me some of the popcorn but as yet no[t] much luck. Do guess maybe they will be here by next Xmas but can't see how they can make it by that time. If Gosch's book is one of the possibilities maybe the corn will have sprouted and died by the time it gets here. Will continue to hope however.

The food problem has been pretty decent. Had a change of cooks and for a while now haven't had tomato sauce on everything. Our diet in general mess has been supplemented by a few 'extras' that were purchased when we were in Pearl. Does help a good bit to say the least. Still however I will be very glad when this month is over and the three months as Mess Treasurer has expired.

The man with the money bags came around today & paid off to the first of March. Took out for chow so the slate is clean again up to the 1st of this month. Had $72 on the books so drew the seventy leaving the books with $2 due. Since he took the pay accounts with him can't check to see whether or not the allotment has been registered but believe it will be for they said it could & would be done. Will check when the record comes back aboard. Considering all in all must also have been paid on the basis of J.G. from Febr 1.

Expect to get to mass tomorrow morning as I understand that services will be held. How many of the flock will go depends on them. Guess the usuals will be there wince it is so close to Easter. However transportation is always a problem & one whaleboat never seems to be enuf for all the trips that seem necessary.

Putting on clean clothes seems so useless for one no sooner gets them on than they look like you've worn them a month. However it is very possible that you aren't so offensive to yourself or others.

Some of the officers have gone on Beach Parties with some of the crew—only recreation however is swimming & baseball plus of course some beer which is enjoyed. Have brot back some cocanuts, seashells as what's in them—would like to go but have too much to do. No natives of course for good reason—

With love to my Three S's always & to Dad & Mother

Al & Dada

A.F Herney

Dear Sweet:

Just so you'll know that I was thinking of you & that your Old Man can't at times keep straight just where his family is located am sending you the whole thing.

Do wonder if the mailman wonders what was wrong with the poor dope when he was addressing the letter—well anyway I wrote is there.

My love always to the "Three"—

Al.

P.S. Am not counting this as a letter—this sheet I mean

Al

19 March 45 March Letter No 13

My Dearest Sweet, Susie Steve Dad & Mother:

Didn't think I would be able to secure a money order but since it can be done will be an extra early bird about three dates & events I don't & can't forget. Am enclosing a $50.00 money order with the following instructions:

(1) purchase a war bond $17.50 for Steve (2) purchase a war bond $17.50 for Susie; these you will purchase on each of their birthdays if at all possible and (3) the remaining $15.00 is for an anniversary gift for yourself. Am sending this now since I have the chance & want to be extra sure it will have been accomplished. (Nice long para. Huh?) The letters for each one of the occasions will arrive in due time so don't worry about my wanting to be early.

One of your recent letters amused me a great deal—the one in which you mentioned reading about Iwo Jima remember? Well Sweet we were there—little as we were doing what we could to see that things were all safe and sound.

After leaving Pearl had a few days at Eniwetok & one hell of a lot of work both leg via boat and paper work for me. From Eniwetok had another leg to Saipan & Tinian & how I wanted to get ashore to see if I couldn't find Bill—but again more work.—From Saipan hit for the objective—an early bird as far as the actual assault was concerned.

We started off with a bang—Dog minus 3 by sweeping the areas off the west beaches. Really seemed like we were on a rehearsal.—The little stinkers evidently felt we were too small a fry to sacrifice a possible disclosure of their locations. Some peashooters decided at the end of the day to see if they could reach us—however no hits, no runs & all errors.

The birthday Day minus 1 [February 17] was spent also in making sure that other units coming to the objective would be safe. Swept off the northeastern beach. This time some of the bigger boys thought they would take a try at it but again no runs no hits and all errors. They finally decided to give it up as a bad job.—

Am relating this "My Sweet" to let you know that it isn't too tough and to dispel any worry that you may have. Weve been thru it and all safe & hearty.

Can't for the life of me realize that the Japs could do such a complete job of digging in—How there was anything left of that island after the beating it took is amazing.

On D day when the hour for the assault to be made arrived your old man experienced an unexplainable emotion—knowing that the "Boys" were going in some to remain, others to return in part torn by the ravages of war & others to be successful & vindicate their faith in Democracy. Guts it takes & much of it, tho it's a crude expression to use but still a very descriptive one. They had the job to do & were doing it as was everyone else. It is difficult to be standing off realizing that this was no rehearsal an actual problem being worked out but the <u>thing</u> and lots of it. Old Glory on Mt. Sirabachi and the control of Iwo and what it will mean to helping make Tojo & his pals call it quits, lets hope, is a vindication of all that those who suffered in taking it, gave to bring it & the enemy on it into subjugation. Its getting mighty close to the Rising sun which should soon be sinking and sinking fast.

NEXT MORNING

The letter Sweet was interrupted so will have to complete it now. The pay records are back aboard—got a chance to look at mine—the allotment has been registered the final deduction to be made in April so the increase will be shown on the check which you receive in May.—Noted also that my increase started as of Febr 1 so that's a big load off my mind. At least someone, the pay clerk, is on the ball.

Evidently the cig. shortage is as bad as ever. Sorry I can't send you some but that just aint possible. However I'll make a deal with you—I'll quit if you will & I can assure you that it's going to be a lot tougher on me than it will be on you. Know that to quit will be good for both of us & the only reason I'm suggesting it.

Again Sweet want you to know that the only reason I've written the part about Iwo is to relieve your mind & of course realize you have been interested in what I've been doing. Don't worry but you & Susie can say an extra prayer just in case it may be needed.

With all my love always to "My Three S's"

Al & Dada

A. F. Herney

March 29 Letter No 12 [14] March
My Dearest Sweet, Susie, Steve Dad & Mother:

Am really ashamed of myself that ten days have elapsed since my last letter. It is now only 8:15 PM but I'm dog tired and doubt if I'll even be able to say I've been completed rested so don't believe this letter will be very long.

On checking my calendar discovered I had missed <u>twelve</u> in my count so as not to have you wonder what had happened to that letter will go back and pick up that number.

The last three days have been the kind, if at home, one would have the urge to get good and stinko but didn't because you were too tired. Sixteen hours gets to be pretty much of a day without much time to relax,—horizontally— that is, so when nite time arrives you bounce into the sack and are soon in a disturbed sleep. However what has been the cause of all this is a new experience and wouldn't care to say that it hasn't been good for me in some way at least.

It won't be long till I will have left my Three Sweethearts six months. Has seemed ages and I'm sure that its been as long for you as it has for me—even tho you have been busy too—and with many more problems than I've had.

Since I haven't written you you can rest assured that no one else has received any correspondence from me & speaking about correspondence will not mention anything that might have arrived since the 19th for we too have received no mail. Do hope tho that that time will come soon.

Would like very much to have one of your special back rubs for surly by this time you must be an extra specialist at it. May I drop in soon for one? Yep would be sure to have taken a shower first before dropping in.

Have been wondering if Dad has had any more experience regarding putting his granddaughter to bed—however don't let it get to be a habit for he might miss Susie too much when you return to Chula.

Just three days away from Easter. It will seem rather odd to be in the position not to be able to attend services but suppose if circumstances permit will join with my Flock. Hope you will be able to go & say a special prayer for me—

Hope you have received my letters written this month—for one of them was my Easter letter to you.

With all my love to you "Three" as always & to Dad & Mother.

Al & Dada

Give the youngsters an extra hug for me.

AF Herney

Friday March 30 March Letter No 14 [15]

My Dearest Sweet Susie & Steve:

Will surprise you by writing again today—possibly this and the note written last night together will pass for a letter.

After writing you last nite took a shower, grabbed an old Time read one column & had to turn of[f] the light for that is all I could take—know that you would be appreciative of that if I were at home.

Here it is Good Friday—planned on having Services early in the evening but most of the men preferred waiting until after the movie—which is so much of a stinker that I left soon after it started—so will met with them then. Would have preferred doing it sooner so the sack drill would be of a reasonable length of time. Sack drill seems even more fundamental than eating if you can imagine that.

From all repots Iwo is secured & all resistance crushed. I'm wondering if History will say that it was worth what we paid for it in casualties? Do hope so for if it isn't someone has made an awful error. However it is certain that Japan has felt the full sting of its ignominious acts and will continually be reminded of her misconduct. Germany too is well on its way to disastrous defeat and possibly soon no longer an enemy to be considered. The news from that front is very good.

The weather there by this time must be such that you realize spring is here—Would give much to see some of the native foliage of the U.S.—one soon gets tired of Atools (?) or volcanic masses which have been occupied by the little yellow stinkers & which we now consider militarily important. Of course any green thing looks attractive after a few days at sea.

Was wondering if my family were going to be all decked out for Easter and go strutting—Do know that they will be a picture and would so much like to see them. Our last one was pleasant & I remember how the Pride & Joy did well in posing for several pictures—but she did get tired of it & decided she wanted a bit of exercise. Do hope you take some pictures this year & will send them along to me.

Do hope that you received my letters with the Easter Contribution for you & Mother & Dad. Very possibly however it was delayed as there was a possibility of it.

Knowing that you miss me as much as I miss you—With all my love to the three of you as always Al & Dada
A.F Herney—

7

OKINAWA AND BEYOND

April 1945
[The invasion of Okinawa began April 1, Easter Sunday, 1945]

3 April April Letter No 1
My Dearest Sweet Susie & Steve:

Here it is two days after Easter—the time however will not pass soon enuf so that it will no longer be necessary to count the time I've been away from you.

The plans to write you a short note daily just had to be forgotten for when the end of the day came I was just too tired.

Easter was spent in a manner very much different than any I've spent before—of course the routine as far as service life is concerned—was so busy all day that any thought of Services were forgotten. However I'm sure that the Almighty will forgive each of us for not having spent the day in his way.

If I'm wrong about that he will let us know in good time but we can only wish for the best.

Both Carl S. & Dutch should be in the area but just where & what chance I will have of seeing them is another questions. It is tough to know they are around and not be able to look them up. Hope they will keep their eyes open for me. Haven't heard from Carl since my last letter which I mentioned to you.

It is tough to be without mail again for there must be some for us some-place but where it is the questions. Would like to find the guy with the an-swer. Mail means so much as that is the only thing that helps the morale when it's low and it is so good to be on the receiving end.

Haven't had the ambition to drop any of the Phi Mu's a note for their let-ters & cards but must do so—However think I'll make it a joint letter & send it to Beth for the group. Hope they don't mind.

Thank goodness the job of Mess Treasurer is over & will no longer be the recipient of the growls about the chow and the personnel problems that went with it—Why don't you do this that—suggest you tell the boys to do this or that.

Corrected the Progress tests of Arnold—Steward mate 3rd class who wishes hopes & prays for a 2nd class rating. Both Gosch & myself had stomach aches for laughing—a sample—"Soups are one of two main types (a) with water and (b) with out it." The correct answer being stock. Both Gosch & myself wondered if there could be soup if you didn't use water. Arnolds spelling generally is phoenetic—however when answering twelve true & false question he spelt false five different ways & all incorrectly—as follows faul, fauls, falus, fauls and faus.

Really a pretty good job—Another—a completion question "Moisture in the air is called " yes ". "Water glasses should be filled with water". "Ser-vice of food should always be from the out side." Am keeping the papers so as to go over them again when the need for a laugh. Incidently his grade was 1.4 Told him today he hadn't done too well & he looked a bit unhappy.

It was quite warm today. Could really acquire a tan if one were permitted to have the shirt off while on the bridge but that just aint in the cards. The evenings however are a bit chilly & a jacket is useful.

Wonder if our tenants are enjoying the old homestead as much as I'd en-joy it and have enjoyed it. Certainly they could be comfortable there & at least get the enjoyment of a house for a while even tho they don't know just how long it will be that they can stay.

Since I've had no mail for such a long time really out of touch with any of the family & know none of the latest news—all of which makes it tough to write a letter that is half way interesting that at least you are glad to know that I'm well & safe & love you a great deal.

Must take a shower and be off for some sack drill—With all my love to the Three of you as Always—

Al & Dada

AF Herney

April 4 April Letter No 2

My Dearest Sweet, Susie & Steve:

Now that most of the days duties are over must get another note off to you for possibly the mail man will pick these up tomorrow and send them on there way to you. I do hope so for you haven't had any letters sine I've had any & that is a long time.

Since I don't know how soon this will reach you will say now that the old man is so low on funds—enuf to get by on—that you will have to take care of "Mother's Day" for yourself & Mother. Didn't want you to think that I had or would forget it but unless pay day arrives before then, which I understand it won't there will be nothing from me. Possibly I was a bit premature in sending the $50 money order but didn't under any circumstances be in a position where I couldn't take care of those three days.

From information received today it will be about another week before we are to get any mail. Somehow things got fouled up a bit—can't understand it for operations should have been able to give the Post Office what info was necessary. Maybe he forgot to ask huh?

Saw a movie tonight in the mess hall—Background to Danger—had seen it before for the life of me can't remember where or when—However it was a bit of a diversion and it didn't hurt any—exciting as usual and Raft is good.

By this time you should be a full fledged aid—an expert at giving baths—backrubs. It has just occurred to me to wonder if your prospective patients are to be of a variety she-males & hemales or only the former. If both will remind you about the bed pan story—just a tip & hope you will act accordingly.

Really if all of the time expended by waiting were capable of being profitably utilized this war would & would be over in short order—but then there is that criticism to make of civilian life also—so will just put it down to the debit side of the ledger and leave it go at that.

Haven't written Alice as yet but hope to do so soon. Would like to know however if she had gotten confirmation from the Dept for it would look silly writing about Fran in the past tense.

Seem always to write long paragraphs about how much I love you my Sweet—seem to take it for granted that you know—however I do remember how you enjoyed being told and can't blame you. However always bear in mind that you've always been the only one and always will be. With my ever-lasting love to the three of you as Always

Al & Dada

AF Herney

Sunday nite April 8 April Letter No 3

My Dearest Sweet, Susie, Steve, Mother & Dad:

I do hope that you have fared better with the mailman than I have for it not you haven't received any mail since the 19th of last month which means better than three weeks—however prospects appear a bit better & possibly we will get some very soon.

Have been terribly homesick for the past week—really give one hell of a lot to have this thing over & be back home with my family. How long it will take and what the final cost will be one can only conjecture but we do appear to be on the upswing and definitely on the offensive.

Post me please on Uncle Jim [Farnham] for if this lasts much longer he will surely be out here. Would at last like to know the ship to which he has been assigned.

Still hoping to get to see either Dutch or Carl or both. Not sure however that they are still here or not but then it doesn't take a whole lot to be out of touch with what is what & when you have our job to do & you do it—squacking doesn't seem to help either.

The weather hasn't been too pleasant topside for the past few days so have been below doing some paper work. Never seems to be finished & never will, tho you'd think that the time would come when you could say—all done.

Saw the "Ghost of Canterbury" with Laughton this afternoon—did enjoy it—Laughton of course was his usual self & gave forth. The young lady wasn't bad either.

Speaking of young ladies how is the Pride & Joy. Of course she is still Grandma's helper and assisting caring for Steve, mostly from the entertainment angle. I am sure she is being very good for her Daddy who misses her very much.

Here it is almost two months since you have been at Lincoln. Am grateful to be kept busy for time passes much quicker that way. Do hope that the two months you've lived with Dad & Mother haven't been too much for them & that they are sorry that they asked you to visit them especially for such a long stay.

Your increased allotment should reach you in May for the deduction was to be made in April. Know that you will be just as careful about the funds with the allotment of $200 as you were at $122—Sweetheart I have one heck of a lot of faith in you and love you equally as much.

With my love always to the three of you

Al & Dada

AF Herney

———

[A letter from Al's uncle Albert Caughey.]

April 10, 1945 2111 Swift, Houston 5 Texas

My dear Albert:

We learn from Hugh [Caughey, Al's cousin, son of Aunt Julia and Uncle Albert Caughey] that he will be executive officer on L.S.T. 1073. Amanda [Hugh's wife] and baby are now with Hugh in Boston. The L.S.T. will leave Boston late this month. Our nephew Donald Caughey, my Brother Rudolph's son is chaplain on the Nutrona, a transport ship. You might run across him.

After six weeks in the hospital following an operation, am back in Charles' home...It was a serious operation for a man of 74 in my condition but I pulled through all right. It will take some time yet for me to regain weight and strength.

Then the next thing will be to dispose of our chattels in Atwood bringing to Texas what we want to keep. Then we hope to go to San Diego to see whether I can be useful to either your sister Marie or to the McAllisters [Al's sister Julia and her husband, Mac].

When an operation was agreed upon, Hugh was in Norfolk where they train for amphibious warfare. He came to Houston, Amanda & baby came from Sulphur Springs…[Uncle Albert describes the operation and his recovery in detail.]

Your brother George forwards your letters to us, so we won't be disappointed if we do not hear from you directly. We know what it is to have a long list of people to whom you think you ought to write and how little time & facilities you may have for writing.

Love from Aunt Julia & Uncle Albert [Caughey]

April 15 April Letter No 4

My Dearest Sweet, Susie, Steve, Mother & Dad:

The mailman at last came thru on the 12th with personal mail— March letters 3 thru 11 with the exception of #5—which seems to have gone astray somewhere. Also received two letters from Marie, one with the Certificate for claiming Tax Exemption & one from Sweetie Pie & George.

Correspondence from this end has fallen off terribly this month—here half the month is already gone and this is only the 4th letter—Shame on me.

So the little feller finally got his shot which Mommie had tried to get for him. Can't blame him being upset about it especially when they give it to him in the leg. From the way he is gaining at cutting teeth it won't be long before he will be a little Feller no longer. You had better start training him now or you won't be having any peace when you do get back home—for your going to have to leave some time for I'm.

Glad you are having the pleasure of the Phi Mu group in Lincoln—it can't however be anything like the S.D group with the Auxiliary. Really to miss those periodic parties.

So Susie Q hasn't forgotten her Pop—Sweet of her to throw the kiss my way and would give a lot to have been there and said "Hi" to her & her Mommie. Sorry that Mother has such a bad time when Paula & Susie decided to cut up. It is good for Susie to have other youngsters to play with & I suppose picking up little tricks are part of growing up so will have to take them in our stride. Ho hum.

The itemized account of the cost of clothes for the youngsters causes one to wonder if they are just youngsters. However the picture indicates that the purchases are becoming—and don't mind your expending the funds. What did Mommie get besides a new hat—for she shouldn't have neglected herself. Sorry I couldn't have been there to parade the family around. Better luck next time.

Marie wrote that Ruths [Al's sister-in-law, wife of Francis] father has passed away. It really is a blessing for he was in such a condition that he was almost helpless. However it is hard to know that our dear ones are no more. Must drop her a note.

We like everyone else here much shocked by the news of R's [FDR] death. While we all were not in accord with everything that he did it is unfortunate that his time was up at this stage when a foreign policy was past the formulated stage but well on its way to being carried out; The S.F. conference will bear some fruit.—Can only hope for the best.

In one of my last letters I mentioned something about your prospective patients. They would put you in the ward with the old men. Did enjoy the story about [the] vase. The recommendation about the bed pan still goes & is something to remember. Am very happy that your interest hasn't weakened but please take care of yourself & don't overdo anything. Yep remember your still a Mommie & you have two youngsters entrusted to your sole care until Daddy gets back to help take over.

Dot and the children, Easter Sunday, April 1, 1945.

Sorry that Alice [Quiggle Ayres] has finally gotten confirmation on Fran's death. It must have been very difficult waiting and yet while waiting there was still hope. Will drop her a note also—however it is difficult to write since I really didn't know him well enuf to say what one should say when trying to put on paper those things which mean so much.

By this time you should have received the letter about which Dad seems so interested. Really isn't much that I was able to tell & the reports you've already received are much more complete & far more descriptive than anything I am capable of giving you.

Havent commented on all of your letters as will take a few at a time so that I will have something for the next letter or two.

With all my love to the three of you as always

Lovingly—Al

A.F Herney.

April 18 1945 April Letter No 5

My Dearest Sweet, Susie, Steve Mother & Dad:

To take up where I left off in answering questions & comments in letter No 4.

Susan's visit with Ann did contribute to Susie's education of growing up—certainly one doesn't get dirt dished on hair face body & "Apple" very often, of course the apple was extra special.

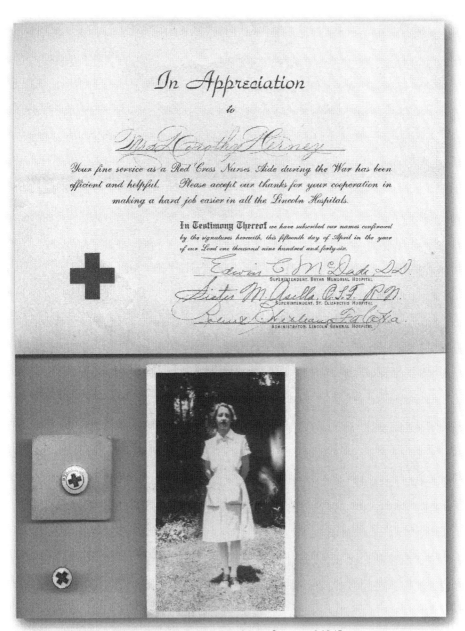

Dot in her Red Cross nurse aide's uniform, April 1945.

Should congratulate you on getting your cap and pin. It is definitely good that you have some interest other than yourself & youngsters for the busier you are the sooner you will be having the time pass for you.—You & Evelyn evidently make a good pair. She sounds like nice people.

Sorry to hear that you are having the tummy aches again for they are anything but pleasant. You can say again you are glad that another junior is not contributing.

To fulfill Susie's wish that she wanted her Daddy to come home should be passed on to the Navy Dept for even tho the El Capt. wanted to satisfy the wish won't be enuf.—Give her an extra special for me for wanting me home.—Sometime tho huh? Sorry to hear that Susie is back on the sprinkler detail. Don't know but what your attempted cure "Bribes" and Punishment aren't a bit inconsistent. However since I'm here & you're there you will have to do what you think best.

The reports of your reaction to "Have or Have Not" and the "Artists" portrayal of their respective parts plus what Time & Newsweek have given Bacall point to a hot time in the old town tonight. Don't think Sweetheart that I couldn't go for some of that too—loving of course—but not or with "Bacall".

So glad that our radio has been repaired even to the tune of $20.03. It would seem that we have some good tenants for which we can be grateful. If Mac & Asa did fix the roof (don't remember) they must have caught the leaks.

Marie wrote that several of the chaps—"Atherton" among them were to go up for physicals early in March—Replacements are needed & the big boys like everyone else want to get the thing over with in a hurry. Please God, in a great big hurry.—Maybe Paul [Allyn] will be lucky & not get took—if he does however think the Navy will be the best bet.—Palma has a good bit of nerve thinking of another however she may be thinking that if Paul is taken it will be too damn late when he does get home. Give them both my very best regards.

Don't worry about Steve being slow—won't be disappointed if he isn't walking talking & have all of his teeth by the time he is <u>one</u>. From experience with the "Pride & Joy" hate to think of them both growing so fast and without being there to enjoy seeing them grow.

In case you don't remember it had been over a year since I had visited a dentist. Had one cavity—old filling which had to be removed & replaced & another new small cavity. Otherwise O.K. Must go back to have the temporary—small cavity filled & the other shined as didn't have time to do that before.

Still haven't received any of the boxes that were sent. Can imagine it is a question of space & can well realize what they will be like when they get here.—Hope the corn has sprouted & I'll find ears of corn—which when shelled will provide pop-corn far in excess of what you sent.

Susie has inherited her father's musical ability for sure. However, what the tune, it <u>ain't</u> so important, but the thought—that is the thing.

Your first day as an 'aid' will be one to remember. Make some good mental notes and give them to me later or when Papa comes home. However Sweet, as you already know, I don't want you to overdo it & should you find it too much <u>give up</u> and you won't be a quitter either for you have yourself—the youngsters & your husband to consider.

Was much tickled by the closing paragraph of letter of 20 March if "Mama" is doing OK but could use her Sweetie—well we won't go into that! Am glad that I'm not the only one that misses some.—Ho hum! Do love you so very much Sweetheart.

With love always to the Three of you.

Al & Dada

A.F Herney

April 19 April letter No 6

My Dearest Sweet, Susie & Steve:

Since I didn't think there would be the opportunity to get mail off to you today didn't write last night—was wrong for which I am now sorry. Must also ask you to overlook parts of my last letter—huh?

The mailman seems to be having a hard time. Did have our mail here at one time—but since he hadn't been advised, yes we have properly damned the guy who should have taken care of that, that we were present he sent our mail elsewhere. It is however to be returned soon—quick we hope.

Saw the oddest sunset the other evening. Old Sol at one moment was a perfect circle of rich orange—the next just the lower portion behind the horizon & soon appeared to be as if poured into the sea—gave the appearance of a red lacquered tea cup upside down & soon was lost to sight.—Something close to amazing to say the least.

This afternoon had a spell of rain—came down as I remember the <u>dew</u> of the Midwest. So solid that visibility was nil or less if that were possible. Such a shame too that all of it could not be caught and stored for water is still & I suppose always will be a problem. Fortunately it didn't last too long. Possibly the sea will not be so salty now since some fresh clean water has been added.

Had hoped that I could get a permanent filling in place of the temporary and the other shinned up—however that may not be possible this time & will have to wait. Thank goodness neither are bothering me at all. Incidently the Dr who did the work was from Miami & he was so busy didn't have the opportunity to ask if he knew Mel Ruliands.

Have you found a "tri" for Susie as yet? With the luck you've had finding the play pen for Steve you should have by this time. Is he still active when in it or did he give up in disgust. I can well remember how Susie did enjoy hers. At times I hate to think of the youngsters growing up for while they are a problem they are well worth the trouble.

The calendar would indicate that Mother's Day falls on the 13th of May this year. Another event that won't find Papa at home to help Mommie celebrate but can only hope there will be others in the future. Will write you a special letter which I will write later, A letter to Mother, too.

The latest word on the war in Germany sounds encouraging. It would appear however that since the West wall has been passed & things look hopeless for the Germans they would prefer the boys from the West to get to Berlin first for the Russians have the answer, maybe not the right answer as what to do with Germany especially those who have much to account for. With Germany gone what a concentration of force could be fixed on Japan. They we could all get home.

With all my love to you Three as always

Al & Dada

A.F Herney

April 20, 1945

My Dearest Sweet, Susie and Steve & Dad & Mother:

The mail man was generous today for he brot me your 12 & 13 for March & 3&4 for April—the latter written the 9th & mailed the 10th. Not bad going.

So glad you have finally received more mail from me—what are you missing. The Febr No 9 as I recollect is the one which I misaddressed to Lincoln Calif was it not? Don't recollect having written you such a wonderful letter about Iwo but happy it was received with that feeling. To add a few more lines on your map—cutting across islands being immaterial if that helps any—you can add a line back from Iwo to Saipan—and then on to Ulithi in the Carolines. Of the two places the latter is preferable for Ulithi like Eniwetok is an atoll—which however differs in that you have palms on the small Islands.

Enjoyed getting the snap of Dad & the Pride & Joy waving to her Dad. Can't say I would enjoy the snow as much as Susie but could take most anything if I could have my family.

Received a letter from Marie, Sweetie Pie & Uncle George along with your letters. Incidently Marie said that improvements at [cabins on Mount] Palomar were waiting for my return and assistance. I too Sweet could take a bit of relaxation at Palomar with you & be more than content just to sit.

Was much amused, again, at you regarding the tenants. You did what I would have done had I been in your place including of course not going home should Dad & Mother want you to remain for a bit longer.

From the description of Steves demanding way & hollering if he doesn't get it Mother's name is quite appropriate. I might add that Mothers supposition and your analysis are both correct. Surely both Steve and his Mommie are glad that the shots are now a matter of the past. Don't you remember my saying that you shouldn't push him for he needn't have all of his teeth before he is a year old.

Don't worry about me & finances. Still have a bit from last payday & since we haven't been paid for March or April should have a bit on the books. Really with no bars, taverns, or <u>women</u> to help one spend what we have be it ever so little, one doesn't need much. However as I said before did want to make sure the <u>days</u> would not be forgotten.

Am not worrying about you ruining the bank account & very happy you purchased some clothes for yourself for I did ask you in one of the previous letters if you weren't going to buy some. Also pleased that you participated in the purchase of the new rug & wouldn't have complained if you had gone for it all.

Did realize that the pictures were taken of the flowers sent for Valentines Day. As for the Orchids think I have the answer & should have realized that possibly it would not have been feasible. We are a mobile unit and sending them would indicate our location. Will write Joe and ask him to check on it however.

Have finally written Alice a short note. Not very proud of it but as I've said before it is difficult to write such a note when I knew him so little. Possibly getting back into her old line of work may be the answer to her problem tho I do think she has a matter to take into consideration before she decided to definitely do it.

Maybe you had better resign yourself to the fact that Susie may have her mother's love of music but her Dad's ability—She does try so let's give her the benefit & hope for the best. I'm sure that Mommie & Susie were very much admired. Incidently Sweet, the lady was not far wrong, and I will add that she might have said that much oftener for you have always been properly attired & looked plenty good to me & always.

So Susan has attended her first movie—or was it her first? Your selection was a good one—won't suggest Dracula or anything of like nature for the next one tho. You might tell her Daddy feels bad when she says "No" when the answer should be "yes"—the "no" should come later when she grows up.

Your experiences on the maternity ward and—sounds like your really interested—now possibly you can fully appreciate what you've had when you accepted the responsibility of making both of our two youngsters possible. Thank you Sweet for both of them and I love you a great deal for both of them.

My love to the Three of you as always.

Al & Dada

AF Herney

April 21 April Letter No 7

My Dearest Sweet Susie & Steve:

Since the opportunity of mailing this may present itself do want it ready.—Don't believe I numbered the letter of April 20—but it was to have been No 6.

Just had a shower & feel clean again for a little while anyway. It however is a matter of taking one when the circumstances are the most favorable. Are to have a show later on this evening & contemplate attending. Really the only relaxation we have now. Didn't tell you this before I don't believe but the electrician who operates the gear wanted to improve it so while trying did more damage than improvement & now occasionally the thing starts jumping so that by the end of the film your head continues the motion—up & down. Sure is a thrill.

Ran into Tom Hamilton today—don't believe you ever met him—an atty from S.D. who had his commission before Pearl Harbor & was called in. Also have seem Harms who was at Tucson when Carl I were there—you remember Mrs. Harms don't you? Harms has been out here since shipping out soon after our release from Bean Town & expected to be going home soon. Can't really blame him if he has been out here that long.

Susie's Bunny Benjamin sounds as if he is pretty much of visitor. I'm sure that he did bring "Easter Eggs" to Susie as he does to all good little girls.

I do remember the group did meet us in Petersburg one Xmas when Marie was in school. Remember Don & Dick but for the life of me don't remember Jean—besides that's been one long time ago—1928 in fact—I'm sure she will overlook the lapse of memory. You four must have had a good time—Wonder how many hands weren't interrupted by a lot of gabbing— would bet not many.

Snow so late in the year can do a lot to hold back the birds & bees— However do remember an Easter in Deshler [Nebraska] also in the dis- tant, distant past when the snow was so deep the drifts were higher than little me.

Thank God you didn't wonder if you would have made a good nurse when you were deciding what to do for if you had had its very possible that I would not have met you for its sure you wouldn't have come to Calif to attend S.C.—Now its too late for you have me and two youngsters to worry about.

Realize that weeks can seem long if the mailman decides not to show up with something in the bag for you. Guess we both suffer equally that way however.

Have been trying to catch a cold the last two days. Believe however I can avoid it—APC pills and a little of the sulpha nose drops should help.

Received a letter from the Mac's written by George. He passed on the information that Uncle A. had decided that he and Aunt J. would make their home in Houston where Charles has his home. Can't blame him for wanting to be there but it would have been nice having them in S.D.

With all my love always to the three of you—

Al & Dada

AF Herney

———

[A letter from family friend Walt Carrell.]

21 April 1945 Saturday—

Dear Al—

Gosh, time sure slips along. I intended to write on your birthday and here two months have gone by.

Mom sent me Dot's last letter and according to that you are number 1 rover boy of the Pacific Fleet. The good ship Scurry must be well command-ed. After all your recent navigating experience you're not apt to get lost going from a bar to the little boys room.

It sure feels good to be out of school and Texas. Am having a great time dusting of[f] my bars and getting out of the habit of being a dog-face. It's a big change and it was well worth the small effort exerted in those 17 weeks.

After ten days at home I came up here for a two weeks course in Infantry weapons. We fired on the range for a couple of days, and I qualified in everything we shot which makes me happy as I want to transfer to the Infantry.

Right now I'm in a training outfit as a platoon leader & instructor. The work is interesting and there is a good deal of field work involved.

Spring is almost here so the country is more beautiful than ever. The whole state is just like one big park.

Well, time to end this. Just wanted to drop you a note. Take care of yourself and lots of luck

As ever

Walt [Carrell]

———

April 25 1945 April Letter No 8

My Dearest Sweet, Susie, Steve, Mother & Dad:

The mailman has finally brot me the missing letters No 5 & 14 for March, latter containing a picture of my "Two Best Girls" shoveling snow and 1 & 2 for April. Still no packages as yet—much parcel post has been delayed somewhere—hope they can break down soon & deliver—Lot of the men aboard still have Xmas packages which are enroute.

Glad to hear that the Reeds have finally come thru. Know that they will be pleased that it was a girl & can enjoy her as much as we have Susan; Blythe however did have to do it the hard way didn't she. I've often wondered if Mother has forgotten the afternoon before Susie arrived. I haven't & doubt if I ever will.

Susie must have been a great big help with the cookies wanting to help & helping are two different things however but guess we will have to accept the as part of the growing pains. Can't remember about the shoe incident either—maybe we're getting forgetful in our old age huh?

When you get some word from Jerry & Elmer [Cawby] be sure to pass it along for I'll definitely be interested in knowing. Do hope they aren't to go wanting at this late date—all the effort & all wasted—would be a huge disappointment I'm sure.

If Steve is going to loose a small bit of his hair do you think he would mind passing it to his Dad so he can cover up a bit of the bald spots—or should I say to reduce the high forehead hair line?

Did miss not being with you for the Easter Holiday—the coloring of the eggs—hiding them and watching the youngun's enjoying finding them does recall the pleasant Easters of the past. I too thought of last year at Boston—yep we got pictures to prove it & what a lady—

Marie wrote that Ed had gotten Susan & Steve the music box. Just like him isn't it—can't say that he doesn't like them a little. Can well imagine your surprise by being called by the family.—From all reports they miss the three of you very much.

Thanks for enclosing the clipping on Walt—didn't doubt but what he would make it—now his problems are just beginning but he as always will be able to cope with them. Should drop them a note but its hard to get up the energy.

Uncle George's letter gave all of the plans for Easter at Julia's. Sounds as if the crowd is increasing rather than decreasing but guess that is nothing to worry about. Mother Styer was to be included.

Ann's letter didn't mention anything about Monica's trip to L.A.—surely she didn't contemplate a fling—however it might have been possible. Helen sent me a program from the Turnabout—still enjoying remembering the delightful evening we had there with her.

Since Mother's Day isn't too far away will make this my letter to you. Have tried to remember the one last year but for the life of me can't. Do believe however that we were in S.D.—Will miss not being with you this year "my Sweet" for I love you a great deal.—because your <u>you, my wife</u> and the <u>mother</u> of our two sweet children.

With love to the Three of you as always—

Al & Dada

P.S. Am enclosing a short note to Mother

A.F Herney.

April 27 April Letter No 9

My Dearest Sweet, Susie & Steve:

Can't promise that this will be more than a very short note for its still AM. & chow will be down in a few minutes.

Have been back on watch for the last week. It's been the 12 to 4 which is a stinker, for you don't get a whole lot of rest at any one time & with the other things that have to be done you hate to be in the sack all of the time.

Expected the mailman to call today but no luck—possibly he will catch us tomorrow—if not will just have to be patient. It was been long enuf so that there should be some mail for us at least. Did enjoy Susie's contribution to the letter of April 3 from herself & Steve. Does she having the writing bug yet or has she given that up. There is some nice wallpaper at Grandma's which she shouldn't try to improve.

Everyone's thought is on getting home—of course this thing must be brought to a favorable conclusion first however. Have been hoping that the affair in Europe will bounce in a hurry so that all of the effort can be concentrated on our little friends in the Pacific. Don't feel Sweet that I want to come home until I can be assured of being able to stay—that of course is a matter for the bureau to decide. It will or would be hard to be home for short while only to be required to leave you again.

Ran across an article in Readers Digest Sept 1943—"Questions on Childbirth"—the last one especially for it such is really the case my, my we really hit the jack-pot, or maybe we are both not one's of the greater percentage.

Was much annoyed at the statistics of deaths & casualties on Iwo—set out in "Time" [March 5, 1945]. Still can't understand how an island as small as Iwo could have taken the beating it did—day & night and yet have the defenders inflict the damage they did. The price paid in the estimation of the strategists was a heavy one but a necessary one. We can only hope that the price to be paid at Okinawa will not have to be as heavy & costly.

Your taking walks with the family makes me a bit envious of you—not being there to join you. Can imagine what a figure all of you three cut you pushing Steve & Susie pushing her doll. Well my time will come & know that it will be enjoyable.

The sea is a bit rougher today than it has been for the past few days. It is pleasant I can assure you to have the sea as calm as that which you would find in a basin set on the good old solid earth. Not bumps—rolling staggering or skinning of shins or hitting of elbows!—

The moon to has been such which might with the right person call for a bit or romancing. As it is only the fact that there is a moon as admitted—nothing more for it is easier that way and you don't get nearly as blue.

The count on the letters for this month hasn't been much Sweet but haven't had the energy to do much about it. Maybe I'm getting old in a hurry & need some rehabilitation—Who know's—could try & see what the bureau thought of it.

Think of you always and every waking hour—love to the three of you always.

Al & Dada

A F Herney

P.S. Gosch also says I snore but he hasn't had the opportunity to determine whether I twitch—

Love Al

8

ON PATROL

May 1945

May 1 May Letter No 1

My Dearest Sweet, Susie & Steve:

    Here it is the beginning of a new month and May Day at that. May I wish each of you a happy May Day even tho it will arrive late? Failed miserably last month on letters to you and have resolved to do better this one for I fully realize that you too like letters coming your way.

    Was wondering if Susan would be interested in today for the May Basket end of it. Most children do as both you and I. Continually regret that so many days are passing by that I'm not home to enjoy living with you and the youngsters.

    One often is surprised isn't one when they aren't bored. Can imagine however that you two had the right to expect to sit & fight waiting until you could make a break for the wide open spaces. The chance meeting after the dinner has opened the way to new relationships & I don't mind at all. In fact I would be a bit disappointed if you just sat and twiddled the thumbs. However as a word of warning don't expect the old man to go galvaganting around when he gets home for he ain't for he is going to sit & enjoy being home.

    Since your last letter is April 5 written on April 12 haven't had word as to the outcome of your final exam but can guess you passed and above the average—you would.

Didn't realize that Dad was so close to retiring. That however is good to hear for then we can expect them to become Californians & be close to us can't we? At least I've always hoped that that is what they would decide to do, when Dad retired. Possibly I'm optimistic about the matter but I expect Japan to fold within 6 months from the date of Germany's unconditional surrender which for all reports should come soon. Nothing to base the optimism on other than the beating the Japs have taken & our own forces so close to home base.

Haven't had much information on the S.F. conference. Have just had a very few skimpy reports. Would like it much if you would send me as detailed report as possibly by way of running accounts from the newspaper. Time of course will give a summary but I want more than that.

Have been averaging darn little sleep in the last week—have too d much paper work for the afternoon to hit the sack so will have to let the lack of sleep accumulate & try to catch it all at once. No sooner did I get to sleep after coming off the 8 to 12 watch than I was awakened for something in my line—then what a time to get back to sleep—Ho hum! Really could have slayed a communications officer I can assure you but fortunately for him he wasn't around.

Your starting Susie out learning her ABC's—quite early aren't you—don't forget there will come a time when we may want to spell & then will be out of luck, and incidently Steve has made tremendous progress in the last few weeks too hasn't he? Pop says "Hi Steve" so glad all of your shots are now a matter of the past.

With a great big hug & kiss to Steve & the Pride & Joy & many of them to my One & Only. With love to the Three of you Always

Al & Dada

AF Herney

4 May 1945 May Letter No 2

My Dearest Sweet, Susie, Steve, Mother & Dad:

Will drop you a short note before hitting the sack for 40 winks—Possibly can get them in before going on watch. Have tried it before but no luck—a good time to relax is right after noon chow but that also is a good time to get some work done.

Today has been one of those grand days—especially after a storm—sun good & warm while the sea is content to remain almost motionless. More like a small lake than the large body of water which it really is.

Haven't had any mail since your No 5 for April was received last week. Do hope that the mailman will be generous real soon again for much has happened to you & the family since April the 12th all of which I will be happy to know about.

Just another week from Sunday & Mothers Day of 45 will be an actuality. It is hard to realize that so much time has passed since the Scurry set sail from the West Coast. Can only hope that the remaining time to be spent away will seem to pass as quickly. Time however has begun to drag—the monotony of it all—doing the same thing over day after day—

While on watch the other night Schnabel & myself concluded that this life is not living—but merely an interlude—which will have been lost to us—but appreciating the enjoyment we have had & looking forward to the future expectantly. Maybe were wrong & just trying to rationalize our dislike for military life as a career.

Haven't had too much news on what has been happening on the European fronts—other than general advances by the Russians & the Western Allies, the story about Hitler death & the capitulation of the German forces in Italy. The sooner that one is over its certain the sooner this phase can be concluded.

We have been fortunate in getting our share of fresh & frozen provisions. Of course we have had to take our canned foods & cold cuts along with the rest but on the whole one hasn't much to complain about. Believe we fare as well or better as the civilians at home on the food problem—but Ho hum I and many others would be willingly sacrifice much to be back home.

Haven't attended either of the last two movies both of which were stinkers to begin with & there were other things that were better done so passed them both.

Can't blame Dad too much for complaining when the Time is late. The latest one is 16 April. Of course that's weeks back but the thing is read from cover to ———. At least we get an idea of what has gone on & where, but, when, now that is the question.

My Sweet I've been lonesome as all hades without you & I'm sure more discontent as time passes until I can get home—however it's one hell of a long way to hitch hike & I'm sure I'm not that strong a distance swimmer. I love you & the youngsters with all my heart always. Again wishes for a very pleasant Mothers Day to you, & Mother.

Al & Dada

AF Herney

Saturday nite May 5 May Letter No 3

My Dearest Sweet, Susie, Steve, Mother & Dad:

Almost one week of May of 45 is almost a matter of the past—which of course means one week less that I'll have to spend away from you. The rest of the time could also be a forgotten matter too—Ah Home?

Still no mail tho there is prospects in the next few days. What makes it so tough is that it is so close & yet so far. It isn't the mailmans fault but it certainly is a matter of organization & somebody should get hep about it.

About this time last year I was either in SD or very close to it during driving home from Lincoln and Mama & Susie enroute via the rain—Steve of course was not as yet a reality but definitely an expected addition—just when was the problem facing us.

The sea has been choppy again today—all of which is disgusting—reminds me much of George F—quiet one minute & restless the next. It should be content for a few days at a time but since it can't it has definitely convinced me of the fact that I do not want to continue to be a sailor & won't care if I never take another trip via the "Bounding Blue".

Took a good nap this afternoon. Contemplated snoozing till 1400 but didn't have the energy to hit the deck at the time the mess boys called me—finally rolled out at 1600—felt a bit more like living when I did get up tho I could have very profitably spent the time doing some paper work—but ho hum who wants to do paper work when its so enjoyable doing sack drill.

Would be in the market for a good massage after a good tub bath—both of which are pipe dreams but certainly something pleasant to think about.

Showers serve there purpose for the usual but the tub bath in the pinches. About the only way to get one out here is to jump overboard & that is impractical for you'd have to take a shower afterwards.

Sunday Afternoon
Dearest Sweet:

Somehow the letter was interrupted so will have to take up where was interrupted.

Still not a pleasant sea—tho the weather top side is warm & pleasant—could very well dispense with the chop—chop if that were possible.

Tho I'm sure you've intended telling me you haven't said how much time you were required to spend as a Nurses Aid—after you became qualified. So is it as much as you feel you can serve or do they expect a minimum? However don't see how they can do the latter as it is voluntary. Of course one doesn't mind doing what interests one but there does come a time when you might feel you'd prefer not doing it.

Should answer all of the Phi Mu's but haven't had the energy to do it. Do hope they will forgive me for not being prompt. Wonder how they are getting along without the Herney's from C.V. but then guess they have & will do without us for a spell longer.

Still haven't had the pleasure of running into Dutch or Carl & guess that the opportunity is past. That's one of the big complaints—can't do what you want to do when you want to do it. Let's call on Sherman again huh?

Noticed in the picture taken of the Three of you with the youngsters in their Easter gad abouts that Susie Q is almost as tall as her Mommie's head which is a bit more than in the picture taken of the "Three" on Susie's second birthday. In other words Dad can see she is getting to be a big girl and acts like a big girl too when Mommie asks her to do something.

As ingenious as the Americans are it is surprising that the principal (?) of a choppy sea hasn't been utilized to rock youngsters to sleep and really much more practical than Ed's method—Will have to give it some thought—there might be a fortune in it. Would dispense with rocking chairs—quite an item.

Don't know how my insurance account stands but the premium on the accident & health policies will be due mine in July & yours sometime after that. Will have to call on you & your account to take care of them—don't want my policy to lapse under any circumstances.

With all my love to the Three of you always for I do love you so very very much

Al & Dada

AF Herney

May 9 May Letter No 4

My Dearest Sweet, Susie, Steve, Mother & Dad:

Back on the old schedule—have been since Monday. Have a lot of paper work to catchup so have been spending a few long hours. Really do wish one would catch up & stay caught up but always behind for some reason.

Suppose that everyone at home are extremely happy about the affair in Europe being off the block as far as further hostilities are concerned. We all of course were excited about it—even tho we like you had a let down several weeks ago when some bloke was a bit too optimistic & passed the word of Germany capitulation. However we can now concentrate for the greater part on breaking Japan which I hope will be soon. If it were only possible to convey to her as we did to Germany—thousand upon thousands of planes overhead constantly—our superiority of men & materiale in the air as we have on the sea & land it shouldn't be long.—How soon we can do this will depend a great deal on what Russia will allow us to do even tho she will not actively engage in war against Japan. The use of the Trans-Siberian Ry would assist a great deal in process of logistics.

The weather was a bit damp on Sunday & Monday morning bit has cleared beautifully. Surprised the non-Californians by saying it reminded me of our wet spell in the winter at S.D.—Ho hum that brings up the matter of home again & I just ain't in no mood to discuss it for I might start swimming in that direction.

Still no mail but have hopes of some within a few days. Of course there will be all of the May letters to be sent off to you so some should be coming your way soon.

It is quite a nice thing that Pres. Truman has set aside the 13th for the Day of Thanksgiving for I'm sure that there are many Mothers & wifes who have not suffered losses & will now have greater hopes that their sons & husbands will return safely to them. Truly a nice Mothers Day gift.

Took all of the pictures and renewed my contacts with the family. Felt much better afterwards for I was blue as blue could be. It helps to know what is waiting for me so far away.

Have you been able as yet to find a tri—for Susie? Possibly since the thing is over "over there" there might be a loosening up & the big boys will again be putting some of the non-essentials & a few of the essentials back on the market—yes & a few of the essentials too which from Time's reports were going to be curtailed. The British plan on loosening up on "VE" Day—however their situation is a bit different since they have suffered a good bit—hm—a concession from Herney—surprise myself.

Sweet while I've had much in life to be grateful for I do so remember the three days I had at home with you & the youngsters and the time we had in Long Beach. I'm still very proud of you the way you "didn't" go into a jag when we said good bye. It is for so many of these reasons that I love you so much & so sincerely and always will. It is this that gives me the drive & will to return to you & our youngsters.

With all my love to the three of you as always—

Al & Dada

AF Herney

P.S. Incidently we are having a hell of a time getting stamps so if you don't want V mail or letters sent free you might enclose a few in your next few letters.

Al

May 10, 45 Letter No 5 for May

Dearest Sweet, Susie Steve Mother & Dad:

Won't promise that there will be more than a lick to this but did want to drop you another note.

Received word today that we have some mail and will have the opportunity in the next few days to pick it up. Happy Days. Still can't understand why some thing wasn't done about it long before this however—almost two weeks now.

The sea was calm again today—almost like a glass top surface. There was a peculiar haze just off the surface which was peculiar to no end. It was warm and pleasant, topside however & wouldn't mind more days like this. Did spend much of the day in the space allotted to me doing more paperwork.

Addressed the envelope before writing the letter—notice where my mind is again. Would have saved the envelope for a letter when you returned to CV but are running short of postage as I told you in my last letter—hope you won't mind the scratching out of 399.

Have accumulated a lot of correspondence—so much that I'll have to get rid of some for I won't be able to carry it with me. Had fun in rereading some of your old letters before disposing of them. Will do a few more tonight.

Saw a movie this AM in the mess hall. For the life of me can't remember the name of it but it had "La Femmes" in it which is of course something to look at. Murder mystery—could it be the "Nine Gals"? Didn't see the one this afternoon Dangerous Blondes but plan on seeing it at its next showing which should be soon.

Didn't get to hear any of the news today as to what was doing here there or elsewhere. Wonder just how many people still have hangovers or need Bromo or Alki for over indulgence in eating for drinking—hear it sizzle—the alki not the stomach or maybe it is at that.

As usual straighten up the drawers in the cabinet & soon everything is again in a mess. Must take time out in the next few days & arrange things so that when reaching for a sox I don't get a pair of shorts or a tie—the latter is really a burden now for haven't worn one since the days of <u>Pearl.</u> Maybe I should put them away in moth balls!

Haven't written any letters except to you Sweet in so long that I'm ashamed. Should drop the family an occasional note if nothing more. Then also there are the rest of the friends who should get a note also—Will see if I can't exert enough pressure on myself to do it soon.

The violets—or what are left of them at 399 should have been all through flowering by this time—don't imagine there is even one stalk of carnations left—will start anew when & if this thing ever is over & I can get back to those good Sundays when I was home with you but you were a yard widow— You won't mind will you Sweet?

With all my love always to the Three of you.

Al & dada

A.F Herney.

May 11, 1945 May Letter No 6

Last night after writing you wrote Joe a long letter—the first since I left Pearl & I did have to write him. Ended up by writing four pages—really longer than any I've written you but then there were four months travelogue which was included so that made up for the length.

Saw "Banjo on My Knee" Joel MaCrea & Barbara Stanwick—if you've seen it I'm sure you can appreciate how much the Old Man wanted to play the "Saint Louis Blues" He finally got to but oh what a pull he had.

Another pleasant smooth sea today. Don't know just how long it will last but do enjoy it anyway—pleasantly warm too during the short while I was on the bridge today or topside for that matter.

Thought possibly that we would be seeing the mail man today but no such luck. Guess he & others have forgotten all about us, dang it, anyway. Which also means no mail at all off to you.

While listening to the radio the other evening the station was offering some Japanese music—sounded as if some had the stomach—Gosch piped up with "Just wait till your little girl starts taking music lessons." If that's what it will be like I'm sure you will have her doing the practicing while Dad is at the office. Incidently has she made up any more songs?

All of us are getting bit touched off at the long hard grind. However there still is a job to do & we can't quit until its finished. Do wish <u>they</u> would get smart and give up now because it will be soon anyway & the price to be paid will be terrific. It is hard to believe that they will be any less difficult to convince than the Germans have been—complete & utter destruction may be the only answer.

Work up to a certain point & think you are accomplishing something & you begin to loose interest. Maybe that's because the remainder of the job is so much in the future that it all appears as a hopeless mess & mess it is. Ho hum—just life, I guess.

Tomorrow however brings prospect of some mail at last—do wish that that were for certain as the story seems to be getting an old one.

You being away from Chula leaves me far away from news of any of the people there—Harvey & Ruth, Doc & Marie and etc.—Will be good to get back & sit quietly in the front room with you Susie & Steve & yes wouldn't mind a piano lesson in progress. Could turn up the radio loud enuf to take care of that.

Have been thinking much about you three—wondering how much the youngsters are going to allow me to fit into the picture without some adjustment on their part—even Susie & the longer I'm gone the more chance of it—however don't think it will be too difficult. Love all three of you with all my heart.

Just one day away from Mother's Day—Will add an extra special prayer tomorrow my Sweet for I do wish I could be with you even for just a moment.

Love Always
Al & Dada
AF Herney

May 13, 45 May Letter No 7
My Dearest Sweet Susie Steve, Mother & Dad:

Finally received a couple of Sugar reports your No's 9 & 10 plus Marie's letter of April 24 & a letter from Fran. However the few letters written last month 9 in no. my record is almost as good as yours & I can assure you I was one hell of a lot busier than you were even with two youngsters—not complaining but explaining—Am doing better this month already so you see if there's time it will be done.

From all reports in our letter No 10 & Susie's telling Mother what will happen when daddy gets home blows away the fears expressed in my letter of the 11th. She must have a memory & too I'm sure her Mother is keeping alive the thought of her Daddy who hates like all to be away from her, Stevie & her Mommie. She has a very correct idea of what her Daddy would like to do & today too. Of course Mommie would be along for this is her day. Sorry to hear that she decided she wanted to go strolling & Daddy will be awfully unhappy if she does it again.

Marie's letter of April 24—with personal note added saw she had received the certificate which was received in time & would be taken care of for us. Glad you thought of it for it will be a saving on taxes & should take advantage of it.

Received a small amount of parcel post but nothing yet for Herney. Guess I'll just have to be patient about it.

Glad to hear about the Coles' even tho the news is not at all good news. Harvey has hit himself hard in more than one way. Don't doubt but what the worries of Lee have helped too—really a shame that we've gone this far & that he is now needed. Of course it would be tough on those who have had a lot of time in not to get back to their families but it would easier than breaking up an additional family to do it. However thank goodness that is for someone else to decide.

Marie wrote that {Armstrong} due to a hernia had been given limited services. {Davis} ought to do well as a Red Cross operator for I still have that deep feeling about that service & Bobs type just about fits in. Not kind I know but I can't help it. {Case} couldn't take it as anyone who knows him can well state.

Dear John some day is going to get himself smacked right on the chin & good & when he does he will regret some of his high handed manners with some of the people who needed medical attention & were refused. What a nature—thank god he's got it & not me.

Didn't some of the Diamonds take advantage of our Domicile at 288 Del Mar when we went to LA one week end?—Seems to me that there was some of that clan in C.V. at sometime.

Sweet you needn't feel that you owe the St Joe folks a visit—if you felt you wanted to go it would be alright with me & nice to show what the youngest Herneys look like but traveling with children and now knowing them too well don't see why you should do it. Do wish we were traveling opposite directions to be meeting at home but that just ain't in the cards at present.

Steve ought to know that the sooner he gets his teeth the sooner he'll have to be visiting the dentist—however teeth do seem to be a necessary thing to enjoy living, like steaks, chew a bit of gum. Don't believe that he should grow up too much either for his Dad will miss that pleasure & he well remembers the enjoyment he had with Susan when she was in that stage. As for knowing that he's talking to or calling for his "Pop" that's another matter.

Doesn't feel at all like Mother's Day on this end. Do hope that my letter to Aunt Clyde arrived in time to see that you had your flowers. Would have like[d] to deliver them myself & hope with all my heart that I can do so the next one that rolls around. I'm sure too Sweet that you miss not having me with you which helps somewhat to take away that low feeling.

Was a bit surprised by Marie's letter in reference to Uncle Albert & Aunt Julia for I had thought that they were to stay in Houston with Charles. However I am very glad to hear that they do plan on coming to SD for they can & will add so much to our lives—help fill in the place left by both Mother & Dad & both of them are so sound—the mental agility of both of them for their age & what they have experienced still astounds me.

Again my Sweet wish you the pleasantries of "Mother's Day" & dreadfully sorry that I am so far away. Apologize for the first paragraph of this letter which might sound a bit harsh but was not intended that way. I love you with all my heart and miss not being with you every minute of the day. Always yours as always

Al & Dada

A.F Herney

May 14, 1945 My Letter No 8

My Dearest Sweet, Susie, Steve, Mother & Dad:

Another day has slipped by & didn't seem to get a thing accomplished. However did have the cavity which was temporarily filled at Ulithi fixed up.

Evidently Dr. Smith found a big one for he worked for quite some time on it & it is tender as all right now. Do guess it will ease up for I hope so.

A bit disappointed for no mail today—there is always the prospects of what the morrow will bring as you well know. Do wish that each of us were able to say that the mailman each day would bring us a note—carrying what news we wish to have.

Had planned on doing so much today & not one of those things as planned is accomplished. Really one wonders at times what good it is to plan—for it will hardly ever be followed. Maybe to do so is one way to kid yourself about being busy.

Mr. Bezold and Krause are in the ward room playing Ace Ducey—occasionally play a game myself but never interested enuf to make a study of the game—want something for relaxation. Mr. Bezold whom you have never met has what he calls his bad days at the game & everybody including Herney takes him.

Was able to buy some stamps from another ship today so you won't have to send me some. What with the delivery doubt if they would arrive in time to be of any value—& plenty stickless too—Have enuf so that I can write you for some time as bought a full sheet.

Relived the twelve to two watch this morning—plan on relieving the four to six in the morning. In this way I can give the other chaps a full nights sleep which I can assure you is very welcome & damned unusual pleasure.

Gosch has now joined the kibitzers & the usual cry is "Boot Him" irrespective who has the play. Not a bad game for some pleasure.

Missed not holding service tomorrow & didn't think to try to arrange for a church party to attend services at some other vessel. I'm sure however that the almighty will forgive me at least I hope so. Was busy in the morning & you soon learn to do things when you have the chance, otherwise you do get caught short.

Has been warm today and a bit wet topside tonight. None too unpleasant however—what with foul weather gear & rubbers you can't get too wet—tho it is preferable to be dry.

It is already time for bed—must sew a button on the pantses—lower buttons seem to take an awful beating in the laundry for some unknown reason.

A bit tired of having part of the flap open so better get out the needle & thread. Another reason why this is a hard life.

Not much of a note Sweet & haven't mentioned that I love you—you do know however what is in my heart and all of the love that is yours and the youngsters. Which [wish] I were close so that I could tell you so rather than having to put it on paper. Fortunately the months are passing & soon this will be over.

Love always

Al & Dada

AF Herney.

15 May May Letter No 9

My Dearest Sweet, Susie, Steve, Mother & Dad:

My God, here it is only the 15th and I've written as many letters in these 15 as I wrote all of last month. Maybe I shouldn't do this for it might spoil you; but seriously Sweet when theres time & a chance to get some mail off to you the letters do get written.

Saw Tom Hamilton again today. In fact sat in his office for over an hour talking about old times, members of the bar, how we both would love to be home. He had seen Dutch who was well & incidently is possibly home by this time. Quite a break for him if he is & envy him for his opportunity. Has been gone now for some time so I'm again running into my usual luck. He, Dutch was on the staff of a commander of Transport Division—still is for that matter as far as I know.

Still no mail. Believe that tomorrow I'm going to make a trip to find out what the hell whose got the mail. Maybe by screaming a little they will dig it out. One of the sisterships received twenty bags of mail a few days ago & I'm sure we have much more than the few bags we have received.

It has been rather a long day. Told you I had the four to six—started out on the rounds & didn't finish until about 1930. Should get a little horizontal drill but wanted to drop you a note first.

The tooth has calmed down today & is no longer too tender. Still not what you could call comfortable but there ain't no cavity there no more so feel happy about that. Next call I hope will be in about six months & won't pass up the opportunity to have them inspected.

While doing some burning off the fantail this afternoon two of the crew were kidding Mr. Bezold about the sex of his expected (next month) on claiming bragging about his girl just new, weighed 11 lbs & believe it or not & the other claimed it took a man to have a boy.—Of course I refuted both claims & said it took a man to have both a girl & a boy—really stopped them for they had no answer to that one. Mr. Bezold married a gal from Chicago, she Catholic, he not however; it didn't take too long to lay the keel for they were married sometime in Sept.—

Since Time has not been coming thru have been reading myself to sleep with piecemeals of thriller & wild wester's. At least helps to relax a bit before hitting the pleasantries of slumberland and dreams of my family. Haven't had a nightmare in a long time so do guess they help a little.

At times one can get so disgruntled—but shouldn't; as said before started out early this morning—had hoped to get my work accomplished before breakfast. Instead discovered that hours were from 0800 on so had to come back aboard have chow & return this later this morning. Shouldn't complain for I did have the nice chat with Tom. He told me that I & Dutch were the only two chaps from SD that he had seen since he had been out here.

Again not much of a letter Sweet but as you've said even a scratch is better than nothing. Do love you so much with all my heart. Love Always to the Three of you.

Always Al & Dada
AF Herney

May 16, 45 May Letter No 10
My Dearest Sweetheart, Susie & Steve:

If I'm not careful I will spoil you for sure for here is number ten already. Would like to think there will be ten letters waiting for me when & if we can catch up with it.

Did hear today that there was twenty eight sacks of mail in the vicinity. This of course made us very happy especially since we have prospects of getting it tomorrow. Why the mix up we can't determine.

Took out all of the pictures of you the children & the family for I had a new prospect—Lt. Kennickle who [is] the Cominrons Engineering Officer and temporarily aboard us. After my display & he admitted that the Pride & Joy was just that—he brought out his pictures of his wife & baby—also a little girl—a brunette however & about two years younger than Susie—Of course it was understood that Susie took after the maternal side for her Dad couldn't have contributed very much to her looks.

Got paid today—up to the first of this month. To allay any thoughts you might have that I haven't enuf money there was $111.00 on the books for me—all deductions including general mess made. Only drew $100.00. While this is for two months March includes the pay as JG without the increased allotment to you for the first deduction was to be made in April & you were to receive the increase for April in your May check. Please let me know if the allotment check was increased as of this month. However before payday arrived was running a bit short but one is apt to have that happen if the times between paydays are so far between. They wouldn't pay us up to the present time that is to include the half month of May.

Am enclosing a 10 yen bit of currency. This I think should be Steve's—but you do with it as you wish. How it happens to be on its way to you or where I got it is another story which sometime soon I hope to tell you.

Finally saw the end of "Honey Moon Lodge"—both the leads played by parties entirely foreign to me—glad that it has finally been shown in its entirely for something always seemed to be interrupting.

Notice that as usual the pen is running short of ink. It does seem that it is always running short when writing a letter tho it would eventually run dry so it might as well be when writing a letter as any other time.

Didn't get much accomplished today at all—did some small amount of work this morning & a little this afternoon. Should have a bit more ambition but can't seem to get really energetic about it anymore.

If—there are some letters about the family in tomorrows mail should be able to have a more interesting letter the next time I write—Until then I know that all my dreams will be pleasant ones for I'll be dreaming of the three of you—my love always to my Three S's—

Al & Dada

P.S. Wonder how many of these letters I would send if I reread them with a critical eye or anything akin to it.

    Love Al

A.F Herney

May 17 May Letter No 11

    My God Sweet—don't let this kill you, fur this will be a letter a day for five short days but all in a row—Hmm—

    Everybody is a bit frisky for we think we are on the trail of our mail & intend to get it or else—Still we can't be sure & everyone will be disappointed no end if we don't catch up with it.

    Spent most of the morning just waiting—first on one foot & then on the another—did get back in time for lunch only to shove off again for another fast trip.—Really fagged but did want to drop you another note.

    Ran into Kirmsey—also a C.O from Harvard—my class—Since you don't have the book with you the name won't mean a thing. He had his assignment the first day when we reported to Frisco. Also on a minesweep—which was already in commission & shoved off immediately. Has been in a few operations of course he like everyone else is quite anxious for it to be all over so he can get back to his family too.

    Is warm today—or maybe its because we did so much in so little time and worked up a sweat who knows.

    I do miss the Three of you so much and love you with all my heart.

    Al & Dada

A.F Herney

    Give Susie & Steve an extra big hug & kiss for me but keep an extra extra big one for yourself.—

    Al

May 18, 1945 May Letter No 12

    Received your May 1 & 2 yesterday & April 6,7 & 8 today plus some of the packages that were sent—intended to arrive on Febr 18 last.

Yesterday afternoon was given permission to go to pick up or mail before taking up an assignment. Got to the spot where we had been told we would find our mail and damned if it wasn't sent back that day to the spot we had just left. If you don't think we are all blowing our tops including your old man you can guess again. Instead of getting the sacks we contemplated ended up with some <u>one</u> bag—which had your May letters included.

Today however we were permitted to return to gather up the mail which we did—a slight increase by now—29 sacks.

To get the things distributed with the least confusion men were detailed to sort & all others kept out. Really what a mess it all was & some of the packages a total wreck—a complete disintegration of wrapping & contents, some packages with all writing obliterated, broken and contents loose. Really a shame & appeared as if some of the bags had been lying in the water.

Received packages as follows—two from you from Chula & one from Lincoln, a package from Mother & one from Lloyd & Etta, that is that was all that showed up till late in the game. Your packages were pretty well preserved & in rather good shape except the popcorn in the cellophane package was a bit on the loose side—did salvage it however. Mothers package with the candy & hankies was still securely wrapped but the candy unsalvageable, too bad for it looked as it might at one time have been real edible. Thank her for the try anyway. The package from Lloyd & Etta candy also— still can't make up my mind just whether to imagine I've already enjoyed it & leave it go at that or eat it. The pharmacist aboard said there was nothing wrong with it however.

The cans in your boxes faired much better this time than last for the lids are still secured—used water on those for Xmas & the wax broke loose— haven't attempted to investigate but will do so at a later time don't worry. Also enjoyed seeing some reading material enclosed—did watch out for the serial & saved them from the discards. My Sweet where did you get the dittie on Wakiki—simply a scream—have read "High Time" but will enjoy reading it again. Really Sweet it is nice for you to take time to make goodies to send don't think I don't appreciate it but everything is so darned uncertain as to when & how they will get here that it isn't worth it—Hard candies & that type of thing in cans go well but even they have a tendency to pick up moisture & soon no longer resemble what they looked like in showcases back in the States.

After reading your letter May 1—the first hint that anything of value was sent for my birthday looked over all of the discards of the packages—nothing there—however there was another small package on the wardroom table for me—still well wrapped but a bit damp. It was so well wrapped with gum tape or something else as effective for I had one h——— of a time opening it. Since it was from Park Blvd wondered what it could be—finally after getting into it thru the side found a pipe & believe it or not mildew in the bowl and in the stem—looked for a card or writing & found something else—two cards & a very beautiful bracelet—with name & serial number. Honestly "Sweet" there were tears in my eyes for I didn't expect anything of the kind either the pipe or bracelet. Can assure you I was happy about both & have intended for a little while to write & say I would now have one if you wished to buy it. It is a bit large but can have that taken are of easy enuf & the pipe can be cleaned up so as to be useable—will have to bum "Dr" for some alcohol.

Also received a letter from Aunt Clyde—very newsy one too—good word about you & the youngsters—Ben, Carl, [Ben Alice, her daughter, and Carl Royer, a nephew] etc & that she had received my letter so that you would have your flowers on "Mother's Day"—just sort of a surprise which maybe you didn't expect to get.

Haven't commented on your letters but will do so later—giving me something [to] write about in some future May letters which I hope to get off to you. Did want to write about the packages before any of the small details about them slipped my mind.

Don't know who picked out the pipe but it appears to be a good one & a nice shaped one—will enjoy smoking it I know—using some of the good tobacco Mr. Johnson left me when he was transferred.

Sweetheart am very grateful for the boxes—the contents and the thoughts that came with them. I love the "Three" of you so very very much. Please thank Mother & Dad for their box also—two swell hankies which I'll save for the best.—

Love to you three S's always

Al & Dada

A.F Herney.

PS. Gosch had to dispose of a box of candy, cookies & other edibles too. Did salvage some stationiery that was still damp so that the envelopes could be unflapped & dried—had them spread all over his bunk & mine too—

Al

Sunday Afternoon May 20, 1945 May Letter No 13

My Dearest Sweet Susie, Steve, Mother & Dad:

Have just completed doing a wee bit of work since it is hot & mucky decided to knock off for awhile and relax—so will do so by dropping you note no thirteen.

Friday nite after finishing the note to you decided to see what could be done with & for said pipe. Got Dr. to break loose with some alcohol which is kept in his safe & proceeded to give the pipe a bath—inside & out. The alcohol of course took the varnish off but that is of little matter for the grain will be much prettier when darkened. Of course the first few smokes were a bit on the tart side but won't take long until it will be an enjoyable smoke.

As for the bracelet had to have two of the links removed so that it wouldn't be down around the thumb & little finger. One of my flock Chief Flesher Chief Electrician did the job for me & while the tools available scarred up one link it isn't too bad & can now wear it. Think time will smooth off the rough spots left on the one link. Yep it sure is a beautiful thing. Did you remember the serial no or did you remember that it was to be found in your copies of my papers which I left with you?

Was a bit amused at your reaction to Ben's having a good time. Sweet don't get upset about such small matters—it may be what he wants and enjoys but that would tend slowly to drive me nuts. You know under what conditions I would want a shore based job and it ain't at some advance base—not but anyplace so that I could have my family & then too think of the miles traveled—ho hum—Do hope that Bev gets some relief from her sinus for that is anything but pleasant.

Glad to hear about Art being taken out of amphib—However most of the boys in it wouldn't trade it for anything else.

Dad with his numerous copies of Time shouldn't have to look for a copy when & if he gets time to read—three copies my what a luxury.

Possibly with a bit of patience & a little time spent in showing Steve just how easy it is to roll from front to back Mommie wouldn't have to crawl out of the sack to put the young man on his stomach.

Gosch just came off watch—announced he was going to take 40 winks—relaxed & is now making audible sounds indicating he is catching those 40 winks & wasn't fooling about his intentions.

To get to the tough life Mommie is leading if you are giving Susie Dr. Wegmens suggested treatment & turning Steve over just when do you sleep. Sounds as if you are up & down all night—or does it just seem that way—Know I'm short on the capacity but—? nuff said.

Popped the corn which you sent in the cellophane bag last night. Wasn't too successful but had enuf for all of the officers—sent some up to the bridge to Mr. Hetzler & Schnable—Gosch had his while in the sack reading (said my this is just like home). Mr. Hanna & I started popping—then the Skipper came down & wanted to assist & did. Think there is some more but haven't investigated. Really feel a bit guilty having it & not enuf for the crew but I guess one can carry that to an extreme.

Am commenting on only one letter at a time so that I will have something to write about—this regarding April No 6—

My love to the Three of you

Always as Always

Al & Dada

AF Herney

P.S—I am very happy to have you assure me Susie won't forget.

Love Al.

May 22 May Letter No 14

My Dearest Sweet, Susie, Steve Mother & Dad:

Getting awfully close to that 15 mark & tending to spoil you for the future but then who cares huh?

Bunged up my knee several days ago—bruised it and it has been sore as everything for the last few days. Nite before last started out with hot water bottle but soon ended up using an ice pack. Crawled out of the sack when no position was comfortable—dressed & relaxed on transom (couch to laymen) with the ice pack—got to sleep soon after midnight.—Last night started with the ice pack & soon was asleep—did however waken occasionally. Has been raining since last nite & that may be the reason for the thing hurting today.

Incidently had on my bracelet nite before last—did a good bit of perspiring—result it, one bracelet well tarnished which of course can be easily remedied. Will have to be a bit careful after this with it.

Among the many sacks of mail or rather included in time were our magazines—some in poor condition. In looking thru the Febr 5 issue of Life saw the "Dido"—attractive, appealing and practical—definitely having it points—You might investigate & see what you think—What was displaying the item wasn't too much of a bargain however. Don't know if its in the same issue or not, but also an article on nice flimsy night wear to the tune of $50 plus which you can overlook—simply from the financial end however.

Glad you were able to get a Taylor Tot [a type of stroller that allows the child to self-propel] for Steve—for the price without bumpers he will undoubtedly get a whole lot of enjoyment out of it besides doing himself some good—getting his legs strong.

From the amount of bridge you have been playing you should soon be an expert "Mickey Mouser" if not an orthodox player—rules sometimes don't answer the need.

The dinner for the Nurses Aides must have been quite a nice affair & while the picture may not have been in the paper when they said it would be it should come later & you can pass it on to me. The lecture was thrown in free & gratis wasn't it?

Am awfully glad that your hours come in the morning & are limited to two days a week. Feel if you gave much more time than two mornings a week would be cutting Susie & Steve short—what without their Pop being around & besides don't want you to be worn out when & if Dad gets home which he wishes could be very pronto.

So the Pride & Joy has another of the <u>times</u> when everybody is in step but Susie. Daddy feels bad he finds out about it & he always finds out.

Sorry to hear about Lloyd—he has been working too hard as has everyone else. Must drop them a note of thanks for the candy and birthday card. He really has been awfully good to the family, we-uns included. Hope we don't loose him.

Must close Sweet for chow is about down & can't miss that even tho the appetite hasn't been too good of late—lack of exercise I suppose. Love the three of you with all my heart always—

Al & Dada

A.F Herney—

MINE SQUADRON 12
FLEET POST OFFICE
SAN FRANCISCO, CALIFORNIA
MAY 23, 1945

From: Commander Task Group (Commander, Mine Squadron TWELVE).
To: Commanding Officer, U.S.S. SCURRY (AM 304)

1. During assault operations against enemy held OKINAWA SHIMA,… at about 1930 on 22 April, your vessel participated in an action against enemy aircraft during which your guns, by their accuracy and intensity of fire, brought about the destruction of one enemy aircraft and assisted materially in the destruction of another.

2. The Task Group Commander desires to express his pleasure in the above results and to congratulate the officers and crew of the U.S.S. SCURRY (AM 304) on the high…efficiency, excellent team work and spirit of are collaboration displayed throughout this engagement.

3. In accordance with reference (b) you are authorized to display a miniature Japanese flag on your bridge structure to represent the enemy plane shot down by you.

/c/ Commander

May 24 May Letter No 15

My Dearest Sweet Susie Steve, Mother & Dad:

The mailman saw that we had some mail again day before yesterday. Brought your April 12 & 13 & May 3, 4 & so that brings me pretty much up to date.—the last letter was mailed on the 10th—only twelve days—which is not bad at all.—Maybe he will be good again today—who knows. Also received a very nice note from Helen written of course in style that only she can write.

Thanks for passing on the word about Uncle Jim—will add his ship to my list and be on the lookout for him—wonder if it will be my usual luck to be near & yet so far from him as it has been my luck in the past.

You were quite an optimist holding on to the last half of the train ticket weren't you? Am glad however that you didn't hang on to it till it was too late—Don't know how much longer than six months you intend to stay but that again is a matter for you to decide. You have been there only three months now.

It is nice that you are getting a good bit of time in the OB ward for you do seem to enjoy it so much. Enjoyed your off hand comment that things happened to be quiet that day—no babies today. My God they can't be arriving all the time—Another thing where one are all the Papa's for they didn't get even a mention.

By this time I do hope all of my family are much better both colds— stomach & streaks—Can feel for all of you for colds can make one so miserable and when a stomach ache is added that really is hell. Do hope they don't hang on too long this time. It's funny but I'm sure you met Mrs. Harms at one of the afternoon gatherings outside the fence at Beantown. She was a blond (not the Hussey however)—but no mater anyway.

Can well sympathize with Elmer and Jerry—a whole house full of needies for the expected problem of stowing them—until the big event & then having them available when it does arrive. July is not too far away—thought it was to be sooner than that but guess they ought to know—we did didn't we but Steve fooled us a bit.

Don't like the advice you gave Steve about the haircut—or he is really the one who should decide when he want his hair trimmed—maybe he'll be a Sampson.

Do remember now about Mothers Day last year & thanks for reminding me.

The Pride & Joy evidently is picking up a good bit of lingo & knows when to use it. Can't quite for the life of me think that she would think to say kids to Mother & Dad—did you correct her—it was sweet of her to think about wanting them to have a nice time.

Wouldn't mind being there to give you a back rub Sweet & for the other thought will have to file that for further reference too—Knowing that my Three S's are all well—Love you always as always

Al & Dada

A.F Herney-

May 25
May Letter No 16
My Dearest Sweetheart, Susie & Steve:

Will try to write you a much more sensible letter than the last few I've written—all mumbo jumble—but that is much as I've felt.

The mailman called yesterday bringing us no mail but was kind enuf to take our mail so that was some consulation. Of course we all would have like him to bring us some—however he was pretty good to us in the past week so we have no great complaint to make.

Enjoyed receiving the picture of your graduates. Not a bad picture either of any exept the lady standing behind Annette—did she have a stomach ache or is that natural & she ain't mad at nobody. Know you have referred to all of your gang Sweet but can't remember anything about any of them by Evelyn— Will you forgive me if I should be pretty much of a blank if I should have the privilege of meeting any of them?

So Susie is going to be flower gatherer is she? Do hope you enjoy the flower water Susie—it's best not to consume the water after you've had flowers standing in it. Also remember it isn't healthy to pick Grandpa's tulips.

Sorry to hear that Aunt Mary [Dot's aunt, her father's sister] has run into the unfortunate circumstance of loosing her husband. Seems a bit cold to put it that way but no ill thought meant—My sympathy to her & hers including Dad & Mother. It is my recollection that he was a nice chap. Leave it to Mother & Dad to see that there is something for the two grandchildren.—

I was nice of Ladelle & Jules [Al's roommate in Berkeley while in law school] to remember Steve. Feel ashamed that I haven't written them but will have to leave it go at that. Your problem my Sweet.

Can't understand who is nuts for Unke wrote me that Uncle A & Aunt J planned on staying in Texas. However Marie's note to the family commented on the fact that she would be glad when Aunt J arrived. Am very happy however that they plan on being in Calif. Maybe Unke had a pipe dream when he sprung the last on me or decided he might make up the Caugheys mind for them—without their knowing it of course.

Your luck seems to be on the rough side too. Can well imagine how much you would enjoy seeing Lois [Hudgins].—As much as I would Ed—Thanks for passing on the info—will certainly add the SS Edwin A Stevens to my list. Don't think your suggestion about yelling is a good one for this Pacific is just too darn big & that ain't no fooling. However it might be one way of establishing the fact that a medical survey is in line, but that wouldn't be fair.

I haven't heard from Carl either & I wrote him while at Ulithi. Maybe all of our mail goes back to Pearl & his distributed from there. Who knows what the hell they do with it.

Am glad you had something in mind to get for Mother. However you generally do pick something that is appropriate. Was sorry that I couldn't have gotten something more than the flowers for you but the bankroll just wouldn't stretch. Maybe next time huh?

So the "Pride & Joy" was presented to the Kier's immaculate in appearance. Maybe it was a saving grace that she was talkative for what she lacked in appearance she evidently made up for in personality.

Was wondering just how long the [Chula Vista] house would be satisfactory. Still think that the roof leaks at the rafters get soaked and swell-down—however there is a good bit of adobe there & could swell from both the bottom

& top. Ho—hum—if we keep trimming that door there just won't be anything left of it.

Very possibly the stomach is a bit like mine. You might see an MD. To see what's wrong. Do hope you don't have what I've got for it ain't funny. Maybe its just the flu & you'll—get over it long before eight weeks. Do check on it tho Sweet.

Yep it won't be long Sweet till our 8th anniversary will be here and soon after that our son will be one year old & the Pride & Joy the ripe age of three. How time does fly—and what nice memories of it all I have except of this time I've had to be away from you. It should soon be all over however & Pop will be home once more—taking up where we left off. God he, Steve, can pat a cake and is beginning to know when to wave by by—I can assure you he won't have to do much of that to Dad except in the morning when it's off to the office.

You hadn't written that you had gained any weight—Helen commented on the fact that you had reported—evidently to everyone except Pop that you had gained ten pounds. Good for the weight but shame on you for not passing on the good word. Your face looks a bit fuller in our last pictures than the picture taken on your arrival in Lincoln. Hope you don't loose any of what you've gained with the flu.

I love you a great deal my Sweet and am still homesick as all—would love to say I was on my way back to you but that ain't so—so I'll just say my love to the here of you always

Al & Dada

A.F Herney

May 27 May Letter No 17

Dearest Sweet, Susie, Steve, Mother & Dad:

Have had rather a quiet day—took a wee nap this afternoon so will drop you a note before hitting the sack for the night drill.

Yesterday was really a toughey—not for any other reason than I awakened early & did paper work all day—quitting about 2230 which of course is 1030

PM laymen time. Did get a good bit accomplished and satisfied with the time spent.

Saw Deanna Durbin in "Hers to Hold" within the last few days. Wouldn't mind seeing it again for I do enjoy her voice and she sings one of my favorites "Shalimar" (?) Don't know whether I can convince Hetzler on a rerun or not but will try. Didn't see either of the other two films now aboard for they really were stinkers—saw the opening scenes until the odor drove me away. Ah to be a fool to be so particular about entertainment.

Haven't received any mail more recent than your May #5 mailed on the 10th. However that isn't so long ago so any news I have of my family is very recent.

Sorry to hear about Leonard Kelly. Too bad too for he was a nice kid. His wife & youngster are not alone in being without husband & father. So far Sweet we have been fortunate—and pray to the Almighty that we will continue to be so. I do remember Winnie but she was not near the gal that Mary Lou was as I recollect them.

We are a bit handicapped with our 16 milometer movie projector in that we do not get the latest film—so it will be some time until we get to see "Fighting Lady". From all reviews it is worth while seeing. While it has been my pleasure to see our aircraft both land based and carrier based operate the scenes collected in that film would be just as new to me as they were to you.

Was very amused at Dad's reaction to Susie's wanting to attend the cinema with you. Of course it was sweet of him to feel that way about it. Do you think we will have to wait until the sandman arrives before we take off to attend or do we just not go?

Had forgotten that Mother & Dad's anniversary was in June. Will drop them a note but you again will have to take care of the remembrance for the only thing I could think about sending at all would be a bottle of "Pacific" and I [am] very doubtful if that would be appreciated—putting salt in Lincoln water would just about be the same thing.

Marie's reference to [family cabins at Mt.] Palomar had the same effect on me—have wished many times that I could take a few days off—do nothing but just relax—can't think of a nicer place to do so—except of course at 399 J—with my Three S's there.

The news reports of late mentioned the possibility of additional amounts of gasoline allowed to "A" holders. This of course is good news and can well indicate lot of things—There will be a gradual relaxing of the restrictions many articles except of course food.—the ravaged must be fed & I agree with many of the big boys that to do what we can is one of the first steps in proving our good faith to the peoples of the world—maybe they will soon forget about it but at present it is important.

Sweet—there is nothing mechanical about sending your love via the written word—I can assure you that if you stopped I could gladly whup you—which I haven't to date—Knowing that you love me & are waiting till that happy day when this is all over is one of the few things that makes one give a damn about wanting that day to arrive.

Love Always to my Three S's as always

Al

AF Herney.

May 30 May Letter No 18

My Dearest Sweet, Susie & Steve:

Almost the end of another month—another down & scratched off the calendar and one less to go before I can be with you again.

The last two days have been long ones—night before last couldn't get to sleep tho I hit the rack about 2200—funny thing about it was that worked all of the time yesterday but didn't feel sleepy—just lazy—Ho hum the interest of it all I guess.

Had word we were getting some mail the other day—yep we got mail—two lousey letters—one each for two of the enlisted men—thank god there wasn't a lot of official stuff which always means plenty of work for me. Maybe soon however—mail all is always good to have.

We've had a good bit of rain of late—that is at least the last three days—it is good not to have to get out of it if you prefer not to—& of course I prefer not to. Incidently most of the boys are now wearing rubbers—Gosch borrows mine—so you see none of them like wet feet—disagreeable things I'd say.

When I'm day dreaming of you three there are always so many pleasant things I want to write you—but when its time to write I seem to go a sudden blank—Maybe I'd better have a secretary to follow me around when I'm in the day dreaming stage huh?—

Have thought of writing Dr & Etta, Father Brown, the family but just can't get around to it—will need a bit or urging I know—will some time anyway & I'm sure that neither of them will be too upset if I don't answer soon.

The greys are gradually wearing out—the four pairs of pants, the only pant I've worn since leaving the states have really worn well. Did buy a couple pair of dungarees & have been wearing them which helps both on the laundry & the pants. Hate to spend any more money on clothes for if my optimism isn't too far wrong won't need any more than I have. Can get them here if I need some.—Shirts are holding out—have been wearing them unironed—they soon have the appearance of being unironed anyway after a very short time.

Have read the serial you were so kind to cut out of the Sat E Post. Was curious that it was ahead of itself in one of the installments or maybe I'm just nuts & right now nothing appears to be in balance—result of fatigue or what ever they might call it.

The knee has finally come around to behaving itself.—will have to be more careful crawling up & down ladders after this or insist they be padded to protect both the shins and knees—Oh yeh?

June this year will be a bit different than last Sweet for it was my privilege to be with you & Susie at least a little—did get down over several of the weekends. Can well remember standing all the way from L.A.—it was well worth it however.

Sweet continue to be awfully homesick for a sight of the three of you and a lot of that love I'm sure is waiting for me. Of course there would be much coming your way too. All my love to the Three of you as always.—include Mother & Dad too.—

Al & dada

A.F Herney

P.S. Sweet all out of Emprin Compound—Would you send me some air mail—helps when I get an headache occasionally. Send several small sizes in metal containers if they come that way.

Love to all,

Al.

May 31, 1945 May Letter No 19

My Dearest Sweet, Susie Steve Mother & Dad:

The mailman came thru with April 11, May 6, 7 & 8 and a letter from Alice A[yres] acknowledging my letter to her.

So glad you enjoyed the roses. Was happy of course to know that you would be getting them for Mothers Day. I might say Sweet that the fact that there is still the problem with Susie shouldn't make that much difference. Whatever any one else might say about the problem forget it—what you know you know. Incidently the young lady is growing up isn't she—even going to nite movies—my my.

So glad you were able to get the tri for her. Agree with Mother that $15.00 seems a good bit of money for one second hand—Was wondering too what Susie would do with it without pedals tho I'm sure you should be able to get some at a Bicycle shop. Incidently what about OPA ceiling huh? Oh hell I forgot they are friends of yours—the OPA I mean.

Can't quite understand why you haven't received more of my letters—possibly they will all come at once.—I can assure you I've written nineteen including this one. However it is possible that they have been delayed enroute—& also there was a two week period when we didn't get any mail off the ship—They will eventually show up.

Appreciate your sending on the Paxton letter. Neither he nor she have had very much education—it was a nice try by him however. They are nice people Sweet. It is good to know that Nick is enjoying his new home with them. Am happy that Ralph Jr. is able to enjoy his Purple Heart—not posthumously.

The news about all of you being ill doesn't make me at all happy—of course I do realize that its nothing serious & that you are taking proper care of yourself & the two youngsters. Recommended before & do again Sweet that you see a Dr. about that stomach of yours.—can see Susie enjoying being waited on hand & foot & enjoying it no end. Ho hum—what I couldn't do for a bit of that myself.

Your reference to cash has been answered in any earlier letter. Do have sufficient for any needs I might have—haven't drawn May pay & I can assure you I have all of what I drew the last pay day so don't worry about it. If I didn't want to do it this way I wouldn't have done it. Also doubt if you have been spending all you've received for you realize as well as I do that we'll have to have something to live on the first few months after I get home.

Am not one bit worried if that son of ours doesn't walk until he is two. He still is short about six weeks which might be the cause—and tell him to quit this long nap stuff in the morning—however can't blame him getting all tangled up in the covers if he enjoys it.

Saw Bob Burns in Alias the Deacon tonight—not bad—did enjoy it. Sat thru about five minutes of "So's your Uncle Dudley" last night which was quite enuf. Wasn't in the mood for a show anyway I guess.

Keep on dreaming I came home Sweet—Maybe if we keep it up long enuf it will be a fact—that is an eternal dream of mine—day & night. I love you Three so very much and hate like hell to be away from you so long—Lovingly as Always

Al & Daddy

A.F Herney.—

P.S. How do you like these small envelopes. Have run out of the long ones—will have to get another supply I guess.

9

SWEEPING MINES AND PATROLLING OFF OKINAWA

June 1945

From Dictionary of American Naval Fighting Ships: *She [the* Scurry*] remained off Okinawa until 8 July, sweeping mines and maintaining antisubmarine patrols around the transports.*[xx]

2 June 45 June Letter No 1

My Dearest Sweet, Susie & Steve:

Can't let today go by without dropping you a note—& I mean a note—have been busy the last two days so that is why no mail—What with nineteen letters in May—most of which I hope you have gotten by this time. I'm sure you will overlook the absence of scribblings from me.

Another one of those months can now be scratched off the ticker—down and out—which of course means one month closer to home.—Doubt if any one at home counts the time as much as we all do for it means one thing & one thing only. Home to our Dear Ones.

Have commenced reading Bob Hope's I Never Left Home which you sent in one of your packages. So far have enjoyed it tremendously—He writes as he talks—Seems to grow on one yet isn't near what Fred Allen could ever be. Of course there is a dispute about that & I suppose always will be.

The letter this morning was interrupted by a trip so will finish here before the boat shoves off on the mail trip & me on it Damn it—

Really I've taken so many trips in that boat that it will be one hell of a time until I'll even step in a rowboat when this is over.—Then when getting where your going there are about 16 dozen other places for the boat to be so you wait—you know how impatient I am. Left the ship this morning at 8 15 and got back for lunch at 1 00—they fortunately saved if for me tho the word was they didn't know whether I would be back—The last word I passed was that I would be back & ready to be picked up at twelve—Really hate to hit port—as does the mailman for it means so much extra work for him—me too—This is & is intended to be bitching—or did you guess?

Your remember Mother—& her planning. All one had to do was to mention going someplace & wingo—everybodies problems were yours—that's just the way it is here—nobody seems to want to go—so Schultz who has to go generally gets stuck—naps are nice & can get one if somebody else does it for you—yep still bitching—hope you don't mind.

The only pleasant thing about getting into Port is that there may be mail for you Sweet & others I like to hear from & about—greatly disappointed when there is no mail for then all one has is the work—ho hum. Haven't had any mail from you since that dated May 17—hope that there will be some today.

Haven't written Mother & Dad yet & can't promise when I will get to it but soon I do hope—don't remember the date of the event but should—yep even had to think hard to be sure of Susie's birthday so you see how many of the dates I've forgotten.

Incidently you might ask Mother if I owe her any money over & above what I sent for the flowers—didn't stop to think that $5.00 might not be enuf to cover the cost of a dozen roses—if there is anything over & above will see that she is compensated.

Must close this short one Sweet which is sour as all but can't help it—do want to come home—Love you all so very much.

Al & Dada

A.F Herney

June 5, 1945 June Letter No 2

Dearest Sweet, Susie, Steve Mother & Dad:

Don't think I'm cheating but believe I have written you a note, which was plenty sour, as Letter No 1 for June. Not doing so well this month so far—but as I've told you before when there's time you'll get a note.

So dog gone tired the last couple of days really don't know whether I'm coming or going—since we had the additional advantage of a rather rough sea last night & this morning decided I'd pass chow and relax instead—took a nap till about 1400 hundred feeling some little better than when I hit the sack—ho hum for home with all its comforts.

Still so awfully blue & homesick—yes even to the point of even trying to swim—Wouldn't be at all unhappy if the little yellow b's would give up right now—could get home to the three of you very shortly if such was the case. Often wonder if it wouldn't be smart of have the letter drafted and all ready to go reference "When Do I get Out"?

Haven't listened to much of the news of late—and still biting into Bob Hope's contribution to Enjoyment before dropping off to sleep—The Time has been read and don't like to start a novel for it takes much too long.

Wondering if Aunt Julia & Uncle Albert have made their appearance in SD. as yet—Do hope they get there for it will be nice having them. Haven't had any recent word from them for I know they are busy too.

Could go for a good tub bath and back massage tonight—fire in fireplace & relaxing on the floor at 399—of course there would have to be Mommie Steve in Bed & Susie on her way.—Quit day dreaming Herney or you'll start bawling in a moment. Well anyway its nice to think those things.

Do hope that Momie is over her middle problem & both Steve & the Pride & Joy no longer have their colds—the last word was that everybody but Momie was improving & she should soon be on her way.

If you would like to know how it feels to be more or less water bound— just ask me—haven't had foot shore since the first part of March when at Saipan—really enuf to drive one a bit looney to say the least—at least however I've been off the ship—but as I've said before that is no pleasure either for all it means is that you go from one to the other—there is the compensation of seeing some new faces.

Incidently met J. Johnson a chap from Harvard in our class. Had quite a nice chat with him—didn't know him too well while there—but then you couldn't be chummy with everyone especially if you wanted to pay any attention to your family. He is on the staff of a commander of an LCT group & much excitement—a bit rough at times however.

Sweet, do hope you will overlook this kind of a note but couldn't do a bit better due to the emotional status I'm in—"Blue—Blue—Blue" I do love you so very very much & do so want to be with you—With all my love always to the Three of You—

Al and Daddy

A.F Herney

"HELLO DADDY! Wish You'd Come Home Soon!

"Home will be the happiest place, Dear Daddy, on the day When you come walking up the steps And come right in—to stay!" Dot's message inside: "The only gift we're sending is our love because all our packages don't reach you and we know our love will. So 'Happy Father's Day' to our Daddy and we only wish you could be here with us. Susie & Stevie"

June 7 June Letter No 3

My Dearest Sweet, Susie & Steve:

Received your May No 9 & 11 and a very nice Fathers Day Card from the two youngsters.

Can well understand why Mommie has been so busy—what with both of the youngsters running such fine temperatures—my God how did they stand it—the temperatures of course not Mommie. Am very glad to hear that both of them are better now and do so hope that their Mommie isn't bothered with the ailing stomach.

Think you were very wise not to think of sending anything to me for Dad's Day and unless another Xmas rolls around before I get home don't think of sending any packages—seems to take a year & a day & oh what a shape they are in when the get here.—Haven't as yet received Helen's birthday package. It is possible that it might have been one of those we received which had practically disintegrated.

Helen in her letter mentioned that we [are] an other Aunt & Uncle or rather that we had acquired a new nephew by marriage. Details unknown— Wonder what connection the LA trip had to do with it? Won't mention the matter until I get further word. [Al's niece Monica married Bill Zens.]

Thank you for remembering Jack's birthday—haven' remembered anyone's & would just as soon forget my own—

Was quite amused my Sweet about the note that you found enclosed in Jacks letter. Maybe Ann was trying to pass some information on to you but think she gave you a wrong steer. Don't know what the note was but any information Marie may have about me did not come from me at all nor to any of the family— for you have had all the information passed out by me. When the time comes will give you a running report of where why & what has happened. Really think Maries note referred to someone else so rest easy about it.

Have felt all day like I think a pregnant woman feels with the morning sickness—the sea has been a bit rough today & I still don't like it—doubt if I ever will. Have worked all day however at paperwork doesn't seem to help it any—think I'll do some horizontal exercise soon.

If Uncle Jim [Farnham, Dot's uncle by marriage] is out in this part of the world now should get to see him soon. As for enjoying the sun always have preferred hot to cold—you can shower the heat or the result rather—away— but still the sun is pleasant wherever you may be as you well know—yes even in Nebraska. When one is talking to a Limey what can you expect but to find out that they won the European war II just like they did W.W.I. Nuts to em—hate to think of actually operating with them for I'm afraid I'd tell a few of them off—ho hum.

With the exception of May 7 & 8 you have received about half of the letters for May—can understand why you receive them in bunches for they are generally mailed at one time—we unfortunately can't run down to the mail box on the corner—Am glad you have been getting them—the others should be along soon.

With all my Love to the Three S's—and so very happy they are over their sick spell—

Al & Daddy

A.F Herney.

P.S. You can really see where my mind was when addressing the envelope— Ho hum—

June 8, 1945 June Letter No 4

My Dearest Sweet, Susie, Steve, Mother & Dad:

Felt a bit better today as the sea she sorta smoothed out a wee bit & the didn't try to do so much close paper work—guess it all adds up to fatigue of one sort or another.

Am thankful I wasn't around at the time of cleaning the venetian blinds— sounds like it really was quite a chore and a bit of exercise too.

So Susie Q has started off to school already—yes even if it is nursery school it is school and means the little lady is growing up but fast. Hate to think that all of this is happening when Daddy has to be away.—but then he is & that's that. Will be good for her in more ways than one—and of course will give Mother C bit of rest too for she will only have one to look out for when

Mommie is doing her volunteering. I'm sure that Susie Q does enjoy it & will more so as time passes.

Sweet feel like a meanie in not being able to comply with our suggestion of sending the Pride & Joy some gum—but since there is a regulation against doing so—foodstuffs including candy & gum shipped to the Islands and beyond are not to be remailed to the states. We don't allow the men to do it so don't feel that I am at liberty to do so either. Would very much like to however & I'm sure that Susie will forgive me for feeling this way about it. Will write Chuck R & ask him to send her some if you wish.

The two young wives should have been told about the story of "Who's Afraid of the Big Bad Wolf" remember? It takes much more than nerve & both of them must have been a bit on the loomey side.—

Haven't seen Hamilton since the last time I mentioned him to you last month Of course he is busy I'm sure you realize this isn't a matter of picking up the phone & passing the time of day—for if it was I'd be talking a good bit to you. I'm sure you won't find out where he is by reading my letters so you might save yourself the time—however you might reread them—the letters I mean, for it does help when the mailman is late—yep just ask me.

Will be glad to receive the article mentioned. Time has mentioned them several times location Rocky Mt. States—not quite so far east—Dad of course will be interested to know about the matter so be sure he gets a chance at it.

Have worn my bracelet at all times except when showering. It must be sterling as its marked for it is practically black in spots now—must clean it I would put some clear nail polish on it if there were any available. Will have to keep looking & maybe soon I'll be lucky.

You'd better tell Steve to knock off this 2100 to 2400 stuff for he will be a night owl soon enuf without starting so early. Maybe he reason for it all was that he had so much sleep & too little real exercise when he was running the high temperature.

Know that the Pride & Joy will forgive her Daddy—With all my love to the Three of you Always—

Al & Daddy

P.S. The mailman just arrived bring your No 13—a letter from Joe K—note from the Reads—will mention them in my next letter.

Love Al.

10 June 1945 June Letter No 5

Sunday afternoon again—they do seem to come and go for which I am very grateful—however never fast enuf for it they past as soon as desired I would be back in CV with you & the youngsters.

Had a shower & shave so feel a bit rested and relaxed tho a tub bath would have been very satisfactory again for a change. The only trouble is that the navy does not furnish enuf conveniences.

The stationary supplies aboard are nill at present so until we can get some aboard or can beg borrow or —— from another ship will have to salvage a few old envelopes from the pile which I didn't discard—hope you won't mind.

Blythe's note—please note—the women seem to be the better correspondents—includes the following information I assume you already know. Chuck is now Officer in charge of the San Diego Fleet Post Office—which of course is a mean job itself. They are much enthused about the new home—have a victory garden & doing much yard work. Margaret is the center of attention with them as Susie was with us and Pop spends a good bit of time with her in the evening—nearly too big for a crib or rather the Pride & Joy's cradle, all of which brings back very dear & pleasant memories. Too bad they couldn't have a red head if that's what they wanted.

The letter from Joe K—contains the following—Soon after I left the money for the orchids was returned to him for the reason I mentioned to you. He asked if there was something else you waned which either he or Vi could buy & mail you—will think of something when I next write him which won't be long distance. He is acting Ass. Staff Judge Advocate Gen for the area arm Service—but as yet no promotion in sight. Has made application for Judge Advocate School at Ann Arbor—do hope he gets it for he has been deserving a break—They are still running the nursery—no longer living there however, but still takes much of Vi's time & Joe's too for that matter. Tots

Joe's youngest sister—you remember her—is expecting next month. Mother Keller isn't well—high blood pressure and of course Joe is worried about her.

He of course was interested in the saga of Iwo which was narrated in my letter to him. Joe at one time was anxious for an advanced base but don't think he would want much of it now since I'm sure he has had much of what he never even really got from Jerry—true love & complete consideration.

Saw the Pied Piper last night which is the reason you didn't get this note as of last night—know you won't mind my missing a few days this month. Really a delightful picture & truly a vehicle for Wooley—he can be the most obnoxious person—all in an uncouth by yet dignified manner.

Here's another note Sweetheart without saying much of anything yet saying that I do love you much for it would be very easy to put off till tomorrow or the next writing you. You & the youngsters are always in my thoughts and constantly want this thing to end so that I can once more take up the pace of breadwinner & guardian of 399 J Street. With all my love to y three Sweethearts as always

Al & Daddy

A.F Herney—

12 June 45 June Letter No 6

My Dearest Sweet, Susie, Steve Mother & Dad:

Hope you don't mind the stationary but that is what we have aboard— beggers still aren't choosers so will have to be content.

Finally received the two links in the letters No 10 & 12 for May—also received Marie's letter of the 22nd which you mentioned in your letter.

The promise of the two months vacation is really something enjoyable to look forward too. Is it necessary that we decide at this time whether we have the pleasure of the company of the children or can't we leave that for a further time when the decision will be important. As far as the taxes—don't feel that Marie should assume that responsibility. Don't think it will make that much difference so when the time comes to pay the taxes we will pay it.

Incidently talking about finances have you written Saunders about our accident & health policies. The way & the numerous occasions of bumping the shins don't want the policy to lapse. Believe also insurance on the car is about due too—ho hum June always was our heavy insurance premium month.

Monica [Al's niece] pulls a fast one on Pop, Mom and relatives doesn't she? Can see Sal [Monica's mother] being up in the air & possibly rightly so but holy gee Monica never was interested in education anyway. Maybe it will be the best for her. How will it feel to be a great aunt?—Good God but were getting old.

Am wondering if the {Armstrongs} purchasing the Frazee place is Keith or his old man—if it was Keith he must have made a pile this last year plus since I've been in or he is darned optimistic. Doubt if he will be turned loose too soon even tho he is on limited service as there will be plenty of boys eligible for discharge and just about as many desiring it.

The air mails arrived in good shape—however as I've told you no need for sending any more. Would prefer that you use them on the exterior of envelopes—hm need any more hint.

Pop hasn't been anywhere where he could have a picture took & besides you know how he loves to have his picture took—looks the same as ever except possible the high forhead is ever sneaking higher. No toupee in sight & non desired—let the sun & moon reflect therefrom.

Unless things change radically real soon don't think you will have to worry about transportation problems unless you want to return to the old homestead—However as I've said before that is a problem for you & you alone.

So the "Little Feller" has started already. He did get a tough beak do be careful of him until he is all better & it no longer hurts to apply pressure on the side. Can well imagine it wasn't Mommie's fault for I remember Susie deciding to take a few all without any help from anyone and did Mommie scold Poppie—remember?

Sweetheart—the nursing may be getting worser & worser but you have at least some part of me—doesn't help much I know but remember I don't even have that—just memories & very pleasant ones at that.

With love to my three sweethearts as always

Al & Dada

A.F Herney

June 14 June Letter No 7

My Dearest Sweet, Susie Steve Mother & Dad:

What do you know—the mailman came again today with our May 14 & 15 which ends up another months correspondence. Of course I still have a credit of four letters in May & the mailman isn't as speedy in delivering your letters—but no matter—you wrote them & they have been received.

Just off the 2200 to 2400 watch—worked all day except for the time I wrote you this morning. Really has been a long day but doubt if I could find time tomorrow so will continue to scribble a few notes, that is before sack drill.

Do wish it were possible & just as easy to go see Daddy as the Pride & Joy made it sound. I can assure you there would be nothing nicer than to make that suggestion possible. Wonder if she would like me in civies or should say rather if she will like me in civies?—She should get used to it of course. It won't take me too long to make the adjustment I can assure you. The "Grandfather" may have been picked up from the neighborhood children or even at school—surprising too what the youngster remembers for it was some time ago that Daddy fixed that swing.

The knee is much better—not the intense pain that I did have—occasionally it bothers especially when it is necessary to sit in any one position for any length of time or when the ups & downs via the ladders are excessive & sometimes they can be—generally needless too.

Just what are you planning on doing—doing into the business of purchase & sale of used children equipment—"we buy & sell anything & everything connected with the pushing, pulling & pedaling of children." My my what a sign—however you might ask Mother & Dad if they mind any.

Saw E. Robinson in the Mr. Winkle goes to War tonight: Rather an unusual part for him to take but it was enjoyable—must say he did it as well as the tough gangster portrayals which were his meat.—

Could use & would appreciate some more pictures—it has been almost two months since Ive had any new ones—those taken prior to Easter—Don't worry about Steve being so serious—takes after Pop in that regard when he is having his picture took.

Thanks for sending the information about the bank account tho wasn't worried about the matter. Quite a sizeable amount you have in the sack Sweet. Is it all in the checking account or rather was a good portion in the checking account on the first Monday in March—for if it was we will get stuck like we did once before—remember? Don't want you to deprive either yourself or the youngsters of what you need—a nice reserve is something to think about and emergencies always can happen—lets hope there aren't any except possibly a hurry up trip back to the coast.

You are right Sweet to be grateful that 8 months are passed—I join in the thought that these next 8 will definitely bring about what will cause us to forget them—they have been long lonely months for me too. I love you so much—

With love always to my Three Sweethearts—a big hug & kiss for the youngsters (being careful of Steve's rib of course) and an extra big hug & kiss for you Sweet.

Al & Daddy

A.F. Herney

P.S. Carrie's problem has my curiosity aroused—could it be Lloyd?

Al.

June 16, 1945 June Letter No. 8

Not doing nearly as well this month on the letters Sweet—but as Ive told you before—when there's time you get—when there ain't you don't—Still don't know how I batted out 19 to you last month.

Wrote the family a letter last night—the first in quite some time—over two months & when I got thru with it didn't have any energy left.

Has been quite warm today—really unbearable or rather uncomfortable constantly perspiring—was some breeze on the shady side of the ship so occasionally went out on deck for some fresh air to get revived only soon to be very uncomfortable again.

It won't be too long now Sweet till our next and 8th anniversary—Steve's & Susie's birthdays. I'm going to miss not being there of course for each of them—had to miss last year too & two years in a row is a bit unpleasant but will just have to think of the pleasures of those to come.

When writing Marie told her I didn't think she should do what she had planned about the taxes—so when the bill comes go ahead & pay then without anything being said. Also told her the news about the two months at Palomar was something very pleasant to think about & hoped that we could soon realized it.

Took a shower & shaved—I believe it while all I have on is the pajama pants I'm sweating so if you see water spots on the paper—it's part of me not the trade marks of the manufacturer.

It was good to hear that your friends husband is alive and on his way home. From what information that has been passed out the German prison camps were on a par with the Jap camps—unpleasant in the extreme—Possibly those boys returning from the prison campus should be place in charge of the camps in our country. Yet too an eye etc. doesn't seem to be the answer.

Still haven't had an answer from Carl S. Don't know where he is or what he has been doing—had hoped to get a glimpse of his ship but no such luck as yet—Maybe the future will bring us together some place. I do hope so for I would like to see him a great deal.

It would be very much of a pleasure to feel the ground under the feet—even if it meant doing leg work which is always does—afraid I will really have sea legs & won't know how to walk properly if we soon don't have the opportunity. Hate to think that this could go on very much longer. However I still will take the Navy to the Army any day.—

The outing at the park on the 30th must have been a treat for everyone—nice to think of green laws, trees & people—especially you three being there—promise to take the children to the zoo when I get back—Steve should be old enuf to enjoy it too & his rib well so he won't hurt when his Daddy carries him.

Won't write a note to Dad & Mother—so will say goodnite Sweetheart—with Love always to the Three of you.—

Always

Al & Daddy

A F Herney.

17 June 45 June Letter No 9

My Dearest & Only Sweetheart:

I am not including anyone else in this letter my Sweet or it is intended as an anniversary letter and as such is intended for & addressed to you and you alone. Know you won't mind it coming early for while I'll be wishing hard that I were with you on the 3rd I'll still be here & you there.

This will be the third anniversary that we will not have been together— the last I was in Seattle & the year before that you were in Lincoln—remember? That was the year I gave you the bracelet.

The eight years since you became the Mrs. H has not really seemed at all long—This of course is undoubtedly due to the fact that we haven't fared too badly. We of course have had our problems—didn't always get what we wanted when we wanted it but on the whole came to an amicable understanding and only once did we have a serious problem.

When referring to faring didn't refer to mundane things so much as just a part of the complete picture—We've enjoyed each other, living as a whole and have two swell youngsters which we can show and say to any and all— Well what have your children that ours lack?—There's a great deal of satisfaction in that Sweet most of which you have made possible.

You are well aware of the fact Sweetheart by this time that I regret all of the time that I have been away & regret more the time I will have to remain away even tho it may be just a second of time. This however is beyond our control and we'll have to be patient and make up for it at a later time.

It is difficult to explain Dot how satisfying it has been that you fit in to the Herney clan. They all care a great deal for you because you are you. Your constant kindness and consideration of Mother did much to endear you to them and something I will ever be grateful to you for having done so. Then too we can't discount being the mother of two very nice youngsters, a niece and nephew.

The many pleasant recollections of our relationship have done much to make the tough moments of a sailors life seem bearable. Realizing what is waiting for me at home dissolves the major portion of any problem into a negative quantity. You too might consider that when you have something that is extremely burdensome but your thoughts will have to be on the reverse "There's something out there who wants to come back."

Writing always seems to lack that which we hope to convey—but must suffice when no other means are available. In case you haven't gathered from what has gone before I love you Sweet with all my Heart—that I'm extremely happy that you are my wife and the mother of our two children.

With all my unchared love as Always

Al.

A.F Herney

June 17, 1945 [This letter not numbered]

My Dear Son Stephen:

It is difficult to believe that you soon will be celebrating the first anniversary of the day that you became a member of the family unit consisting of Sister Susan, Mother and Dad.

Out of the many days of that year your Dad has had the pleasure of being with you only three days. He of course is ever thankful for even those three days and yet extremely sorry that it could be for such a very short time, for it is one of the inherent privileges of parenthood to enjoy seeing a youngster grow from being a wholly dependent being to an independent entity by a slow but ever constant process. Every and each stage in that process being a wonder in itself.

Mother has kept me well informed as to your progress, your problems, ills, pains, and aches—all of which are normal. Yes even a broken rib. It is good to know that you are gradually overcoming that slight handicap with which you started life for you were such a little feller.

A very Happy Birthday to you Steve—with hopes that this coming ear will bring you every thing that is good for you and that Dad will be able to actively take his part in caring for you. I am indeed grateful that you are my Son

Lovingly

Dad

A.F Herney

COMMANDER MINE SQUADRON FIVE
UNITES STATES PACIFIC FLEET
18 June 1945

From: Commander Mine Squadron FIVE
To: Commanding Officer, USS SCURRY (AM 304).
Subject: Commendation.

1. This Command as recently received from the Commander Minecraft, U.S. Pacific Fleet, a commendation which is quoted in part as follows: "The Commander Minecraft, Pacific Fleet, takes pleasure in commending the Commander Mine Squadron FIVE, and through him the officers and men under his command, for outstanding performance of duty as Commander of the Task Group of minesweepers engaged in the amphibious assault operation at IHEYA SHIMA, OKINAWA GUNTO.
   "The effective application of professional skill, ingenuity and seamanship are reflected I the precise planning of the minesweeping phase. The courage and determination displayed in the execution of this phase while facing determined Japanese air attack are indicative of a high quality of leadership."

2. This Command also takes pleasure in expressing extreme appreciation or the wholehearted cooperation and careful devotion to duty extended by you and the officers and men under your command. This Command would deem it a pleasure to serve with your ship in any future operation to come.

3. It is requested that the above expressions of appreciation and commendation be conveyed to your officers and men.

G.W. ALLEN

June 19 June Letter No 10

My Dearest Sweet, Susie, Steve, Mother Dad:

The weather is still warm & Poppy continues to perspire. However have had the pleasure of a shower almost every day so that should help.

Have taken care of a bit of the correspondence—have written Mother & Dad—the family—an anniversary letter to you and marked as such on the envelope—a birthday letter to Steve and a note to Lloyd & Etta—Many more I should write but don't seem to have much energy left. Just relaxation is all I want.

Cleaned the bracelet today—don't believe it will last long and didn't get much of a job done on it for didn't have the cream for silver or the equipment. The polish I did use didn't hurt it any however. Can now tell it is silver and not cast iron as it appeared to be.

You by this time should have all of the letters written in May for your have reached me. In one of them thought you had mentioned the dates of birthdays & anniversary for Mother & Dad. In the letter to them apologized for not re-membering about Mother's birthday but believe it is in Oct—Is that correct?

The boys have put up a cartoon in the mess hall about censors—of course it is a bit extreme & maybe they are right but what the hell—it ain't no fun reading other peoples mail and while they want to let their one's at home know they love them that's their business—Ho hum.

One of the news broadcasts within the last few days carried a release by a Rep—who commented on the fact that some of the high military officials expected Japan to surrender within 90 days and if they didn't to expect some-thing. As for that they can expect continued attacks by the big boys overhead with all the nice little incendiaries that appear to do much to devastate the homeland. Do hope he is right about the surrender and a bright prospect for getting home before too long if it is true.

Hate to think Sweet that there is this coming anniversary that we will have to be apart again—a bit different than the last for you were then carrying Steve & as I remember almost expecting him then—& of course me in Seattle without knowing anything about it.

Wrote your anniversary letter & Steve's birthday letter early as I wanted to be sure that both got there on time—can't send either one of you a remembrance except some salty sea water or maybe a few sun rays or moon beams and of course my love with you have always anyway.

It will be nice if Uncle Jim can secure his discharge & return to his family. He has had a good shot at it already and it would be tough on him to make him ride the rest of it out way out here tho being on the type ship he is or he has much better prospects of getting back at least once in a while. Would like to get home but don't want to be over age as yet for there are still a lot of things I want to do before I reach that age.

With love always to you Three Sweethearts—

Al & Daddy

AF Herney

21 June June Letter No 11

My Dearest Sweet, Susie, Steve Mother & Dad:

Well the mailman came thru with our June 1 thru 4 and 6—left No 5 someplace else—can't guess where it is but it will eventually show up. No 6 was postmarked the 11th so it isn't too tough or long a wait.

Was quite amused at the difficulty that you had about the emperine [compound]. Should have suggested sending a bottle of 100 airmail which I'm sure could be done. Inquire about it anyway if you will.

Wrote a letter to Father Brown last night after finishing your letter—just one less to write & possibly will get the due's down to nil. However if one expects mail it is necessary to carry out your end of the deal too but oh what a chore it can <u>bee</u>.

You seem to be playing a good bit of bridge which I don't blame. Mickey Mouse should be your game after playing with so many different partners—I still like that kind of game and to hell with the rules—the unexpected is generally the most exciting thing about the game anyway.

As for selling the car use your own judgment about that. What will happen after this is all over is another matter & I assure you I haven't the slightest guess. As you say however it would be hell being caught in Chula without a car.

Expected that the slowdown on production would follow the capitulation of Germany. Some reconversion must be permitted for if not there would be chaos economic political & social—for you just can't throw thousands into the unemployment status without repercussions. Hope that Fran can stay on—but that a lot of those small parts get bounced right out on their ear so that they can go back to where they came from—yes some even from Nebr.

Very happy to hear that Steve has nothing more wrong with him than the rash—He does have a hard time of it. The cry baby part doesn't bother me much for believe he will be able to take care of himself & yet not be pugnacious about it like his Dad has been at times.—

As for Susan wonder who she takes after as for being mischievous—can't understand her attitude with Steve & that will require some attention—Do you think she will be the tom boy type?

Papa hasn't put o too much weight to without much exercise has gotten a bit flabby. Will have to try some exercises again. Haven't had much of an appetite lately but that isn't to be wondered at for it has been warm and my stomach too still is treated gently for it not I can be uncomfortable as all get out & I mean out. Sorry to hear yours is acting up once again—Do take care of it. Please also keep putting on a few more pounds as you'll need it.

Mailman about ready to depart so will say once again that I love you with all my heart always

Al & Daddy

AF Herney

21 June 45 June Letter No 11 [Letter No 12]

Since I don't remember if the letter finished his morning was No 11 will assign that number to this one. In that way won't be cheating anyone but myself.

Was warm again today—didn't over exert myself doing anything either I can assure you. Did what I felt should be done—yet was busy all day.

Took time out to see Rudolf Menjies (?) Catherine Hepburn & Ginger Rogers in an old number—subject theatrical boarding house. Nice diversion & hot too—that is the mess hall was so as a result you enjoyed while you sat & sweat or you just sat & sweat.

It is quite amusing of Susan & the Swing. No doubt Dad was a bit disgruntled about her hesitancy in using it after he had taken time to make her one especially after she had asked him for it. The neighbor children must be darling children or do their folks know it already? There is always the possibility of asking them to stay home or had you thought of that?

Glad you finally got the answer to the joke you had forgotten. Have forgotten most of my repertoire—but then this is a good place to forget them—you don't mind, you shouldn't.

Can well imagine how excited Chris was to know her Poppa was to be home the middle of this month. I wonder if she appreciates how much he wanted to be there. Don't blame her for passing up a hen party for the prospect of getting further word.

Think possibly the trip to Riverton will be good for Alice—in more ways than one—getting out on her own with the responsibilities of a mamma & seeing old friends. Some satisfaction in knowing too that people are glad to see you.

Your mentioning 2322 Haste [address of Al's rooms while at law school in Berkeley] brings back some mighty pleasant memories Sweet—both of us worked hard that summer but enjoyed it too.—Celebrated our first anniversary too I believe in full fashion—It was the St Francis wasn't it that we spent the evening? Ruth & Bill Baily aided in the pleasure of the afternoon. Have been trying to place 2132 Haste—someone really got stuck—since San Fran is the regional office of the OPA can't understand why those conditions should be permitted. Bet that veteran believes he was <u>fittin'</u> for the ones back home.

If Susie likes [pop] corn as well as you & myself I'm afraid we will have a youngster who is going to demand some should she hear the popper going after she has retired.—the answer of course will be to start early but that isn't too good either for it will be so soon after diner or an alternative pop some corn in the garage—more fun.

Enjoyed the clipping about Crosby & Hope—Did I remember to tell you that Hope's "I Never Left Home" held some enjoyable moments of reading— sounds like him—or what remembers he sounded like on the air—especially how to differentiate between the female Officers of Britain's Shemales—the Lt had two buttons—he knew because he had been out with one she had had two.—Well who knows—

Here is another day gone Sweet—one closer to being home with you & the youngsters—something that I wish would be mighty mighty soon—I do love the three of you so much—

Love always

Al & Dada

AF Herney

June 24 June Letter No 12 [Letter No 13]

My Dearest Sweet, Susie & Steve:

Since I didn't get this written last night there will be only a short note— have some post cards if you would prefer those—oh yeh!

It continues to be warm—Really believe I perspire more than I take on yet don't seem to be shrinking away. Can't quite understand what it is all about—could enjoy this weather if I were at home I know. Still prefer it to cold any day.

Incidently about the notice on Mother's Probate—the notice was sent to the Legal Residence—in this case properly addressed whether it was done by Gee-Gee or another secretary.

Palma seems to be getting on quite well without poppa—a mother–in-law & roomers. She does have energy, enuf for many of us. She has it however & we don't so why feel bad.

As far as the big problem of worrying about getting home on a days notice—doubt if that will be one you'll have to meet—especially very soon. Of course I don't know & all conjecture on my part. Don't know what kind of duty this chap Wright has but guess he is on one of them thar ships that gets back to the States occasionally.

Wonder if the telephone Co is happy about you going into the second hand business—wear on the equipment—time of the girls and all that else that is to be considered. You did get a good price for both vehicles so guess you can be a bit proud of that. If Susie isn't too crazy about having the tricycle can you afford to wait until we can get a new one for her later when we won't have to cart it around too much.

Sweet don't care if you won't write each day—however as you know even a note is nicer than nothing at all.—Write when you have time include what info you have.

It is nice of Ann to have Monica and her husband with her. Will seem strange to Jack & Joe to have Monica & her spouse there at the house. What reception did they have & where—you did forget to mention that.

Am pleased that Susie Q has gotten so she enjoys school. The more she can accustom herself to other children the more social graces she should acquire and the more tolerant. It is good also to know that Steve & Susan both are feeling better. Have you tried to apportion the maternal & paternal contribution to Steve's temper? If it, the temper, has been induced by too much lap exercise remember I have only three days to be blamed for—Don't know what has who buffaloed.

Here it is almost another month gone—do wish they could all scoot by in a hurry for I do want to get home to you three Sweethearts—can't be soon enuf for me—will gladly take over my share of the responsibilities of the household—paternal care and _____ and all of the rest that goes with it.

With love always to the Three of you as always

Al and Daddy

AF Herney

24 June 45 June Letter No 13 [No 14]

My Dearest Sweet Susie, Steve, Mother & Dad:

Lucky me—the mailman brought me your nice letter of June 14—No 7 but still is holding out on No 5 or did you miss that one as you went by—Well no matter still up pretty well on the news of my family and that is really what matters.

Another warm day—thought a shower might help but just as wet as before I took one—there is the possibility that I'm not as offensive to everyone else now however.

Quite amused by the opening sentence of your letter "These last two days got by me etc." Time must be going in a hurry for your no 6 letter was dated the 10th—Am just as glad that they are passing so quickly for that means only one thing.—

My you are getting to be a gad about—nice if you can do it and don't blame you. However don't leave the whole burden on Mother and don't go so the much the youngsters will wonder if they actually have a Mother as I'm sure they are wondering if they have a Pop.—

Regarding the Gal with the card tricks—she didn't say that everyone was going to get their wish did she? It might be she was merely practicing up on you gals for cheering up the poor little Soldier Boys which she will undoubtedly entertain since she is too a Red Cross worker. Just kidding Sweet for I'm sure too your dream will come true—just when however is another matter but keep right on hoping & hoping hard—I'll have to add more too for you didn't want me home any more than I want to be there.

Had wondered if they hadn't had some kind of commissary there in Lincoln. You would think they would with as many personnel that they have stationed there. Were you fortunate enuf to get the Pride & Joy some gum for I still feel like a heel not being able to send her some. A gold mine as far as cigarettes too huh?

So poor Steve is getting his first crack at being told off in no uncertain terms. Holler he can & holler he does—meanie Mommie & Grandma just let him holler.—It should be noted however that a years, or almost a years training can't be untrained in a day so I do hope your ears will get accustomed to the din of it all. Since the little feller has made his start don't believe it will be long before he is on his feet instead of in a horizontal position or on all fours. Am not worried about it—did you think he might be just a bit on the hesitant side.

Do hope Susan won't get too daring with the swing—such as standing in the thing—do hope the two falls out in the wrong direction won't frighten her of it tho.

Odd that you should hit a Dr who knew Lloyd wasn't it. So glad you decided to do something about yourself for all you have just got to be tip top when Pop gets home for were going to crowd a lot of living into a very short space of time making up for what we've lost. Yep & see that the youngsters have stored up a reserve on the sleep side.——

With all my love to you Three as always—regards to Dad & Mother— Yes Sweet again a Happy Anniversary if it can be one with your old man so far away—

Love

Al & Daddy

AF Herney

25 June 45 June Letter No 14 [June Letter No. 15]

My Dearest Sweet, Susie Steve Mother & Dad:

The mailman let me down today—no note or even a Time—do I feel left out in the cold—tomorrow is another day & will just have to hope.

Am just a wee bit red this evening since I've had my shirt off for two hours while topside today. Its either getting a bit tan or too hot to stand it—which is worse I wouldn't know. Even in the evening when things should begin to cool off the clothes become sopping wet without any exertion at all. Or for some of that sea breeze as it comes in off the bay at home.

In looking over the wardrobe may have to invest in some new trousers soon. The four pair I started with still have some life in them yet & may hope that they last me out. When out have worn dungarees which of course haves saved the greys—they tho of course—the dungarees being blue don't show the dirt nearly as soon as greys—you start with no press & end with none so your not at a loss there. The supply of shirts is still adequate & won't have to worry about that little matter.

Visited with Larry Cuba today—took time out to take another whale boat ride—don't believe you met him but he was the chap who had stayed at the Calif Hotel in Long Beach—remember. He has had a youngster since he went west. His main thought like that of the rest of us is to go home but quick. He has an application in for photography interpretation & hopes to get it to it may mean getting home to the states for about 10 weeks & back out again. Think he is foolish for as I've said before I want to go home to stay. The second time out will be plenty tough.

Have seen several movies lately—but for the life of me can't even remember the titles—strictly a release from the daily monotony of it all. The one this evening starred Allan James and _____ Carlisle. Not anything right up to snuff or now playing on broadway. However they do have there place & fill in some of the spots.

What would you like to do on our anniversary Sweet? Take the few days and go to Palomar or just sit at home and take it easy? Both of course would be enjoyable and the choice is a hard one—then too there is always the gas problem or could we afford the amount needed.—Nice dreams what? It is going to be one hell of a place to be celebrating & will be wishing hard on that day.

Who has won out the great tussel going on at 2315 Ryon—Steve or the combination of Mommie & Grandma. Bet he can wait both of you out & still holler & be as mad as he has been when you think you've won.—Children are that way.

As for the Pride & Joy know that she is being a good girl—nice to baby Steve, sweet to Mommie, Grandma & Grandfather, does what she is told and loves her daddy as much as he loves her.

Hating like everything to be so far away from Sweet—important too to have this all over so I can come home. Love you with all my heart

Always

Al & Daddy

AF Herney

June 26 June Letter No 15 [June Letter No. 16]

The mailman was good today—brot me your June No 8—mailed on the 17th which isn't bad for time—just nine days and Marie's letter with all of its news.

You don't mean that my Pride & Joy was sort of naughty—what does she want Daddy to be—disappointed for he will be if she continues to be a bad little girl. Maybe he won't want to come home—oh yeh? With the evenings as long as they are it a bit difficult to put her to bed when its still light.

As for polishing the car remember one anniversary that I polished the car—of course I started before my Sweetheart was up or do you remember. Glad you were able to get something that Dad & Mother wanted for there anniversary and something for Dad. As for as anything for "Pop" it was just another day. Ho hum and didn't miss not having a package. In fact think it is easier that way—the less one has to remind one of home the better these days for you can get so damn homesick. Had forgotten that I was home last year for Father's day that then I've forgotten a lot of things.

So Dad got the treat of playing nurse maid again last nite. Do wonder if Susie gave him another tough nite of it or whether she was a little lady as she can bee. Suppose Steve amused him too try not going to sleep and making all of his different kind of music.

Do hope that the old town won't be too quiet for you with some of the gals leaving. Three weeks until Caz gets back shouldn't be hard to take especially if they are calling you for extra duty at the hospital. Indicently the Mr. "Hopkins" hasn't anything on me for my Chickadee is a Nurses Aid too. (See March "Readers Digest" pages 89–90). Don't take too much time out doing that work Sweet to deprive yourself or the youngsters.

Sweet as for wondering or worrying where I am don't—for I'm safe & have been in the past & feel sure I'll be all right in the future. Will let you know where what & why when the proper times comes & please don't be impatient. Just remember always what I've said before Come Hell High Water—Japs or no Pop will Come Home.

Heard today about one of the Comm Officers on a sister ship getting orders to return—another CIO job. Haven't talked to him but don't think I would want that—still think it would be better to ride this thing out so that when we do go home we can go to stay. Think it would be mighty damn tough to say goodby the second time—maybe I'm wrong but that's the way I feel about it.

Sorry that Ann hasn't had that trust deed signed over. Thought I had done so and my Sweet am sure I gave you a power of Attorney plus executing all of the other necessary papers. Believe it may be in the safe deposit box or at the Office. The power of atty sent Marie was a limited one—limited to making to the tax declaration only.

Speaking about the p of a [power of attorney] given to Marie it was nice of them to accept her word on the matter and darn the exemption. As for the stocks & bonds believe the bonds referred to are bonds other than government bonds of the baby type with which we are blessed. There are the Northrup stocks however which I believe cost us $312 dollars or do we still have them—see how forgetful Pop is getting.

Disappointed to think that the wait for the pictures is going to be as long but guess there's nothing I can do about it. Something to look forward to anyway.

So glad that Uncle A & Aunt J have arrived. Quite a reprise too that George decided to take another trip to Calif—all of which should be good for them. Nice too that Hank [Gawers, Al's brother-in-law] has gotten the assignment to Clovis and can be home for a bit—Hate like everything of course to miss the reunion & believe they will all miss us.

Envy Helen having the time to spend at Palomar but our time will come—wonder if Helen is really needed or the heart throb "Bill" is the attraction. He must be quite a boy for Helen's standards are high—hope he doesn't spoil the friendship by wearing yellow sox with ox blood oxfords—remember?

Didn't know that Monica's Bill was expected to join the army so soon. A little tough on the kids for there ain't no time like the present is thee when your just newly married—ho hum Sweet does it seems like almost eight years ago?

Just one week left Sweetheart of the eighth year of our relationship as Mr. & Mrs. Much has happened and much will happen in the future all of which I'm sure will be as pleasant or more so than that which has gone before—can't wait to get home to start making the future one huge dream come true—I love you with all my heart as always

Al.

A F Herney

June 27 '45 June Letter No 16 [June Letter No. 17]
My Dearest Sweet, Susie Steve, Mother & Dad:

Another warm day so I guess it is here to stay for awhile—summer time anywhere even in Nebr is warm—sometimes hot. Dot's letters indicated that Nebr is however having some unusual weather—could slow some of Calif's especially San Diego unusual weather.

Wrote the family a note—hoping it might get there for the reunion on the 2nd—doubt if it will but just hoped it would.—It is quite unusual to have one so soon after our last one in '43—That was a nice gathering and pretty complete as far as the Herneys were concerned. This one will find Mother, Al Dot with their two youngsters absent but the addition of Uncle Albert & Aunt Julia.

Have pretty well broken in the pipe the youngsters & you Sweet sent for the birthday—gives a nice sweet smoke—of course there never will be any-thing quite as satisfying as a cig however.

Don't know if I mentioned that I cleaned my bracelet last week—had it looking just about new—and believe it or not it at present is just as black as it was before I cleaned it—do guess that I'll have to be patient and wear it that way until I can get some nail polish to protect it.

The Time's are coming through in pretty good order now. Have already received and about digested all of the June 18th issue. Have saved the article on China until bed time—just a reserve. Doesn't take long for the sandman to call once you convince yourself that the heat won't diminish any. Irrespective how hot it may be can't stand a fan blowing directly on me. Don't know what there is about it but don't like it. Gosch of course benefits by reason of that fact.

Remember the name of the movie two nights ago "Larceny in Music". Last night saw ___ Montgomery and Annabelle in the "Bankers Moon". Neither one worth raving about but something to do. Would like to state now Sweet that irrespective how many bum ones I sit through now won't mean I'll go just to be going when I get home—for there are too many other things that need catching up on.

Mr. Bezold has been in a dither for the last couple of weeks. He is expecting and is quite anxious to hear. He takes a good bit of ribbing because of it. He wants a girl as badly as I wanted a boy—but I'm sure that what ever he gets will eventually make him happy.

Don't know what they are having by way of Cinema this evening but thought I'd write this before they started as I could shower & hit the sack afterwards.

You know If I'm not careful I will have written you a goodly number of letters again this month—get you in the habit of expecting them and disappointed if you don't—that's ungood Sweet—but don't mind if you are. Would like to be home so as to do a good job of it.

With all my love to the Three of you as always

Al & Daddy

A.F Herney

28 June 45 June Letter No 17 [June Letter No. 18]

My Dearest Sweet Susie Steve, Mother & Dad:

Just completed another session in the sweat box—crew mess seeing "Orchestra Wives". Good music and not too bad a plot—It seems that the last few pictures we've had aboard—all ancient if not in time in use—do not have the endings with them so you really are left high & dry—much like "The song without words" or whatever it might be.

Took a shower this afternoon before chow—plus a bit of horizontal exercise. Not much but something of a refresher at that. While you feel fresh for only a short while after a shower you feel worse if you skip it. The amount of water you can consume amazes you no end. The good book says eight glasses a day—but that is far from sufficient.

Opened up some—one can of your cookies the other day—tried one not bad—investigated a second & saw lots of nice little bugs crawling around which means only one thing. Haven't investigated the other but will to see if they can be consumed or must be disposed of. Real sorry about it but can't be helped. All the time & effort it took too to make them and ship them wasted—Did let me know tho that you were thinking of me especially when you were so busy.

Have for the life of me tried to find Ed & Maries home address but all I can remember is Keating so number at all—yet not even the hundred block. Oh well what a memory anyway.

The last few times in the anchorage have only been off the ship as little as possible—refuse to take any unnecessary trips. Went aboard another ship today for about ten minutes but the vessel was close so didn't mind too much. Will let some of the other chaps do some of their running around and see how they like it for a change.

Think we will be paid some time after the first. Haven't been paid for two months. Have drawn up to May 1—still am very well fixed as far as Herney is usually concerned and didn't draw all that was on the books for me when last paid, don't therefore worry about Pop and his sheckles.

Am playing with the idea of rereading "High Time" again for there is too much humor in the thing to get all of it the first time. Just wonder how much time Mary Lasswell spent in San Diego—must have been considerable for the story isn't something one can dream up about of thin air.

The article in Time by Congress Judd on China is pretty much a contradiction to the article in Saturday Evening Post of Febr 24 "Vinegar Joe & the Reluctant Dragon" Possibly they can be reconciled in that one is the viewpoint of a military man—and a smart one from the record, & the other a politician.—

Only two days left until we can count the ninth month as down & out since I've had to leave my little family. Nine months that will never be recaptured or regained but possibly & very much so, make living with them mean so very much in the future. I miss you three so much and so want to come home.

With love always to the Three of You

Al & Daddy

AF Herney

29 June 45 June Letter No 18 [June Letter No. 19]

My Dearest Sweet:

Time only for a short note—increase the count by one & will keep up the score of last month—providing of course that I get to write you tomorrow.

Received your No 9 today. Won't comment much about it—other than its nice to hear that Jerry & Elmer are now parents and good to hear from Vic. Wondered if he hadn't been around on either the Iwo or Okinawa invasions for that would set him about the right time. Thanks for sending on his letter—do wish I could write a nice note like that—incidently he went a long way around to get to Okinawa didn't he?

Received a letter from Ann today—enclosing an order for full reconveyance. Have executed it—wrote a note so it will be on its way tomorrow. The letter is newsy as usual & much about the youngsters. She seems to think that there might be something serious between Helen and Bill—Will wonders never cease for I'm sure that he must be the essence of many things if Helen is in a serious mood. Maybe that is the reason she thinks she is <u>needed</u> at the Library [at Los Angeles City College] for the late summer session.

Joe [Tex, Al's nephew] has a Planter's wart on his foot which is to be taken off—quite painful Ann said. Do hope it won't bother him too much. Said also he has made some good grades this semester—finally getting serious.

Jack [Tex, another nephew, Joe's brother] is to become a real worker this summer—plans to work for Balboa Laundry. Ambitions kid to say the least—has tried for a commercial drivers license too.

Don't know why I'm passing this on for I'm sure Ann will write you & you can get it first hand. So nuff of this.

Finally had another picture with an ending to it tonight. Crosby and Martin in "Rhythm on the River". Ancient as many of the others but always like to hear Bing sing. Really did too little of it in the picture but I guess there is no right to complain. Had the usual sweat while enjoying the picture of course. What a pleasure it will be to attend a Cinema in an air conditioned theatre.

Back to Anns letter it seems Jane is going to do what she has always wanted to do—raise her cockers commercially. Surely she will enjoy it and will give her an outlet for all that energy. Not bad prices either $45 per is good clipping.

Only one day left of this ninth month Sweet. If the scuttlebutt isn't that the future looks bright & rosy—However am looking at it, the future in view of the Scuttlebutt with very dark glasses—not pessimistically however.

With much love always to my Three Sweethearts
Al & Daddy
A F Herney

June 30 June Letter No 19 [June Letter No. 20]
My Dearest Sweet Susie Steve, Mother & Dad:

It really is good news to hear that the youngster is here—Surely they will be as pleased with her—quite nameless huh—as we were with Susan. No doubt Elmer [Cawby] was as surprised as everyone including Jerry that the youngster was early. If she is as small as Steve there is no question that she must be a little thing. Jerry must have had a very easy time of it from her report to you. Elmer of course was saved that seemingly unnecessary prancing up & down the corridor waiting the good tidings. The bottles & net did arrive just in time didn't they?

So Steve is finally coming through with a few of the signs of being a bit independent. The procedure must amusing and yet pathetic—so much effort & so little accomplished Wonder if he realizes that it will eventually be simpler to do. Can't blame him preferring the bed for the antics—for the floor can be awfully treacherous and a rug rough. Can well remember Susie not being content to have diapers quietly placed in position. Has his rib pretty well healed by this time? Do hope so for that may be the reason too why he has been hesitant about moving around too much.

If Susie as learned to go quite high in the swing Daddy will have to move the swing at home for it certainly isn't in the most desirable spot—concrete can be so hard and the edge so sharp. Wouldn't want to think that the "Pride & Joy" would be hurt by Daddy's lack of forethought so it might be smart to have it taken down before you get home—A promise of another should satisfy her & if I'm not there possibly Uncle Mac can fix one which can be set up in the middle of the yard.

Have said before Sweet that while I'm sure you enjoy your work at the Hospital and I'm very proud of you doing it please don't take too much on yourself and especially don't let them impose on you, for it one thing to be generous with your time and another to take time from the youngsters—Those two cherubs are dear to me as they are a part of yourself. Possibly a bit selfish but we do want them to be just a little bit better than the next—not in the manner of "Keeping up with the Jones" either.

Where did you get the little story about the Officer, the gal and the Scotch? It would seem that she knew her business and was ready willing and able and not the least bit reluctant nor did she need much of a sales talk.

So glad you were able to get Dad something for his Dad's Day that he enjoys. From your letters he doesn't get much time at home any more but seems to be on the road most of the time.

Still want to come home so bad Sweet but know that will be impossible so must be happy in the thought that you Three will be there waiting for me. I love you with all my heart

As Always

Al & Daddy

PS. Will drop Jerry & Elmer a note before hitting the sack. Should have done so long ago.

A F Herney

10

ARTS AND CRAFTS WHILE OVERHAULED AT LEYTE

July 1945

From Dictionary of American Naval Fighting Ships*: "She [the* Scurry*] remained off Okinawa until 8 July, sweeping mines and maintaining antisubmarine patrols around the transports. The minesweeper underwent overhaul at Leyte, Philippine Islands, from 13 July to 17 August.*"[xxi]

July 2, 1945 July Letter No. 1
My Dearest Sweet, Susie, Steve, Mother & Dad:

Your No 11 showed up today—not too bad time since it was mailed the 23rd. Still have not received No 5 nor No 10—Evidently still enroute.

The idea of the picknic sounds very inviting. You will be quite a picture with all the trimmings you plan on taking with you. Of course Dad & Mother can properly show off the grandchildren—do hope for their sake that both Susie & Steve on their best. Would very much like to be with you but that is impossible—some time soon however huh—go someplace on a picknic where theres lots of good green grass & much shade.

Are all of you who went to the commissary eligible purchasers—if so you did make your trip worth while & much more fun battling together than going alone.

Those Friday afternoon get togethers must be something. Not much of a quiet afternoon is it—however—since most of you are Mothers I assume you can properly care for the children & still gab to your hearts content. What Mother doesn't when it comes to talking about their off spring.

Missed writing you last nite—quite tired after seeing DuBarry was a Lady & the usual sweat out. Just crawled into the sack & that was all there was to it. As for the picture it will pass—could have gone for more songs by the gal who sang about Solami (?) & for looks had it all over the gal whose name was given top billing.

Can well imagine how Rob Roy [Dot's younger cousin, son of Heral and Jim Farnam] is looking forward to the summer on the ranch at Cody. Do think I remember Helen but wouldn't swear about anything right now except I've been so burn't up all day that I've been swearing—period.

Mr. Bezold received word today that he is now the papa of a baby girl— Just what he wanted too—tho we have been kidding him about getting a boy. Doesn't know much about anything except that mother & baby are doing alright. He has been quite upset for the last week in not hearing.

Guess it will be my luck to take the Beach party tomorrow—take enuf for 2 cans for each man—just something else to do & god only knows there is enuf already but go I must. If its that important then there are things that will justify letting them slip on too—but for that oh well!

So happy that Susie Q decided she wanted to add her note—Thank you "Pride & Joy"—you really don't know how much Daddy misses you & wants to come home & be just another guy that lives at 399 J Street in Chula Vista with Mommie, Susie & Steve. Do hope it will be soon for Daddy is getting tired of being a Sailorman.

This time 8 years ago Sweet <u>Poppy</u> was putting on the final touches to jumping off into the briney deep. Never have been sorry for having taken that leap either but then might now only the pleasures of the part & the expectancy of the future are realities Its hell to be away—so far away from you & the youngsters—I love you with all my heart as always—

Al & Daddy

A F Herney

July 3rd 1945 Letter No. 3

My dearest Husband—

This is our 8th anniversary—and it seems we are some distance apart—just a few thousand miles or so. Shall we say, "better luck next year?" Marie & Ed are at "Happy Holler" [Mt. Palomar cabins] and I know we'd be there too if we were in San Diego—New gas coupons just in yes, I think we'd be there—with Susan and Steve both. I haven't let myself thing too long on the subject today—it brings the tears too close too easily.

I can't even remember if I told you what I got last Saturday as your present to me—instead of the flowers—a very lovely pin and earring set—it is most beautiful and goes with my bracelet so nicely. It will outlast the flowers many many years and will remember it as this particular year.

I worked at the hospital this morning—when I arrived at 8 I told Sister Francesca (in OB) that I was celebrating my wedding anniversary by working— she laughed—she's so nice—young and full of fun. About 10 A.M. one of the nurses went sailing down the hall with a cake in her hands—said to me as she went by—"birthday in one of the private rooms." It didn't think much about it. I hadn't been at that end of the hall & didn't know who was in there. Then Derringer— student nurse began shooing all nurses, aides, etc. down there saying we're all invited for cake. I kept protesting saying I didn't know the patient—I'd stay back and watch lights—but I was shoved along & in the room—it was empty—no patient—and the cake a surprise for me for my anniversary. Sister and Derringer had cooked it up and were so pleased that I was surprised.

I came home and read your letters that came today No 14, 15, 16 and then read the anniversary letter—no 9—which I had saved for today. I just can't be that wonderful Sweetie—you're blinded by the blue Pacific—but I'll try and live up to the best of it. I've learned an awful lot in 8 years—that I needed to know—I've learned a lot in the last 10 months—particularly since February that I think will add materially to the smoothness of our home life from now on—providing my mind holds up until the strain of discipline of a 3 yr. old with one coming up for some but stiffer treatment! Of one thing I'm very sure—I'd never change my mind could I go back to the Spring of '37—I'd never want anyone different—I just want you always.

Has Mr. Bezold's baby come yet or the notice thereof. Don't leave me hanging in space—one must know!

The C.V. Star came today—and almost didn't look at the second section to see Floyd's face starting at me. Quite a boost and a nice one. Bobby was given Legion Award at Jr. High graduation too this year for outstanding Citizen so Lena should be proud. Am glad for them.

To get back to the anniversary gift. I finally located the card in the desk today you had sent Mother to put with the flowers because I saved that too for today—when looked in it—the $10.00 was there. Then Mother told me she as a bit worried because she didn't find money in your letter—she didn't want me to mention it to you because didn't want you to send more money but she wondered if you had forgotten to put it in—or it had dropped out when censored or what—& of course I didn't look in envelope until today—she had just given me $10.00 the day I went to the Base so I had no idea she hadn't found it—All is well and accounted for.

My pictures got mixed up tonite on the table because wind came up while we were on front porch. I had them all separated in bunches and now I don't know which two I haven't sent you. This is one of them I know but can't decide which is the eighth. If you can tell me now which ones you have I'll send the missing one.

It would be nice to have you back for a CIO job but as you say, parting again would be something I'd hate to face. We're grinding out the days—just hope our dispositions last.

Well, last year at this time I was in bed but most unhappy with a sharp pain in my right side which I <u>thot</u> was appendicitis—and a year ago tomorrow I was in Mercy Hospital for a brief sojourn. Well, there are 4th of July's & then there are others. Hope the next one is a reunion for us.

Here we go Sweetie on the 9th yr—they say the first <u>10</u> are the hardest you know—so maybe we won't be bothered much longer! I love you so much—I can't tell you how much—but I'll be here waiting to prove it—so hope that helps the days & nites a bit out there.

Always, your loving wife.

Dottie

—————

July 3——45 July Letter No 2

My Dearest & Only Sweetheart:

Even tho I've written you a note for this occasion previously so it would reach you by this date I can't help dropping you another note on this "Our Big Day."

You, I am sure have been extremely lonesome even tho you do have the two youngsters with you, and don't relish our separation but you can know Sweet that your lonesomeness & unhappiness is multiplied many times on my part so many miles of land and sea away.

Do not know what your plans are for the day but those for this end are the usual routine of the day, and routine it can get to be, monotonous as all. Do hope that there will be something that you can do that will at least help make the day appear at least as of old.

Quite warm again today—really wonder what they do during the heighth of the summer, yet come to think about it, it is summer isn't it. Again what I couldn't do for some of that Calif weather with the cool breeze coming off the bay.

Didn't have to take the crew on the beach party today as the one yesterday was cancelled. Suppose that tomorrow will by "My Day"—guess I can take at least one day in tending to the boys. It will at least mean hitting the shore & taking advantage of the bit of shade that is visible on the beach. No swimming permitted however because of pollution, which possibly is just as well. Can however play a bit of ball and get some exercise too.

The conference in the passageway—Hetzler, Gosch, Gates & Hanna has broken up so won't have that interference to contend with. Just bulling is all they were doing—tho when you come to think about it there is not a whole lot else to do.

Haven't as yet received any of the recent pictures you have taken—Am quite anxious to receive them for the lift the morale. The bestest thing of course would be to know that the Scurry was pushing her nose thru the waves Stateside to you & the youngsters.

My Sweet, tho I've said before & will many times more—You are the "One & Only". I have meant it and greatly appreciate these eight years tho they really seem less than that. You are what I do want to come home to and stay home to in the future. Am sure I didn't know what I would have done these nine months without the assurance that you were mine & tho the parting was necessary you will be there waiting for my return and at the same time given a greater meaning to you and what you have given me. Have never questioned your love for me but have at times strained it a bit because not always being the most thoughtful and considerate husband. For these shortcomings I am sorry and ask your forgiveness.

I love you with all my heart Sweet—Will love you always in the future. Do so hope the letter, card and flowers have reached you by now.

Lovingly

Al.

A F Herney

6 July 1945 July Letter No 2 [July Letter No. 3]

My Dearest Sweet, Susie & Steve

Here it is almost one week of the 10th month already gone—wouldn't mind one bit it the 10th et sq. months had gone by and the Scurry was homeward bound—discharge awaiting me when we arrived.

The mailman finally came thru with our No 10 and twelve—neither of which will comment on at this time. Where is No 5?

Told you in my last letter that the fourth was to be my day on the beach— It was—in more ways than one. Shoved off for the beach with 18 of the crew—beer enuf for 2 cans for each man—about noon. Picked up Mr. Handy a Comm Officer on a sister ship who said he would like to go.

Dispensed the beer soon after hitting the beach so that it would still be cold and could really be enjoyed. Of course it didn't take very long for it to disappear.

Mr. Handy had taken his camera, ships photographer, with him. He suggested hiking around abit. Investigated a few of the caves that had been investigated by our forces previously—really not much left of them.

Then off to the races for just around the corner were some things that might be of interest so Mr. Handy said.—

However it seems that the previous time the tide had been out & the beach could be easily negotiated. The first part of the trip was easily negotiated but— finally came to a small gap between the rocks—about ten feet deep—and about five feet wide at the base of the cliff gradually widening as it neared the beach.— All with about four feet of water at the bottom. After discussing whether to leap or stretch Herney tried to stretch—having declined the offer of a push by Handy—result the stretch was too long—Herney gave way in the middle— down & into the drink—all wet except for the cap. No injury to person but certainly ruined the package of cigs and put the lighter out of commission. Crawled out the other side—disrobed & wrung as much of the brine as I could out the clothes including shoes that I could get out of them. Mr. Handy learning from experience wadded across ala nude—having passed his clothes & camera to me. What disgusted me was that just a little later two army chaps came along nice & dry—they had jumped it which we should have tried & didn't.

After a few more hazards including wet feet and pants legs finally arrived at the spot for which we were headed only to be told that we were out of bounds unless we had pass and would have to leave. Did however get to see the remains of a native village a few prisoners of war but no pictures. Do guess we can live without them but will try to have to remember them in the minds eye. On finding out we were in forbidden country of course scooted out of there post haste.

Not much of a way to spend the 4th Sweet when one wants & wanted so much to be with his family.—but then there will be 4th s in the future which will be so much more pleasant.

As always I send the Three of you all my love—be sure to give Steve an extra kiss & hug for me on his birthday which isn't too far away.

July 8 July Letter No 3 [July Letter No. 4]
My Dearest Sweet Susie & Steve:

A letter which I had started last nite was interrupted by several things so started afresh today—

— 319 —

The first "You can't Ration Love" strictly a stinkey yet so bad it was funny. Can forgive them for making it for it did give some pleasure at least.

Next on the list was the 8 to 12 watch & didn't have the energy to do anything about letter writing when I did get off watch.

Still as warm as it had been for the past several weeks—makes one so uncomfortable—no sooner hit the sack and the mattress & pillows are sopping wet. Finally in desperation you just give up & let the sandman grab you.

Was a bit surprised to hear about Chuck. Really wonder what the story is for Blythes letter said he was the Officer in Charge of the San Diego office. Seems odd that he would be receiving orders first in charge & then changing the place of duty—tho it does seem that something has happened. It was nice that they had a stag party—really would have liked to been there!

Ann sent an order for reconveyance which I have signed & returned to her post haste—don't know whether I have told you about this or not. But it has been taken care of. Again will say I believe I did give you a P of A. among other this but no need to worry about it. No reason to go nuts over such minor things Sweet for it doesn't do any good.

Sorry to hear that Ann isn't doing too well again tho I'm sure you couldn't keep her quiet if you wanted too for she is Herney & always will be. Don't believe she would be imposed on if she didn't want to be so don't worry about it.

You've done much better than I for I'm still waiting for a letter that Ed was to have written me before Xmas. Mentioned that fact in my last letter to them. Please send it on when Dad has seen it.

So glad you have the gum problem solved for I still feel badly about not being able to send some to the "Pride & Joy". Do hope the luck continues and that you can get some film too.

Now that Steve has started his process of maneuvering it won't be too long until he is on two's and all of the trouble that that will mean for Mother, in drawers etc remember?—

Poor Susie is learning to give & take because of the swing—all which of course will be good for her—what a picture she must make when asserting that she isn't a baby.

Didn't want to disillusion you Sweet but when writing about not needing transportation. When you plan on returning to C.V. is of course your problem except you'd better be there when Pop gets home or at least on your way—nuff said about that.

Will try to do better the balance of the month on letters.—have fallen down on the job so far but know you will forgive me.

With love always to the three of you

Al & Daddy

A F Herney

10 July 1945 July Letter No 4 [July Letter No. 5]

Dear Sweet: Since the spirit was willing but the flesh was weak—very week.—You didn't get a note dated the 9th—Hope you won't [mind] too much being neglected this month with so few letters to date.

As you read before it has been quite warm. The least exertion causes the body to give off sufficient moisture to dampen every stitch one has on & from the looks of things it will be a bit warmer still. Didn't seem to mind the heat at Eniwetok or at Manus but come to think of it was fall in the northern hemisphere at that time.

The nights have really been beautiful topside even tho old man moon hasn't been out with all of his light—the stars however are there peaking between & thru the clouds. One is conscious of the fact that the sea catches and reflects some of their light. If the sea would continue to be as calm as it has for the past few days can't say I wouldn't mind being at sea until this thing is over & I could come home and hang the old hat on the peg & keep it there.

At last you are going to have some luck on the tricycle—or at least that would seem to be it. Didn't think there was any chance of getting gyped after you first experience of being too anxious to buy even tho you didn't eventually loose anything on it.

Sorry you didn't send on the portion of the Star about Dutch—is good to know that he did get home and was quite glad to know that he could. Possibly with Kelly back things might again be a bit different with the force in Chula.

That picnic must have been a huge success for the "Pride and Joy" tho Steve is really too small to have gotten much real enjoyment out of it. Can well imagine that she was quite pleased that you could stay & did stay until 9. One can't blame her for not being too interested in the food when there are so many other interesting things to do at the park especially have someone's attention most of the time. Surprised that she & Ann weren't interested in eating berries instead of exercising.

Carrie's problem intrigues me a good bit for several reasons—have wondered how long she could stand being wed to such a selfish person as Lloyd—possibly he can't help it but could at last make the effort. Where is the big lug now, is he still at Pearl where & when? Shouldn't be catty but there's one guy that is hard to appreciate.

Tomorrow is Steve's first big day, tho I'm sure he won't appreciate anything except the added little attention that he might get. Wasn't he all pooped out after the long haul across the bedroom. Not worried about his lack of locomotion at all for he will get there soon enuf. I'm sure you will give him an extra big hug and kiss for me who so wishes he could be there.

Do hope that the Japs will get hep to the fact that they are definitely behind the eight ball proper. Germany of course suffered the result or rather effect of concentrated air attacks but nothing compared to what the Japs have already started to receive. Oh why in the hell don't they say all right were down—what's the penalty so we can all come home.

Will soon write you that long letter which I have promised you for some time but never got around to writing.

With all my love as always to the Three of you—

Al & Daddy

AF Herney

July 11 '45

My dearest—

Hardly seems like a whole year since I shocked everyone out of a yr's growth by having our son ahead of schedule—but no one the worse for it now.

Alice is coming around soon—we are going to meet Caz's train which comes in about 10:30. Alice, Elaine & I went out last nite to mail a letter for Alice—ended up having a glass of beer & trying to help Alice decide which of several things she would do. Think it will be the 18 month course at U of Chicago (on scholarship.)—we all think she would be rather silly to pass up that chance—even tho she could get a job without the degree now. It was Elaine's wedding aniv. Yesterday so the beer was our toast to her. With Pete safe in Paris for the future—& a slight chance of her going over—she wasn't too depressed.

So cool today and this evening, have the doors closed again—may well turn out to be the coolest July on record.—Not complaining—it's wonderful—like Colorado—or California.

Susan has suddenly taken a great love for the kitten—she lugs it around like a sack of salt—cat doesn't seem to mind at all—never offers to scratch much to my surprise.

Our loot at the base consisted of some synthetic gum called "Yank Gum"— small box of Lux flakes (priceless at the moment)—can of Dole Pineapple and something that passes for a bathing cap—looks better than what I've seen in town.

I don't know if I ever told you that on July 3rd I received a telegram from McAllisters—sent to Lt. or Mrs. A.F. Herney—sending their love for our anniversary—they were supposed to mail it out but haven't done so yet so will stop by & collect it.

Have a note to write to Jerry—have mailed her several things & better tell her about them.

Susie was very nice to Stevie—singing Happy Birthday Cake to him all day—and she knew he was to have only 1 candle on his cake but she will have 3 on hers. Somehow I've sort of thought you'd be back for Susie's birthday—don't know why—but now any hoping for Christmas—with my fingers crossed.

Love you so much

Dottie

July 11 '45 Letter 9

Dearest Daddy:

Today I am one year old—tho' frankly, whey they make such a fuss about my age I don't know. They keep insisting I crawl—or try to stand up—I'd much rather just sit—sometimes its sort of fun to wriggle across the floor on my tummy after Sister's doll—but today they put a new fuzzy bunny in front of me—guess it had something to do with my birthday— nice and soft anyway. I was real good this morning—didn't mind my play-pen at all—made them sort of coax on the milk at lunch because I could see Mother was in a hurry and trying to frost a cake & be ready to go to the Base with Palma at 1:30. I was sleepy anyway so finally ate my lunch & went to bed.

When Mother came home I just woke up—and she dressed me up in a brand new suit—red pants and a red & white striped polo shirt—some stuff—Auntie Ree & Uncle Ed gave it to me for Christmas. Then she took me out in the yard where she had a white frosted cake with one pink candle in the middle of it, on a stool. They stood me up beside it—so decided it was up to me—I reached out and took a hunk—whereupon everyone was very pleased so I ate the cake & frosting in my hand while Mom took pictures of me. Then Palma & Ann & Tommy came & all ate cake—that is Tommy and I didn't—we sat in the playpen—and let the rest of them chatter—you know women.

Grandmother held me after dinner out on the porch for a long time— but I was finally put to bed tho's its fun to lie and gurgle awhile before go-ing to sleep. Altogether it was a very satisfactory birthday except for one thing—someone isn't with us that should be—that's why I'm writing this letter. Mother shows me a picture of such a nice looking guy who she says is my Daddy—then she hugs me real hard & says he'll come home someday and play with me—I was sort of little when you last saw me I guess but shucks I'm ok now. Guess I fooled everybody a year ago because they didn't expect me quite so soon. Do hope Mother is right—that you'll come home soon to be with us—'Cause I need a Daddy and sister Susan always looks so happy when they talk about Daddy. I know you must be a lot of fun, we're doing ok tho—and hope you are too.—Incidentally—I feel sort of in the money—a bond from you, Grandpa & Grandma & Mother—pretty good intake—don't you think?

Just to let you know I miss you too—

Your son,

Steve.

Top photo: Stephen with his first birthday cake, Lincoln, Nebraska; Bottom photo: Susan with Ann Allyn and Stephen with Tommy Allyn.

—

July 11, 1945 July Letter No 5 [July Letter No. 6]

My Dearest Sweet Susie, Steve, Mother & Dad:

Here it is the 11th already and Steve's birthday. I'm sure this day will be much more exciting for him even tho he is too too small to appreciate than it will be for his Dad.

Just the usual routine of the day—including everything including the warmth of it all irrespective of where one may be it is hot. Still however can't bear to have a fan flowing directly on me but doubt even that would help.

Taking a shower doesn't seem to be much of a help either for your wet before you take one—wet during the time our taking one and all wet again as soon as you dry off. Had a bit of rain from the heavens this morning but had been busy working so really didn't know about it until it was all over.

Some of the crew have been sleeping topside for which you can't blame them. However it is a bit hard to appreciate the unwillingness of the steel plates of the deck fitting themselves to the contours of the body. Yes even I may attempt to convince them that they should be a bit more cooperative.

Haven't had any mail from you now for about a week—however that as usual isn't too unusual—no not meaning that you probably haven't written but just the nature of being a navy man. You also will be on the short end— even tho at the present time may be receiving some of the letters previously written.

Enjoyed your remarks about the different reports from the different members of the family. I may say however you shouldn't limit your remarks to the Herneys—Wonder how many of nine people of unrelated families would report the story—will say that the Herneys are destructive in this that they may plan for each other tho at times it may be a bit awkward for the one who is on the receiving end of the planning. By way of reminder you knew that before you married me and took me for better or worse. Ho Hum.

Back on current events since the last two issues of Time ain't as yet arrived. With as little actual news as we gleam from the air waves "Time" is about the only thing that keeps us really in on the know. Its going to be good to be able to pick up a newspaper again and read yep including the funnies even to it will take a bit of time to get back in the groove.

Enjoyed the Pride & Joys description of the ice cream cone—when you stop to consider it wasn't too bad a job either—She is getting so she knows all of the enjoyment and pleasure of childhood—& I least of all begrudge it to her to am sorry I can't be there to help her appreciate them.

Still have a bit of something to do before hitting the sack so will say good nite—pleasant dreams—maybe at least we can get together in them.—I love you three so much as always

Al & Daddy

A.F Herney

July 12 July Letter No 6 [July Letter No. 7]

My Dearest:

Can kill two birds with the one stone this evening—soaking my right foot in a pan of hot water and <u>writing</u> you this 6th letter.

As for the foot only the big toe & joint are sore. Was conscious of every-thing not being all right yesterday but didn't think anything about it except thought I had tried to push thru the bulkhead during sack drill. However this morning it was really swollen and a bit worried. It is much better after four soakings today so do guess there is nothing to be worried about.

There has been no appreciable change in the weather—still warm enuf to sweat the usual amount only to take on more fluids & get rid of that too. As I've said before please some of the cool sea breezes at Chula. I'm more sure now Sweet that no one could sell me any other climate than that of Southern California—Pooh on the four seasons too of the mid-west.

Should have written George—which as usual I didn't do. He said in his last letter that he was to write you. Am awfully glad that he had the oppor-tunity to visit the folks in Calif again for I'm sure that he has missed Mother about as much as any for she was about the only one who really corresponded with him regularly.

Ran across an old Newsweek of early June. The article really raised hell about many things including the meat shortage. Of course the OPA was to blame—and probably they are right. However I doubt if the blame will ever be placed where it really belongs. Henderson just happened to be too good a soldier and allowed the "Boss" to influence him too much—but that's politics.

Nothing has been said about the tenants recently so wondered if we still had some. Remember the last time they were mentioned was in regard to the door—the usual one—front. However if they do decide to find a home of their own can't blame them. Don't think under those conditions the house should be rerented but that again is a matter which you will have to decide.

Wonder if the Coles have made their trip north and are back home again. Harvey by this time should be contented that he couldn't get into this thing for I'm sure that he like Uncle Jim would feel free to take advantage of the age limit. Will drop them a note soon. Something else to put on the must do list.

What I wouldn't give for a sight of you Susan & Steve—however the next best thing is to take out the pictures I have & wish & maybe do a bit of day dreaming but then its such a shock to come back to realities. Life away from my family is hell. Should take consolation in the fact that there are many thousands like me—but that's just a bromide.

Love you with all my heart as always

Al & Daddy

A F Herney

13 July July Letter No 7 [July Letter No. 8]

My Dearest Sweet:

Word has it that we might expect some mail tomorrow. I for one however am still a bit skeptical about it so won't feel too badly if there isn't some for us.

It is quite a bit cooler top side this later afternoon. Possibly that is due to the appearance or more rain clouds which of course mean only one thing— hm—the possibility of more rain—very deep concentration caused that.

I'm really getting as bad as the crew—haven't a whole lot of interesting things to say tho you see amusing incidents but which for the present can't be related. However will try to remember them for future correspondence.

Plans are for the movie topside tonight—that is of course if it doesn't rain. Can't understand why the Almighty won't give us that much peace at last for be alone knows what & how much hell one can take. Irrespective of all that it will be sorta nice not to be sweating while trying to enjoy the movie for a change.

From all prospects don't intend to be taking or making too many boat trips on business very soon—not that there won't be the chance but just don't have the energy nor the drive—except of course off toward the beach which they say is quite nice—will do & let you know.

Have been keeping my eyes open for Uncle Jim's ship but no luck as yet. Wondered if you weren't a bit wrong on your speculation as to just where he was. There is also the possibility that he might [have] moved around a bit too. Who knows just what is in store for them at what time.

The big toe is much better today. The soakings it got yesterday must have done the trick—very little pain today even with a shoe on—still would like to know what was the matter but since there is usually something wrong guess it will have to be taken in stride.

Continued after the show—

For a change no interruptions except to change reels—Saw "Dragon Seed" which I think you saw in part in more ways that on in Long Beach. Not too bad at all—even tho the emphasis on really have been amusing Hepburn isn't too bad an actress & rather enjoyed it.

Report from Gosch is that the beach is nice so will plan on spending some of the time there. Really don't plan on doing any more than is necessary in any way shape or form—Don't plan on doing it the hard way either.

Well Sweet over one third of the eleventh month is already gone by the boards. Do so wish they would scoot by the way like lightening so I could get home to you & the youngsters. Miss you so darn much it isn't at all funny & so want to be with you.

With love always to the Three Sweethearts—way back there waiting for me—no more impatient to have me home than I am to be home.

Lovingly
Al & Daddy
A F Herney

15 July July Letter No 8

My Dearest Sweet, Susie, Steve Mother & Dad:

Almost one half of this the tenth month already gone for all of which I am mighty grateful for it means one thing at least—that I is just that much less time that I need to be away from you.

Didn't write you last nite as I had had the watch with Mr. Schnabel during the day and after seeing the movie had no energy left for letter writing. Should be ashamed to admit it but that is the way it was.

The movies have been of a bit better selection—possibly due to a movie exchange being in the vicinity. Nite before last we saw Dragon Seed as I told you—last nite Mickey Rooney and Judy Garland in "Girl Crazy" and tonight the same two in Strike up the Band—neither of which I had seen. Both light and enjoyable which is something of a relief in itself. The movie tonight was interrupted by a good fast rain so the completion of the picture was indoors but still enjoyed it.

Went ashore today to see what could be seen—not much I'm sure but it was good to be on land once again to stretch the legs a bit. Even tho there were cokes available they weren't selling them that way so really had to drink beer. Broke down and had the second can tho would have preferred cokes. Two beers is a big dissipation for me for there is no fire or desire for it or anything stronger—actually the last thing I'm wanted.

After the two cans of beer Van Ott a comm officer from a sister ship and myself took a stroll along the little beach picking up a few odd shells. Nothing out of the ordinary I can assure you but something to do. Couldn't interest anyone even in a game of horseshoes—hm—how well I remember one day at Palomar when I played so much and got blisters. Plan on going back again & see what else I can find—but no blisters and not much more beer either.

Still haven't written you that letter I've intended to as yet but just to whet your curiosity a bit more will say that you can draw that tentative line to Okinawa in permanently—would you like to know more? Be patient—I'm sure you'll be happy when you receive it.

The mail is as yet holding out on us. No mail again today but can hope for better luck tomorrow. Mr. Bezold is dying for some for tho he received word that he was the father of a baby girl & that Mama was doing fine too he hasn't as yet received a letter from her—he can hardly restrain himself when he finds out there just ain't any mail—not even official stuff. Possibly will have to make a personal call on the post master & demand some pretty soon—heh what's the delay? That of course would be influence needed for him to hand over what he has been holding out on us.

Needless to say that I miss you all more & more as these days slowly pass into that from which they cannot be recalled—how nice it would be to be able to turn the time back after this is all over so none of life would have to be sacrificed. I love you with all my heart as always

Al & Daddy.

A F Herney

July 16 July Letter No 9 [July Letter No. 10]

My Dearest Sweet, Susie, Steve

Some very disappointing news today—viz—not to expect any mail for at least two weeks—not good but ungood to say the least especially when news of you & the youngster is what I'm looking forward to at least.

Since things are as they are I'm just going to have to imagine that I've received the letters you've written—telling all about Steve progressing better than expected on his navigational problems is well & gradually being unspoiled. That he has at least two more of the teeth that will eventually be replaced in just a few years.

The "Pride & Joy" is as usual taking over wherever she goes—is attending the nursery school still & enjoys it as much as ever and of course does many things which are astounding in more ways than one but above all that she has been a very good little girl.

Mother of course is well—continues on with her nurses aid work, enjoys it and when needed generously gives more time than she agreed to give. That her problems with the two offspring multiply daily all of which tends to give her gray hair. She had better say that she still loves Daddy & misses him a great deal—for all of which Daddy loves Mommie very much.

Have spent the day in getting absolutely nothing accomplished. Don't intend to do much but today has been a total waste of time. Just piddled around and not a bit sorry.

Tomorrow is another watch day so means will be restricted pretty well to the ship. Maybe can get some work accomplished then.

Thought I could accomplish a small job I had in mind with two dog tag chains as the one you bought for me in Boston but for the life of me couldn't find a dog tag chain at any one of three ships service—Hence I'm going to ask you to purchase and send to me two plain silver chains—for women and one for a little girl and one for a big girl. The links should be a little longer than the links of the dog tag chain. Think you could send them airmail without much question. Would suggest that the chain have a clasp on in the back. They needn't be too expensive but would suggest they be sterling if you can buy such a thing. My what a long paragraph and clear as much as to just what I want.

Really—the nights have been lovely. A shame that they must be spent without some romance with the "One & Only" thrown in but that will have to come at a later date. What a shame that all this time will have to be wasted. Ho hum doubt if I'll even be able to catch up on my romancitizing.

Another letter Sweet that doesn't have much of interest in it but you know it wouldn't be written unless I loved you a great great deal. It is so very difficult to write anything but a dull note when one doesn't have some late information of his loved ones.

With all my love always

Al & Daddy

A F Herney

July 17 July Letter No 10 [July Letter No. 11]

My Dearest Sweet, Susie, Steve, Mother & Dad:

Another warm day. Could very easily have gone around with just a pair of shorts but you don't do that when you have the deck—certain attire is required and it isn't always comfortable.

The show last evening was rained out on the forecastle so we displayed it in the mess hall. I stayed only long enuf to get good and warm and then left because it was what I call a stinker "Put Your Best Foot Forward" and they did it in Technicolor—Really what a waste of film & the gal Lucille Ball—they don't need her in "Hollywood". Hit the sack.

Even tho the days are fairly hot the evenings are cool enuf to be good sleeping & that is just what everyone does. It is good to be able to do some of that horizontal exercise without being uncomfortable while your doing same.

Tried to do some paperwork this afternoon. Soon gave up however since they were chipping the deck above me—was going slightly nuts so gave up in disgust—result nothing accomplished but an effort at it any way. Wonder what the deck hands would do if they didn't have to chip & paint, chip & paint.

Spent the balance of the afternoon deciding and trying how I could most effectively use the chains I asked you for in yesterdays letter. Think I have it pretty well worked out and will be able to do a rather nice job of it too. Only time will tell & it will take some time but then a diversion from the humdrum and I don't have any unfinished furniture which I can spend time on so ———.

Still no mail today. Do hope the mail clerk wont get to the point where he dreads to go after some but comes back with nothing. Wouldn't blame him if he did for no mail brings growls as it always has and always will.

Susan's birthday will soon be here—not much more than a month away and already three years old. God how she's growing up and Daddy missing so much of the pleasure. My shoulders still ache every time I think of the Sunday we went sight seeing via trolley in Boston and poor Susie's discomfort because of the wet disposables. What a day and Dad was so disagreeable. Don't know if I will be able to get a small remembrance to her in time but will try hard to do so.

Most of the chaps with who I've talked recently about the future are quite optimistic too. Their optimism like mine is based on no hidden or dark secrets but just general news. Do hope they are right and we can all be some so very very soon for I don't enjoy being away from you one bit and am chaffing at the bit to get back and be Daddy & Husband in fact. I love you with all my heart as always.

Al & Daddy

P.S. Wonder if I'll forget that the permanent address of "The Younger Herneys" is 399 J Street Ch.V. for I've addressed so many envelopes to 2315 Ryons St.

A.F Herney

July 18 July Letter No 10 [July Letter No. 11]

My Dearest Sweet:

Another long day and still no mail from you—tiresome I know but just as unsatisfactory for us on this end and as usual we all are disgusted about it.

Today was another warm one which when added to the chip chip not much work was accomplished. Piddled again this afternoon which if it doesn't stop will mean much more in the near future which will be bad.

Took the opportunity and had two pairs of shoes and the Romeo's resoled and new heels—not too bad a job either and not too expensive. Supplies of soles are few and far between so am lucky they could be taken care—Shined up the old shoes look pretty good & are comfortable so won't have to invest in some new ones.

Had a double header last evening. "Two Girls & A Sailor" which was good entertainment can quite see why the women go for Van Johnson. The second the name of which now evades me together with the players was definitely second class but had some good lines—P.S. the little "Doughgirls". Story about the crowded life in Wash D.C. as was the plot of tonight's diller called "?" also a diller. However must say that both evening were pleasant topside without interrupting showers from above.

Have started the letter to you—just started—and do plan on mailing much before the middle of next month. Do hope that you won't be too disappointed either in the content or the time you will receive it. Plan on making a few carbon copies to send to the rest of the family.

Had a shower just before chow tonight. Did little good except to get some of the dirt off. Nothing unusual to be as wet after as before and during the shower & should be used to it by this time.

Plan on taking another trip to the beach—however plan on having some cokes' this time for I understand if you holler long & long enuf you'll get them. From your having lived with me for some seven years you know I can do plenty of that.

Our news is much more complete & often recently—however there is still only one thing we are anxiously awaiting—Toyiko quits—new spelling of Tokiyo but left it as it is. Have quite a few rebroadcasts of many of the old familiar programs too but they for some reason just don't have the appeal that they used to when—some long time past.

Forgot to mention that I again had my hair cut yesterday—by a barber and once again sat in a barber chair. Rather a nice feeling after sitting on a stool and having one of the many men perform the operation. Actually the clippers change hands so often you want to sing the old ditty "Button Button"—paraphrased of course.

Another day Sweet which is of the past and one day closer to being home with you. Should be and am grateful for that at last. So want to come home as I'm sure you want me to be there.

With love always to the Three of you

Al & Daddy

A.F Herney

July 19 July Letter No 12 [July Letter No. 13]

My Dearest Sweet:

The Gods were good bringing mail from you—July letters 3 thru 7 inclusive—where the rest of the mail is no one really knows but cares, I hope. We do.

Pleased to know that my anniversary letter arrived in time & that the letter to Mother did too—sorry I forgot to mention that the ten spot was in with the card. Do wish Sweet that you would have gotten the flowers—of course if you are happier with our selection I too am happy but you could have had both couldn't you?

Thanks Sweet for the very nice anniversary letter and I ain't blinded by the Blue Pacific or anyone or anything in it. Anything learned in our eight years together has been mutual. It is gratifying to know my Dear that if a choice was offered you Spring of '37 you would not choose differently.

The surprise party on you at the hospital sounded like it was good fun and mighty sweet of Sister Francesca. Evidently they like our Mommie at the hospital and appreciate her being there—all of which goes to prove it doesn't hurt to put ones self out once in a while.

So glad to hear that Floyd F is doing so well,—he has worked hard and deserves it. Bobby too has contributed to the family honors & Lena the nice little person can rightfully be proud.

As for the pictures to date the only recent one received is the one of the "Pride & Joy" in the swing—so until the rest of the mail shows up we will have to let the matter rest. Just can't be of any help to you. She does appear to be having a very good time.—God love her.

Missed being at Palomar on our Day but then Sweet there are going to be so many many more that we can enjoy there that our appreciation of them will be oh so much greater. Wonder if Eddie & Marie missed having us there as we missed being there—do hope so for would feel bad if the latch string was not open to us.

Your fourth appeared to be a quiet one and yet pleasant too for you were doing something that pleased you & of course Dad. There is a great deal of Satisfaction in being able to do what you want to do when you want to do it. Teaching Susie to enjoy the pleasures of swimming was an excellent idea for the afternoon. She too will enjoy swimming as does her Mommie You didn't expect her to get want to get out of the pool when you know how much she enjoyed, and I hope she still does, her bath.

Am or rather will be looking for the polish mentioned. Hope you have included some nail polish to insure that the silver polish will not have been used in vain for it don't take long till the salt bin again has it blackened till h____ won't have it.

Hope you haven't the pull cord of the cartoon as a gadget in mind—for if you do I promise to clean out the closet every day—so there—.

Am very pleased Sweet to know that you have made the start in July of writing every day. I haven't done as well I know except spasmodically but write every chance I get when there is the chance of getting it off to you.

With love to you always "My One & Only" and to the Pride and Joy and the "Little Feller" too.

Al & Daddy

A F Herney

July 20 July Letter No 13 [July Letter No. 14]

My Dearest Sweethearts:

Don't think I'm in any condition to write but can't & shouldn't pass the opportunity.

—Played a bit of ball tomorrow—that was yesterday, and feel that to-morrow, that's today—I'll be slightly stiff—about as still physically as I am in other ways right now—for after the game wandered into the club had two beers and ended up with three scotches—not much as a total but more than I've had in a coons age.

Bezold was with us today—plays piano—tickled a few keys and was Poppie blue—as could be for he remembered some might pleasant moments when Mommie sat down at the baby grand at 399 J street. The piano wasn't too good & Bezold can't play as Mommie can so—but did it enjoy it at that for it was a circumstance where one couldn't have all he wanted, when he wanted it.

So Steve has decided to cut another of those things we insist on calling teeth—however he would miss having them, wouldn't he. Since Dad isn't there to help suffer thru them Mommie has to worry about them all herself. Do hope he won't want to play with dolls when I get home tho his time will come I'm sure—and hell and high water won't stop him.

Can't quite understand your statement "I got the wedding presents off to Monica and Pat today." My God—don't tell me that the favorite niece [Patricia] done and did it too—thought she had so much before her. Can un-derstand why I'm in the dark since there is mail missing but am amazed is such the case. Dreadfully interested in knowing when & to whom, where and why. If she did decide to do it can't really blame her for Pat will do OK in any company—a bit surprising to say the least.

Saw a la femme today Sweet—white and American but didn't phase me one bit for there is only <u>one</u> that is you and you alone. Whistles and such may go for some but to me that's all wasted effort and rather humerous too.

Helen's boy friend incidently is <u>Bill</u> Lemon I believe who is a prof of math at Helen's college—a widower with two youngsters. Surprised you hadn't heard about him from some of the family and am sure I'm not telling any secrets. Really believe Helen is quite taken for a change—and maybe thing will run in threes—who knows.

No doubt the <u>Pride and Joy</u> looks fine in her new dress as she would look swell in anything.—Would like to see a picture of the ensemble for Mommie Susie & Judy modeled of course when the work is completed. Good to hear that Susie's training is progressing and no more bed problem. Can't blame her as I've never blamed Mommie for wanting to crawl back into bed at 7 AM.

Your brief description of the swimming suit or what could do for one has me intrigued.—just how do you know I wouldn't approve—If I were the only one to see it being worn of course.

With love to you three as Always

Al & Daddy

A.F Herney

July 21 July Letter No 14 [July Letter No. 15]

My Dearest Sweet, Susie Steve, Mother & Dad:

Not more than one third of this month left—not complaining at all but more than happy that this much is gone.

Have been trying to find the name of the ship you gave on which Ed Hudgins is doing duty but for the life of me can't locate the letter. At least it wasn't in the ones I reread before disposing of them which I hate to do but would have to eventually. Thought I had written down the information when I received the letter but evidently didn't. What makes it worse can't remember the name of the ship.

Con't Morn of July 22

A short interruption due to the show being called—"The Falcoln & the Co-eds." Amusing in more ways than one—second rate to begin with and missing the middle reel. At least we weren't showered out so that helps somewhat.

Think I will be able to get Susie something nice for her Birthday & get it away in time too so that she might have it for her birthday—that is of course if someone doesn't rearrange the plans made.

Still no sign of our mail that seems to have gone adrift somewhere. Should catch up with us soon for there are many things I would like very much to know about.

The body is a bit stiff today from the game of baseball of two days ago. We should learn Sweet that we are growing a bit old—too old for much exercise when your so soft. Maybe its good that we can & do take a few of the kinks out of us once in awhile however.

Don't know if I will go to the beach today or not—would be a nice afternoon but no heavy stuff like he last time ashore—that too I can't take for being out of trim and I hits you like a ton of bricks.

Attended Mass this morning—arrived soon after 7:30 when Mass was to start so was late—Didn't have time to gather the flock so that they could attend too if they wished. Evidently they didn't look at the plan of the day either.

If this is to be mailed today will have to cut it short. Love you with all my Heart as always

Al & Daddy—

A.F Herney

July 22 July Letter No 15 [July Letter No. 16]
My Dearest Sweet:

The mailman finally came thru with your 13 & 14 for June the latter mailed on July 1 and your July 1 & 2. These of course had the pictures in them so after commenting on them you will know that you have sent eight. The other enclosures too will bear mention.

Also received a note from Marie—as the one you enclosed & a letter from Virginia with two more clippings of our niece & new nephew [Patricia and her husband, Robert Menke].

What a shock to find that Pat had gone & done it for I was quite sure that she was going to be a career woman like her Aunt Marie—so much charm that she radiates it. How ever I had been told by someone that she wasn't near the student. Don't think, as you, that she wasn't sure of herself before taking the step—however wonder a bit in light of Marie's letter that she hadn't before dated the chap. Don't think Tommy even had a chance for reasons which are rather apparent tho he was a nice kid. Imagine the distinction of wearing a wedding dress made of the silk of a parachute—My my—what this younger generation won't do. The party or reception at Marie's must have been something huh?

The pictures four of Steve with his hat in the Taylor Tot are both very good as is the one of Mother in the background. He does look as if he was getting to be a problem. However all boy. The one without the hat is amusing—is that two or three hairs I see on his head. Sure he's waving at Pop and the sun in his eyes. He too looks like a Charleson—maybe its something he'll be grateful for when he gets a good look at his Pop.

Am glad you have sent on some nail polish—for I partially cleaned the bracelet today & without it there wouldn't be much use of doing it—just took the worst off so with the silver polish on its way will do a good job when it arrives. Thanks for the emperine—sorry it caused you so much trouble.

I'm glad that the letters are reaching you within a weeks time. At least in that way you know I'm still at this end straining to get home. Your letters unfortunately are a bit on the longer line but they eventually get here—except still haven't received your June 5—or did you write one.

Don't know what to expect in the letter from home—and we would be away so as not to be able to properly enjoy them but our time will come Sweet.

My love as always to the "Three Sweethearts" of Pop who hates to be so far away for so long.

Al & Daddy

A F Herney

July 23 July Letter No 16 [July Letter No. 17]

My Dearest Sweet, Susie, Steve Mother & Dad:

You are keeping up the very good start for I received July No 8 today—written the ninth. Ho hum do wish I had your ambition but 16 to date isn't too bad either.

Believe you have received all of my June letters if you received No 19 for believe that is all I wrote.

Had already received the picture of Pat which you enclosed. She is a beautiful young lady isn't she and just as wholesome. The young man is lucky tho he may not know it—maybe we ought to tell him huh?

Wrote Ge-Ge a note this morning—to answer both this last letter and one or two previous ones which were unanswered. She's such a good egg and have included her in on the letters written to S.D.

You didn't expect our oldest to be immune to mosquitoes and chiggers did you? Unfortunate for her to attract them—blame Pop for he was susceptible to both too—just one of the things she inherited from the paternal side.

Your mention of the Hawaiian girl admitted for delivery is interesting. There will be much of that for Joe K told me that there had been a tremendous amount of marriages in the Islands and quite a problem. It will be worse as time goes on and the number increase from many standpoints including the social. One thing more we have to worry about. Why some men can't keep their _____ well no good mentioning it.

Don't worry anymore about the deed for Ann Sweet as the order for reconveyance has been executed and mailed. However if you wish you can return it to her. Agree with you that the ushering job will be far better for Jack but one the other hand will mean some late hours.

Wonder what is Hanks trouble now. It would be their luck to have him ill on furlough time. Do they still plan on being in Clovis or is he to remain in Kansas.

Marie wrote that Amanda Lou & youngster [Hugh Caughey's wife and daughter] were to arrive the 29th. Will be nice for Tanta & Uncle A to have part of the family near. Hugh too will be along soon and then out into the Blue Pacific for him—no one as yet has told me what the No of his LST is so I can add that to my list.

Think Steve is doing alright on his locomotion—needs time is all and besides he will be in things soon enuf as it is—Don't worry for I don't one bit. Very clear drawing of the position you found him in the crib.

Have hopes of doing a bit of sight seeing tomorrow and maybe a bit of shopping. Can't promise too much as the value of the dollar seems to have gone down—our own fault for money at times does seem valueless. Have several things in mind & hope I can find them.

With love always to my Three Sweethearts so far far away.—

Al & Daddy

A F Herney

July 24 July Letter No 17 [July Letter No. 18]
My Dearest Sweet:

Very disappointed for several reasons—first because of misinformation didn't get to take that little jaunt today as planned and secondly no more mail today. The latter reason is rather childish since no one else received any either.

To soften the harsh disappointment went to the beach this afternoon—ended up having three rums and much much cokes—my my—such dissipation. I'm sure will put me in the pink. Can feel the tummy growling now but like something else is oh so the essence. Tsk! Tsk!

Last evening was a lulu—to start things off had a sprinkle—let off so as the troupe would say "The Show Must go On" it did. Whistling in Dixie with R Skelton & Co. Half way thru it rained—not hard but rain in any mans language. Having prepared for same with a few others stayed with it till the end. A chief sitting behind me said "My God, my wife had a hell of a time getting me to take her to a movie & here I am sitting thru one in the rain." Was I self conscious and ashamed of the times I too had deprived you of the pleasure of entertainment.

Previous to the movie the boys played a command performance record—had a selection of & rendition of "Pistol Packin Mamma" which of course bought memories of a very pleasant week-end and thoughts of you—"My One & Only". Would like some time Sweet to return to the Rancho Grande Ranch for another of those nice weekends—when of course Pop is tired of just sitting and no longer remembers being a wander-luster on the high seas. That was a nice week-end wasn't it and of course accounts for Steve? As I remember Pop was a bit on the amazed side when he found out that Steve was on his way—but that of course was a temporary matter.

Believe arrangements can be made for the jaunt day after tomorrow. Am working on it and hope it works out for would like to see that the "Pride & Joy" does get something for her birthday—Mommie & Steve being on the short end because of location. However will say that Mommie & Steve too are on the shopping list—Have sufficient to take care of them too even tho we haven't been paid since the middle of May and then only up to May as far as recollection takes me tonight.

This is the end of this tablet my Sweet as possibly the next letter written will be on scraps or other than letter paper until our ships service puts in another stock.

Do love you so much & want you so much & want to be home but can't— With love always to you Three

Al & Daddy

AF Herney

July 24 [This appears to be an incomplete draft letter.]

My Dearest Pat & Bob:

What a surprise to find that "Best Wishes" are in order for you Pat, still the favorite niece, and Congratulations to you Bob. In case, & just in case you don't know it Bob your quite a lucky fellow for you have snagged the eldest Herney niece or nephew and a probably but now less probably career woman.

Dot had written that she had, on a jaunt to the business section of Lincoln, purchased wedding presents for both Monica & Pat. Since we had had several weeks mail missing this of course raised several questions in my mind.—1st was Pat actually married 2nd was Dot suffering from war nerves having had to re-main on the home front? The matter was answered of course when the missing mail finally showed up—letters from dot—letter from Marie & one from Mrs. Caperton all with clippings & pictures of a very sweet bride and bridal couple.

In mentioning the bride as having been a probable career woman was us-ing career in the sense of its normal connotation—however—it can be said that marriage can and is a career in itself not only from the feminine but also from the masculine viewpoint. Constant adjustment & compromise are in order and a requisite, not so much with your moral standards but rather what we all feel are our personal...[letter ends]

July 25 July Letter No 17 [July Letter No. 18]
My Dearest Sweet, Susie Steve, Mother & Dad:

Thought I would write this after the show bur cut it short for one very good reason—it was a stinker Abbot & Costello in "In The Navy". Comedy is always good entertainment but some things can't be irrespective of how much you would like to enjoy them. The movies for the last three nights have been stinkers.

Had another warm day—as usual—no rain however for a change—but then it always seems to be a bit hotter after the showers anyway so why have them.

No mail again today but did get some parcel post—a package from George with a dozen boxes of licorice. Still seems to be fresh and in pretty good condition. Didn't know when he sent it but it did finally get here.

Started to write Pat a note last nite—didn't get very far with it because of several interruptions. Will finish it and send it later.

As you can see have run short on stationary again so much resort to this but know you won't mind.

Nothing new by way of news for you—but did want to get off a note to you.

Love you "Three" with all my heart always.

Al & Daddy

AF Herney

July 26 July Letter No 18 [July Letter No. 19]
My Dearest Sweet:

Darned close to the end of the 10th month—which doesn't make me at all sorry that at least that much time has elapsed since we had to call living together off for a spell.

Took that little jaunt I mentioned in my letter of night before last. Gates & myself left at 710 this morning and didn't get back till after 5 tonight—What a day, tsk tsk!

Was limited in selection of things for several reasons—some of the stuff you wouldn't have—others the prices they wanted were outrageous—However did get something for the family—or most of them rather—I should say—forgot about Tanta—and especially for the two married nieces.

Purchased a belt for Susie—made of coconut husks cut into hearts & painted with pictures of people from many lands—believe it or not it doesn't look like much—but bet you can't guess what it cost me—tried to get some leather thongs to restring I but no luck so will get it off as it is. Will send it to you together with something purchased for Mother & Dad. Hope it will get to you in time for her birthday.

Hand-painted coconut-husk belt Al purchased for Susan in Tacloban, Philippine Islands, which became the prototype for similar items he handcrafted for members of his family during the time the USS Scurry was undergoing overhaul in San Pedro Bay, Leyte, PI.

Your gift purchased today—like Mother & Dad's will send on to Marie with the others—no sense you packing it around. Where they were purchased will have to come later.

During the purchases today discovered well that the value of the American Dollar just isn't worth a damn Did enjoy the day for several reasons and came back $29.00 poorer than when I hit the beach—Don't mind and I am not complaining.

Was very much interested in the village, identity later, as wanted to compare it in part with Tijuana which is clean in comparison. The local market place is back away from the busy military thorough fares—food including meat exposed to the flies—the odor was something and very happy we had eaten before we hit that street. Really not much of the village we didn't see.

We stopped to view some pictures the itinerant urchins peddling pictures on the street of course. Saw a picture of an old church & on learning the approximate location started off. The traffic on the dirt roads constantly raised annoying dust but a half mile hike got us there—It turned out to be an old Catholic Church—which like everything else suffers from the element of time and too the desecration of vandals and man.—Much like the Missions of California—the statues, unlike those to which we are accustomed, having painted robes, had robes of material—velvet—heads of hair & the like. Some too were partially glassed in. However the amusing thing to me was the sign indication that a new church was the plan of the day. Wonder if history is so that it means nothing at all.—Think the Society that rebuilt the Missions in Caliph should write the "Padre" a note.

Never did I expect to see the time that grownups as well as youngsters would use the by ways to answer the call of nature that too was revealed today—Forgot to mention in the comments of the picture salesmen—Where & How they get them is beyond me—but they have them wherever you go so I guess—not just 'art' pictures but the filthy kind they used to try to peddle in the heads in Tijuana. I have not as yet started a collection and don't plan to either. I hope!

Know that you also would have enjoyed seeing the village and missed not having you with me for I'm sure that you could have gone everyplace I went without embarrassment—and you would have had your camera to take some of the pictures that would be nice to have for the future. Tired from the hiking but its good to be physically tired for a change.

Tried to find some chains today so you wouldn't have to send me any but no luck so will wait for yours—hum!

Please don't mind the scraps for that is all that were left.

With all my love always to my own Three Sweethearts

Al & Daddy

A F Herney

July 27, 1945 July Letter No 19 [July Letter No. 20]

The mailman is holding out again for he brought your July 10 last but no sign of No 9 as yet!

Forgot to enclose the picture of the church I mentioned in last nights letter—will do so in this one. Think the photographer could have moved the trash cans—yep both of them. In the building of which you see only the corner on the left, looks like a wing of a church, there is being offered a first year college course. An inducement to stick around and go back to college—yeh?

Photo/postcard of Saint Nemo Church in Tacloban, which Al purchased from an itinerant vendor.

Am surprised to find that the bonds are nearing the $1000 mark—that is of course the maturity value. However it is just another means of savings—Thought the youngsters had more than Pop & Mommie but those monthly bonds do begin to add up.

Understand that Pat & Hubby were to spend their honeymoon at Rancho Santa Fe. Can't imagine anyone wanting to write letters on their honeymoon but then it's a good time at that. Nice that Bob can be under "Willie" even for a time. Don't remember "Willie's" last duty or whether it was changed because of his promotion. Bet you Julia had an idea that Willie might be home. Will wait for more details on Pat & Bob when & if Marie's letter arrives.

Sorry to disappoint you but you know how I love cats—don't trust the little stinkers. Evidently Steve follows Pop in this regard. Might compromise if you promised to have the cat or kitten out of the way when Pop gets home from the office.

What with the meat problem it is you were diplomatic to listen to him orate on the end of the war with Japan. Think he is a bit pessimistic about the date or month for if Russia felt she were ready to join in the treaty would be meaningless. Think Peason will come closer to it & have many hopes on it.

As for the cradle think a note to Blythe at her old address might clean up the whereabouts. Certainly Monica would like to use it as much as we would like to have her. Still time to get the matter straightened out. Wonder how soon Pat will be making us great uncle & Aunt too?

Sorry to hear that Marie's [Carrell] leg is bothering her once again. Walt's transfer to the infantry looks like he might be in on some of the stuff our west—when, where or how is still conjuecture to most.—

Didn't get any of the heavy stuff asked about in the post script. Did however know about it. Will write you about that too.

With all my love to the "Three" of you & Steve please get that tooth that's bothering you.

Al & Daddy

A F Herney

P.S. Enclosed is the label out of the purse sent you from the Islands.—Al

July 28 July Letter No 19 [July Letter No. 20]

My Dearest Sweet, Susie, Steve, Mother & Dad:

Another warm day—which makes for inactivity unless you want a bath—in which event the slightest exertion is the answer.

The mailman again today passed us by—not even a card from anyone or anybody.

Don't know if I mentioned that at the last mail call I received a "V" letter from Harvey C—Not to delay further wrote them a letter last night. Have intended doing so for some time so that is another one off the due list.

Restrung Susie's belt today. Used strips of chamois so everyone will have to be a bit careful with it. Will try to get it off in the mail tomorrow together with the little remembrance for Dad & Mother. Haven't wrapped either as a present so that will have to be up to you.—don't think Mother will mind not having tissue and blue ribbon or stuff.

If you haven't purchased and mailed the chains I requested forget it for I think I have an answer to my little problem. Should be as attractive, maybe more so, if I don't use the chain. You may however have to wait months for it anyway.

Gosch, Kraus and Hanna and Gates took the little jaunt I took the other day. They too were tired when they got back aboard tonight but I'm sure they didn't see all there was to see. Plan on going back soon after the first primarily for official business and will then get something for Pat & Monica—not included on either the grown up or youngster list—it's hell to be halfway between isn't it?

Tomorrow is the first year birthday for the Scurry—just a year of sea duty and much has happened since then—one thing certain, that my love for you has deepened and strengthened tho I never thought it could for I've always loved you, oh so much.

Continue to be an optimist as to this thing winding up soon so I can get back to my Three Sweethearts who are always in my heart.—

All & Daddy

A.F Herney

July 29 July Letter No 20 [July Letter No. 21]
Dearest Sweet, Susie, Steve, Mother & Dad:

Very close to winding up the 10th month that I've had to be away from you, and of course the Scurry's first birthday. Had a very fine dinner this noon including turkey—and a few left overs tonight.

The pamphlet, "in Memorium" [including the *Saga of the Scurry* written on the ship's first anniversary] prepared for the Scurry carries the menu as well as some other information. Will send that on to you together with some other menus from the past which I found in the drawer the other day.

U.S.S. SCURRY

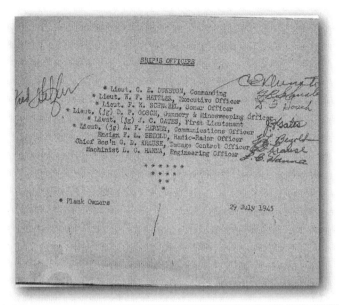

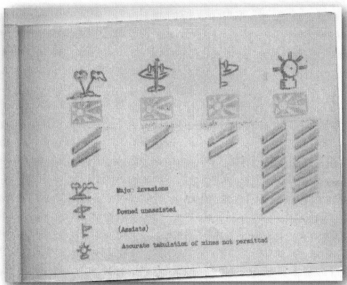

Two interior pages from the USS Scurry's *first-anniversary program booklet include signatures of officers and notations of ship's wartime accomplishments.*

From "Saga of the Scurry: The First Year," the ship's first-anniversary program: Noblesse Oblige—

In one year the ship has become a true veteran, having experienced the Baptism of Battle her men now wise in the way of the sea. Nearly eighty percent of the present crew are plank owners, shipmates of a year. And what of the men of our proud veteran? Have they become "toughened" by war? Only in a sense of realizing maturity, by having belonged "to a fraternity where men are closer to each other than they are to their own blood brothers, to a service whose only purpose and mission is to protect the common rights of man, to the comradeship of a group where there are no eight-hour days and no five-day weeks, where loyalty is the watchword and where 'well done' is duty's compensation."[xxii]

Did get off the package to you today. Sent it first class mail—costing 73 cents but did want it to get there in time. Must also write Susie's birthday letter soon for that too should be there it time.

Another warm day—which of course will call for a shower tonight just before hitting the sack.

Again the mailman passed us by—why we don't know for by now we should be on his regular call list—at least he should know where we are—we do.

Sent some laundry to another ship in the vicinity—had hopes of getting a decent job done—clothes were returned with the final touches of a rough mangling job—and six pairs of wool socks natural grey, 40 cents per so small think Susie might wear them. No more of that for me. Missing three kerchiefs too. Think I'll send the socks to Jack & Joe for I doubt if I could ever stretch them to the size where they would be comfortable.

We were paid last week—had one hundred twenty some dollars on the books but only drew $75—Did need some for my little trip to the beach which set me back $30.00 for something for most everyone. Money always did get away from me even tho I never lost it physically. It isn't of much value if you don't enjoy having it to spend however, yes sometimes even a bit foolishly.

Since our projector is being repaired imposed on a sister ship last night. "This is The Life"—not bad. Peggy Ryan had a part—she has been in quite a number of the pictures seen recently and can that kid dance.

Seems I've set a new high this month on letters Sweet but I can't promise it will continue.

My Love Always to my Three Sweethearts.

Al & Daddy

A.F Herney

July 30 July Letter No 21 [July Letter No. 22]

My Dearest Sweet, Susie & Steve:

The mailman finally came thru with another letter from you No 11— with the pictures of the little feller on his first birthday and a letter from Marie. Still have not received your July No 9.—

You seem to be slipping on the letters even tho you promised it might not continue. Ho hum mothers are busy people aren't they?

Glad you sent the pictures of Steve. Like his "Oh Hell" attitude—and he really took a big hunk out of the cake while he was doing it—and what complete enjoyment.

Wonder how much 'jam' there was in the session between Myers, Moore and Howard. Don't know the name of his ship or would be well on the lookout for him too. It could be that he was assigned that area to operate out of, in which case I possibly would never get to see him tho would very much like to see that area.

Possibly its just as well that you haven't seen most of the movies we've had aboard for on standards most of them are strictly "B" pictures, but one learns to enjoy what diversion is available. What a joy, too, it will be to sit in on a movie in which there are no breaks, changes of reels and repairs. Did get our machine back again today so will have a movie aboard the Scurry tonight.

Think I'll write my friend W.W and tell him to keep S.D off his stinkey program. Where, why or what does he or anyone else think that J. Roosevelt is qualified for the gubernatorial seat—? If he wants to play politics let him go back to the home state.

Worked this afternoon, instead of going to the beach, on something for you. Don't know yet how it is going to work out—Susie's belt gave me the idea. Have a few sore fingers but nothing that time won't heal. When they are finished you won't have to wear them for my feelings won't be hurt.—My communications now the sand paper widows.

Love Always to my Three Sweethearts

Al & Daddy

A F Herney

July 31 July Letter No 21 [July Letter No. 22]

My Dearest Sweet:

Here is the last day of July almost at an end. July is an especially nice month for several of its days are days that are pleasant to remember—the day you traded Miss for Mrs—and eight days later when our son decided he would make his entry into this topsy-turv world. Hate to see it pass so quickly yet and regret it too much for it means getting back to you and the youngsters.

The heat continues on—sweat, shower, sweat, shower infinitum. Heat rash attacks at odd places but Herney of course can't have it where it won't show—no he has to have it on the head—just above the hair line—yes in between the three hairs—Ho hum what fun. Would try powder but then I would look like hell running around with powder on the bald spots. Don't want to be accused of trying to break up the reflection from the shinney areas. Your favorite tincture too would do the trick but what a sight & mess.

Took a turn on the beach today for about an hour. Had nothing but coke and four of them. Would have done some more work on your & Susie's gadgets if I had staid aboard—just gave the fingers another day to readjust themselves to physical labor.

The news sounds encouraging—that is for the Pacific standpoint. Can't see how Japan can take much for with convoys in between Japan & the Asia mainland being wiped out. National death, total and complete is not too far away unless of course they cry "Uncle," loud and quick. Surely, even the militarists must recognize that fact—or shouldn't one give them that much intelligence.

Now if that isn't a nice thing, to remember dreaming but no remembering what you dreamt. Must have been very satisfactory but thanks anyway for mentioning that you did dream, tsk tsk.

Don't think you need worry about Pop making an unexpected return to the States, knowing of course as he came in another wouldn't go out the window wardrobe in hand, for that doesn't seem to be in the cards. Still some work to do when where and how we still don't know. Agree with you however that you need not worry the head about it.

With love always to you Three, who are always in my thoughts.

Al & Daddy

AF Herney

Installment Two [undated; missing Installment One. Written on same paper as letters written in late July 1945]

The last installment One left the Scurry swinging on the hook at Ulithi anchorage—which I may say is huge and just as undesirable for even tho there was a recreation "Island," no natives, available it happened to be a half hour whale boat ride away—and besides there was just too much else to do in order to be properly prepared for the next big venture. As a result Herney didn't go ashore.

So—with much pleasure the Scurry's anchor was aweigh and away we steamed on the morning of March 19 to the destination—Okinawa Gunto. Even tho we knew that this operation would be much more intense and of longer duration than Iwo yet all of us were looking forward to being up there where the land forces could use some help from a rather small but yet a fighting unit. Arrived off Kenama Retto early on the morning of March 26.

No time was lost for we swept a channel west of the Retto on that day without much success—however we did sweep in accordance with instructions & as a matter of precaution. No enemy opposition which of course while gratifying still was a bit disappointing.

The next day found us sweeping north of the Retto and again without results. Everyone was a bit excited late in the day for word was received that we might get to sweep the beaches of Hagushi the next day—but alas that fell thru.

Our spirits came back the next day for orders were received to sweep the Hagushi beaches on the 29th which incidently was Love minus two. Every precaution was taken against any eventuality that might arise by reason of opposition from the beaches. We were at last to see just how good the little yellow fellers were—the five support lying to seaward were a welcome sight. Did our job and a good one too—sweeping our first mines and assisting in sinking some floaters, of which there were many. Nary a bit of enemy fire from the beaches which when it was allover was something that we again were grateful about. Odd how one's viewpoint changes.

Love Day April 1 and Easter found the Scurry assisting in Sweeping operations of the beaches north of Zanpa Misaki, which if you'll check the map is north of the Hagushi beach. What an Easter not so bad for ourselves but for the boys riding in on the Hagusih Beach. We were all very happy to know that we had assisted in making their short trip beachward safe and were exceedingly glad when we heard that opposition to their landing was almost nil. With the fine support in back of us and air support overhead we attain were safe from shore fire. Do really believe that the Scurry has carried some good fortune with her.

With the sweep of April 1, the Scurry's gear was stowed—any other duties were assigned.—Patrol. Back & forth, back & forth till time will not have it. Tiresome, that's true but the days were eventually passing. It was while on this duty Dot that I saw that unforgettable sunset—Old Sol one minute a firely ball—the next melting into the horizon appearing as a Chinese Red teacup upside down and at last just a orange reflection against the clouds. It was things such as this that helped one keep his balance.

The islands of the Gunto are attractive and inviting—at least the Japs made them appear that way. Beautifully terraced and [narrative ends here].

11

JAPAN SURRENDERS: HOPING FOR HOME

August 1945

August 1—Aug. Letter No 1

My Dearest Sweet, Susie, Steve, Mother & Dad:

The first day of a brand new month is like each day of the past coming to a close—uneventful and nothing to report except ———

It was hot again today. Had planned on doing some of the paper work but fate was with me—the radio technician was painting the coding room so—I got out of it nicely. Of course I could have worked elsewhere.

More trouble with the movie machine. Just started (slight delay, since the word is the movie machine had been fixed) and wingo it went on the bum. The show "Girl Rush" and did it turn out to be a stinker—better to have had no interruptions.

Luck is with me so far—Gosch, Bezold and Hetzler have colds—with a touch of sore throat. Suppose I won't be able to avoid it but ain't wishing for one. Gosch just started his this afternoon.

Another day without mail—can't understand why it doesn't come thru. Really had better service at our last spot and expected to be left out in the cold occasionally. Think I'll load the 45 and go gunning.

Awful homesick for my Three Sweehearts—my love always to them.

Al & Daddy

A F Herney.

Aug 3 Aug Letter No 2.

My Dearest Sweet:

Won't promise more than a note for I'm in no mood for letter writing—just plain low—The mail man yesterday & today produced your No 9, 12, 13 & 14 for July. Don't know what your no is for the month but time will tell. Did enjoy the note from Steve and of course the contribution from the "Pride & Joy."

Can't say I don't agree with Mother about Susie's hair but then you are the one that must care for it and make her comfortable.—A shame to sever such golden curly locks but then they should grow back again.

The four pictures were all very good ones, two of Steve with less on than his "Pop" is used to running around in—a bit envious however; the one of Mommie is course very nice as usual—my, but she does look dressed up in her uniform—Of & regarding our oldest don't believe I have a picture in which she is not precious.

Sorry Sweet to hear that you are having trouble with your throat. Know how bum you can feel especially when you have it with a cold.

Avoided a summer cold so far—Started sneezing yesterday morning but took some pills and a shot of nose drops which I brought from Cambridge. Evidently caught it just in time.

The rash on the head is not much better—did have Doc paint the things—mostly little things—with tincture of merth—makes me look like an indian with a war paint job but does ease the itch. However it really doesn't make a lot of difference how the appearance stacks up if there's some relief.

Didn't plan on a shower tonight but since the shower is to be secured tomorrow—new paint job—guess I had better hit it for sack drill.—

Will likewise comment on your letters in my next one.

With love always to my Three Sweethearts

Al & Daddy

A.F Herney.

Aug 5 Aug Letter No 3

My Dearest Sweet, Susie, Steve Mother & Dad:

Started a letter last nite after the movie but gave up as in no letter writing mood which isn't unusual. Still haven't finished the other letter

I had intended getting off to you in a couple of days—Will try hard to finish it.

Just back from the beach—a ball game, yes another—the fifth in a series of how many we don't know—won the first three, lost the last two & todays a stinker—10 to 4—my my—but seriously your "Pop" is getting much too old to be playing such a hard game. Will be stiff as hell tomorrow.—that of course is my own fault for not taking some regular exercises. Do feel good at present after a shower.

Don't think I mentioned it before but the announcement of Pat's wedding was received day before yesterday. Still have unfinished a note to them too.

Susie's assists on Steve's birthday is a new wrinkle isn't it?—Why the cake added but then it does make sense for that's what the cake was for wasn't it. Those pictures of Steve & the cake are excellent—a story in themselves. Of course you can tell which of the four youngsters are the better looking—the two on the left without a doubt.

From the amount of bridge you are getting to play you should be pretty good by this time—yes including the time out & between hands for a gab fest.

Don't tell me that they are having unusual weather in Nebr?—God forbid—yet if its cool at nite you can at least be comfortable which is sometimes a bit difficult here—hot during the day & almost as hot at night. The pillow & mattress get aired as much as possible for they do need it.—sometimes wet in the morning—no cracks—from perspiration no less.

Won't mind taking the "Pride & Joy" and the "Little Feller" on a picnick or picnicks for that matter but on one condition—that you won't insist I eat any cold meat sandwiches. The Navy has an uncomplimentary name for it & I've had so much of it that it is much like the army's version of "Spam"—A broiled steak won't be bad to look forward to however.—

While my optimism is still the same about the war ending don't think I'll be able to make it home by Xmas, unless of course the Gods are good. Would of course like to be there now with this thing all over.

For your information "Sea Duty" from the date of commissioning but oversea's only from the time of leaving—"Oct 2"—does that help.

Have high hopes of seeing Dutch in the near future—just where or when is still a problem. Will however be very good to see him—at last some first hand news of old friends.

With love always to my Three Sweethearts

Al & Dady

AF Herney

P.S. Can't understand the delay in my mail for I have written most every day & they were mailed not later than the next.—

Aug 7 Aug Letter No 4

My Dearest Sweet Susie & Steve:

Don't know what is wrong with the mailman again but he has missed us three days running again. Difficult to understand why our mail is so irregular.

The little project for you is just about completed. Have a few more things to touch up and will then get them off to you. The belt, necklace and bracelet are for you and the single necklace is for Mother if she wishes. Had to use some pieces I wouldn't normally have used but wanted the three things to match if possible. You needn't wear them unless you wish to for I won't be hurt if you don't. They did give me something to do & rather enjoyed playing around. Susie will have to wait for hers but plan on making her a set too— have enough material to make a matching set—however don't want to take the time right now.

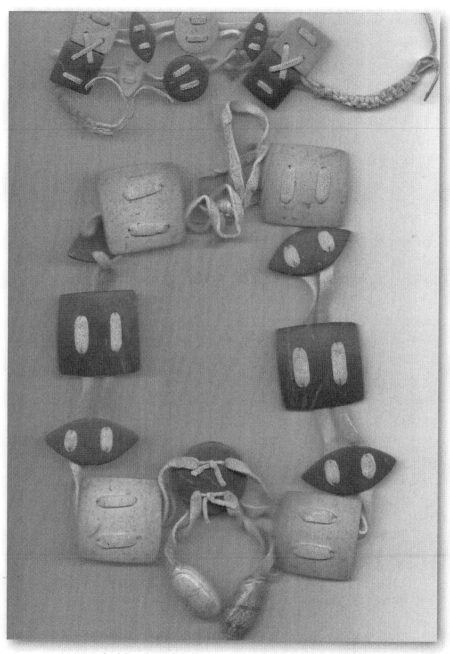

A coconut-husk bracelet and necklace Al crafted for Dot using chamois lacings.

More warm days. Thought I had the heat rash licked but it was uncomfortable as all this morning. Had the deck this afternoon & was it warm—irrespective of that had Doc apply some more tincture and did I look like an Indian—somewhat better tonight.

Saw a very good movie tonight for a change Gregory Peck & Greer Garson in "Valley of Indecision"—good supporting cast too. Had a run of stinkers recently—so much so that it is no longer fun to spend the time & wasting it in that way—

Was a bit optimistic about getting to see Dutch—don't know where or when he went but went he did—am I disgusted as all hell about it.

The news broadcasts sound encouraging especially with the new type of explosive. Possibility of actually blowing the home islands right into the Pacific. Actually that might be the answer to our immediate and Asia's problem in the near future. Still think my small bet about Japan seeing the light within 6 months of the time Germany decided she had enuf is a good one. Hetzler came back aboard today with news that an officer on another ship had $600.00 he wanted to wager that the war would be over by the middle of next month. Hope he is right for then we at least can begin to make some definite plans.

Must get that birthday letter written & off to the "Pride & Joy" or it will be late & that can't happen.

Don't know where you ever got the idea I would be home to help her celebrate tho of course you know I would like nothing better. I do hope that this will be the last day of much interest to any of us that I will be away.

With all my love always to "My Three Sweethearts"

Al & Daddy

AF Herney

Aug 9 Aug Letter No 4 [August Letter No. 5]

My Dearest Sweet, Susie, Steve, Mother & Dad:

Not much of any news today except the big news Russia declaring war on Japan. That of course was just a matter of time anyway & if not an open declaration passive resistance—for Russia's future requires the end of Japan—Good to know however that Japans Day is fast approaching.

Received your No's 15 & 17 yesterday plus a letter from Uncle G—The in-between No 16 is missing but will show up eventually. No 17 had the chain in it—supposed No 16 had the first one mailed.

Still no sight of the two parcels mailed first class. Will let you know when they are received but really look for them real soon as we still have a good bit of official mail being hidden someplace—

Evidently Susie is much more at ease in the barber chair at her age than I was—my how I hated to go—still do for that matter as it does seems such a waste of time just sitting—a massage would be appreciated however.

The article about the Lt. <u>Super</u> Grade is not new & saw it in print long before it appeared in Time—in fact as early as the first week in June.

Sorry to hear that Pat & Bob's honeymoon is or should I say [was] cut short. A bad break to say the least—Nice that Pat got to go to Frisco with him for that is a swell place to let down the hair.

Don't remember whether Bye Bye Baby was a number in "Strike Up the Band".

Went over on the beach yesterday for another game of ball—the opposition defaulted so we played one o cat—got as much exercise. Afterwards Pop had a good time—so good in fact he outspelled a good speller—tsk tsk. Thank God felt alright today. Don't plan on doing it again real soon however.

Poor Steve with the heat rash—can sympathize with him—the chiggers haven't bothered me so can't fully appreciate your itch. Not too many bugs here either & as yet no sign of mosquitoes—can sit topside without a shirt & be perfectly comfortable.

To my knowledge we have no more expectant fathers—tho there might easily be since we have had a few new men report aboard.—They might have taken care of <u>their</u> home problems before shoving off for the west—haven't asked them about it but will if you would rest easier about it.

Your last letter took only 10 days to arrive—maybe they have finally located us. Will likewise be interested in knowing how long it takes my package to arrive. Bet it makes better time than yours.

Still must put a few more touches on the necklace with Mother's name on it & will get it in the mail.

Love always to "My Three Sweethearts whom I miss very much
Al & Daddy
AF Herney

Aug 11 Aug Letter No 5 [August Letter No. 6]
My Dearest Sweet:
The very good news we heard early last evening [Japan agreed to unconditional surrender and accepted Potsdam terms after the atom bombs were
dropped on Hiroshima on August 6 and Nagasaki on August 9] means one
thing—that my separation from you and the youngsters is in sight. Just when
the dept will see fit to say "Go home to your loved ones" can't be too soon for
me that is still undetermined. There is however this hope that at least one of
the factors—can be transposed from the unknown to the known columns.
Don't see how the Allies can do anything but accept the Nips offer.

The news came during the movie—"Standing Room Only" remember?
McMuray was left in the position of the would be employers room, the em-
ployer on his way to change after getting the soup bath by Arnold & the dinner guests at the table. No one was interested in seeing the rest of the show
but took in the spectacle which was unfolding before our eyes here in the
harbor, truly a beautiful sight.

Searchlights, crisscrossing against the heavens, running lights, adding their bit, pyrotechnics of all descriptions and various colors parachute
flares, whistles tooting sirens contributing to the din.—Gave one the impression of standing in the center of a huge gigantic carnival. Don't believe I
will ever forget it but irrespective of what the sight did to the emotions there
was some deeper meeting Sweet—at that of course meant—"home" with all
its blessings—you Susan & Steve would again be a reality rather than just a
hope—tears were close as they are now from the mere joy of the thought.

Finally got the box off to you this morning. Tried to pack it so that nothing would or could be broken & addressed it to Lincoln for didn't know that
there might be the possibility that you would be heading west before it arrives. Includes some menus from days past and the anniversary booklet on the
scurry which has been signed by all of the brother officers. The necklaces &

belt are adjustable so you can fit them to suit, on the bracelet however I failed to allow much room for that but judged the size as best I could. Can secure it by fitting the ends thru the center of the thongs on the opposite side & believe it will be sufficiently secured. Sorry that the thongs on the necklace for Mother looks like it had been handled a lot which it has but didn't want to take a chance on washing it which is possible for it is chamois.

Don't know what you have in mind Sweet about getting yourself and the youngsters back home. Am hopeful of being home to stay not later than six months from now and of course will do my utmost to make it by Xmas which would be the only gift I would ask of anyone. Do wish you will plan on getting there and settled at 399 before then for that will be the essence of homecoming—returning to our home & finding you and the youngsters there.

Haven't done a thing this morning which isn't unusual for neither has anyone else—too much excitement & there must be time for day dreaming with much possibility of those dreams being realized real soon.

Realize Sweetheart that you like many others are overjoyed at the news of the day—feel sorry for those of you who will have some accounting to do when the men get home. It is grand to know "My One & Only" that I have had no doubts about you and your love for me—it has been mutual & tho while a trim ankle is always a sight never to miss there has never been anyone but you and never will be.

With my love always to "My Three Sweethearts"—

Al & Daddy

A.F Herney

Aug 15, 1945 Aug Letter No 6 [August Letter No. 7]

My Dearest Sweet, Susie Steve, Mother & Dad:

The mailman while I was absent from the ship delivered your No 16 with enclosure, the very newsy letter from Beth, your 18 & No 1 for Aug—plus a letter from Sweetie Pie (picture enclosed too.).

At last the news we have been waiting for has finally been received—hostilities are to stop—occupy Japan—learn them their lesson then everyone can go home. A problem and a big one for us'ns that want to get home soon is not only the problem for us but for the big boys too—Hell lets decide real quick huh?—

Some of the ships in the harbor are trying hard to be celebrating tonight but not nearly the show that we had last week. Really is anti-climax for we knew they were breaking & breaking fast.

Have been a bit lax about any correspondence even to you for the last few days. To be honest guess it boils down to the fact that I didn't want you to be self conscious again this month—that is about me writing more letters than you—tsk tsk.

Just beginning to get over a stinker of a cold—had a sneezing jag for two days & if you know how mean one can feel when the cold is just in that stage. Still sniffle a bit but not too much & not enuf to be uncomfortable. Quite a few of the fellows seem to have had them.

Went again today to do a bit more shopping & pick[ed] some thing for the kids. Couldn't find any more decent table sets for Monica, Pat, Tanta & Mike so guess they will be left out in the cold. Will only hope I can pick up something else for them later.

Your guess is a good one—you are an astute astuter to say the least—can't understand how you came to the conclusion but then oh then—

Am not awfully fond of that picture of Susie—didn't do her justice—something lacking even tho I can put my finger on it. Incidently did get the letter off for her birthday which isn't too far away is it? Know that you will give her an extra big hug for me—& assure her that her "Pop" will make up for those that he missed—Of course Susie is the only one who will be in on the hugging—yeh?—

Sweet very anxious to get into civvies & stay there—just another way of saying that I want [to] come home to you & the youngsters & stay there—you won't mind having a strange man around the house will you.

I love you with all my heart as always

Al & Daddy

A.F Herney.

Aug 16, 1945 Aug Letter No 7 [August Letter No. 8]

My Dearest Sweet:

The "Navy" Dept as you know came out with their generous policy today. I like Gates have only 38 points which is just 11 points short of having any action taken on a "Request." Since no credit is given for overseas duty think there will be a hell of a noise & quick, so don't expect the plan to be final for more than a month & am willing to bet I will be home for Xmas & a civilian or darn close—

Didn't comment about any of your letters in my note of last night.

Don't see how you could have been so unfortunate as to get the jits when it was so warm—however going from one extreme to the other could do most anything to you.—sorry to hear that it effected you that way.

You were wise in having your teeth checked—wise to be sure & though it is uncomfortable while it lasts you are mentally at ease afterward. Haven't been since I had my work done about three months ago & unless I'm wrong will wait until Doc C can work on me if that is necessary.

So Steve is getting real ambitious on the exercises—display of physical strength mental determination and persistent too—hm—just like his Pop— but Sweet you ain't seen anything yet.

The [silver chains] necklaces both arrived in good order—both pretty much what I originally had in mind. Will do tho I could have gotten along without them if you hadn't purchased & sent them before my letter cancelling the order was received.

Alice will undoubtedly be happier digging into the work now that she has decided what to do. Will give her that emotional outlet one in her position needs. Wish her much luck from me if she is not already gone.

Susan's urge to be "It" is understandable for it is been fed to her by all yes including Daddy & Mommie too. Should be easy to take care of that tho or is that to be Dad's job?

Wouldn't worry too much about regular hours for the youngsters Sweet for you might as well know that everything is going to be topsy turvy for a short while after Pop does get home. If Steve enjoys singing at three in the morning who knows but that he might have a partner in crime. Do have to make up for lost time.

Still haven't finished that letter about the travels & doubt if I will do so—Yet you will still want to know I'm sure. The big thing now of course is when can I tell you in person.

The cold is still hanging on—blow & blow with little result. The drops I brot from Cambridge are all gone so don't know what will do if it continues to hang on—suffer with some sinus—yeh man what fun.

Scurry's plans are still indefinite but there is a possibility that I may get to see some of the area I have wanted to see since we are so close—tho I'm sure it won't be the same as it was prior to the Nips—nothing could be.

Hiro's speech to day would indicate that we're still heels—but since we were the more powerful we didn't get licked—that is that's the story to those who don't know but to us that do know he's trying to save face—hm—what for an opportunity to boot him in the posterior—could use my best kicking foot too—

Still riding high in hopes of being with you at Xmas Sweet—my love always to my Three Sweethearts—

Al & Daddy

AF Herney

Aug 18 Aug Letter No 8 [August Letter No. 9]

My Dearest Sweet:

Have a few minutes this morning so will use them to drop you one of the few notes you have received so far this month.

Raining this morning—not too hard but enuf to make it uncomfortable if you plan on being out doors. Did have to make a trip this morning but that has all been taken care of now.

Was fortunate to be able to buy some stationary today—war over means of course letting the hair down—will make a difference with many of them of course—Played around with the chains last nite—do think they will work out if & when there will be time. Also have gotten material for Susie's belt, necklace & bracelet. Will try to make them match yours but it all depends on the material.

Things are still pretty much in the air—everyone on edge wondering just when we can get home and sever our present relationship with the armed service. Would of course be much happier if we knew just when—Still hopeful of Xmas—we communications have this to our advantage & that is that we are still specialists & do think they can get along without us.

Wonder if Pat's Bob was shipped out before the news arrived for it is our understanding that those in the states on leave would not be sent out again but retained in the continental U.S. Do hope he gets the break & wasn't as yet sent out.

Was not surprised about C & L. Had expected just that & can't say that C is much at fault. Frankly she has been patient as hell with "The Big Shot"—It would be like the selfish conceited guy to think it was all her fault and stabbing him in the back. Knowing him don't think he twiddled his thumbs while in Pearl—would like to know where he shacked up & with what kind of gal—hm—Of course there is the problem of the youngster.

The analysis of Cal was quite amusing. Maybe he has changed a good bit since he has had the privilege of staying at home & riding the gravy train—Still don't envy him or the others like him & no money could pay for the experiences since Oct 15 1943—which of course has cost us not so much from a monetary stand point but something priceless—time & separation from you & the youngsters.

{Davis} was lucky to have hit the bright spot about the right time—I'm sure you would like me to remember you should I get the chance to see him. Might be interesting to say the least.

With love always to my Three Sweethearts—yep all of it

Al & Daddy

A.F Herney

Aug 23, 1945

Aug Letter No 10. [August Letter No. 11]

My Dearest Sweet Susie & Steve:

Have been a very poor correspondent this month—Have intended writing each nite but then couldn't drive myself to it for I've felt in no mood for writing. Quite a time between letters too but then the latter isn't my fault.

Have been bothered again with the heat rash—broken out in more places than on the head. This morning seemed to itch all over—feel fairly good in the morning but it doesn't take long to upset that for as soon as one starts sweating bingo—there it appears.

Just four days until Susie will have her third birthday. Surely that will be the last one that Dad can't help celebrate. Am sure you will give her an extra big hug and kiss for me. Do hope the package with my little remembrance arrives in time.

Am sending a cigarette case—which came from the same source as the currency I sent earlier. Enclosed in the case am sending some currency and coins—and the chain sent with Susie's name on it. Have made a necklace of coins originally scheduled for Susie. The loose coins especially the silver are for Steve. As for the necklace if you feel it worthwhile would have the links soldered for it will be impracticable unless they are as I had to cut the inks to get them thru—the coin—.The currency you can divide between Susie & SteveStill haven't made Susies set but have the material & should have some time soon.

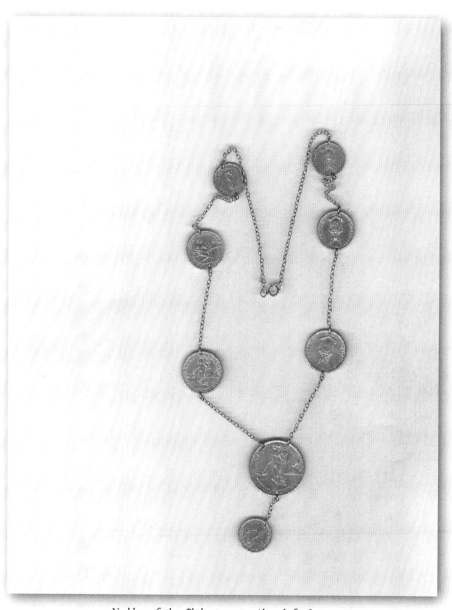

Necklace of silver Philippine coins Al made for Susan.

Am so damn anxious to get home its funny. Have lost absolutely all ambition to do—USNR to transfer.—here is one for sure who wants no more
military life—its for them that likes it which aint me. Do really wonder how
many would like to stay? Wish they would speak up quick so every thing could
really get down to normal.

Sent four of the enlisted men off for home last week—those that had the
points—(none of the reserve officers—eight in no were eligible) & were they
delighted to be on their way as no one really knows the plans for the Scurry.
It is at least encouraging to know that the Japs are to sweep the area around
Tokyo tho it might be interesting to be there when the occupation forces arrive. Of course Halesy's idea of riding down the streets of Tokyo on Hiro's
charger was as asinine as Tojo making the peace terms in Washington.

Don't know what you have planned on regarding returning to C.V.—Still
have hopes of getting there by Xmas myself tho I may be optimistic beyond all
dreams yet its better that way—my 6 months from Germany's surrender was
optimistic too. Gosch had the boys play "White Xmas" for me the other evening
but I told him at Xmas he could laugh if he saw me—otherwise hold his humor.

Don't know if I mentioned enjoying Beth's letter—newsy as all hell and
full of her wit—could go for some of it real soon.—

With love always to my Three Sweethearts—whom I want to see very
very soon.

Al & Daddy

AF Herney

Aug 24 Aug Letter No 11 [August Letter No. 12]

My Dearest Sweet:

So that you will get another letter will write before the body is too
weak—

The mailman brot your letter of Aug 15 with word of your realization
that the war was practically over. It was a good feeling wasn't it and o how
grateful one can be for just that news. Realize how you felt.

Any question about your plans on getting home to C.V have already been
answered. You of course have your problems of transportation and the like to
determine your date of sailing homeward. Of course I still have someone else

saying when I can start but it won't be too soon. Most of the fellows are a bit pessimistic about when we/they will get home but I can't be downed—for I've got too much waiting for me there to tarry the least bit.

Glad the package reached you in such good time. Don't really remember when I mailed it but believe the latter part of July. If the other package for you makes as good time you should have it soon. The package mentioned in last nites letter was mailed today. It wouldn't be necessary to remove the pieces but you could adjust them on the thongs.

Haven't written to the family in quite some time. Feel guilty about it but that is really as far as I can get with it. Maybe the spirit will move me later.

The party sounded as if it might be good fun. We had an impromptu one too—and with trimmings. Who wouldn't what with prospects of getting home eventually? Nice that you gave the soldiers the pleasure of some piano playing—could appreciate some of it myself.

Must send some of the pick me ups to the family in S.D.—will be sure to inform Marie about your luncheon set and will ear mark it for you and then you can get it when you get home.

Don't see how any spot could have been as beautiful as the harbor in which the Scurry was anchored on the nite we were told of "Japs" wanting to quit. Can't remember how I described it but what a sight—will never be another like it.

Sweet there is only one thing that's deep in my heart and that is to get home to you and the youngsters in a short short time—will crack that bottle for sure.

With love always to my Three Sweethearts

Al & Daddy

A F Herney

Aug 25 Aug Letter No 12 [August Letter No. 13]

My Dearest Sweet:

Didn't get the mail off today nor a chance to see if there were more for us—so will add this to the collection to be deposited tomorrow—winging its way off to you.

Just out of the cinema—not bad "The Rains Came" a very old picture with Myrna Loy, George Brent and Tyrone Power. Had it in the mess hall as no movies topside (why no one can figure out)—added a few more bumps to the heat rash but the movie was good.

The day has been quite busy but can't say a whole lot was accomplished. My sins of the last month are catching up with me—meaning the rest & recreation for I have a good bit of work piled up.

The Capt received a cut out from the "Time" regarding the Navy and the need for 30,000 officers who wish to continue "Navy Life." The outspoken chap voiced my opinions more than adequately. However he failed to add that since the Reserves fought & won the war for the Regulars I can see no need why the Reserves should continue to be held finish up the work so they, the Regulars, can immediately take their leaves & when their ready return to the good old days of keeping the guns in good order. Ho hum.

A friend of Gosch's was aboard last nite. Really believe I've met my match in "Bitching". He said that he has gotten so that he now analyses everything to see if there isn't something he can Bitch about. He is on a Y.M.S. and evidently they have more to complain about than we on the big 180 footer. They have been in the same area for five months & the crew has had recreation parties twice in that time and then to hear keep up the morale is really pathetic. Hope I don't go writing letters thru official channels regarding my sentiments for feel I might be Seaman 2nd class right smart like.

On the smoother side hope to take a shower after completing this and look over a few funnies that arrived in the mails yesterday. The pictures in Life—subject—Bathing suits & the French version thereof (different issues) I can't see are worth much more than a glance and a shrug of the shoulder (?).

Sorry that I let go Sweet for it isn't good reading but couldn't help it—won't mind if you tear it up without reading it.

My Love Always to My Three Sweethearts

Al & Daddy

Aug 26 Aug Letter No 13 [August Letter No. 14]

Dearest Sweet, Susie & Steve:

Not much news from this end tonight at all—again no mail for us and about two weeks of mail for the first of this month hasn't caught up with us.

Everybody is quite pessimistic about when we will get home as there seems to be so much to do. Can't see why some of it or the greater part left to the Nips under supervision. If things don't break pretty soon & favorably think I will play with the idea of resigning my Commission.

This is not such a bad idea since I can't see taking my annual vacation cruising around on the Pacific—which of course would also mean you would have to take yours alone too. Besides haven't liked the idea of playing monkey to the Regulars for that time. Just a thought. Think under the circumstances that they might accept a resignation. Believe the only penalty is loosing the mustering out pay amounting to three hundred dollars. Could easily sacrifice that instead of spending months out here.

Did get in some good licks today. Didn't get accomplished what I would like to have done but there are never dues anyway.

Have finally gotten over the cold—the sinus still drains a bit which is & can be annoying.

Yep and the heat rash still continues. Have tried face lotion on it but that doesn't seem to do too much good. Will try tincture of merth. On it if it doesn't get better soon.

Attended the movie tonight "The Falcon Goes West." Quite a thriller to say the least. The general run of Sea Films are very poor—definitely class B—but guess we shouldn't mind too much as they are some entertainment.

The news tonight indicates Truman considers the state of emergency to exist even tho VJ day will be declared, this of course to keep in effect certain powers vested by Congress. Also that OPA has set the price on the cans to be or expected to be delivered in about seven months. Think they are a bit optimistic to think that it will still be a government agency in operation at that time.

Wouldn't mind being in on the formal signing of the terms in Toyko Harbor. We of course being little fellers don't & won't have a chance—we can stick around and do the dirty work—Doesn't seem quite fair but then everyone can't be there.

Don't know who the damn fools are still speculating on whether Halsey still plans on riding Hiro's Horse. Think it about time they knock it off but quick.

Wonder if the military have set up "no Fraternizing" with the gals on the home islands. Bet many of them would like to satisfy their curiosity—hm!

With all my love always to my Three Sweethearts

Al & Daddy

Aug 27 Aug Letter No 14 [August Letter No. 1]

My Dear Sweet, Susie, Steve Mother & Dad:

Your No 9 dated Aug 17 finally arrived. Your letter writing this month has just about been at the rate of mine.

Am a bit perplexed about the dinner party mentioned. Could that have been the one you had on the 15th or some later time? No doubt everyone that could made a holiday of it & for good reason.

No doubt it is good to be able to get about all the gas you can use. Strange feeling to be able to do so. Wonder how many of the family have driven to Palomar to enjoy the cabin? Can't say I wouldn't mind being there to help them drive. Understand tires still are & will be rationed for some time. If it isn't one thing its another.

Sorry you are as depressed about the point system as your letter indicates. On the present basis don't think Sweet that they could keep me in this thing for 22 more months—need 11 instead of 10 points.—Have already answered your question about returning to CV so will say no more about that.

Have had an unpleasant day with my right lower antrum (?sp)—has been draining since last night and it is anything but pleasant.

Enjoyed the clipping you enclosed even tho I don't know all about every thing mentioned. Helps to keep up on the news somewhat at least. Approximately what is the time it takes for you to get the paper?—Local news even if a week old helps to keep up to date.

Time Aug 20 issue arrived today so will have something to keep me busy for a few nites after hitting the sack. A couple of pages and lo the old man is asleep.

[The cover of the August 20, 1945, issue of the Pacific Pony Edition of *TIME* magazine featured a single, large red orb on a white background, similar to the Japanese flag, but with a thick black "X" imposed across the red image.

The cover art clearly conveys the definitive end of the war with Japan. Inside pages of the magazine feature articles on the atomic age and US Army Air Forces photos of mushroom clouds at Hiroshima and Nagasaki.]

Had "Cabin in the Sky" tonight. Didn't quite enjoy it as much as the stage production for several reasons—first you weren't there & then too they left out that bewitching dance by the gal who played Georgia Brown.

Haven't heard from the family since the Japs decided to quit so don't know how Fran & Ann stand but do know that someone is going to get a sad awakening on this reconversion. Wonder if Consolidated has made any post war plans except for commercial planes?—Kaiser has taken his steps & believe that he & his pal will force a revolution in the automobile industry—no doubt but what he is an ingenius operator.

Don't loose heart fair lady for Pop is going to be coming home long before he could expect to on the present point system. There's too much waiting for me at home to dally out here.

With love always to My Three Sweethearts

Al & Daddy

Aug 28 Aug Letter No 14 [August Letter No. 15]

My Dearest Sweet:

The mailman finally gave out with the back letters Aug No 2,3,5 & 6—don't know where 4 is—maybe I've received it & will have to check back—a letter from Unk G & a copy of Marie's Letter. Still no packages.

First thanks for remembering to enclose the name of Ed's ship—Have entered it in the address book before I forget it & forget that it is in one of your letters.

Am much amused at Uncle Jim & the letter. Doubt if he is still there but wouldn't hurt to look around if and when & just in case tho for the life of me don't remember what he looks like for that was back in 37 remember when we went back to show of the practically brand new husband.

As for the article in Time on Ulithi read it—can't say I feel much the same way as the author as he must be prejudiced for while I'm against. Thank god that isn't where we had our rest and recreation.

— 379 —

Didn't even expect that the folks would decide SD was the place in Calif tho I had hoped they could see the light. However even LA would be so much more accessible than Lincoln.

What with all the social activity—strictly the ladies—even one day at the hospital—you have taken on a job of sewing getting the youngsters ready for when Pop does get home—for I'm sure you aren't going to have too much time when he does get there. Don't believe I would spend much on winter clothing for the youngsters as my last letters indicate.

Surprised that Susan isn't very tolerant with Steve at least with Steve's toys. Rear approaches might help if you could see fit to use that method for she should learn to be generous. Steve will get his training in that regard when he is just a wee bit older and begins to comprehend.

The description of few washdays indicated the training of the Little Feller is well on its way. Will be nice if we have a bit better luck with him than with Susie. Still don't feel badly that he isn't walking as yet but he's getting around indicates it shouldn't be too far away.

Good to know that you have the teeth all taken care of once again. Believe I should have mine checked again just in case for I'm sure its been a long time since I've had any greens or fresh vegetables & damn little fresh fruit, canned too for that matter. As yet however don't believe I'm falling apart.

Can see Elmer & Jerry home via the train—wonder what or just how soon he will get his discharge as I'm sure he has enuf points and of course his line is such that they might not need relief.—Could forego his vacation & pack up & head for home to stay—Oh day.

Still haven't had an answer from Carl S to my last letter. Had begun to think we were in the dog house for the house—Do hope Carl got home for he did have a larger shot [at] it than myself & then too was in on the Philippine deal which wasn't pleasant. As for Hank don't think he has enuf points to get out, nor Carl either—both too young & not enuf service to make up for the difference.

No just where in the hell do you think I can get any Calamine lotion—I'm sure ships service doesn't carry it & don't believe it's a standard in the navy stock. Now have the stuff—itch on my back. Ain't pleasant—Toots. I can assure you.

With all my love to My Three Sweethearts—oh so anxious to get home to you.

Al & Daddy

A F Herney

From Dictionary of American Naval Fighting Ships*:*
The minesweeper underwent overhaul at Leyte, Philippine Islands, from 13 July to 17 August and, after escorting a convoy to Okinawa, sailed from there on 30 August to clear minefields off Japan.[xxiii]

Aug 31 Aug Letter No 15 [August Letter No. 16]

My Dearest Sweet:

Your No 4 showed up on the 28th—too late of course to be answered for there were so many things to do as always. Just had a chance to glance at the clippings so will have to read them.

In case your interested only purchased things for the female of the specie except one thing for Ed—a soup stirring spoon made of bamboo & coconut— cost all of 50 cents—besides you aren't going to talk me into doing the Xmas shopping and you know it.

Wonder if the tenant is using my gopher traps for I had better luck than four with them. Of course one can't use gopher traps on cows—but there are other ways of convincing them to leave the hedge alone. The morale of the story would be—our yard rent the place—do bet it looks nice.

Glad to get the news about Carl. Have been looking for him everywhere I've been as far as Dutch—Nice that he got as much time with IJ & Steve. Would like to see him with that youngster.

It started out a bit rough and your Pop was pretty sure he was going to be one sick boy but no such luck. Have been working steadily—catching up on back stuff since underway & when feel a bit woozy from too much close paper work take a walk out on deck for some air.

You should see me now. Do bet Steve was fortunate—my back is a pain— feels practically raw—both arms and same on my right leg. Thought maybe a change in latitude might make a difference in the heat but nothing noticeable yet.

Glad to know that at least one of the youngsters is going to be musical—if it ain't going to be Susie it will have to be Steve—if so he is going to be the lucky one. Susie & I will just join in on the choruses that are if you two will allow us the privilege.

Have read that long article in Aug 20 issue of "Time". I like you hate to think of the horrible possibilities—there are however tremendous benefits that can be derived from the principle—let's hope the efforts are concentrated in that direction.

Wonder if a letter to the Sect. of the Navy to the effect that "My Mother Didn't Raise ME to Be a Sailor" would help for I'm sure I have never been one—never want to be one and damned if I will be once this thing is all over. For a time anyway you had better planning on raising Susie & Steve in Marie & Ed's boat.

Was so busy that I had even forgotten to mention Susie's Birthday on her Birthday. However do know she will forgive her Dad who is suffering from wantacomehomeitis so bad he's beginning to be a problem.

Love always to my Three Sweethearts—

Al & Daddy

A F Herney

12

The Yellow Sea and Visit to Nagasaki

September 1945

From Dictionary of American Naval Fighting Ships:

Scurry swept mines in the Yellow Sea between 1 and 7 September, and then helped to sweep the approaches to Sasebo and Nagasaki, Japan. She was one of the last American ships to enter these ports after the war. Between 17 and 26 September, she acted as pilot vessel at Nagasaki for transports repatriating Allied prisoners of war.[xxiv]

Albert Herney's Officer's Qualification Report from his personnel jacket, September 1, 1945.

Sept Five—45

Dear Family & Sweetie Pie:

It would seem that news from Calif is coming thru a bit more regular now that another correspondent is added to the list viz George. His letter of Sept 19 [August 19?] arrived yesterday.

The mailman also delivered a letter from Uncle Albert postmarked the 12th of April as well as a letter from Walt Carrell dated about the same time. Satisfactory service huh? Did enjoy getting the letters however if a bit ancient.

Quite odd that Uncle A's letter with the information as to the L.S.T. on which Hugh [Caughey] was seeing the Pacific, reached me the day I did see Hugh. On arriving here at Sasebo for some availability received a visual from Hugh. Since he was leaving for the PI's at noon hurried over and had the pleasure of visiting with him for about a half hour. Needless to say I did enjoy it immensely. Even tho it had been some time since I had seen him don't believe he would have been hard to recognize for he does have UA's features.

Unfortunately neither of us knew that we were at Nagasaki at the same time—we moored in the middle of the stream & they on the beach adjacent to us.

Have been ashore here at Sasebo. The waterfront area unlike that of Nagasaki does not appear to be damaged to any great extent. The industrial & business section however is leveled due to the B 29's and incendiaries.

In the residential sections small plots and every inch is utilized for gardening. On a hike up the hill noticed carrots lettuce, radishes and what appeared to be sweet potato vines. The residential sections, except for the merchant who lives above their business establishment are all on the sides of the hills sloping up from the waterfront.

The business section or rather what is left of it, appeared to be quite dirty to our standards. Small stores with low openings for doors—wares anything but attractively displayed from the street—didn't even stick our head inside the door for fear of being yanked out by the MP's.

Dress seems much like that of the people at Nagasaki—women just as unattractively dressed tho did see several who were dressed in good taste. Guessed that they were of the better class but I could have been wrong for they might have been a 'Gal' without knowing it. Haven't seen anywhere that they have to carry a placard stating that fact.

Don't know what good we are doing out here—or what the immediate future holds. Scuttlebutt is running free & some of it good to hear.

As far as Xmas box will say the same to you as I have to Dot—don't send a box for if I'm not home or close to it will be pretty much of a wild man and remembrances wouldn't add to morale one bit.

Has been cool for the past few days—a blanket is pleasant tho a bed partner would be much for satisfactory. A cold front in the area accounts for it.

Undoubtedly there is not a dull moment for the Herney clan. Do hope that the Caugheys won't find it too much & leave before I get home.

Marie that trip to Mexico sounds interesting—should hurry home so that you can take that trip but can only say that I will get there as soon as possible—plus of course a short lazy spell that I plan on spending with my family trying to crowd into a short time all that I will have lost—most of it spent at 399 J Street however.

Have a booklet for each of the boys—should have sent it before this as well as some things purchased at Tacloban, Leyte Island P.I. when there. Will try & get them off in the near future.

Plan on writing Helen very soon for I hear that she's to have an operation to haven't been told if it is to be done in LA or SD.—but since there is an attraction in LA will send it there.

With much love to each & every one of you

Al Always

Al

Sept 6—Sept No 1

My Dearest Sweet:

Didn't realize that it has been such a long time between letters since this is the first in September.

Have been very busy & when day is done or so called done your Pop is not in either a frame of mind or physical condition to be writing.

Then too there is the matter of the Sea—never seems content to be calm very long & while I have not been sick to the point of getting rid of the last meal it is always more comfortable & reassuring to be in a horizontal position.

Censorship is off—which while for reasons other than security I haven't written you can't & won't make too much difference. It will mean however that every morning while in port & just before getting into port you have had to read someone elses mail. Quite a relieve from that point of view.

Did think that this cooler climate would soon drive the heat rash away but today have been bothered again. Find a sharp corner to rub the back on— much like Nick used to use the hedge—real satisfaction, even tho momentary, in scratching it. Took a shower tonight & had Doc use a goodly amount of tincture seems to have left the noggin thank god.

Can't quite understand the clipping on Fred R—didn't refer to him as being in the service tho that might have been merely any oversight. Don't see how he could be out of the service already—if he is he is quite fortunate.

Enjoyed the clipping on Driver. Tried to get a chance to get ashore over a week ago to contact him for it would be nice to see some of the Island even tho most of the villages have been razed—maybe soon however.

Haven't been able to get any news on Carl or Dutch either from operations so may be will have to wait till I get home to see both of them—Who the hell wouldn't I like to have seen but both of them—All in all this damn Pacific is a pretty big place.

Started work on Susie's belt, necklace & bracelet & that's all—Will have to wait till things slow up a bit for while the war is over there is work yet to be done.

In case you don't know it your Old Man is known as Home by Xmas Herney—He does want to get there damn quick.

With love Always to My Three Sweethearts—

Al & Daddy

Sept 7 Sept No 2

My Dearest Sweet:

Just in case there will be an opportunity to get this off to you will drop you just a short note. Even tho there is a chance to get some mail on the run we may not get any mail off—do hope there will be some for us for we have had none for over a week again this time.

Thank goodness the sea is again on its way to behaving itself—passed up chow tonight for a combination of reasons—one didn't feel too hot & secondly didn't care much for the menu—chili con carne & can the cooks do things to it.

As for food will be very happy to get some home cooked food again. Absolutely a minimum of preparing food—all one can say is that it is cooked. Possibly that is due to the number of men to be fed but hell I know I can make better stew than what we get.

Bezold passed the word that the blackout restrictions for all vessels at sea was to be raised tomorrow night. Sounds much too good to be true & doubt it for more reasons than one. Will be good to enjoy the air on deck after dark & have a smoke before hitting the sack.

Had a movie in the mess hall tonight—title "B" picture—musical & helped ease the strain somewhat. However doubt if sitting there did the heat rash much good.

Have a training film projector mounted on the bulkhead in the passage-way just next to stateroom 102—whenever we go up & come down or vice versa the bulk head creaks—is annoying but not much to do about it.

Am interested to know what your plans are about returning to Calif. Still very much an optimist but, returning as to time is your problem. Don't blame you for not wanting to sit out there all by yourself when you are still welcome in Lincoln and it is much nicer for you. Come to think of it that short visit has turned out to be almost a whole year hasn't it. Do hope it hasn't been too much for Dad & Mother.

Am getting so tired of being a sailor I could scream—still can't quite understand how they've got the fortitude to expect us to do the work so that in a short space of time they can return to peace time schedule. Hell we've got the adjusting to do while there still in what they chose as their vocation.—

With love always to My Three Sweethearts

Al & Daddy

From The Navy Department Library—"US Navy Personnel in World War II":
Between 7 Dec 1941 and 31 Dec 1946 there were 4,183,466 officers and enlisted
personnel that served in the Navy...There were 3,793,429 enlistments and a total of
3,546,179 persons entered the Naval Service during World War II.
Peak strength of Navy overseas (as of 30 June 1945)—198,383 officers and 1,923,910
enlisted...In the Pacific (ashore & afloat) there were 1,366,716 on 31 Aug 1945...The
average length of service of officers and enlisted in World War II was 2 years 6 months...
During World War II, the USNR outnumbered USN personnel on active duty by a 3 to
1 majority...On 31 July 45 the month in which the Navy hit its peak strength, USNRs
on active duty composed 87.4% of all Navy personnel.[xxv]

Sep 10 Sept Letter No 3
My Dearest Sweet:

Well the good old Navy did come out with a new point plan today—however not much help for your old man—still 8 points away—Plenty put out about it too—think they could demobilize us a lot faster than they are except of course it might take the regulars too long to get back to their peace time swinging on the hook if we didn't stay to do most of the cleaning up.

Have seen some more areas—not what I wanted to see but then something anyway. Know you have read about the boys setting themselves up in Korea—chalk one up for the Scurry in seeing that part of their passage there was safe.

The mailman brought your No 7–10 & 12—some between are missing but right at the moment don't know which ones for sure except no 11—for you mentioned the Booklet in 12 but said nothing else about the other contents wondered how the package had arrived & when. Your packages of July are still enroute & when they catch up with me God alone knows & I don't think he will tell.

Quite surprised about our son doing his stuff before the radio. Could go for a sight of him and Susie; and you of course. Will be content to have him accompany the orchestra if he so wishes.

Has been cooler the last few days—taking a shower every nite—some tincture and powder—helps too—haven't itched much today as a result. A few more days of the same kind of weather will help too.

Didn't expect to get back right away & hoped as a result that we might—faint hope—get in on the sweep to Toyko but no such luck. That would have been worth while doing & the ceremony if from a distance would be something to remember. The Scurry unfortunately was detailed with others to do the job mentioned before.

Expect to be able to get this mail off within the next couple of days. That will mean that there will be several weeks that you will not have received any & then too because I've been delinquent in writing the picking would be more than four letters. No one else besides yourself have received any letters nor have I written anyone else.

It would seem you've had a good bit of social life in the couple of weeks before Alice left for her new job. Am glad you were able to do so—that trip to Omaha sounded interesting—know you had one for me.

Thank goodness we have been permitted to have movie's topside—had a double feature tonight Hop Along Cassidy & Princess O'Rourke—the latter a pleasure the former a stinker—Where we got it—hm—give it back but quick.

Can quite imagine Evelyn Andersons happiness when her old man showed up unexpectedly. Would be nice if he didn't have to shove off again.

Wouldn't invest in any shirts until I get home. Am quite certain my civies will fit & I may be able to get into my 13 ½ shirts if they don't send me home before too long—fretting & fuming. Am afraid that they won't want me in the service if I write in a letter of resignation for I'm sure I won't be choosey in my language or phraseology. Ho hum—Do want to get home so bad.

Love always to my Three Sweethearts who are waiting for me.

Love Always again

Al & Daddy

Sept 11 Sept Letter No 4

My Dearest Sweet:

Just a short note to add one more to the few which should be off to you in the next few days.

Rather a depressing day for several reasons—is raining & your old mans prospects of getting out damn soon are slim.

Glad Susan still remembers that she has a home & that she will be heading that way in not to long a time. If she wants to get as badly as her dad she wants to get there bad as everything.

Four of the officers aboard are now eligible to be <u>freed</u>—Capt Hetzler, Schnabel & Bots Kraus—lucky fellows all but then they were in some time longer than I have been. Don't know just how soon they will be on their way for they can be held 4 months on the request of the administrative command. This whole thing is so topsy turvey that no one really knows what it is all about.

The news indicates that the occupation troops are just about completing the disarmament of the Japanese. Hope the whole thing is over soon—can't say I envy any of the occupation troops for they do not have a (pleasant) prayer for discharge or replacement real soon.

Haven't been paid again for several months. Planned on getting paid the 15th of Aug for that time had about $130 on the books—Still have about 50 with me so am in pretty good shape & god knows when we will get somewhere where we can spend some. Would of course like to spend it in the States & think I will save it up for that purpose.

Wonder if Joe K [Keller, Al's friend at Pearl Harbor] is out by this time. He should be for he has had a good bit of service—married & a good bit of service over seas.

Must close & get this off & back to work—just after noon chow—

Love and all of it as always to My Three Sweethearts

Al and Daddy

Sept 14 No 5 September

My Dearest Sweet:

Have been able to get our mail off to you but we have received none at all since that delivered to us on the 8th of Sept. Should have some pretty soon.

The weather has continued to be favorable for the heat rash—rather wet & damp but cool so that now I am almost free of it from all portions of the anatomy—still a few spots high on the shoulder and arm.

It has been pleasant to see some topography that is not composed of sand and a few palms & especially just sea. The terracing of the least tillable soil indicates that the little fellows we had around Chula have had it bred into them for generations. One can find about any shade of green which you wish on a hillside. Rather odd of course to see a cultivated field amongst the shrubs which are or seem to be familiar on the foothills back of S.D——

Would very much like to see the results of the second & last atomic bomb that was dropped but that for the present seems to be out of the question. Possibly some time later if ———. Ho hum that is one of the penalties of being a sea faring man—get there first but after getting there there seems to be no place to go.

It would seem that the Scurry's bow is always pointing in a direction away from the States. However if we get much further east it might be just as short to continue to go west tho it might take a good bit longer. However doubt if that is the case.

Have been trying to do my work but find that I have little heart for it as I have one thing on my mind & that is to get home. Still have hopes of getting there by Xmas or shortly after & stay too. These mines can't last forever & it's a cinch your old man ain't going to sit out here while the USN boys take their leaves—Haven't written that letter soon but it won't be long unless something is done about it & soon.

Should write the family but haven't the desire or will power to do it. Even tho the war phase has terminated there is much to do and must be done. Would like to say otherwise however.

Old man Neptune has been irked again and has been showing his ire. As a result didn't have chow yesterday noon—got up in the morning with a wicked headache & that may have helped things along.

While at Okinawa the first of this month had an awning for the boat deck made. Now we can have our movies there instead of on the forecastle should it rain. Yes we have had them topside which is a blessing.

Anxious to call it quits with the Navy & to get home to you.—With all my love Always

Al & Daddy

Sept 16 Sept Letter No 6

My Dearest Sweet Susie & Steve:

Should be writing much more than I have but that doesn't seem to be possible for several good reasons—one of course is that my last few letters have been nothing but gripes & them aint the kind of letters to write.

Then too we have been busy and when the end of the day arrives there doesn't seem there is that much energy left. Oh for the day when I can say all the things I would like to put in a letter—all nice & about my Three Sweet hearts.

Is raining again this evening & as a result are having the movie indoors. Not too bad for it has been rather pleasant both day & nite—not that heat which brot on the rash. Entirely free if it now.

Still no mail tho we should have some soon. Thought the Gods would be good today but no luck. More should accumulate as time passes so that is something pleasant to think about anyway.

At least we have gotten into the inside for once—a break for us for as usual we are always on the outside looking in. Even here what amazed me was not so much the destruction, tho it is apparent, but rather the ever present terraces—intensive cultivation—all pleasant on the eye too. They don't seem to have what we refer to as marginal land or anything akin to it.

Now the next step is a bit of shore party to see what ticks—doubt if that will be possible to do but something to be expectant about anyway too I would prefer China & always have.

Our supply of cigs has gotten a bit short—rationed to a carton a week & reduced to Chesterfields—even out of talcum—have some good face powder but you don't use that for after bath. Getting in training for being a civilian again—short of this & that tho I'm sure I could bear a few shortages on everything except some loving.

Wondered if the small package—cig case—chain coin & currency have arrived? Has been about a month now so guess it should be there.

All of my dreams have been of home and the Three of You—can't get there soon enuf. All my Love Always

Al & Daddy

Sept 20 Sept Letter No 7

My Dearest Sweet:

Had intended writing last night after the movie and a shower but a discussion naval etiquette—authority and what have you went late into the evening. As usual Herney was the lone wolf but by God I'm sure I'm right. Ho hum more fun and all in good spirit.

Has been raining again today—not too hard but enough to make it uncomfortable topside if you wish to stick your nose out. The evenings too have been rather cool so that a jacket isn't too uncomfortable at the show on the forecastle. Was tempted last nite to call it quits at the end of the first reel but decided to sit it out.

Have promises of some mail soon—do hope so for it will help me get out of this slump I'm in & I can assure it is one. I'd better get out of it soon—have worked hard during the day but that hasn't seem to do it at all.

The left arm is a bit sore today & was last nite due to a cholera shot given yesterday afternoon. Don't think I'm a pig but they said take it so that's that. Get another in a week.

Have had the opportunity to be in the harbor several times—Of course the oftner there they more one becomes conscious of the rubble—Mitsubishi & family of course are a lot less wealthy for all of it—large structures once shops now nothing but skeltons with the steel ribs exposed to view.

Sampans their occupants & movements are of interest. Slow progress over the bay but eventual success. Yes even the women take their turn at working the odd shaped oar off the stern or gunwale—pushing & pulling for the side giving it that peculiar movement which is just as odd as the shape of the oar. As yet haven't seen any of the femmes which might be classed as Geisha Gals but then maybe I wouldn't know one if I should see one.

The essence of futility I believe is the fact that there are several ships hulls—apparently just off the ways resting neatly on the bottom of the harbor—only part of the hull & the superstructure visible—Evidence of our bombers activities no doubt.

Expect to have a more interesting letter to write after tomorrow for maybe we will get a break.

Did a bit of work on Susie's assembly yesterday so may eventually get it finished.

With All my love always

Al & Daddy

Sept 22 '45 Sept No 8

My Dearest Sweet:

The mailman finally delivered one letter from you—No 13—and a letter from George written on the same day.

Was glad to know that Susie had such a pleasant day even tho a day premature—tho it couldn't be otherwise with such a nice Mommie. With all of the activity and extras that are required Mommies are bound to be worn out at days end.

Very pleased to know that she keeps wanting to know when Pop is going to get home—difficult for a youngster to understand these separations but then it won't last forever. Incidently did some more work on her ensemble & should have it off before another week is over.

The mail prior to your no 13—for the middle of Aug is still missing as is all of the mail since then. We have been getting it as irregularily as our is regularily being sent out—that is if one writes.

Glad you enclosed the excerpts from Connie's letters. Have already told you what I have thought about it—all my sympathies with Connie. It is odd but I've often wanted to ask Connie if it was to her liking to have been left alone so much while Lloyd was satisfying his whim of doing this & that—alone of course. The description of Lloyd's reaction is typical of him—ho hum he probably is to be pittied and kicked in the pants at the same time. Might do him some good. Too bad Connie doesn't know his shipmates at Pearl for I'm sure they could give her some information to shove down his throat and make him like it. Do hope that Connie didn't allow her emotions to run away with her in her relations with Bill for that might put her on the defensive.

We finally got a break today for we were given the opportunity to see the effect of the atomic bomb. [truck tour of Nagasaki] Complete & utter devastation with the exception of few buildings in the area—they of course are mere shells—no windows or roofs. Steel framed buildings with no walls & the frame works twisted and bent—some still upright but askew. Frame or brick or masonry level to the ground—exposing portions of the machinery or equipment housed. Rather grotesque to see still standing granite archway among the rubble—Saw pieces of china & tile which I would have liked to recover but weren't permitted to leave the truck. No crater or excavation since the bomb was to have exploded prior to reaching the ground.

Everyone including children seems to be busy cleaning away rubble or otherwise engaged in doing something useful. All along the road passed all types of both sexes coming and going. Most of the women wore trousers of some shape or description & I will add that none of the attire appeared to be flattering to the shape of the women and none that raised the wolfing in your wolf of a husband.

Forgot to mention that the effect of the bomb appeared to do little damage to the crops growing on the hillside in the immediate vicinity tho some trees that were aren't no more—a picture much like a mountain slope ravaged by a fire.

Hetzler who was on the trip I made after viewing countless ill dressed, scrawny appearing Japs made the astute statement "And with that they expected to defeat us?" While they didn't & never could defeat us they did give us a bad time and upset a darned happy routine for a whole lot of us.

So the Little Feller is getting to the point of wanting to walk. It shouldn't be much longer before it won't be necessary to lug him every place & when he does—hm—wonder who will have to worry about him being in this & that. Just so he isn't all grown by the time I get home.

Don't know yet whether you have gotten the Cig case etc which was the last package I mailed—still haven't received your two mailed the first of July.

With all my love as Always—haven't even worried about your fidelity Sweet—

Al & Daddy

Sept 22 '45

Dearest Family & Sweetie Pie:

Can't recollect when I last wrote but for certain it has been much too long ago.

Like everyone else I've had a single tracked mind "When in the hell do I get out of here" and as a result the correspondence has suffered even to Dot.

Have received your letters of 8 Aug Marie—Sweetpie's of July—a nice letter from Uncle G & G.H's of 27 Aug—all of which were more than welcome. The box of Licoice arrived from George—in good shape—am still nibbling on it too—thanks much.

In case I haven't written about the unforgettable picture presented in San Pedro Bay, Leyte P.I. when news of Japan accepting the terms of the Potsdam Declaration with the reservation was received—here it is—

The Scurry's crew was enjoying a movie topside—this of course came to a halt but quick. Human emptions displayed themselves in different ways—some I'm sure said a fervent prayer in thanksgiving. There were sufficient kindred souls so that before long the whole harbor was brilliant with searchlights crisscrossing the sky flares and rockets of many colors gracefully tracing their trajectory thru the sky finally to extinguish into nothingness. All of which was appealing to the visual sense.

The auditory sense was not neglected for it seemed as every ships siren and whistle piled themselves one on the other resulting in a bedlam of sound.

Gave one the feeling of being in the center of a gigantic carnival. A spectacle thoroughly enjoyed and one I never expect again to see.

From Leyte back to Okinawa for a few days before off to do some sweeping which of course we knew would be a bit different since they were no longer assault sweeps. Cleaned part of the way for the boys going in to occupy Korea—way out in the middle of nowhere.

The Scurry finally did get a break—and off to Sasebo and Nagasaki. Didn't go into Sasebo but still have hopes.—

Nagasaki and its harbor well protected has been of interest for several reasons, the main one being of course the atomic bomb.

All along the waterfront one is conscious of the destruction our high fly-ing boys did with just bombs and as a result the Mitsubishi family is a lot less wealthy. Shipping both completed & uncompleted resting on the bottom—really the heighth of futility launch a hull & have it sunk. Structures gutted, windowless naked frames exposed to the elements. Part of the price of war to those who decided they could destroy us.

Today we had the opportunity to see the results of the atomic bomb—no crater but a complete and total wreckage, with little exception of everything within its orbit. Steel framed buildings—steel frames twisted and bent—bricks & masonry and frame structures leveled to the ground and only piles of rubble. Those structures of masonry still standing are roofless, windowless and burned or seared.—Machinery & equipment, utensils, china part of the rubble—It should be some time before Japan is in need of scrap iron from the U.S.

People coming and going—hurrying to avoid the passage of the truck that carried us over the area. Weren't able to get out of the truck—would like to have salvaged some bits of china and tile saw close to the road. The women—or a majority of them wear slacks—and the size & cut of them are not very flattering to the shape as there is generally a large baggy section in the rear. As it was raining most of them, men & women carried parisols—one was a plutocrat for he had two—using neither at the time.

Everyone seems to be engaged in doing something even the children—odd little urchins—generally dressed in combinations of things.

About the only traffic here on the harbor outside of our boats is that of the sampans—fitted with an odd shaped oar or oars—not rowed—and the movement used to propel the sampans is as odd as the shape of the paddle. Yep even the women take their turn at it. The work is done from a standing position. The traffic between the two sides of the harbor was quite heavy this noon. Saw one man pushing & pulling his sampan with about 20 customers—slow but steady progress. How much longer the Scurry will be here is a ques-tion none of us aboard know.

It has been nice that George has been able to stay so long & nicer of course if he could see his way clear to stay in S.D. Someone ought to be able to convince him & Mike of that fact—will have to leave it up to you in S.D. for my chickadee nor I are there to do it.

Would add Hugh's & Bob's vessels on my list but as yet no one has told me what they are. Don't get around a whole lot but there is a chance that we might end up in the same spot.

Our mail is again on the backlog side of the books—today is the first we've had since the 8th & that was little when we got some. Do guess the only way to straighten out this mail problems is to see that there is no need for it—

Was optimistic about Japan quitting within 6 months from the time Germany threw in the towel—and as equally optimistic about being home before too long a time—Xmas or soon thereafter. Surely not on the basis of the present point system but they can't use all of us little fellers or a great percentage for a lot longer—Should leave a little for the regulars—hm—

Much love to each & every one of you

Al—

———

A typewritten letter from his friend, Carl Stadler:

23 SEPTEMBER 45 HAGUSHI BEACH, OKINAWA

DEAR AL:

I SUPPOSED THAT BY NOW YOU HAVE REALLY THOUGHT THAT STADLER HAS FORGOTTEN YOU COMPLET ELY BECAUSE OF THE VERY SMALL AMOUNT OF CORRESPONDENCE THAT HAS BEEN GOING BACK AND FORTH BETWEEN THE TWO OF US. WELL AL, IF I HAD A NICKEL FOR EVERY SHIP'S PRESENT LIST THAT I HAVE SCANNED AND EVERY OFFICER CLUB THAT I HAVE TAKEN MUSTER IN, LOOKING FOR YOU, I'D BE ABLE TO RETIRE WHEN I GET OUT OF THIS DAMNED OUTFIT. WHERE YOUR SHIP HAS BEEN KEEPING ITSELF MUST BE A DEEP DARK SECRET.

WE GOT A BREAK AFTER THE OKINAWA OPERATION AND MANAGED TO GET BACK TO THE STATES FOR REPAIRS. I GOT 30 DAYS LEAVE AT HOME AND ANOTHER 30 AT PORTLAND WAITING

FOR THE SHIP TO BE READY. IT WAS WONDERFUL, ESPECIALLY SINCE I GOT A LOOK AT THE YOUNG SON AND HEIR FOR THE FIRST TIME. WE LEFT THE STATES AROUND THE FIRST OF AUGUST AND WENT DIRECTLY TO MANILA. WHILE THERE I HEARD A RUMOR THAT YOU WERE AROUND THOSE PARTS AND I REALLY LOOKED FOR THE SCURVEY OR IS IT SCURRY? WE WENT UP TO TOKYO AND ARRIVED THERE ON THE 13TH, AND FROM THERE WE HAVE COME BACK HERE TO GOOD OLD OKINAWA. NOW THAT GIVE YOU CAN IDEA OF WHERE WE HAVE BEEN...WHERE IN THE HELL HAVE YOU BEEN KEEPING YOURSELF?

HAVE YOU EVER HEARD FROM HANK? THE LAST I HEARD OF HIM HE WAS ON MIDWAY AND STILL DOING ALRIGHT BY HIMSELF, BY THAT I MEAN KEEPING NEAR TO A BAR AT ALL TIMES. HE IS PROBABLY LONG GONE FROM THERE NOW HOWEVER BECAUSE THAT WAS JUST PRIOR TO THE LINGAYEN OPERATION THAT I GOT HIS LAST LETTER.

HOW IS THE POINT SITUATION WITH YOU? OR ARE YOU GOING TO SHIP OVER. I HEAR THAT THE NAVY NEEDS GOOD MEN LIKE YOU...AND JUST THINK OF THE OPPORTUNITIES THAT YOU HAVE BY ENLISTING. I HAVE 46 POINTS AT PRESENT AND FIGURE THAT I CAN BE OUT BY FEBRUARY 1ST UNDER THE PRESENT SYSTEM AND BELIEVE YOU ME AL, I'M REALLY COUNTING THE DAYS AND MINUTES UNTIL THAT HAPPY MOMENT ARRIVES. I'M PLENTY SICK OF BEING A MEMBER OF THIS OUTFIT. I.J. TELLS ME THAT DOT IS PLANNNING ON COMING BACK TO SAN DIEGO ABOUT CHRISTMAS TIME, AND I TAKE IT THAT THAT MUST MEAN THAT ALBERT IS THINKING ON COMING HOME BEFORE TOO LONG. I HOPE SO AL.

HOW DO YOU LIKE THE COMMUNICATION BUSINESS BY NOW, OR ARE YOU AS SICK OF IT AS I AM. I FIGURE THAT IF I WORK AT COMMUNICATIONS FOR ANOTHER SIX MONTHS I'LL REALLY BE ABLE TO QUALIFY AS A SINGING TELEGRAM BOY FOR WESTERN UNION, OR BE DECLARED MENTALLY UNFIT FOR NAVAL

SERVICE...I'M PRETTY SICK OF THIS GLORIFIED MESSENGER BOY BUSINESS.

THIS HASN'T BEEN MUCH OF A LETTER, AL BUT I JUST WANTED TO SAY HELLO AND LET YOU KNOW THAT I HAVEN'T FORGOTTEN YOU COMPLETELY. SAY HELLO TO DOT AND SUSIE AND TO THE NEW MEMBER OF THE FAMILY WHEN YOU WRITE TO THEM FOR ME. I'LL STILL BE LOOKING FOR YOU. GOOD LUCK AL, AND I HOPE THAT WE SEE EACH OTHER SOON, IN CIVILIAN CLOTHES.

Carl

Sept 28 Sept Letter No 9

My Dearest Sweet:

This has been rather an unusual day to say the least.—Arrived at Sasebo Harbor to find Hugh's C. LST in port—sent a visual over—but since he was leaving this PM I had to see him this morning—finally got about a half hour with him—now I know what LST he is on at least & I wouldn't have known he was in unless he had signaled over.

He is fortunate enuf to have 51 points and has sent in a request for discharge & feels quite fortunate that he will get it. Can't say I blame him—will be a break for he has been in for some time. My—how he looks like Uncle Albert—has the Caughey features. Would of course liked to have had more time but then it was nice to see him.

The mailman was good today too—mail twice in a big way—believe I have all of your back letters—Marie's letter of Sept 12—a letter from Sweetie Pie, Lee J, the [San Diego State College] Aztec newsletter and two requests from Cal Alum for a 4.00 donation—and one of your packages emperine and nail polish.—Quite a good bit of fortune I should say.

To top it all off a good steak dinner and a double feature—"Hostage" & "Wrecking Crew" the latter quite old I should say. Had King Kong last nite. I staid or could stand just a short amount and left long before the thing was over.

Sorry to hear about Helen not a pleasant thing to have bothering you—
will drop her a note if nothing more. Wonder if Bill is the inducement to
wanting it in L.A.? Won't again make the mistake of calling him Lemon when
he is Orange.—

Very much surprised to know that the package with the booklet and all
only took ten days. Your supposition about airmail service must be correct.
The material used was coconut shells. Took some time and sanding to shine
them but since I had no gardening to do it was relaxation from paperwork
& rather enjoyed it. Have most of Susie's set completed and should get it off
before very much longer.

Didn't send a copy of the booklet to the family but have one for each of
the four boys which I will get off to them soon with a piece of currency—
from the Philippines. Haven't as yet acquired Jap currency except that sent
earlier the ten yen—piece. Both the yen and the cigarette case are from the
same place—Okinawa & the story about them—hm.

Glad you liked the necklace of coins. Laughingly told Gosch that Mommie
would wear it—it really is too heavy for Susie when she is so small, relatively
speaking.

Regarding George—if you remember Marie's letter of Aug to both of us
she mentioned trying to induce George to stay in S.D.—of course for Mike
to come when she was thru nursing her mother who is ill. Would be nice to
have all of the family in one area.

I'm glad I.J. didn't write you that I was going to be at Okinawa. It
wouldn't have helped you knowing we were there. It wasn't pleasant I can
assure you but that's all over now & of the past. A bit amused tho for you
should have known that being in on the Iwo deal we very probably would
have been in on Okinawa as we would have been in on the next one too if
there had been one.

Haven't commented on your letters but will give me something to put in
my next letters so that they would [not] be just all bitching.

The resignation as a way out as been discarded for the present, besides
they said few resignations will be accepted. Will wait a little while longer to

see what gives before doing anything. Besides they can't keep all of us little fellers out here too much longer. Still hopeful of being home by Xmas.—

Lovingly as always to my Three Sweethearts

Al & Daddy

Sept 29 Sept Letter No 10

My Dearest Sweet:

Haven't had time today to reread your letters or get the questions in any sort of orderly manner so will just ramble on.

Neglected to write Dad a birthday note in fact had forgotten all about it—apologize for me and wish him a belated birthday for me.

As for Xmas don't want you to send a box for several reasons—first I don't think it will reach me in time—and mainly because I still have hopes of being with you or so close to it that a remembrance won't be important. Should I not get there don't feel that a box would do the morale any good and I don't want to feel bad about not getting one off.

Scuttle but has it that we may have a chance to get ashore for a sight seeing trip. Had hoped that that would be possible for a shame to be here & not get to see anything. This of course will not be anything as spectacular as Nagasaki. Generally we of the sea have not been permitted to get ashore and for good reason.

Sorry to hear about Footsie I. Would like a few more of the details as to when & where for it might be possible that it might have been close to home. We didn't go alongside each ship to ask for a roster of officers. DO's of course as Time has said take a beating.

Lee J. wrote me much the same as you had heard. Wonder if they plan on sending them back out here again. Don't see it for we have much larger & faster tonnage which could satisfactorily do the job. Nice that he did get home & with good fortune shouldn't have been bounced off the plane.

As for the linen from the Philippines am sure I saw some but such did not appeal to me. Not too expensive either & not much more than the heavier material like that sent to Mother. Sorry I didn't know you had that in mind for I would have gotten some for you. Will remember if we make another trip in that direction, tho I do hope not.

Had "Captain Courageous" this evening. Enjoyed it tho I may have seen it previously. Helps make up for King Kong which someone else was gracious enuf to accept, but why is a mystery.

Have several cartoons which I think you might enjoy but don't think I'll send them via the US mails—Esquire—remember?

Slowly digging into & thru three back issues of Time—helps me to sleep.

The "Three" in the gallery weren't bad for 30 cents—tho they didn't do justice to any of you.

I love you with all my heart as Always

Al & Daddy

Sept 30 Sept Letter No 11

My Dearest Sweet:

The mailman gave again today with your No 7 of the 17th—a letter from Uncle A of April 12 & Walt C of April 23—both of the latter first class service to say the least.

Glad of course to get them even tho they are a bit old, tho I can't see why first class mail is so slow in getting to us—they (the Dept's) wonder why we use air mail.

Uncle Albert related about his operation—interesting to say the last tho I'm sure he is very happy that it is all over.

Will enclose Walt's letter so you can get the stuff straight off. Assume that he was in training for the proposed operation after Okinawa which never came off—lucky for Walt and any many others for it would have been a tough assignment—as they were bound to more intensely resisted the closer we got to home base.

The reports from the liberty party today Gates & Bezold escorting indicated that a trip ashore will be worth while even tho no trading with the inhabitants are permitted.

Thought I had a lead on Dutch the other day but again can't quite make the grade. Do guess I will have to wait until I get home to see him.

Don't remember if I told you that we had two guests, females, while at Nagasaki—off the "Haven"—both, in fact all of the Red Cross nurses. Both seemed pretty good eggs. Staid for chow but shoved off early since they were due back aboard before 6:30 P.M. The Skipper brot them aboard. Nice to see women again tho don't worry your old man didn't go overboard for there is still just <u>one gal</u> for him.

Have about completed Susie's ensemble & hoped to have it in the mail before we leave here—for what or where no one seems to know the scuttlebutt is running free.

Had "Jam Session" for our movie tonight. Short intermission for a sprinkle. That gal Ann Miller has a nice pair of gams—her chest ain't bad either—do you mind?

Did enjoy Lee's letter—his always have something in them so that one can't help but appreciate receiving them—definitely Lee all over.

The "Pride & Joy" seems to be banging herself in some way or other. Was a mean knock she must have gotten—now you gave it an extra kiss for me to make it well quicker.

With Love Always to My Three Sweethearts.

Al & Daddy

13

SASEBO: SHORE EXCURSIONS

October 1945

Oct 4 Oct Letter No 1

My Dearest Sweet:

The days seem to be slipping by so fast for here it is the 4th already and no letters off to you.

Have been busy as all doing this & that plus extras which have been added due to the demobilization. Really it has been no picnic—too damn much extra to do.

Received a nice note from George again today—still in SD so I expect that they will keep him there.—Will be nice to have all of us in such a close vicinity—nice for the family but maybe a bit rugged on the in—laws.

Has been a bit more than cool for the last couple of days. A cold front is in the area. A blanket at night is pleasant tho a bed partner might be a bit more comforting.—ho hum. Please don't plan on the twin beds for awhile for I'm sure that I don't want to keep the floor shined. Naughty ain't I?

Had the movie on the forecastle again tonight. "Hi Diddle Diddle." Good entertainment but almost unpleasant to be topside even with the jacket on. Breeze blowing around the ears.

Scuttle butt is still much and varied—most of it pleasant to hear however. Still an optimist however all the way along and hopeful of being home by Xmas or soon thereafter. From where I sit don't see how they can efficiently

& effectively use us small fellers. Of course it is nice to have company but hell our time is just about up.

The family wrote asking if they should get a Xmas box off. My answer to them will be the same to them as it was to you—negative.

Still at Sasebo—tho why I couldn't tell you. Did get ashore & as usual took are of some business ashore that should have been taken care of by the Exec—but who expects him to do much.

The area along the bay is unlike that of Nagasaki, in pretty good condition. Small amount of damage. Our B 29's & the incendiaries did however take care of the industrial part of town—burned as badly as Nagasaki was demolished, block after block & rubbish. Had to hike, no transportation. Hanna & I took 25 of the crew. Walked here & yonder gawking as was everyone else. Hiked to the top of a hill to see a cemetery—disappointing but the view comprehensive.

Homes are much as in pictures—small amount of furniture—numerous mats on the floor & sleeping floor slightly elevated from the main floor. We were not permitted cameras, to trade or converse with the inhabitants.

Residential sections are on the slopes of the hills which seem to rise from the harbor areas except that occupied by the industrial section which lies in a valley. Quite steep inclines too. Noticeable how few streets there are but many walks & stairs.

The business section & what is left is unclean according to our standards. Chinese section of SC is clean in comparison. Shop keeps evidently live on the second floor of their establishments.

Dress is comparable to that seen in Nagasaki—saw only two women who looked as if they might be of the better class & dressed it. Surprising good taste in choice of colors.

While passing a barber shop couldn't help but noticing that many of the barbers were she's—& in one a he was shaving a she. Didn't know they had bearded ladies in this neck of the world. Accidently wandered into forbidden area but wasn't long until we were shooed out. Understand, but don't believe, that there's a dispute about price—the gals want $6 but the management thinks a $1 is a fair price. If true is interesting but none of that for me.

Have finished Susie's ensemble—tho not quite satisfied with the shells attached to the necklace. Have also about finished with a shell necklace for you using the chain you sent. Hope it will prove satisfactory. Will send them together.

With love as always to my Three Sweethearts

Al & Daddy

Oct 6 Oct Letter No 2

My Dearest Sweet, Susie & Steve:

Nothing much that is new to report—only that as usual am only waiting word that will mean home & you—with all the pleasant things that go along with being husband & father.

Have had no mail from you in the last few days. Of course there is always the future & hopefulness that there might be some mail.

Susie's ensemble plus a sea shell necklace for you is ready to be sent on its way. Not entirely satisfied with the accessories on Susie's necklace but can't be too choosey as can't go along the beach at Samar [island in the Central Philippines] & look for more. Do believe that everything including the bracelet will be too big for her but you can adjust if you want her to wear them. Wouldn't suggest allowing Steve to chin himself using the shells on your necklace as the source of pull.

Wrote the family a note last night advising them not to send a Xmas box. Told them also about seeing Hugh and the visit to Sasebo.

The authorities are now allowing regular liberty at Sasebo with trading. As yet none of the men have found silks for sale. Maybe the merchants are waiting until the price goes up. In case I do get a chance to get back will see what I can find for my Sweethearts.

An officers club is set up too—ice & water provided—each officer to provide his own special refreshments. Laid in a small supply while at Pearl and was able to get some Canadian Club here. Don't however know when the opportunity to go see will be provided but maybe.

Have as usual been doing a good bit of paper work—would like to chuck it all damn quick but—. Who knows?

The weather has warmed up again yesterday—slept without a blanket & not too uncomfortable except early this morning rolled & tossed a bit. Maybe it wasn't the climate or weather—hm?

Omnibook of Jan has had my attention the last few nights—"China To Me" by Emily Hohn especially. She must be some gal—cosmopolitan and Democratic at the same time.

Didn't get to attend Mass today as we are out—was able to attend last Sunday. The Padre was a young chap & seemed to have a practical approach. He was late for service & as a result of hurrying was perspiring freely all during the service—wanted to loan him my kerchief.

Won't be too long now till you will be heading towards home where I want to be badly.

With love always to my Three Sweethearts as Always

Al & Daddy

Oct 8 Oct Letter No 3

My Dearest Sweet:

A short note before the mailman shoves off with the mail—will be several days until another note will be winging its way to you.

Another rainy day & a busy one too—spent a good bit of the morning at the Issuing Office.

This afternoon was consumed on administrative matters so in fact can be considered as work.

Haven't had that opportunity to get over to the beach again so nothing for you three.—

Understand that there is an establishment approved for officers. The charge is 100 yen per hr rental. The entertainment is provided by gals who sing & dance for you. Tea too is provided. Don't think it isn't legitimate so plan on looking in if the opportunity is presented. No business however for that is not what I'm looking for away from home.

Scuttlebutt is still running riot. Also news of a new point system soon. What it will be or mean will only be known when released. Do however feel that the Navy is a bit afraid of the public's reaction to their general requirements—which of course will be shown in Congress's attitude.

The news about the number of strikes is a bit disturbing. They, in peacetime as well as during war lead to economic instability & an abundance of social unrest—or maybe strikes are the result of them—well any ho who's got the button.

Did received some mail aboard the ship today for the latter part of Sept—none in the bunch for Herney tho he isn't complaining as he hasn't been too good on the letter writing & admits it—however he does love you just the same—and much.

With love always to my Three Sweethearts

1Al & Daddy

Oct 12 1945 Oct No 4

My Dearest Sweet:

Have felt like hell for the last two days—underway during the day but swinging on the hook at night. The sea has been quite rough & as a result uncomfortable. Didn't loose my cookies but maybe it would have been better if I had.

It has been cold again for the last few days—this cold front & the condition of the sea is all a result of the big blow which passed to the east of the Island day before yesterday. Certainly glad we don't live where they normally expect to have them.

No mail now for about a week. Don't believe they have established air service to Sasebo as yet but should soon. Ships coming from Okinawa bring mail or what there is of it.

Still haven't wrapped our package or the one to be sent off to the family in S.D. Should do so & will try to get it off or wrapped so it can be mailed when we are thru with this little operation we are on now.

Anchored last night & then again tonight in a small cove—no interest to find out where—The area above the beaches all seem to be inhabited and cultivated. More terracing—would be interesting to go ashore to see what they have in the many plots.

Don't know how long or what will come after this but for sure am getting so sick of this horsing around. Symptoms of war fatigue, delayed, are becoming even more evident. Somebody is fooling themselves if they think this is being done in an expeditious manner. Maybe one can put it down to "Service" and let it go at that—Doesn't help much however if you don't want to stay in it but have other plans for living.

As usual started writing a letter & the pen goes dry—had to buy a bottle as all out. Hope this will be the last I'll buy aboard the Scurry & the last from the Navy.

Have been having the movies topside when not raining. Did last night & it was cold. Reminds one of the crisp air in the mts—which of course would be pleasant to take in comparison. Wrapped up in jacket rain pants, muffler gloves & still was uncomfortable. O well it can't last forever.

In case Susie is still wondering when her Daddy is coming home to her you can tell her he is wanting to do so damn quick—post haste & all that.

With love always to my Three Sweethearts whom I love with all My Heart.

Al & Daddy

Oct 15 Oct Letter No 5
My Dearest:

Since I just dropped a note to Helen & there is a possibility of getting this off will also write you a short note.

Now that the typhoon is past & things have calmed down a bit feel a wee bit better—still get that weak feeling in the middle when underway—hell who wants to be a sailor anyway.

Still no mail from you. Do hope that it wasn't lost because of the storm. From all reports there is that possibility—Certainly glad I wasn't at Okinawa when she hit. We just caught the outside of it—which of course is sufficient.

Scuttlebutt is still good & of most any you want to hear. Haven't changed my opinion nor have the hopes been bashed any as yet.

The nights & mornings have still been cool. The mental attitude hasn't been prime, to enjoy it however & don't think that will be possible except if they could be enjoyed in the mts at Palomar.

Have been sweeping passage off the northwest of Kyushu between Iki Shima & Fukuoka. How much longer we are to be here don't know—in fact they can have all of it more.

Have been showing the movies topside the last few nites. Hs been cold enuf to go wrapped up in the winter clothing issued to us. Had Laughton in the "Man From Down Under" last nite & did enjoy it.

Hetzler, Schnabel and Kraus all are impatient to get started home. They are in line waiting. Think their best prospect of getting home is in staying with the ship until she heads homeward which shouldn't be too far distant.— hmmm—Wouldn't mind if we were on our way tonight but that doesn't seem to be in the cards.

Anxious as ever to get home to you and the youngsters—Love you with all my heart as always

Al & Daddy

Oct 15, 1945

Dear Sis: [Helen Herney]

The past few weeks have been such as to remind me of fall in Nebraska— cool & nippy in the morning & evenings but warm in the sun during the day. Needless to say a blanket at night is a comfort—would much prefer a bed partner however.

Both Dot & Marie have written that you expected to undergo an operation sometime this month—just where you were to have it done they didn't say or who was to do it.—Do so hope that it will be completely successful and that it will not be too much for you. Upon recovery & <u>when</u> I get home you can tell all about "Your Operation."

Don't know if Dot wrote you about me calling your friend Bill "Lemon" or not. However I'm sure he won't mind if I'm a bit confused for more than one reason.

Since the family might have passed on my last few letters won't retell of the ashore visits at Nagasaki or Sasebo. Regular Liberty is now permitted at Sasebo so would like to get ashore to get a few <u>"nick naks".</u> To my knowledge no one has found any silk, really about the only desirable thing to bring home.

For the past few days have been doing a bit of sweeping off the northwest coast of Kyushu—between Iki Shima and Fukuoka to be exact. How much longer we are going to be here we can't find out as no one knows or won't tell.

Still very hopeful of being home by Xmas or soon thereafter. Rumors are free and varied & some of them sound pretty good. Of course always believe those that that to prove our hopes.

Had hopes of getting to China before coming home but believe that out of the question. In what sweeping we have done since the Nips surrendered have been conscious of the difference between those sweeps & the assault sweeps at Iwo & Okinawa.

The last typhoons—of late Sept & the one of last week fortunately were on a track which missed us. Did however catch the outside of them and caused a bit of discomfort. From the news was very grateful not to have been at Okinawa. Don't believe that I will ever be a good sailor. Still feel much like I assume a pregnant woman feels, every time we get underway & feel that way most of the time we are underway. Thank God for the benefit of anchoring at night, even tho it is just a short respite from that feeling.

Movies—16 mms aren't too bad & sometimes sit thru some that would hold no attraction if you had to move ten feet to seem them if at home. Have had them on the forecastle when weather permits.

Again Sis do hope that the operation won't be too much for you & that you'll be all well by the time I get home.

Knowing you will give my regards to all in L.A.

Lovingly

Al

Oct 16 Oct Letter No 6

My Dearest Sweet:

Another chance to get mail off to you so will drop you a note. Word is that we have some mail somewhere—not lost in the typhoon that hit Okinawa. However from all reports our administrative command could profitably take a kick in the pants for a lesson.

Have finally wrapped & Mailed the package to Susie Q—Hope it makes as good time as the last package I sent. You will find that everything may be a bit too big for so bit a little girl but then maybe not. Sent the sea shell necklace too & hope it meets with your approval. Almost went nuts getting it squared away.

The tobacco tin Al used to store the shells he gathered from beaches throughout the Pacific arena, and the necklace he crafted for Dot using some of the shells. He labeled the box, "Ye Old Sea Shells."

Spent the day swinging at anchor—all in that nice little anchorage I mentioned before. Wasn't interrupted & got a good bit or work accomplished.

The Scuttlebutt seems to be getting better & better & if correct my hopes won't be far wrong. Am praying of course that it isn't just scuttlebutt & that I can soon be with you.

From the continued cold mornings & evenings would say that autumn is here for sure. Don't like either the intense heat of the P.I. nor the cold of this climate—still much of a <u>Southern Californian</u> even if it does rain for days during the months of Dec & Jan.

Don't know if I mentioned getting a card from Lois H. [Hudgins] mailed from Boulder Dam Dated sometime in April. This was received when the other old mail came thru about two weeks ago. Now that the Armed Guard is of the past doubt if I will get to see Ed.

Wondered if Uncle Jim had as yet arrived home & been discharged. If he was at Guam word has it that it is one hell of a place to get out of. We have transferred several fellows but believe I would have preferred staying & riding the Scurry home. Lost my leading Radioman H Goldstein, from LA & a blow it was. Ran a good shack & took much off my shoulders. Do so I hope he got away from Okinawa before the recent storm for life there now would be anything but pleasant.

Have been trying to keep myself busy to prevent going nuts—can think of nothing but terminating my relationship with the service & returning to the old haunts which hold pleasant memories & which I'm sure will offer many many happy moments in the future.

My Love Always to my Three Sweethearts since I haven't included Dad & Mother for some time share some with them huh?

Al & Daddy.

Oct 18 Oct Letter No 8
Dearest Sweet, Susie, Steve, Mother & Dad:

Life at last is proving to be a bit more pleasant—the end now for certain does not seem to far away—the end of course being no more military life. Haven't as yet seen the Alnav reducing points but that in conjunction with other factors makes my hopes of being home by Xmas or soon thereafter much stronger.

Underway back to Sasebo & some mail I hope. Don't know how long we will be there but have only a minute for a note—have as usual many things to do before getting into port.

Would of course like to know when you plan on starting home so the letters, if & when written will be mailed to the proper address. Do hope the package gets to you in Lincoln before you leave.

The news of the last nite indicated that the railroads planned on handling about a million men during Dec;—most of course will be going east from the West Coast thank god so your problem shouldn't be too difficult.

Must close but did want you to now I still love you always
As always
Al & Daddy.

Oct 18 [number 2 with that date] Oct Letter No 8 [October Letter No. 9]
My Dearest Sweet:

At last the mailman on this end broke down and gave forth with your 8, 9, 10 & 12 of Sept 1& 3 of Oct, a letter from Carl S, a nice long letter from Marie H & one from George H.

Carl's was written on Sept 23 from Hagushi Beach, Okinawa—then off to Tokyo on the 13th of this month. Doubt if I will get to see him for he has sufficient points under the new system to get out now—Do hope he gets out in a hurry & doesn't have to wait for relieve.

Hetzler & Krause received their orders today for transportation home & discharge. Relief for Krause only is being sent.—While the two replacements clouds the picture a little still hopeful since I was low point man aboard & I will be eligible by Dec 15 on the basis of 44 points. Can't see how they can keep all of us out here & they must have some of us to take her back—Would prefer to ride her back anyway as being pushed around on another vessel isn't at all pleasant.

Your letter writing has been about as sporadic as mine. I however haven't kept track of the total written but do believe it will top yours. Can well imagine that you haven't waited to write thinking I may have been on my way home but "Baby" remember when the Scurry starts skidding eastward I will write you to that effect.

It wasn't necessary to report that others consider Susie <u>Superior</u>, that's a foregone conclusion as far as I'm concerned. As for being mischievous at times that's from the Paternal side—he has been at time too but don't let it worry you.

Sorry to hear that Steve is going to be a knob turner for I'm sure that will get him into difficulty with Pop especially when relaxed, horizontally, listening to some program. Really can't wait to get home to add <u>My Spoiling</u> to that already handed out. You really can't expect me to take an active part in discipline for at least a month after I get home.

Have been trying to figure out the office arrangement mentioned in Marie's letter. Can't for the life of me do it but guess I can get accustomed to it in time. Plan on doing it snazzy like too huh?

Carl asked to be remembered.

With all my love as always—will be satisfied if you get home by the middle of Dec—then you'll be there waiting for me.

Al & Daddy

CERTIFICATE OF DEMOBILIZATION FACTORS - ALNAV 295-45

DATE ___18 October 1945___

1. ___HERNEY_____ ___Albert_____ ___F.___ ___303567___ ___Lieut(jg), (C), USNR___
   Last Name   First Name   Initial   File or Ser. No.   Rank or RateClass.

2. U.S.S. SCURRY (AM-304), c/o Fleet Post Office, San Francisco, California.

3. _____A_____ : _____B_____ : C : D : E

4. ____18 February 1912____ : _____34_____ : 1/2 : 17 :
        Date of Birth   :   Years of Age :   :   :
5. ____15 October 1943_____ : _____23_____ : 1/2 : 11½ :
   Date of Reporting for Act. Duty : Total Mos. Act. Duty :   :   :
6. _____ :   : 1/2 :
   Date of Active Duty With Any Other : Total Mos. Act. Duty :   :   :
   Armed Force Than U.S. Navy. :   :   :   :
7. _____ : _____13_____ : 1/4 : 3¼ :
   Active Duty Outside Continental US : Number Months :   :   :
8. Dependency Status as of 8/15/45 : _____Yes_____ :   : 10 :
                                   : Yes or No   : 10-0 :   :
9. _____Total Points_____ :   :   : 41-3/4 :

10. Eligible for immediate discharge ___No___ . Reason: ___Insufficient Points___
                                    Yes or No

11. For Officers Only: Total number of days taken as leave or delay counting as
    leave since 9/1/39 or date of first commission or warrant, whichever is
    later ___21___

12. _____San Diego, California_____
    City and State to which entitled transportation upon discharge or release
    from active duty.

"Certified to be correct to the best of my knowledge and in accordance with
the information available this date."

                                        Signature of Individual Reported On

                                        C. E. DUNSTON, Commanding,
                                        U.S.S. SCURRY (AM-304)

*Certificate of demobilization factors showing Al's ineligibility for immediate
discharge due to "Insufficient Points" dated October 18, 1945.*

Oct 19 Oct Letter No 9 [October Letter No. 10]

My Dearest Sweet:

For the first time today saw the true dope on points—Alnavs are slow in getting to us. Had heard that points were to be reduced to 44 as of Dec 1 but I'm from Mo.

Most everyone is quite hopeful of being home—that is aboard the scurry—by Xmas—even the Capt who has been unsocial about it before admitted this morning that there was a good chance that we would be there. Just where we would light I don't know—Am crossing my fingers for the Des[troyer] Base in S.D.—not impossible either.

Thought I had a lead on Dutch but haven't been able to pursue it to the end. Maybe tomorrow I can do it myself. Asked Hetzler to make an inquiry for me today—would have taken him five minutes but it appeared he was too damn busy for himself—he is really a very selfish & spoiled little boy & I mean little in that respect.

Noticed from operations that Bob M Pat's husband was at Agoo on the 16th. Haven't checked but believe it is in the PI's someplace. Don't know where he is going from there. Noticed from Marie's letter that Pat is working at Martin-Verbs on 5th. Wonder if the proprietor (?) remembers a client of ours gave her a bum check—client only after the check had been given.

Have been short on water again so showers have been few and far between. Will try to sneak one tonight or I won't be fitten to live with or near.

Sorry to hear that you have had trouble with your knee again. Do hope it is again all well & won't bother more.

A bit surprised over Walt C getting married. Must have found something to his liking or he wouldn't have jumped off into the briny deep—or maybe she was a good inducer. Can't say I blame you for felling unkindly about the correspondence. I am on the owning end as for letters to them as with others.

From the clippings on the Judgeship there is quite a problem. Is you Is or You Aint seems to be the theme song. Feel sorry for the Capt getting in such bum condition but he has had a colorful life & a full one.

Nothing more has been said about Monica's date of presentation nor about Helen's operation—have both been postponed on bum dope?

My but the Casey's must be family inclined. Believe this must be the 4th—Should well afford the fourth for he was making the jack.

Off to that shower & then to bed with Sweet Dreams of all Three of My Sweethearts as always

Al & Daddy.

Oct 20, 1945 Oct Letter No 19 [October Letter No. 11]

My Dearest Sweet:

Received your No 11 today with the picture of the "Pride & Joy" & another on a pony. The packet of letters which yours was wrapped had been slightly wet & as a result the print stuck to the envelope—didn't do too much damage however.

The picture is good of Susie as always. Can agree with Palma that the other could just as well have been left off—was she troubled with dyspepsia (?) at the moment.

Plans for tomorrow include a trip down the coast via "Jeep". Hetzlers cousin in the Sea Bee's over at Sasebo to provide the transportation. Capt, Hetzler Gosch & Bezold went today. Bought a bit of China ware—silk was non existent. Commander Wilson friend of Hetzlers cousin told of an officer finding a Kimino & paying $50.00 for it—hm what price for the work of the cocoon. Maybe it was fancy huh or the price included what wears it? The merchants even on China seem to know what the score is—oh boy here come the suckers.

Received a new officer aboard today—the relief for Kraus—an Ensign with the grand score of 26 points. God how I would hate to be in his shoes.

Even tho you could get that ride to Santa Ana with the neighbors think you are wise to go via train. The more I think things over feel that you should if you can be home around the 1st of Dec. The house I understand is to be ready for your occupancy. Nothing as yet is official or akin to it but more hopeful than ever of getting there by Xmas. Can't tell you all of the details or reasons & don't want you to be too disappointed if I don't.

The movie tonight again, third sitting was "Tampico." Did have an excellent tho old one last nite—Ruggles of Red Gap with Charles Laughton & Charles Ruggels.

Please get all of the winter colds over with before I get home—for sure I'll be catching it from them. Would feel mean to be unsociable because of it & don't want to be that way.

Glad you are buying all of the Xmas gifts early. An excellent idea for I'm sure you'll be busy as hell getting ready for the Old Man.

Tried hard to find Dutch today. Discovered that he is no longer on the Montrase but transferred with the staff to the Donohue APA 107. Also he is now a Lt. Commander. Must have gotten a spot promotion for I'm sure no alnav could have caught him, glad for him.

With love as always to All of You—

Al & Daddy

Oct 22 Oct Letter No 11 [October Letter No. 12]

Dearest Sweet, Susie, Steve, Mother & Dad:

Just a little after the start of this a new day & the rounds having been made should squeeze in a short note to you.

Left this morning for that excursion & excursion it was. Bezold, Schnabel, Gates, Hanna & myself from the officers & 15 of the crew. The latter did not have to hang on to our coat tails nor we theirs—thank goodness.

Drove down along the coast to some small town. Looked everything over trying to find silks first & some nice pieces of china. The efforts were futile so as a result came home empty handed except did get something for those left out when buying at Tacloban. Did see a vase that I would have purchased for the office but too large to pack around.

Spent a good bit of time inquiring prices & making them understand it was too damn much.

Children were everywhere. No sooner did the trucks stop then there seemed to be many of them asking for Cigs of all things. Fellows who have been out before say that chocolate, gum & cigs do wonders on bringing the price down—package of gum will bring you 5 yen—which is about 1 cents.

Thought I had located a kimono for you but on second look discovered it was of a rayon material & not too good at that—price $10.00 or 150 yen.

Some of the boys bought back things that you normally hide away in the closet unless of course that you wish to display it above the mantle or hang it from the ceiling. We have quite a bit already in the box in the garage.

Didn't get any propositions at all today—of course wasn't looking for any but understood they were available—reasonable too 15 yen or 1.00.

Next morning after Sack Drill

As is usual when the sleep is interrupted have a headache much like a hang over.—Even a couple of emperine hasn't seemed to help.

Might as well warn you now that in several days there will an interruption in mail to you. This does not mean I am enroute to the west coast but have another small job to do which of course we all hope is our last. Will of course let you know about that phase of it later.

Still no word from you as to when you wish me to address the mail, whatever there might be of it to 399 J St.—Maybe I had better make carbons & send one each place from the 15th of Nov on—tho that will mean typing & I don't like none of it.

With love always to my Three Sweethearts

Al & Daddy

Oct 24 (AM) Oct Letter No 12 [October Letter No. 13]
My Dearest Sweet:

Very disappointed to say the least for day before yesterday received a good bit of mail aboard & not even a note from you tsk—what the hell?

Hetzler & Kraus got away this morning—reported yesterday for transportation & were fortunate to catch some thing going direct to the states. Shouldn't be too long until they are home & civilians once again.

As a result of Hetzler leaving & Gosch in line for Exec Officer spot he has moved into Hetzlers quarters & I moved down to the lower bunk. Krause's relief Asper moved in with me.

Will have to start cleaning out drawers, disposing of correspondence and getting ships files etc. in shape so that if & when won't be too darn busy so that extra days will be spent aboard.

Am having a sea chest, small, made up for the things won't be able to squeeze into the bag. Am glad didn't bring my good bag with me for they do get a beating for they are generally on the bottom. More convenient that way.

The mornings & evenings continue to be snappy. Do hope it doesn't get much cooler for or if it does will try to find some red flannels somewhere. Hate to think of getting frostbite too.—

Schnabel is still waiting for his relieve. Has been on his way for some time now & Schnabel of course keeps wondering where he could be. Surprising he has been so long underway in getting here—maybe possible he is stalling as long as possible & guess he can't be blamed for it.

Our turn over of men is beginning to be a problem. Has meant a good bit of extra work as is demobilization. Can't understand why things are always or appear to be so complicated. Guess it's the military.

With love as always to My Three Sweethearts

Al l& Daddy

14

HOPE SUSPENDED

November 1945

From Dictionary of American Naval Fighting Ships*:*
*She [*Scurry*] then returned to mine clearance operations, sweeping in the Korean Strait until sailing from Sasebo for the United States on 10 December.*[xxvi]

From Falls Church Veteran Stories website—Quartermaster Third Class Bill Rankin:
I was assigned to the Port Directors office in Sasebo, Japan, which had been set up immediately after the surrender...It took 28 days on a Naval transport ship to get there... We arrived in Sasebo in November 1945...Japan had heavily mined the coast and the US Air Force had dropped 5,000 mines in the Inland sea. There was no way of knowing where they were. Minesweepers were brought in to clear channels to the ports...We were advised of where the mines had been cleared and plotted courses for the ships to take to deliver the supplies...not one ship was blown up.[xxvii]

Nov 3 Nov Letter No 1
My Dearest Sweet:

Don't remember when I did write you the last note about a week ago but it has been some time. Wouldn't have gotten to you any way so you will have to be satisfied with this one to make up for it.

Can't say the last week has been an exciting one even to unique to say the least—more about that later.

The first few days out were rough as hell. Had a touch of the old trouble which I believe was due to the condition of the sea. At one time took as much as a 40 degree roll & as usual most everything was on the deck.

Had even quite a time to stay in the sack—tho the horizontal position was by far the most pleasant position to be in. Just sort of hung on for dear life.

It begins to look like this little job is about over & grateful we will be too. However what comes next is a big question & one we all want to know the answer to. Please God make it quick.

Have been out in the East China Sea. If you can spot 30 degrees north and 127 degrees East that is just about where we have been—not moving out of the immediate location.

Fortunately we have had the good fortune to be dropping the hook at night which meant of course no underway watches at night—Helped to ease the problems of the day which were strenuous ones & long too. Have spent all day on the bridge & as a result little paper work which might be a blessing at that.

Have had movies on the forecastle even way out here. Honestly if someone had said that Herney would be on a ship anchored in the China Sea miles from land seeing a movie topside he would have claimed that they were insane to the nth degree. However that has been the case & seems odd to be doing it.

The weather has been cool and at times unpleasantly cold. Even a jacket during the day is comfortable & should be pretty well worn by the time we get home.

Susie & Steve take turns being out front (their Valentine pictures) in a picture frame I've made. Would very much like to have then to spoil & cuddle with—of course there would be much time spent with their mother too—huh?

Must get to some sack drill Sweet as tomorrow will be another hard day as will the day after that—then?

With love always to My Three Sweet Hearts

Al & Daddy

P.S. Will try to get a note off to the family before getting into port again.

Nov 9 Nov Letter No 2

My Dearest Sweet:

Tho your No 1 should have gotten off to you the other day we were fooled—no one wanted to take mail off—however we did get some from you—which helped of course—received the first two colored photos.

Can't quite agree with you on the merits of colored and black & white. The natural effect is attractive but there is something lost in the color of the subject. Possibly I'm too critical—but that is how I felt about the group picture. Steve in his <u>sole</u> seems to have more of the detail & my how smug. A good picture—did you have him squinting in the sun.

Have grown very discontented with this whole mess & the more I see of it the worse it becomes.

Our little operation was extended a few days so instead of getting in on the 6th we continued on—should get in now tomorrow as we have completed the assignment.

The status of the querrie—When are we going home has been further complicated by discovery that our Administrative/Command seems to have no conception of just what his problems are or are going to be & as a result no plan tho expressing a policy—intangible as hell—snafu is a mild term to be used & in fact used.

In addition the skipper, bless him, had put in an application for transfer to the regular navy mainly for a reason. He of course was thinking of Dunston & Dunston only. Seems however to have gotten caught & now in a position where he will be stuck even tho he doesn't finally go USN. Because of it he has been unbearable—concluded a long time ago he was a boor, ill bread, selfish, temperamental unpredictable, egotistical and childish in many ways. Am now sure of it and not at all in a generous mood.

He is to be transferred within the next few days which of course will mean a lot of extra work for all of us. Not that we're or any of us sorry to see him go—He has pulled a lousy trick on Schnabel & Schnabel seems to be holding the sack—Oh well live & learn. Of course being of the nature he is his present circumstance is everybodie's fault but his—(not referring to Schnabel).

With all this on my mind you can see why I haven't written oftener—shouldn't even mail this letter I know but had to get off some steam. Schnabel of course is plenty upset about the position he is in too.

The last mail received from you are No's 5 & 6 for Oct—also received Mother's nice note.

Am ashamed to think that I have neglected everyone's birthday including Dad & Mothers. In fact have forgotten what months they fell in tho I'm sure they will forgive me for neglecting them.

Halsley's reception and the hub bub about "Navy Day" has & will have its repercussion—Nice show but think the Navy will rue the day. Boys, Army, Navy & Marine are waiting to get home & it hasn't left a good feeling with so many of the ships on display.

It would seem that CV is really growing too big for its pants. Don't believe that the building now occupied by the PO is Fedl owned—however if it is <u>why</u> in the hell build another.

A previous clipping about Footsie F indicated he was killed while serving on a destroyer—believe the latter to be true. Sorry for the youngster for he would have enjoyed his Dad.

Good to know that Uncle Jim is in fact home. Can well imagine his family's pleasure in knowing that now it won't be too long.

In view of not having received the package mailed in June or July wonder if I will ever receive the alleged Xmas package. Can make a guess what it will be but will look forward to receiving it.

Am pleased to know that Connie is satisfied with her treatment at H & H [Herney & Herney law firm]. Evidently the bull of the woods decided to pull in his horns. Easier for him that way I know & much more pleasant. I like you don't even think Susie or Steve will have to worry about split affections. Its tough on Brad and will continue to be so.—

Do hope I'm not going to make you be the "Last Little Injun" but only time will tell.

Love you with all my Heart Always

Al & Daddy

———

Nov. 12 Monday No 5 Steve 16 months old yesterday

My dearest—

Wonder if you are remembering that just two years ago today I arrived in Tucson—along with I.J.?? Would give to lot to know just where Lois & Ed are. Maybe Christmas cards will get everyone located again.

Not too peppy today after the spree last night! We gathered at 5 at Elaine's and by 7 we had finished off <u>several</u> frozen daiquiris a piece—and then were off to the Cornhusker for dinner which was unusual too in that we had Pork Tenderloin—pork being very scarce we all enjoyed it thoroly. We got into a very involved discussion on the pros & cons of twin beds <u>vs</u> a double bed. I think it call came up because someone said you couldn't get twin bed or ¾ bed sheets at the PX. <u>Anyway</u> we were all in favor of the twin beds and <u>Elaine</u>,—trust her—said "Well—she had never slept with anyone till she got married and that she had been <u>most</u> unhappy ever since—as far as the sleeping was concerned!" The way she added that last phrase sort of as an afterthought—just slayed us—we got hysterical. After dinner we went to see "Rhapsody in Blue" story of life of Gershwin and it was wonderful. It was a grand evening and Elaine such a peach to do it. She also gave me a pretty linen hankie. I wore my new suit creation & everyone agreed it was most beautiful. Saved you $100. On that deal! Aren't you glad???

Aunt Clyde & Uncle Tom [Dot's aunt and her husband] came by just as I was taking a bath before getting dressed to go—so I donned some slacks for a brief while before had to dash—Aunt Clyde is leaving in the morning for California!!! Jeanette Mickey (remember Janice Mickey—Visiting Nurse in San Diego friend of mine & Ruth & Mark Young?) is driving out to return to her duties as a Marine at El Toro—and has Janice's car so Aunt Clyde is going with. I'm awfully glad for her—She is as thrilled as a little kid and don't ever think she won't enjoy every second. Don't know how long she'll stay. Janice—by the way—is in the Public Health in Honolulu—just went over a short time ago.

Uncle Jim was home again this wkend. I went over Sun A.M. to get some pinking shears & there he was—so stayed and talked a while over some coffee. Thanksgiving dinner is to be at their house—he plans to be here if not home for good.

The Quigles are back from Second visit to St. Louis. Alice will fly home for Christmas. Has her reservation already. I'll relax more when I know we have a place on the train.

Caz was so <u>sure</u> Ralph would be home by this wkend, she was very disappointed—even tho we had all told her not to expect him so soon. I made a <u>find</u> Saturday. I found the metal swing brackets for drapes for our Venetian blinds. I got 3 prs: $1.50 a pair & am now hunting for drapes.

It has been trying to cloud up & storm for 3 days now but can't make up its mind. Consequently very dreary outside.

No mail delivery today since yesterday was Armistice Day—which <u>irks</u> me. Finally got hold of some Navy Day stamps but can't say I think they're very pretty.

Gotta get busy—have a deadline now of Dec 1 to meet & it's going to keep me hopping. Hope by this time you have a date to look forward to.

Love you Sweetie—

Yours

Dottie

Nov 12—Nov Letter No 3

My Dearest Sweet:

From the looks of things, tho as yet I have received none for No, you won't have to go very far to beat me this month.

Your mail is coming spasmodically & in anything of a chronological order. Rec'd your No 1 for Oct—two days ago & Nos 7 & 9 for Oct today. With pictures 3 & 4 which I must say are much better than the first two.

Most apologize for that last letter. Was plenty burned up & couldn't seem to get off the subject.

Schnabels relief has finally arrived & he is to be on his way soon. Have given him our home no & Marie's and asked him to call collect person to person. With good luck he should be there soon after the first of the month.

Do so hope that Dad & Mother can make the trip with you. Would be a bit hard on them but then guess they would enjoy it—especially if the co-passengers were willing to comment on the two beautiful well mannered grand children.

The prospective new skipper is aboard but Dunston still hasn't indicated that he wants to be relieved. He is however going to make up his mind soon or else someone else will make it up for him. Smith is in a hell of a position too & in the squeeze which isn't pleasant for him as he was eligible for discharge on the 1st of the month.

Word was passed today that several of the AM's [Admirable-class mine-sweeper such as the *Scurry*] were to be off for the Islands Pearl on the 20th of this month. The Scurry none of our squadron included. However since the trip is to be to pearl & may mean a transfer of personnel, officer & enlisted, just as glad we aren't included. Understand there is to be another group going in about two weeks.

Can't quite understand just what Commpac has in mind. We are to go out on another operation on the 14th—will not however be as long as the last one we were on. Sweeping all of the mine fields is just one hell of a waste of time and effort.

Maybe you should take Steve to get his haircut every week—that would be once every two weeks for he & his Dad. Haven't had one now for several weeks & the sideburns are getting a bit long. Have been reading all of the old correspondence & discarding all but a few letters which I am keeping—trying to get things in shape just in case things work out to my liking. However when the time comes it wouldn't be too hard or too long to get packed.

With all my love as always to my Three Sweethearts.

All & Daddy

Nov 13 Nov Letter No 4
My Dearest Sweet:

Received your letter No 10 for Oct—dated Oct 30—which isn't too bad traveling time.

The mail from here is taking longer than usual passes thru Tokyo instead of Okinawa—the latter place deserted almost & not of any future importance as naval base.—

The tenants moving makes things a bit more convenient doesn't it? Hope the family will be able to have it spic and clean for your arrival.

Had forgotten all about the festivities of Halloween and the Jack O'Lantern. Just another of those things that are forgotten when one is so far away from the normal life. Do hope Susie enjoyed it. Can well imagine she did her coaxing to have Dad fix it & right now.

The last day out on the last operation saw another of those unforgettable sunsets which I intended to mention before this. Old Sol of course as usual was his intense yellow—spherical only to be in part lost behind the horizon to take the shape of a yellow fish bowl upside down with that portion nearest the opening red instead of yellow. Hard to describe those things but something one can't forget.

Schnabel is to leave the ship tomorrow morning. Has his name with the Port Director for transportation & will have to await his turn. At least the first steps have been taken.

As to your suggestion to meet me when & if the Scurry or Herney sails homeward—don't think it would be such a good idea for I assume that all of the West Coast cities are more than crammed. In addition there is the problem of transportation. Don't think I wouldn't love to have you but there is too much in doubt. Will however, you can rest assured let you know when were are on our way & destination.

Not surprised you can't find the two little islands—not really of much importance except that there is where we were and will be going back to on this next operation. Really a gold mine for running up the score but would gladly dispense with that.

Dunstan finally after much insistence got a stay on his change of duty. Think he will be sorry in the end & some of us too will be on the shorter end. Wish he would have saved us future embarrassment by his almighty ways.

Your package with the polish in it finally arrived today—havent received the letter about Joe K however—think that is No 8 that is missing.

Will be a few days again before you will hear from me as we are to pull out tomorrow—Hope this doesn't go on too much longer.

With love as Always to my Three Sweethearts

Al & Daddy

Nov 17 Nov Letter No 5

My Dearest Sweet:

Expect to get this off on a ship going back to Sasebo tomorrow so it will be short.

Well at last the Scuttlebutt has boiled itself down & out to the simple equation of homeward bound soon. In fact sometime the first part of next month. This then is to be our last operation.

Are now out in Tsushima Straights sweeping a few more—In about the same area we were before—west of Iki Shima Tsushima Island—made up of two islands—Kamino and Shimano Shima. Shouldn't be too difficult to locate.

The only difficulty or problem yet unsolved is just where we will end up. There is a possibility of the east coast which makes me very unhappy. Realizing the Navy Way it isn't improbable so will just have to keep the fingers crossed.

Since you couldn't make reservations until today I assume you have made your trip & made them. Fortunately you shouldn't have the problem as if you were eastward bound as I assume the bulk of the traffic is in that direction. Very interested in knowing whether Dad & Mother will make the trip with you.

Have expected to hear word that Hugh C is home but no recent letter from S.D. Should guess that he will be there soon if not there now.

Not mailing this to Lincoln as doubt if you would get it by the 1st when I assume you will be leaving so when you receive this "My Pride & Joy" will have had her train ride. I remember the last one I took with her.

This operation isn't too bad as we do go into a small harbor to anchor each nite. Helps to relieve the monotony of things.

The weather has turned darned right chilly even during the day in the sun. Nites call for two blankets & could use a bed partner very nicely—especially to get the feet warm.

Have had the movies on the forecastle as usual when not raining. Gets so snappy both a jacket—winter pants & helmet are comfortable. Just getting us acclimated for Stateside I know—Oh yeh?—

Still haven't received your letter mentioning Joe K's last letter—should drop him a note care of his folks—have their address.

Will drop the folks a short note so—

With Love Always to my Three Sweethearts as Always.

Al & Daddy

———

Nov. 30 Friday No. 10

My Dearest—

It is a good thing I had to come to the Beauty Parlor to get my wig washed or I don't know if you would have gotten another letter from Lincoln!

Seems I don't even have time to go to the bathroom leisurely. The trunk and 2 large boxes are ready to go to the depot to be checked tonight. Of course, not the least of my worries is the fact that Stevie came down with a beauty of a cold last night. Susie's had one but is getting over it. His nose was all stopped up last night so had to burn or steam some water. Hope his lets up some by tomorrow night.

Denver is going to be no problem. Merle Burkholder [Dot's cousin] is going to meet us & take us out to their home and later in the day am to meet Effie & David. I can't remember but don't think I told you—Jack has just been transferred to Ft. Devers, Mass (about 30 miles out of Boston (!!!) and aren't you glad we aren't going to Boston?—altho if it got you home any sooner I wouldn't care.)

Monday night Caz & I entertained for Elaine. First we were at Palma's Sunday nite and she had such a nice Sunday night supper for the four of us. They insisted I play the piano for so long that we didn't play much bridge. Mon nite we met at Caz's—she had made frozen daiquiris but her jigger must have been like yours—too much rum so they didn't freeze but oh brother were they good—& potent—we really were floating. We went to the Cornhusker for dinner then and then to a show—which wasn't too good…"Spanish Main."

Tuesday nite I was out again "Chick" Barber—an old time school chum asked Brita Peterson & Georgia Covey Stone & myself for bridge. Chick's husband is just out of regular army after 12 years. Georgia Covey is the girl who with 2 others came to our front door in Chula Vista looking for rooms—their husbands stationed at Ream Field [near Chula Vista] and I did some calling to try & find something for them. Her Dad is Nose & throat D. here. Georgia's first husband was Navy flier, killed on the Siscombe Bay. She has remarried— also Nay flier—former school acquaintance—now out of Navy.

Wednesday A.M. I took Elaine to the train. She really looked wonderful and excited—who wouldn't be? By this time she & Pete should be together.

Last nite Caz & I went to see the double piano concert on the Artist Series. It was wonderful and I'm glad I got to hear them. That finishes my social life—altho Caz wanted me to go to dinner tonite—I said "No"—Everything is about done—but Dad is such a fuss budget & old maid really. The slightest things which might entail a bit of work sends him into a tirade—and all he has had to do is rope the trunk. I really got a bit peeved myself last night at him—told him I did all of it myself when I came home including roping the trunk and putting it in the car—I try not to cross him—but one can stand just so much—how Mom puts up with it all the time is remarkable.

After I get out of here I have to dash downtown to see if I can get the leather stitched on one side of one of my bags I didn't know it was ripped until I got it out. If I can't it will be alrite but would just like to get it done.

I don't look for anymore mail from you until after I get in Chula Vista. Reread thru 4 Nov letters yesterday in their correct sequence which makes a little more sense. I can't remember now how many points you have to have by Dec 1 & Jan 1. I know you'd have 43 by Dec 1—43 ¾ by Jan 1. But how many do you need? My favorite past time to put me to sleep is figuring those points to be sure I haven't cheated you!

I really haven't been at all excited about this trip—maybe I will be when I get going. I expect to enjoy this trip more than I did coming.

Don't you pick a ship like Ralph Robert's coming home. He still isn't here & has been 41 days—they must be paddling. Were in Pearl Harbor on the 12th. I think they must be going thru the Canal.

It has turned colder and is really nippy out—but no signs of snow. Susie has been hoping it would snow before we leave.

I'm about baked so should be dry—will try & drop a note enroute—and so until next time—I love you Sweetie, & hope something clicks pretty soon

Dottie

Train ticket for Dorothy and children from CB&Q Station, Lincoln, Nebraska, to Denver, Colorado, and continuing on to Los Angeles, departing December 2, 1945. Rail and Pullman fare totaled $92.68. The train ticket jacket notes, "Cooperation will help win the war. Materials, labor and plant capacity are so urgently required...that the American railroads and civilian pubic have been asked to help win the war by getting along without additional passenger equipment for the duration."

15

HEADED FOR HOME

December 1945

Dec 2, 1945 Dec #1

My Dearest Sweet:

You didn't have to write many letters last month to beat me on the correspondence. Won't try to apologize for not writing more.

Here we are back at Toushima Straits. This time we have been working in the western part of the Straits—anchoring in Tadei Po anchorage in Koje To—Korea. Koje To for your information is a small neck of land extending out into the Straits from Korea just south of a line between Fukoka Kyushu and Fusan Korea.

Just when we will complete this little job is still a question. Expect to be darn soon so that we can spend a few days at Sasebo & then homeward bound. Ho hum please God make it quick.

No doubt we are at present acclimated to the weather of the northern coast of US. The last few days have been cold—in fact believe there would be frost on the punkins if we had punkins. If two pair of socks foul weather pants, jacket & helmet plus gloves aren't sufficient to make it pleasant on the bridge. Have to take the hot water bottle to bed to get the feet warm.

All of which of course convinces me more than ever that there ain't no place like home. Snow in the mountains if that is what you wish & relatively pleasant weather on the home front with a fire in the fireplace enjoying all the comforts of home at home.

Tho I haven't heard should say that you should be on your way home. Do wish I could say I was speeding eastward as fast as you are speeding westward for then it wouldn't be too long until we would meet.

Finally received your No 8 for Oct with word about Joe K He should be out by this time. Envy him being a civilian in spirit & in fact. Seem to remember meeting Fratis. Must drop him a note for haven't written in some time. Hope he gets to S.D but wish he would wait until I got home.

Besides your No 8 for Oct received your No 6 for Nov—Marie's Nov letter, one from George H & a July letter from Uncle G—the latter with a 3 cent stamp—first class mail. Of course all of the info so old it was almost forgotten—also received a V mail from Harvey C—you of course will remember me to them & impress on Harvey for me that I am <u>not</u> thinking of the Navy as a career.

"Mrs Zilch is" right—hob nobbing with Mrs. Abeb. However I'm sure that the fact that you are a sister-in-law of Marie M brot you the invitation—don't really mean that Sweet as you know you yourself are a nice person to know. Do hope that you enjoyed the luncheon & time spent with her. You should have displayed youngsters too—just in case she should have shown the least interest.

Can't for the life of me know who had called you unless it could have been Hetzler or Krause who would be there in Omaha about that time. Sorry they didn't leave their name. Don't remember giving either your address however before they left.

Sorry you didn't think we were rich enuf to buy one of the musical cig boxes if you wanted one. You should know that I wouldn't have complained or thought you were spending the money foolishly.

Still wondering if you received the last package I sent you with Susie's belt etc—maybe the typhoon interfered. You should have had it long before this.

Darned anxious to be on my way home to you & my two little Sweethearts—

Love always to the three of you—

Al & Daddy

Dec 4 Dec No 2

My Dearest Sweet:

Well at last we are heading toward Sasebo—Don't know for sure but it is almost certain that this will be the last visit to that very fine port in the Empire waters.

Don't expect any of the ships in our Squadron with whom we will be traveling homeward will want to take too many days for availability—I'm sure we don't.

Have heard definitely that we will hit S.D—just what the personnel condition will be by that time God only knows. Haven't planned too strongly on being able to remain for discharge & not go to the east coast, but have had an inkling that that might not be necessary.

Did write Joe K a Xmas letter—should get one off to the PM's too—think you will be going to the Xmas party this year won't you?

Haven't thought about anything except being on my way home. Actually have done very little work—paper, but have spent a good bit of time on the bridge during sweeping operations. Sometimes it got a bit exciting dodging the floaters from the ships ahead—some so close you could see the marine growth on them.

The few days in port and all underway are going to be busy ones—just in case I should run into a bit of luck. Would hate to think that night & day at the last moment would not be sufficient time to accomplish everything that had to be done.

Gosch has received his orders & would very much like to catch other transportation home—maybe could make it by Xmas for which you can't blame him since he hasn't spent one there since 1941.

Things are really beginning to tighten up a bit for Com 5th Fleet has put out a directive on uniform of the day—yes officers included. Liberty calls for blues or aviation greens—ho—hum; ties too are to be worn when on station in port. You know how I love the sound of that. Think I'll sign up for thirty years—! ! ?—Nuts.

If nothing more will get off a letter to you before shoving off from Sasebo—

With love always to My Three Sweethearts—

Al & Daddy

Dec 4, 1945

Dear P.M's [Phi Mu Alumnae] and <u>Auxiliary [the husbands]:</u>

Here another Xmas party is in progress & Herney can't be there to enjoy it with you—You however have the nicer half of the Herney combination back so know you will be happy to have her back with you.

Haven't written any of you for a long time—won't apologize for the delay in thanking you all for the birthday cards and letters. Did so much appreciate getting them even to the mailman didn't deliver them until the early part of March for it seems that U.S. hadn't established mail service at Iwo Jima until a short time before that. Should Chuck R. [Reed] still be in Pearl around Xmas time may get to wish him greetings for rumor has it that the Scurry will soon be on its way home—will seem good too after fourteen months away from the States.

Needless to say I have missed the pleasant times of the meetings and hope that when it comes time to resume the civilian status I will again be welcome. Merry Merry Xmas—

Always

Al

Dec 10 Dec No 3

My Dearest Sweet:

I am sure you will forgive me for not being a better correspondent—but things must be done & what with the turmoil of it all your husband tho loving you much hasn't been in the mood.

The time is almost here for the Scurry to point her noise eastward toward the shores of the US. Tho the routing instructions aren't definite—think we are to go via Eniwetok tho I'm sure we could make it direct to pearl. Then to Pearl & what we don't know—maybe some overhauling before proceeding to the States—How long we are to be at Eniwetok & Pearl is yet undetermined as far as we are concerned. In case I had forgotten to tell you we shove off from these parts tomorrow sometime.

The skipper allowed Gosch to depart several days ago so he should be home by the 1st of Jan—then some terminal leave before discharge—terminal leave in case you don't know is all the accumulated leave you have coming. Can act as a civilian but continue to draw pay & can't be discharged until the terminal leave expires unless of course you wish to forego the pleasures of that money.

Gates & Bezold are eligible as the 1st of this month & their request has gone into adcomunpac for action. I will be underway when my time comes but may send it in from Eniwetok or carry it up to the office personally when we hit Pearl.

It begins to look like we may be underway on Xmas day. Have been hanging around here for the last five days bidding time—damn the foolishness anyway for we should have been in Pearl by that time anyway.

Went back yesterday for another sightseeing trip via Jeep—The skipper drove & had a look at the rural part—result of taking a shortcut. Did get something for you & only you.—Nope no silks as they had no bolt silks & their kimonos were way out of line. Hope you like what I got you just as well.

My Sweet it is almost too much to think that another Xmas is to pass without being there with you the youngsters and our fine family—yes one and all. The God's evidently didn't have it in mind when they were arranging the pleasanter things this year so again will have to look forward to the future. There is one consolation in knowing that that won't be too far off & too the appreciation of the Xmas of the past.

I am sure that the "Pride & Joy" will again be much the center of attraction & fully delighted in all the attention to be centered on her. The "Little Feller" too might be old enuf to begin to realize what the Season means.

Happy that you were able to make such fine arrangements for yourself & the folks all the way to California. Do hope that Dad & Mother can make equally good arrangements going east. I of course will be sorry that I won't be there to see them so should write them a Xmas note.

Well "My One & Only" the Merriest Xmas possible. Wish each of the youngsters a happy holiday for me & give them an extra big hug & kiss for me—there are many in store for them & for you too when Daddy gets home.

My Love Always to "My Three Sweethearts."

Al & Daddy

P.S. Will enclose a note to the family—will write Mother & Dad but extend Greetings to any & all our friends.

My Dear Family & Sweetie Pie:

It appears that the Scurry with I'm aboard will be at Sea on this the Xmas of 1945. Did so want to be with you but military necessity made that wish anything but a reality.

There will at least be the knowledge that the bow of "home" for the last fifteen months is plowing eastward towards the shore of the US, the satisfaction of knowing that the military life will soon be over and the realization that the coming year will not hold the added uncertainties of 1945. For these things I am of course grateful.

While the loss of the "Empress" [Al's mother] still softens the complete enjoyment of the Season, there will be George [Al's brother] & the Caugheys [Al's aunt and her husband] adding to and participating in those pleasures present in all of the gatherings of our clan. A true appreciation of this is not realized until one is deprived of them.

I at this time wish to thank each of you for your many kindnesses, courtesies and helpfulness shown to me and mine this past year. Knowing that you were willing to assist Dot should she have needed help did much to ease my anxiety at having left her with so much responsibility.

Wishing each of you "A Merry Xmas and A Happy New Year"

Lovingly

Al.

Dec 9 Sunday No 2

<u>Home</u>

My dearest—

If you are <u>not</u> on your way home by this time—you will be <u>very</u> impatient I know since it's been a week—and that last letter I wrote was a lulu—I hope you realized that under the strain I had to explode—and the result was ungood! It was a trying trip—that you may be sure of—not so much the children—as Dad. Well, anyway, we made it—in fact the train pulled in to L.A. 5 minutes ahead of schedule—and who was there to meet us but [Al's sisters] Marie and Anne—that was a thrill. I heaved a sigh of relief to know the folks didn't have to buck the crowd and it was lucky since they weren't letting civilians on. I had fed Steve before we got off—so didn't have to worry about his lunch. Marie & Anne had gone up on Mon. to shop for office furniture—and Marie had a few errands yet—so parked the car in a parking lot. Mom, Dad and I and the kids had some lunch while Marie & Anne shopped. Jerry [Cawby] didn't get down to the train as both she & Elmer had colds and the baby too—but I called her & it was good to talk to her. Helen [Al's sister] was at a school luncheon so we didn't talk to her.

We pulled out for S.D. at 2 P.M. Believe it or not I had to direct Marie out over our old route and I could hardly remember—it's been so long since I'd been over the road. Steve finally gave up—fell asleep & so did Susan. They woke up at Laguna Beach. We got to S.D. about 15 of 6. It gets dark so much earlier here than at home it seemed like midnite and Steve had been standing on my lap the last 50 miles till my legs were almost raw from him sliding around.

What a reception I got! I could have wept! The kitchen is painted—it's beautiful—white with cupboards red inside. [Al's brother] Francis did the painting. The fence has been painted white—(George & Karl) [Al's brothers]—the yard—well, words fail me yet—the yard George has completely overhauled is all I can say—it has never looked this good—and he is still working on it—the girls [Al's sisters] all came out—unpacked the dishes, made the beds—well, it was wonderful. I'm so thrilled I'm still gasping. This week has been so full—I kept thinking—I'll get a letter off to Al today—and there just wasn't time—I can't tell you all the details in this letter—(but by God—you'd better get this letter!)—but will try & sketch briefly what we've done.

Steve cried constantly the first 3 days—I guess tired—and everything strange—he about drove us all crazy—but he's been so much better the last 2 days I think he's getting adjusted—(I hope.)

Of course we are still very much in the midst of unpacking. It will take me a month to sort everything into its right place since everything was just stuffed in drawers and it takes me hours to find everything—(Mother's method—not mine.) During all this—I dash around trying to remember where I packed away this & that—& George popping in the door—what should he do about so-and-so—I assure you I'm not bored! Dad has been fidgety since we're stuck & no one to go places with him—and Al—he really is past going alone—we've had to handle him like a crate of eggs—I'm terribly worried about them getting home—they can't get reservation so will have to sit up [on a chair car on the train back to Lincoln]. They leave here Wed. morning.

Yesterday was our first outing. Since Charles Caughey [Al's cousin] was here Marie had Charles, Hugh, Amanda & baby, [Al's cousin Hugh and his wife] Julia Mac [Al's sister and her husband] and us & Aunt Julia [Al's aunt], Uncle Eddie for dinner.—(Ed [Marie's husband] in the mountains seeing about Xmas trees). We got there about 5:30 so I could feed Steve. He & Amanda Lou played during dinner—then put them to sleep. Anne came by & she and I went to the Phi Mu party. I wouldn't have gone but Blythe [Reed] leaves Tuesday. She sails Dec 18 for Honolulu to join Charles—he's staying in the Navy. If you come home by Pearl—you must contact them—he at District Navy Post Office, Pearl Harbor.

Susan had the time of her young life. Karl, Catherine, Butch, Fran & Ruth, Aunt Anne [Al's relatives] came later and she had the most wonderful time. Of course she is still the apple of her Aunt Marie's eyes—and at 11 P.M. she was still going strong. We got home at midnite—. George came out this A.M. and worked all day on the yard. After the kids' naps we drove in to Julia's. I ran over to Karl's [another of Al's brothers] to leave the sterilizer.—Guess I'd better pause long enuf to state you are a great Uncle—Monica had a baby girl (81/2 #'s) on Dec 5—Cheryl Ann—day after we got here and went home today (4th day) because her husband got emergency leave and got here last night. Sally [Monica's mother] is still in Nebr. Pat's Bob due in Tues.

Steve scared to death of Duchess [Julia's cocker spaniel]—but got a little used to her before we left tonight.

Tomorrow Anne & Aunt Anne are coming out to look after the children so I can take Mother & Dad out. Dad wants to go to Tiajuana—have to check a grip—will go around the strand. At this point I'm getting a bit crazy from the constant excitement. Ruth & Harvey glad to see us—Carrell's apologizing all over the place—more about them later.

Bev & Hank left 3 wks ago for Wisconsin—he's out. Carl [Stadler] due in San Francisco about the 12th—Pop Stadler [Carl's father] going up to get him.

And then of course the mere fact that your letter was here for me—saying you <u>might</u> be on your way home by the first wk in Dec—well—that made home coming <u>almost</u> perfect—it can only be complete when you get here—even the prospect of the <u>east</u> coast didn't dampen my spirits—just get started home. Pat [Al's niece] has a friend who can find out where your ship is—if between Guam & Pearl or Pearl and the coast so she is going to start checking tomorrow. I know you'd never make it by Christmas but it can't be long now—I'm on the last month on my little calendar that I've had ever since you left—and by golly it had better be all I'll need. It was wonderful to talk to Hugh [Caughey]—to someone who had <u>seen</u> you—talked to you.

I'm asleep on my feet—or fanny at the moment—I gotta quit—maybe if you <u>are</u> on your way this will catch you along the way someplace.

It's wonderful to be home—all we need now is you Sweetie—Home Sweet Home is waiting and <u>almost</u> ready. I still am puzzled as to whether your clothes will fit—so that I know whether to have them cleaned & pressed—etc. etc—but will find something to put on you.

Susie is so thrilled at being home—it's like a fairy tale to watch her.

Come home quick—

We love you,

Dottie,

Susie,

Steve

———

10 Dec 45 <u>Nite</u>
My Dearest Sweet:

Well it is finally definite that we are to sail homeward tomorrow—getting underway at 0900.

Arrangements are that we are to parade for the Admiral tomorrow before leaving—an exchange of Havanas—That is something for I'm sure no one has done it before this—& all because we have been good boys & this squadron tops on mines swept—over 5000—yes there are four digits in the number. Evidently the Admiral is proud of us even tho he has been tough. Your Xmas package arrived today and all in good shape. It is not necessary to say that I was thrilled to hear your voice & that of "The Pride & Joy" even tho not too distinct at first. The coaching on Mommie's part wasn't bad either. Had thought from your letter it might be a picture—am very glad you thought of it. Will play it again tomorrow—Will try not to wear it out before getting home.

Much much love to the "Three" of you—and again the merriest of Xmas's. I love you with all my heart.

Al & Daddy

P.S. Have extended the Subscription to Time for two years for $6.00 bill to be sent to 399 J—I gave notice of change of address.

Typewritten Letter with Navy Day Envelope from Lt. C.J. Read, District Postal Office Pearl Harbor
16 December 1945
Dear Dorothy:

Received your Airmail letter of the 11th this morning.

According to our information here Al was due to depart Sasebo on 12 December and should reach Pearl on about the 22nd via Eniwetok. Will be looking for him there, and I hope he will be able to spend Christmas with us.

I expect Blythe and Margaret to sail on the USS RESCUE from San Francisco on the 18th and arrive here about the 23rd. This will get them here just in time for Christmas. The USS HAVEN, another hospital ship, sailed from San Francisco yesterday, but for some reason Blythe did not get on this ship.

Things are folding up here fast. I have volunteered to stay on until 1 July 1946, but stipulated that the duty would have to be here in Com14. I could go home on 1 January when postal officers are unfrozen, or 'defrosted', as the common expression here goes, but thought that Blythe and Margaret would enjoy a trip to the Islands.

You can compute Al's points as follows: ½ point for each year of age to nearest birthday, ½ point for each month of service completed to accrue on the day of the month it is due, ¼ point for each month of sea duty, 10 points for dependency. The critical point score (score required for release) is at 44 points. This will drop to 43 points on 1 January 1946. No information is available at this date as to what the points will be after 1 January, but it is believed that they will drop at least one point, and possibly two points, per month. I would estimate that Al would have enough for discharge on 1 January, or at least pretty close to it.

Will arrange for Al to cable you on arrival.

Sincerely,

Chuck

*Dot and the children sent this Christmas card to Al on the Scurry
as the ship headed for home in late December 1945.*

Dec 19—45 Dec No 4

My Dearest Sweet:

Just now starting in to the anchorage at Eniwetok—all of which means that about one third of the trip is behind us.

Still don't know how long we will be here or when we are to be on our way to Pearl.

If the last eight days are an indication of what the sea will be for the rest of the way your old man will be plenty unhappy for it has been anything but pleasant—more than just rough.

Have my application of releasing in the mail & ready to go. The Personnel Office at Pearl will have it soon & can be working on it pending my arrival when of course I intend dropping in to see them.

Neither Gates nor Bezold have gotten their orders as yet—their applications went in about the 5th of the month. Maybe we all will get a surprise when we get to Pearl. I hope huge.

Do so hope that since I won't be home for Xmas nor your birthday that you will make the most of Xmas—mine will come later.

With all my love to the "Three of You" always.

Al & Daddy.

Dec 25—45 Dec Letter No 5

My Dearest Sweethearts Three:

Have just finished our Xmas dinner—consisting of turkey & rice soup, roast turkey, baked potatoes cranberry sauce, asparagus, hot rolls ice tea and traditional pie. Not a bad menu for being underway and more of a step child now that we are on our way home.

Left Eniwetok on the evening of the 20th—only there for a day—logistics—however did get on the beach & a chance to stretch the legs and visited the officers club for a swim (in my shorts) and several cokes—still not too enthusiastic about anything stronger.

While at Eniwetok visited the dispensary to get some fortification for the rough seas we anticipated. Glad I did for even tho the sea as not ben too rough would have been much more uncomfortable than I am.

Dec 28

The letter was interrupted by a call to a pinochle game with Bezold and Aspen—Do hope you don't mind.

To continue where I left off most of my thoughts on Xmas were of you and the youngsters. Seemed to be plenty low & blue & can't seem to work myself out of it.

Haven't a bit of ambition & while I have things that should be done can't quite get into the mood for it.

Tomorrow we pull into Pearl—sometime in the morning. Then we should know a bit more than we do now.

Neither Gates nor Bezold have heard from their application for discharge—which were sent in the first of the month. Plan on going to see the personnel officer when in.

Mail has been nil since the second day before leaving Sasebo. Sensible not to have sent it on to Eniwetok as we can pick it up at Pearl. Yes Sweet—do hope there is some there for us.

This not knowing if & when I can shatter the shackles of the navy off from around this neck. Practically going nuts—not good for I'm bad enuf under normal conditions.

The news reports about the pile up of the military on the west coast sends chills up & down the spine thinking about Mother & Dad getting home. Do hope that they were able to avoid the rush. A shame that so many were so close yet so far on Xmas but then that is what happens when they waited till the last minute to accomplish what should have been accomplished some time ago.

Don't know if I told you wrote Joe K a Xmas note & Other & Dad a Xmas letter before leaving Sasebo. Haven't done too well including mail to yourself but can't help it much.

Do guess that celebrating your birthday which will be soon will have to be postponed as is Xmas & New Years. These of course will be the last that will be spent apart.

Plan on contacting Chuck Reed if he is still at Pearl tho he should have sufficient points to be out of the service. Also may call the gal in the "Public Health" Dept.

It is odd to think that almost twelve months have elapsed since leaving Pearl.—It's going to take a whole lot to get be away from civilization for some time to come & no sea cruises.

Doubt if I will get word from you as to how the "Pride & Joy" and the "Little Feller" enjoyed Xmas but you can tell me as we enjoy our own fireside.

A Happy Birthday to you Sweet & remember I love you always. Ask Susan if she won't give you a hug & kiss for me.

Al & Daddy

WESTERN UNION TELEGRAM DEC 27 TO DOROTHY
Received letter nineteenth expect al twenty ninth Blythe arrived Monday.
Charles
Navcom. Pearl

WESTERN UNION TELEGRAM DEC 29 TO DOROTHY
ARRIVED TODAY PLEASURE TO BE WITH CHUCK AND FAMILY. HAPPY BIRTHDAY TO YOU ALL MY LOVE.
AL
NAVCOM PEARL

——

Dec. 29 1945   The END
Top note: Gosch called me Xmas Eve but couldn't come out, they sent him up to Camp Pendleton & from there home.
My dearest:—

I hope I'm not being too optimistic but at any rate imagine this will be my last chance to write you—and I have one 6 cent airmail left so will hope it really is the last one I need. Your wire or cable came at 9:30 this morning—Chuck's came Thursday—I was sort of dumb—didn't realize I could send you one until just a moment ago thot I'd call Western Union and find out—so hope you get the one I just sent. I guess I should have had more mail awaiting you at P.H. but I just couldn't write more—was so impatient to hear when you got there.

Christmas & Christmas Eve was a big affair again & the only thing we needed was you—Pat's Bob was there, Monica's Bill and Sheilah's Bill. By the way Sheliah [Al's niece, Julia and Mac's daughter] is wearing an engagement ring and there will be wedding bells in January I guess. It really is a pathetic situation Al—and it isn't just my observation—so that you'd best be prepared. Bill is a swell boy,—and everyone in the family feels <u>sorry</u> for him—and Uncle Albert finally took Bill aside and told him Sheilah was lazy, incompetent and a spendthrift. Marie, George & the rest backed him up. You know what a blow that is to Julia's pride. I am not supposed to know this, but like most things I hear them before long—and it goes only on to you—so you must act wise and surprised at everything you hear and see. I do.

Helen [Al's sister] had her gall bladder removed yesterday (Dec 28) A.M.—and I saw her last night at 9 P.M. and she was fine. Geo. Had been out here all day working & we went out to dinner & then I took him home. Marie was at the hospital & when we got to 545 San Antonio then there were flowers there for Helen so I took them up to the hospital. She is so crazy about our two babes—yes Steve is getting his share of affection tho Marie favors her Susie. Julia, Catherine Herney & Joe Tex went to L.A. today to move Helen into the Brigg's apartment so it will be all ready for her. Geo. Is waiting for you to return before he goes back (I think). He never mentions Mike—he has been wonderful—you'll marvel at the yard—he has worked like a fool out here and has been such good company. Fran [Al's brother] has been out of work for some weeks and taking his Social S rather than the jobs they offered since they offered nothing better than $26.00 per wk he took a job as a Ticket Agent with Greyhound and is crazy about it Ruth says. Marie left for the mountains this A.M. with Kay & Bill Frazier—Ed went yesterday & think the Wards are to be there—will remain over New Year's. Sweetie-Pie Caperton was beside herself when she heard you had arrived at P.H.—The Carrell's have asked me to keep them informed—I saw Mickey Salmon yesterday— Manny left OPA last August and they have a Taxi Cab Co in Coronado now! Fred Longworth is out—and manager of Victory Lumber Co here in Chula Vista which Geo. Johnson bought out recently. It is after 12 noon—but we slept till after 9 this morning as children were up late last night—guess I've been lazy, incompetent & a spendthrift too since I've been home—but I feel good & eventually I get things done too.

The Ackerman's left the stove in terrible shape—not damaged but an inch thick in grease—so I worked all day yesterday on it & Geo. is coming out Monday to help me finish it up.

I hope to meet your ship if it comes in here so if you can give me some idea of when you leave there I can find out the rest on this end. I'll probably expire of excitement but want to be there anyway.

So glad you could see Chuck, Blythe, Margaret—they certainly have been wonderful. It almost seems impossible that this long, long, seize of letters is almost over—that you will really be home soon—it really will mean a Happy New Year for now on so until I see you—aren't those wonderful words—

Your loving wife, daughter & son

Dottie, Susan & Steve

MEMO DATED 30 December 1945 from
COMMANDER
ADMINISTRTIVE COMMAND
MINECRAFT
U.S. PACIFIC FLEET
To: Lieutenant (jg) Albert F. HERNEY, C, USNR
Via: Commanding Officer, U.S.S. SCURRY (AM-304).
Subject: Orders—Release from Active Duty
References: (a) ALNAV 198-45
          (b) SecNAV ltr 21 June 1945, N.D. Bull. 45-692

1. You are hereby detached from duty on the U.S.S. SCURRY (AM-304) and from such other duty as may have been assigned you; will proceed to the nearest Staging Center for transportation to a port in the United States and upon arrival report to the Commanding Officer of the nearest Officer Intake Station, then further proceed via such transportation as may be furnished by the Commanding Officer of the Intake Station to the Separation Center at Los Angeles, California and report to the Commanding Officer for temporary duty.

2. Your attention is directed to reference (a) and (b) with reference to certification as to home of record at the time of call to active duty and as to place from which ordered activity duty and mileage payable in advance of travel.

3. Your attention is invited to the paramount importance of having in your possession your records and pay accounts, failure to have records and accounts will result in delay of processing to inactive duty.

4. Upon completion of this temporary duty you will, when directed, regard yourself detached and proceed to your home for release from active duty in accordance with instructions to be issued by the Commanding Officer of the Separation Center.

J.H. BRANDT

1<u>ST</u> ENDORSEMENT 12 January 1946
From: Commanding Officer.
To: Lieutenant (jg) Albert F. Herney, C, USNR
Subject: Orders—Release from Active Duty.

1. Delivered and detached this date at San Diego, California.
2. Carry out basic orders.

C.E. DUNSTON

———

Dec 31 My Dearest Sweet:

Here it is 1945 is almost all over and grateful we should be, even tho you know it would be so much pleasanter to be with you—but that won't be too far distant now.

On returning from the base today found that relief for me had arrived—all of which means of course that your "Old Man" will be getting off in SD to stay—no east coast—thank goodness. Of course I was overjoyed to know that when I did get home I wouldn't have to leave.

Both Gates & Bezold have their reliefs aboard too so they likewise should feel as happy as myself—I say should as Bezold doesn't as yet know about it since he has been ashore since yesterday morning. Both Bezold and myself have orders to be discharged—Gates as yet have not arrived.

On tying up at a dock, as usual very accessible for transportation looked out on the deck and there was Chuck R. was very happy to see him. Stayed for lunch & then came back for me at 5 PM & off to home to see Blythe & youngster. Slept on the floor on an air mattress but didn't mind as it was pleasant to be away from the ship for the first time is almost one year.

Arrived back aboard the next morning at about 8:15 to find that we were due for a surprise inspection at 0900—everyone was happy to see me of course—Do think we surprised them with the condition we are in & a good report followed. Have an idea why they picked on us but that is water under the bridge.

Chuck & Blythe at present, awaiting quarters on the base are living in a one room apartment. Chuck told me that the youngster, and she is good but of course can't compare with our girl in beauty, slept in the head. Thought he was kidding but he wasn't at all. Had a small box built which sits on the floor—so the head ain't used after the youngster retires. Use the outdoors please.

Thought I would be able to see them again, tho will be plenty busy from now on so that I can be ready to debark at S.D. & be all through.

The orders for routing arrived today plans—leave P.H. on the 3rd at 1400. From your last letter assume you will be able to discover our estimated time of arrival. Will leave that up to you or have others get the information.

Happy you got to see Schnabel. Don't let Schnabel upset you about clothes for I'm sure the suits will still fit so get them out & have them cleaned & ready for I'll want to be wearing them. Will try to get a few more 14 size neck shirts just in case the supply of 13 ½ won't fit. Think if necessary that I could squeeze into them. Think I have enuf shorts & skivvies. Of course with the grey will have enuf mountain clothes.

Chuck delivered your letter—also received your letters of 2 & 3 of Dec. You have done almost as well as I on letters this month. Won't promise to write again before leaving.

Love you with all my heart as always and looking forward to the time that I can tell you so—

Always and always

Al & Daddy

WESTERN UNION TELEGRAM TO DOROTHY JAN 3 1946
LEAVING THURSDAY AND NO EAST COAST AIR THE CIVIES AND
COOL THE CHAMPAGNE
LOVE.
ALWAYS.
AL
NAVCOM PEARL

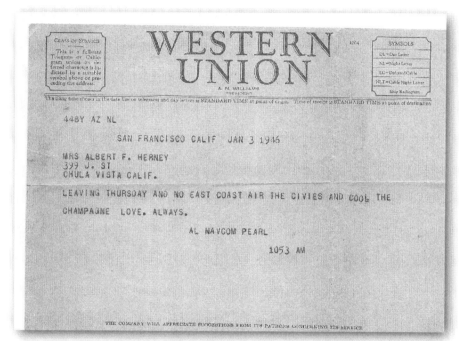

Al's final wartime communication with Dot was this joyous homecoming telegram.

16

Homecoming Epilogue

January 1946

According to the Dictionary of American Naval Fighting Ships, *"* Scurry *received 4 battle stars for her World War II service."*[xxviii]

From a newspaper clipping January 12, 1946—Possibly *Chula Vista Star-News*
Will Arrive Today

Lt. (jg) Albert F. Herney USN, will arrive today on the USS Scurry, a minesweeper with the first squadron of large minesweepers to return. Lt. Herney was communications officer on the ship and has been in service for two years, 16 months of which was spent overseas. He expects to be discharged soon. His wife and daughter, Susan, and infant son, Stephen, reside at 399 J St.

Mrs. Herney and children recently returned from Lincoln, Nebraska, where they had spent the past year with her parents.[xxix]

From a newspaper clipping January 12, 1946—Possibly *The San Diego Union*
26 Ships Arrive Today

The fourteen vessels that comprise famed Minesweeper Squadron 12 head the list of naval craft arriving today with overseas veterans, more than 2400 of whom will be discharged by a total of 26 ships.

The squadron, which swept hundreds of mines from the waters of Iwo Jima, Okinawa, China and Japan, is scheduled to moor at bays in the channel about 8 a.m., the navy reported. It will send 262 passengers ashore, and remain in port several days before proceeding to New Orleans for duty with the Atlantic fleet. Ships in the unit are the Skirmish, Scrimmage, Scuffle, Sentry, Serene, Shelter, Signet, Scurry, Specter, Staunch, Strategy, Strength, Success and Superior.***

Clippings from local papers noted the arrival of the minesweeper squadron in San Diego harbor, January 12, 1946. Dot, the children, and several of Al's relatives were there to help welcome him home.

From the *San Diego Union*, Sunday, January 13, 1946
Minesweepers Tie Up in Bay By Ken Bojens
Their upper structures patterned with hashmarks telling the story of spectacular accomplishments in foreign waters, the 12 surviving ships of Mine Squadron 12 steamed into San Diego yesterday—home for a brief rest before resuming a journey to New Orleans and eventual assignment to the Atlantic fleet.

The 180-foot vessels carried approximately 1200 crewmen and 262 Pacific veterans who came aboard as passengers in Pearl Harbor. They comprised the first large group of minesweepers to return to the United States together.

Flying "homeward bound" pennants which streamed from trucks to fantails, the gallant little ships docked at Navy pier to unload and moved out in the stream to tie up at mooring buoys. How long they will remain depends upon what repairs are necessary before the squadron can get under way again, but it is believed their stay will be short.

Enthusiasm of many of the men over their return to familiar scenes was tempered considerably soon after lines were secured when they learned a long-awaited payday could not be arranged. It was their second such disappointment in the last two weeks, and the liberty-hungry bluejackets anticipated a dismal sojourn in San Diego.

It seems that many of the ships haven't been paid since early November. When they reached Pearl Harbor just before New Year's, attempts were made by commanding officers to get funds for the men, but the big base couldn't help them—it was starting a four-day holiday. Except for those fortunate enough to borrow from more affluent friends, the heroic minesweepers spent a quiet New Year's eve.

ASKED FOR PAY HERE
Hoping to avert a recurrence here, a dispatch was sent from the squadron several days ago, requesting that the men be paid immediately after arrival. There was no disbursing officer on the dock to meet them. The navy has a semi-holiday on Saturdays, and the ships were informed they can't be paid before Wednesday.

Yesterday afternoon officers who had served overseas and in combat with their men for from one to two years were digging into their own shallow resources and trying to see that everyone had a bit of cash before he went ashore. Depleted ship's welfare funds, already tapped by loans at Pearl Harbor, were being used to help others.

Because of the strong possibility that the squadron may not be here more than a couple of days some of the sailors were reconciled to prospects of waiting until they reach New Orleans before refurbishing empty wallets.

FOUR SHIPS MISSING

Four of the original ships of Squadron 12, made up of Divisions 34, 35 and 36, were missing. One was sunk, another was damaged so badly it had to return to the shipyards, and two others have been decommissioned. The remaining sweepers are the Skirmish, Scrimmage, Scuffle, Sentry, Serene, Shelter, Signet, Scurry, Specter, Staunch, Strategy, Strength, Success and Superior.

They have compiled one of the most brilliant records in minesweeping history, with approximately 4800 swept mines to their credit. They saw action in the Marshall, Philippines, Iwo Jima, Okinawa and also cleared large areas off the Japanese home islands and China coast...[xxxi]

From the *Tribune-Sun*, Monday, January 14, 1946—with photo
WELCOME HOME
Lt. (jg) Albert F. Herney of 399J. st., Chula Vista, returned home Jan. 12 after 15 months of service in the Pacific theater aboard the U.S.S. Scurry, AM 304.

Herney, who was graduated from San Diego State college with an A.B. degree, was associated with his sister, Marie Herney, in a law office here before entering the service. He wears the Victory Medal and four ribbons, the American theatre, Asiatic-Pacific, Philippine Islands campaign and the occupation of Japan and Korea.[xxxii]

INTERIM
OFFICER PERSONNEL INTAKE STATION
U.S. NAVAL TRAINING AND
DISTRIBUTION CENTER
Camp Elliott
San Diego 44, California
Second ENDORSEMENT: 12 January 1946
From: Commanding Officer, Intake Station, TADCEN, Camp Elliott,
San Diego 4, California

TO: Lieut. (jg) Albert F. Herney (C) USNR 303567

1. Reported. 12 January 1946 Detached 12 January 1946
2. Proceed to 830 Lilac Terrace, Los Angeles, Calif. via transportation arranged for you and report to the Commanding Officer, Separation Center, for temporary duty to arrive Not later than 13 January 1946
3. You (are) assigned government quarters in the B.O.Q. of this station and will vacate same on date of detachment. There are no quarters available for assignment to your dependents at this station.

U.S. NAVAL OFFICERS SEPARATION CENTER 8646/w4
830 LILAC TERRACE
LOS ANGELES CALIFORNIA
14 January 1946
3rd ENDORSEMENT
to ComAComMinecraft Ser. 61-5250, orders of 12-30-45
From: Commanding Officer
To: lt. (jg) Albert F. Herney, C, USNR (303567)

1. Reported   13 January 1946
2. Examined and found physically qualified for release from active duty 14 January 1946   R.W. EMERICK, lt. (MC), USNR
3. Civil Readjustment Process completed. Veterans rights and benefits made known.

14 January 1946   G.H. FIELDING, LT. Comdr. USNR
Civil Readjustment Officer
By direction of the Commanding Officer:

4. Detached   14 January 1946. Proceed to your home. You
Are granted 1(one) months and 15 days leave, upon the expiration
of which, at midnight of 1 March 1946, you will regard yourself released from all active duty.

5. Immediately upon detachment you will furnish the disbursing officer
of this Separation Center a copy of these orders, bearing all endorsements, including the date of detachment. Forward a copy of these
orders bearing all endorsements to the Bureau of Naval Personnel and
to the Commandant of your home Naval District.

6. During the period of leave granted you under these orders you may,
at your option, wear civilian clothes; and, while wearing civilian
clothes, you are authorized to engage in any occupation not contrary
to law.

7. You have stated that you were called to active duty from Chula Vista,
Calif.

8. You have stated that your official residence is 399 J.St., Chula Vista,
Cal. (San Diego Co)

9. The Chief of Naval Personnel has determined that your separation
from active naval service is considered to be under honorable conditions and that you are entitled to a Certificate of Satisfactory Service.

10. There are no government quarters available and none were assigned
you or your dependents. You were authorized to procure quarters at
your own expense.

J.C. HUNTER

———

Al received an IRS form 1099 for calendar year 1945, showing he earned an income of $2,186.77 for his service that year in the United States Navy.

In addition to his 'good conduct' ribbon, Al was authorized to wear the Victory Medal No. 2; the American Theatre ribbon; the Asiatic Pacific ribbon with two stars; the Philippine Campaign Liberation ribbon; and the Occupation of Japan-Korea ribbon. The USS Scurry, one of the 147 Minecraft Vessels participating in the East China Sea Operation, received an operation and engagement star for that service.

Some of Al's navy ribbons, insignia, uniform buttons, and other mementos of his service during World War II.

THE

President of the United States of America

Expresses the sincere appreciation of his fellow-countrymen for the loyal service rendered by

Lieutenant (jg) ALBERT F. HERNEY

on active duty in the United States Navy during World War II. In testimony whereof I am privileged to bestow this

Certificate of Satisfactory Service

Done in the City of Washington, D.C. this First *day of* March *Nineteen hundred and forty* -six.

For the President:

James Forrestal

Secretary of the Navy

Al received a "Certificate of Satisfactory Service" signed by James Forrestal, secretary of the navy, dated March 1, 1946, and a certificate, "Heartfelt Thanks of a Grateful Nation," from President Harry S. Truman.

Top photo: The Albert Herney family, 1946; Bottom photo:
Al in his "civvies" with his children at home.

About the Author

Susan A. Herney, born and raised in Chula Vista, California, was just a toddler when her father, Albert Herney, received his commission in the United States Naval Reserve in 1943. She discovered the collection of WWII letters and other memorabilia following the death of her mother, Dorothy.

A communications and public policy graduate of the University of California at Berkeley, Susan served in senior marketing and communications capacities at California community colleges for twenty-five years, following a public relations career in the private sector. Her master's degree is in organizational management.

She was elected president of the National Council for Marketing and Public Relations and received that organization's Communicator of the Year Award. She was also named the California Public Relations Organization "All Pro." Her marketing materials have won more than twenty-five first-place awards in juried competitions. She also served as a member and chair of the City of Chula Vista Board of Ethics, and as a member of the Board of Directors of the Chula Vista Chamber of Commerce.

Prior to her recent retirement, Susan served as primary editor and project manager for the development and publication of *Rio Hondo College: Our History*, a fiftieth-year commemorative text.

STEADFAST is her first commercial manuscript.

BIBLIOGRAPHY

Bojens, Ken. "Minesweepers Tie Up in Bay." *San Diego Union*. January 13, 1946.

Crew of the USS Scurry. "Saga of the Scurry: The First Year." Leyte, Philippine Islands, July 29, 1945.

Forshaw, Louise. Interview with Fernando Salazar. "Experiencing War: Stories from the Veterans History Project." American Folklife Center, Library of Congress. May 16, 2008. Accessed April 8, 2013. www.loc.gov/folklife/vets/stories.

Mooney, James L.; Naval Historical Center, et al. *Dictionary of American Naval Fighting Ships (online)*. Washington, D.C.: U.S. Department of the Navy: Naval Historical Center. Accessed May 3, 2014. www.history.navy.mil/DANSF/s8/scurry.htm.

Rankin, Bill. "Falls Church Vet Stories Quartermaster 3rd Class Bill Rankin." Falls Church Veteran Stories. Accessed April 17, 2014. http://fcveteran-stories.us/index/php.sasebo-japan.

Spangler, George. "Ulithi." USS Laffey (website). Accessed April 4, 2014. www.laffey.org

"US Navy Personnel in World War II: Service and Casualty Statistics." The Navy Department Library. Accessed April 12, 2014. http://www.history.navy.mil//library/online/ww2_statistics.htm.

"WWII Command File of the Operational Amphibious Operations Capture of Iwo Jima." The Navy Department Library. Accessed May 22, 2015. www.history.mil/research/library/online.

Author unknown. "Iwo Jima Operation, February–March 1945." US Navy History and Heritage Command Online Library. Accessed March 5, 2015. www.history.mil/photos/events/wwii-pac/iwojima/iwojima.htm.

Author unknown. "ARMY & NAVY, Supply, Tropical Lagoon" *TIME.* November 6, 1944, pp 65-66.

Author/Artist unknown. "Cover image" *TIME.* August 20, 1945. Pacific Pony Edition, printed in Honolulu, Hawaii.

Author unknown. "Mine Warfare Vessel Photo Archive." Accessed April 9, 2013. www.navsourc.org/archives/11/02304.htm

Author unknown. "Will Arrive Today." Unknown but possibly *Chula Vista Star-News.* January 12, 1946.

Author unknown. "26 Ships Arrive Today." Unknown but possibly the *San Diego Union.* January 12, 1946.

Author unknown. "Welcome Home." *Tribune-Sun.* January 14, 1946.

NOTES

i. Mooney, James L.; Naval Historical Center, et al. *Dictionary of American Naval Fighting Ships (online)*. Washington, D.C.: U.S. Department of the Navy: Naval Historical Center. Accessed May 3, 2014. www.history.navy.mil/DANSF/s8/scurry.htm.

ii. Crew of the USS Scurry. "Saga of the Scurry: The First Year." Leyte, Philippine Islands, July 29, 1945.

iii. Mooney et al. *Dictionary of American Naval Fighting Ships*.

iv. Author unknown. "Mine Warfare Vessel Photo Archive." Accessed April 9, 2013. www.navsourc.org/archives/11/02304.htm

v. Crew of the USS Scurry. "Saga of the Scurry: The First Year."

vi. Ibid.

vii. Mooney et al. *Dictionary of American Naval Fighting Ships*.

viii. Ibid.

ix. Forshaw, Louise. Interview with Fernando Salazar. "Experiencing War: Stories from the Veterans History Project." American Folklife Center, Library of Congress. May 16, 2008. Accessed April 8, 2013. www.loc.gov/folklife/vets/stories.

x. Author unknown. "Iwo Jima Operation, February–March 1945." US Navy History and Heritage Command Online Library. Accessed March 5, 2014. www.history.navy.mil/photos/events/wwii-pac/iwojima/iwojima.htm.

xi.   "WWII Command File of the Operational Amphibious Operations Capture of Iwo Jima." The Navy Department Library. Accessed May 22, 2015. www.history.mil/research/library/online.

xii.   Mooney et al. *Dictionary of American Naval Fighting Ships.*

xiii.   Forshaw, Louise. Interview with Fernando Salazar. "Experiencing War: Stories from the Veterans History Project."

xiv.   Crew of the USS Scurry. "Saga of the Scurry: The First Year."

xv.   Forshaw, Louise. Interview with Fernando Salazar. "Experiencing War: Stories from the Veterans History Project."

xvi.   Crew of the USS Scurry. "Saga of the Scurry: The First Year."

xvii.   Mooney et al. *Dictionary of American Naval Fighting Ships.*

xviii. Forshaw, Louise. Interview with Fernando Salazar. "Experiencing War: Stories from the Veterans History Project."

xix.   Spangler, George. "Ulithi." USS Laffey (website). Accessed April 4, 2014. www.laffey.org

xx.   Mooney et al. *Dictionary of American Naval Fighting Ships.*

xxi.   Ibid.

xxii.   Crew of the USS Scurry. "Saga of the Scurry: The First Year."

xxiii. Mooney et al. *Dictionary of American Naval Fighting Ships.*

xxiv.   Ibid.

xxv. US Navy Personnel in World War II: Service and Casualty Statistics." The Navy Department Library. Accessed April 12, 2014. http:// www.history.navy.mil/library/online/ww2_statistics.htm.

xxvi. Mooney et al. *Dictionary of American Naval Fighting Ships.*

xxvii. Rankin, Bill. "Falls Church Vet Stories Quartermaster 3rd Class Bill Rankin." Falls Church Veteran Stories. Accessed April 17, 2014. http://fcveteranstories.us/index/php.sasebo-japan.

xxviii. Mooney et al. *Dictionary of American Naval Fighting Ships.*

xxix. Author unknown. "Will Arrive Today." Unknown but possibly *Chula Vista Star-News.* January 12, 1946.

xxx. Author unknown. "26 Ships Arrive Today." Unknown but possibly the *San Diego Union.* January 12, 1946.

xxxi. Bojens, Ken. "Minesweepers Tie Up in Bay." *San Diego Union.* January 13, 1946.

xxxii. Author unknown. "Welcome Home." *Tribune-Sun.* January 14, 1946.

Made in the USA
San Bernardino, CA
04 September 2015